EVALUATION OF ENVIRONMENTAL DATA FOR REGULATORY AND IMPACT ASSESSMENT

Studies in Environmental Science

Other volumes in this series

Studies in Environmental Science 41

EVALUATION OF ENVIRONMENTAL DATA FOR REGULATORY AND IMPACT ASSESSMENT

S. RAMAMOORTHY and E. BADDALOO

Standards Research and Development Branch, Environmental Assessment Division, Alberta Environment, Edmonton, Alta. T5K 2J6, Canada

ELSEVIER
Amsterdam — Oxford — New York — Tokyo   1991

ELSEVIER SCIENCE PUBLISHERS B.V.
Sara Burgerhartstraat 25
P.O. Box 211, 1000 AE Amsterdam, The Netherlands

Distributors for the United States and Canada:

ELSEVIER SCIENCE PUBLISHING COMPANY INC.
655, Avenue of the Americas
New York, NY 10010, U.S.A.

363. 732
R16e

ISBN 0-444-88530-7

© Elsevier Science Publishers B.V., 1991

All rights reserved. No part of this publication may be reproduced, stored in a retrieval system or transmitted in any form or by any means, electronic, mechanical, photocopying, recording or otherwise, without the prior written permission of the publisher, Elsevier Science Publishers B.V./ Physical Sciences & Engineering Division, P.O. Box 330, 1000 AH Amsterdam, The Netherlands.

Special regulations for readers in the USA – This publication has been registered with the Copyright Clearance Center Inc. (CCC), Salem, Massachusetts. Information can be obtained from the CCC about conditions under which photocopies of parts of this publication may be made in the USA. All other copyright questions, including photocopying outside of the USA, should be referred to the publisher.

No responsibility is assumed by the Publisher for any injury and/or damage to persons or property as a matter of products liability, negligence or otherwise, or from any use or operation of any methods, products, instructions or ideas contained in the material herein.

This book is printed on acid-free paper.

Printed in The Netherlands

PREFACE

Because of increasing concern for the state of the environment, collection of environmental data has increased several fold in the past two decades. Although this is encouraging, it also raises concerns with regard to the quality assurance and quality control of the data gathering process, from sampling to analysis. The evaluation of environmental data in terms of quality, and relevance for use in the management of toxic chemicals in the environment, has reached a critical phase. Enormous volumes of data are being generated, on both residue levels and their effects, to meet short- and long-term needs for regulatory procedures and (environmental) impact assessments. It is therefore important to verify not only the quality of the data collected, but also the choice of relevant test parameters.

This book deals with the evolution of analytical methodologies to the current state-of-the-art techniques, quality assurance/quality control of data acquirements, and testing procedures for screening of toxic chemicals including their hazard identification, persistence, and fate processes in the environment. The models currently employed in environmental impact assessment and risk assessment are also discussed in detail. Public involvement and participation in regulatory decision-making processes are also described. This book is intended for managers and scientists involved in environmental management and research of toxic chemicals in the environment.

S. Ramamoorthy
E. Baddaloo
Alberta Environment
Edmonton, Alberta, Canada

UNIVERSITY LIBRARIES
CARNEGIE MELLON UNIVERSITY
PITTSBURGH, PA 15213-3890

ACKNOWLEDGEMENTS

We gratefully acknowledge Mr. Vance A. MacNichol (Deputy Minister), Mr. K.R. Smith (Assistant Deputy Minister), and Mr. F.J. Schulte (Director, Environmental Assessment Division) of Alberta Environment for their support of this undertaking. We would also like to acknowledge, Dr. H.P. Sims (Head, Standards Research and Development Branch) for his continued encouragement and support of this project.

We would like to acknowledge our deep appreciation to Ms. Meliza Roberto for typing the manuscript which included many drafts. We are particularly appreciative of her outstanding help for thoroughness and completing typing on schedule. We would also like to express our appreciation to Mr. Roy Swenson and Mr. Terry Zenith for the preparation of figures, and to Alberta Environment Library staff for handling our requests. We are very thankful to Sita Ramamoorthy for proofreading the various drafts and providing editorial assistance in a most gracious and professional manner.

S. Ramamoorthy
E. Baddaloo
Alberta Environment
Edmonton, Alberta, Canada

CONTENTS

CONTENTS (CONTINUED)

Chapter 1

INTRODUCTION

Priorities in environmental monitoring and management change with time. In the early 1970s, we were largely concerned with the gross pollution of our air and water which we could see, smell, and feel. Although most scientists were aware of chemical injuries and diseases, this area of research did not get the attention and resources it deserved. Consequently, there have been many "chemical surprises" involving exposures of humans and other environmental organisms to such chemicals. Some of the most significant examples include the Niagara River and Lake Michigan incidents (ref. 1) and the closure of commercial fisheries in the lower Great Lakes. In the early 1980s, the focus changed to address toxic chemicals and their effects on human health and that of the ecosystem.

1.1 ANALYTICAL DEVELOPMENT

In the past decade, the detection limit has been improved by more than six orders of magnitude for the analysis of both inorganic and organic compounds. Both the instruments and analytical methods have become more sophisticated and in many cases automated. With ultra-trace analysis in routine use, it is hoped that there will be very few "chemical surprises". However, the increased ability to detect chemicals has resulted in the "list syndrome". This syndrome has created a dilemma about how research is to be conducted. The two scenarios currently operating are, firstly, the analyst after having detected a new chemical in an environmental sample could initiate an extensive monitoring program, followed by toxicological studies to assess the impact. Secondly, the field biologist observes a biological impact in the natural environment and transmits a request to the chemist and toxicologist to search for the cause through diagnostic services. The question which emerges is which scenario should be followed in order to be cost-effective in environmental protection. For example, the discovery of Mirex hiding beneath a PCB peak was a brilliant example of analytical sleuthing (refs. 1,2). But subsequent toxicological testing showed that Mirex was not of any toxicological significance to the biology of Lake Ontario. However, this turn of events did divert scarce resources away from the search for the chick edema factor during the late 1970s (ref. 1). To be cost-effective, we have to keep our focus on critical compounds.

Another disadvantage with the "list syndrome" is that clients request the analysis of every compound in the list without realizing either the complexity of the resulting database, or the limitations in the identification or quantification of compounds in the absence of proper scrutinizational techniques involving the use of authenticated reference standards, intervention by experienced analytical chemists, etc. (ref. 3). With the exception of priority pollutants, qualitative and quantitative inaccuracy is a widespread problem in environmental chemical data gathering (ref. 3). In addition, interpretation becomes convoluted with respect to toxicity data when the mass balance, if at all performed, shows that the compounds analyzed constitute only a small fraction of the total dissolved organic matter.

The technical data, however complex, have to be communicated adequately among the different disciplines involved in environmental monitoring and management decision process. Analysts have the responsibility of clearly (i) explaining the limits of their knowledge; (ii) indicating the margin of uncertainty in their estimates; and (iii) identifying the information gaps that might be closed by further research. This will facilitate consensus in the decision-making process and likely reduce the possibility of misinterpretation or misuse of data.

1.2 EVALUATION OF ENVIRONMENTAL DATA

Our objective in writing this book is to provide regulators and scientists with criteria for evaluating the available database for use during monitoring impact assessment and decision-making processes. To begin with, the book evaluates the current analytical techniques, and toxicity testing methods. The toxicity end points considered are the acute, subchronic, chronic, genotoxicity, and ecotoxicity effects. This is followed by a detailed treatment on the determinants of the quality of the analytical data such as end use of the data, methodologies used, sampling techniques, quality control and quality assurance programs, criteria to be used in determining the limit of detection, quantitation and reporting the analytical data. Next, the book examines the determinants for the quality of biological data.

The earlier perception of solving environmental problems with money alone changed with ever-increasing number of chemicals in the environment and the enormous cost associated in dealing with them. The challenge was to make scientifically sound decisions about the environmental and human health risks posed by the myriad of chemicals of concern and which chemical to address first.

This brings us to the next chapter in the book which discusses the screening of chemicals for their presence and distribution in the environment, exposure potential, fate processes and toxic and genotoxic effects. Scoring systems used by some regulatory agencies are described in detail. Surrogate approaches to estimate the toxic potential of a chemical in the absence of data are presented. The next chapter provides detailed analysis of hazard identification, threshold and non-threshold hazards, dose-response and safety factor for chemicals exhibiting no-observable-adverse-effect level (NOAEL).

The next chapter deals with the specific needs in chemical and biological monitoring, to identify the adequacy/inadequacy of existing database in meeting those needs. Case studies on chemical and biological impacts to evaluate the database and to assess the need for comprehensive monitoring data are reviewed. Also, the use of mathematical models to evaluate the severity and longevity of impacts are discussed. Final chapters examine non-threshold hazards, merits and demerits in extrapolation of laboratory animal data to humans in ambient environment along with the analysis of the current methods to estimate the total integrated human exposure to chemicals. Methods of cancer risk assessment of chemicals are critically examined. Various elements involved in the regulatory decision-making processes are discussed including strength of data, risk communication, control options and strategies, and acceptable risk.

This book is also aimed to aid research workers in interdisciplinary teams to plan and design experiments to generate valid and reliable environmental data.

REFERENCES

1 M. Gilbertson, J. Fish. Aquat. Sci., 42 (1985) 1681-1692.
2 K.L.E. Kaiser, Science, 185 (1974) 523-525.
3 K.C. Swallow, N.S. Shifrin, and P.J. Doherty, Environ. Sci. Technol., 22 (1988) 136-142.

Chapter 2

EVALUATION OF CURRENT TECHNIQUES

2.1 ANALYTICAL TECHNIQUES

Analytical chemistry is defined as "the qualitative and quantitative characterization of a material or materials". Apart from the conventional functions of an analytical chemist in the areas of pharmaceuticals, natural products, cosmetic and detergent industries, analytical chemistry plays an important role in the identification and quantification of trace organics and inorganics in environmental samples. This analysis provides an estimate of the exposure potential of these contaminant chemicals for which a toxicity profile can be developed based on the toxicology data available. This will provide an estimate of risk to human health and environment on exposure to these chemicals.

For several years, analytical techniques were focussed on the chemical properties of materials analyzed, such schemes served well in the past and were useful in teaching reaction chemistry and also to carry out qualitative and quantitative analysis. The most important analytical fields involved were volumetric and gravimetric analyses that demanded a high degree of skill, care and patience of an artist.

Because of the exploding growth of modern industry, the analytical chemists of the previous generation, who could not become mechanical, were replaced by routine, automated analytical chemists. The analytical techniques were also evolving to perform "non-destructive" analysis by which they do not alter, destroy, or blemish the material under investigation. The non-destructive methods have become an integral part of analytical chemistry in recent years.

In responding to the demands of the industries and environmental analytical needs, analytical chemists have turned to the physical properties of the chemicals (under investigation) for quantitative and lower level of detection. This quantum leap in analytical chemistry has resulted in lowering detection limits from parts per million (mg/L) to parts per quadrillion (ppq = picogram per litre); in addition, specific information on the chemical constituent such as isomer specific information, species information, mass ratio, etc. can be determined. The last two decades have seen a phenomenal growth in the analytical industry with new equipments with on-board computers, menu-driven mode of operation, cook books, hands-off operations, continuous-non-attended performance.

All these are valuable in generating massive data banks, of course, not thoroughly verified by external checks, spectral patterns, etc.

In order to gain an optimum use of the ever-exploding analytical techniques, the end users should know what information is available with sufficient quality control/quality assurance (QC/QA) checks and also should know what information is not available or available but not quality-tested. Knowledge of analytical chemistry is highly recommended in all end users of analytical data so that they know what they are getting as data, ability to question the laboratories, including the overworked "consulting laboratories" about positive identification and QA/QC programs in generating the data. This will avoid the "dreadful" scenario of interpreting the "set of data" that should have been rejected in the first place because they were never validated nor properly identified.

The modern analytical chemists should be aware of and contribute to new developments in chemistry and physics. Their most important role is to harness the new developments for analytical chemistry so that useful and reliable information can be provided to the end users of data.

Qualitative Analysis

This is the branch of analytical chemistry that provides answers to the questions "what is in the sample". There are several instrumental ways to provide results to the question. Elemental analysis with impurities assay is adequate and methods detection limits (MDL) of 1 parts per billion (1 ppb) has been in use for several years. The most used methods in qualitative elemental analysis are: (1) emission spectroscopy; (2) plasma emission; (3) activation analysis; (4) x-ray fluorescence; and (5) other methods (ref. 1).

If the sample is organic in nautre, qualitative analysis for structural formula could be carried out by infrared (IR) spectroscopy, nuclear magnetic resonance (NMR), or mass spectrometry (MS). Mixtures of compounds can be separated by gas-liquid, or liquid-liquid chromatography, depending on the molecular weight.

Quantitative Analysis

This analysis determines the concentration of each component that is present in a given sample. The results of quantitative molecular analysis is shown to provide information to determine: (1) percentage distribution of particular compound in a mixture; (2) the type of functional groups in the molecule; (3) the stereospecific arrangement of functional groups in the molecule; and (4) all other information required in the complete characterization of the sample.

The frequently used analytical methods include MS, NMR, IR, UV, X-ray diffraction and thermal analysis.

2.1.1 Electroanalytical Techniques

The original analytical applications of electroanalytical techniques were potentiometry, conductivity, amperometry, coulometry and polarography. Each technique is useful for particular applications.

A species that undergoes reduction or oxidation is known as an electro-active species. The electroanalytical techniques are now used not only for trace metal ion analyses, but also for the analysis of organic compounds and for continuous analysis. Applications have been developed for quality control in product streams in industry. Normal detection limits will be around 1 ppm (1 mg/kg), but the use of electrodeposition and anodic stripping techniques (by reversing the current), the species can be identified at subparts per billion (ppb) levels.

The electroanalytical techniques provide not only the elemental and molecular analysis, but can also be used to acquire information about equilibria and reaction mechanisms. The analytical calculation is based on the determination of current/voltage/resistance developed in a cell that reflect the concentrations of species under study. Electroanalytical measurements are amenable for easy automation because they are only electrical signals. It is more cost-efficient than spectroscopy units.

The Nernst equation mathematically expresses the relationship between the potential of a half cell consisting of a metal in contact with its ions and the variables as follows:

$$E = E_0 + \frac{RT}{nF} \ln \left(\frac{\text{molar concn. of ions}}{\text{molar concn. of metal}} \right) \tag{2.1}$$

where E =   Potential (emf) of the half-cell

           E_0 =   emf of half cell under standard conditions

           R =   Constant ($8.314 J/{}^{\circ}C$)

           T =   Absolute temperature

           n =   number of valence electrons involved in the reaction (= valence change of metal)

           F =   Faraday number (96,495 Coulombs)

           $\ln$ =   log to the base e

Substituting the values for R,T,F and expressing in $\log_{10}$, Equation 2.1 becomes:

$$E = E_0 + \frac{0.0591}{n} \log (\text{molar concentration of ions}) \tag{2.2}$$

In fact, the potential developed is proportional to the activity rather than to the logarithm of the molar concentration of ions. Hence, Equation 2.1 can be written as:

$$E = E_0 + \frac{RT}{nF} \ln (\gamma \times \text{molar concn. of ions})$$
(2.3)

where γ = activity coefficient of the ion

At very low concentrations of the ion, Equation 2.3 reduces to Equation 2.1, since $\gamma = 1$.

The Nernst equation can also be written in redox form since metal is the reduced form and ions are the oxidized form:

$$E = E_0 + \frac{RT}{nF} \ln \left(\left[\frac{OX}{Red} \right] \right)$$
(2.4)

by substituting values for R,T,F and expressing in $\log_{10}$ Equation 2.4 becomes:

$$E = E_0 + \frac{0.0591}{n} \log \left(\left[\frac{OX}{Red} \right] \right)$$
(2.5)

Most electroanalytical measurements are based on this relationship between E and concentrations of ions. The potential of the complete cell is the sum of potentials of the standard half-cell and the measurement half-cell. The E_o of the standard half-cell (reference cell) is known and is subtracted from E (of the total cell) to give the potential of the measurement cell. This potential is a measure of the concentrations of the components in solution.

Potentiometry

Potentiometry measures the potential or voltage of an electrochemical cell. Accurate measurement of the potential developed by a cell requires a negligible flow of current during measurement stage. The potential of the half-cell of interest is determined by connecting to a standard half-cell to complete the single cell. The potential of standard cells are available from reference tables. With the knowledge of E (total) and E (reference), E (sample) can be calculated. Common standard cell which is widely used is the calomel electrode. The Equation 2.1

$$E = E_0 + \frac{RT}{nF} \ln \left(\frac{[M^{m+}]}{[M]} \right)$$

is reduced to Equation 2.6 because [M] of the pure metal electrode is equal to 1.

$$E = E_0 + \frac{0.0591}{n} \log [M^{m+}] \tag{2.6}$$

which shows a logarithmic relationship between emf (E) produced by the half-cell and the concentration of metal ions in solution. Since values of E_0 and n are known, metal concentrations in solution can be calculated.

Analytical Applications

Potentiometry is used in the determination of metal ion concentration, changes in ion concentrations and pH. It is also used in the analysis of gases and organic compounds.

pH Measurements

pH which is the negative logarithm of hydrogen ion concentration is measured by the potentiometric principle. Measurement of pH is important in drinking water supplies, water in swimming pool, and water-contact sports or in industrial processes where pH has to be measured and maintained accurately for process control. Commonly used hydrogen cell is the glass electrode in combination with a saturated calomel electrode (SCE) as follows:

$$SCE \parallel [H_3O^+] | \text{glass membrane} | [H_3O^+] \parallel 0.1 | AgCl \cdot Ag$$
$$\text{unknown} \qquad\qquad \text{internal reference}$$

The potential developed is given by
$$E_{(cell)} = E(H^+) - E(reference)$$

$$E_{(cell)} = -E(reference) + E_0(H) + \frac{0.0591}{1} \log [H^+] \text{ at } 25^oC \tag{2.7}$$

$E_0(H) = 0$ by definition, $E(reference) = +0.241V$ vs SHE (Standard Hydrogen Electrode); therefore $E_{(cell)} = -0.241 + 0.0591 \log [H^+]$

On rearranging:
$$-\log H^+ = -\frac{[E(cell)+E(reference)]}{0.0591}$$

$$= -\frac{[E(cell)+0.241]}{0.0591}$$

When the observed voltage is -0.6549V vs SCE, then

$$-\log [H^+] = -\frac{(-0.6549+0.241)}{0.0591} = 7 \text{ or } [H^+] = 10^{-7}M \tag{2.8}$$

$$pH = 7$$

pH measurement is also used in determining alkalinity of water samples using acid-base titrations.

Ion-selective Electrodes

Ion-selective electrodes have greatly enhanced the analytical value of the potentiometry. These electrodes are very sensitive to changes in the concentration (or more precisely, the activity) of a particular ion in solution and less sensitive to other ions present in solution. Corrections must be made for interferences if very accurate results are required. The first ion selective electrode to be used was the glass electrode for H^+ ion. The other categories of ion selective electrodes are the (1) metal-ion selective solid state electrodes; (2) anion-selective solid state electrodes; and (3) liquid-liquid membrane electrodes.

Electrodes are available for the measurement of iodide, bromide, chloride, perchlorate, sulfate, and phosphate ions. But a separate electrode has to be used for each ion. It has been shown that these electrodes are virtually insensitive to other ions present in solution. For example, the response of the iodide-selective electrode is about 200 times greater than its response to bromide ions and more than a million times greater than its response to sulfate ions.

The solid-state ion-selective electrodes have been developed for a variety of cations such as Cu^{2+}, Cd^{2+}, Pb^{2+}, divalent cations, etc. and for anions such as fluoride, sulfide, chloride, bromide, and iodide ions. They are easy to assemble, use and maintain, and are used routinely in water analysis. Micro electrodes are now available for low volume samples such as body fluids (urine, blood, serum, etc.).

Quantitative Applications

Ion-selective electrodes are used to analyze aqueous and non-aqueous solutions alike and hence, have found increasing applications in organic chemistry, biochemistry, medicine and environmental analysis. Since the response time is relatively very fast, these electrodes are valuable in obtaining rapid results with no loss of samples. These electrodes can also be used with periodic calibration in continuous monitoring studies of ambient waters, industrial plant streams and effluents. The potential measurements show a perfect Nernstian response to free ions down to parts per billion range; for certain cations such as Cu^{2+}, Cd^{2+}, etc. the detection limit is around 10 ppb (ref. 2). For monovalent ion, a change of 28.6 mV represents a ten-fold variation in concentration and for divalent ion, a change of 59.2 mV for a ten-fold concentration change. Some of the specific analyses used currently include the determination of Na^+ and K^+ in bile, nerve and muscle tissue, kidneys, blood plasma, urine and other body fluids such as sweat, etc. The electrodes have also been used in the analysis of marine muds, seawater, river water and industrial waters as well as for the determination of Na^+, K^+, Mg^{2+}, Ca^{2+}, Ag^+, Cr^{2+}, Rb^+, NH_4^+, I^-, F^-, Cl^-, Cd^{2+}, Pb^{2+}, and CNS^- in organic samples. In aqueous samples, the following ions Br^-, Cd^{2+}, Ca^{2+}, Cl^-, CN^-, Cu^{2+}, F^-, I^-, Pb^{2+}, NO_3^-, ClO_4^{-}, Na^+, CNS^-, S^{2-}, and Ag^+ have been determined at very low levels with ion-selective electrodes. Coulometry, which is based on Faraday's laws of electrolysis, can be used to measure the quantity of electrolyte reduced in electrodeposition and electroplating processes. It is known that 1 faraday (96 495 coloumbs) of electricity is required to reduce 1 gm equivalent weight of an electrolyte. By measuring the quantity of electricity required to reduce (or oxidize) a given sample exhaustively, the quantity of electrolyte reduced can be determined, provided the reaction is 100% efficient (or of known efficiency). Mass or charge i(A) x t(sec) can be used to indicate the extent of the electrochemical reaction.

Polarography

In this technique, a controlled potential is applied to the working electrode. In polarography, the working electrode is a dropping mercury electrode or hanging (static) mercury drop. The counter electrode is the platinum wire or foil. The third electrode or reference electrode is used to control the potential at the working electrode.

Differential Pulse Polarography (DPP)

Although this technique has the most complex polarographic wave forms of the polarographic methods, it is the easiest technique in interpreting them for analytical purposes. The applied voltage is a linear ramp with imposed pulses added during the last 60 secs. of the life of each drop. The pulse height is maintained above the ramp and is called the modulation amplitude, which may vary from 10 to 100 mV. The current is not measured continuously as in normal pulse polarography. Instead, it is sampled twice during the mercury drop lifetime; once just prior to the imposition of the pulse and once just before the drop is mechanically dislodged. The simplicity of the DPP method is due to the fact that the peak height is proportional to the analyte concentration. It is possible to analyze several ionic species with each method, provided adequate resolution is available. The DPP is very useful for trace analysis and the limit of detection is typically 1×10^{-7} M or better. The functional groups that can be determined by polarography is listed in Table 2.1.

TABLE 2.1 Typical functional groups detected by polarography.

Functional Group	Name	Half-wave potential $E_{1/2}$ (V)
$R - C\overset{\displaystyle 0}{\diagup} - H$	Aldehyde	-1.6
$R - C\overset{\displaystyle 0}{\underset{\displaystyle OH}{\diagup}}$	Carboxylic acid	-1.8
$R - C\overset{\displaystyle 0}{\diagup} - R$	Ketone	-2.5
$R - O - N = O$	Nitrite	-0.9
$R - N = O$	Nitroso	-0.2
$R - NH_2$	Amine	-0.5
$R - SH$	Mercaptan	-0.5

(Source: Reprinted from ref. 3).

In short, polarography can be used in the analysis of heterocyclic compounds, many biochemical species which are electroactive such as Vitamin C, fumaric acid, Vitamin B factors, antioxidants, N-nitrosoamines, keto-sugars and steroid aldosterone. Polarography is very useful in analyzing the speciation of chemicals, free ion, complexed ion and solution equilibria. This provides valuable information on the kinetics and concentration levels of the toxic species of a heavy metal in particular and any electroactive chemical, in general.

Stripping Voltametry

This technique may be used in areas requiring trace level analysis at parts per billion level. It is very useful in heavy metal analysis in natural waters or biochemical studies. Although anodic stripping or cathodic stripping are possible, anodic stripping voltametry (ASV) is commonly used. The stripping analysis involves two stages: (1) the electrolyzed product is preconcentrated by deposition at an electrode at a fixed potential, followed by (2) rapid stripping off by applying a rapid reverse potential sweep to get the products back into the electrolyte. Analysis time is in the order of a few minutes. Sensitivity is increased by using the differential pulse wave form and peak currents on the reverse sweep determine the analyte concentrations from a standard addition calibration method.

Applications

ASV is applicable in the analysis of those metals which form amalgams with mercury such as Ag, As, Au, Bi, Cd, Cu, Ga, In, Mn, Pb, Sb, Sn, Tl, and Zn. Metals which form intermetallic compounds and alloys within the amalgam cause interferences. Examples are In-Au and Cu-Ni. This can be circumvented by proper choice of electrolytes which will complex the interfering metals and electrochemically inactivate them. The elements of Periodic groups I and II can be analyzed with difficulty by ASV but better by atomic absorption methods for increased sensitivity and ease of analysis. The following anions at the molar concentrations specified can be determined by ASV; chloride (5 x 10^{-6}); bromide (1 x 10^{-6}); iodide (5 x 10^{-8}); sulphide (5 x 10^{-8}); chromate (3 x 10^{-9}); tungstate (4 x 10^{-7}); molybdate (1 x 10^{-6}) and oxalate (1 x 10^{-6}).

Stripping voltametry is an inexpensive, highly sensitive technique in the analysis of multi-component systems. In fact, ASV is not recommended for metal ion samples whose concentrations are greater than 1 ppm. It is less sensitive for non-metallic and anionic species. Recently, flow through and automated systems have been developed for continuous monitoring needs. ASV is being applied at increasing rate to environmental analysis; impurities in ocean waters, rivers, lakes, and effluents; body fluids, food items, soil samples; airborne particulates and industrial chemicals. ASV requires very little pre-analytical preparation of the samples.

2.1.2 Spectroscopic Techniques

Spectroscopic techniques measure the emitted radiation or the absorption of radiation by a sample. The parameters that need information are: (1) the wavelengths of absorption or emission; (2) the intensity of emission as a function of wavelength; and (3) the degree of absorption by the analyte. All spectroscopic instruments have more or less the same basic design. They all have a monochromator (wavelength selector), sample holder in the path of the monochromatic light and a detector which measures the light intensity after its passage through the sample solution held in an optical cell of known length. The instruments also include source of radiation for light absorption studies and display of the signal intensity in some interpretable form. There are two systems: (1) single-beam optical system (Fig. 2.1); and (2) double beam-optical system (Fig. 2.2).

The essential components of the single-beam optical systems are:

1. Irradiated light source;

2. Monochromator (a) prisms; and (b) gratings;

3. Optical slits;

4. Detector.

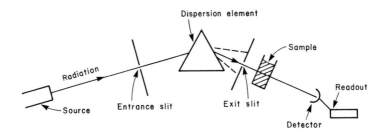

Fig. 2.1. Single-beam optical system.
(Source: Reprinted with permission from ref. 1, Copyright (1987), Marcel Dekker Inc.).

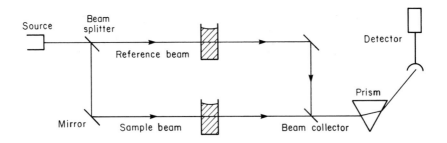

Fig. 2.2. Double-beam optical system.
(Source: Reprinted with permission from ref. 1, Copyright (1987), Marcel Dekker Inc.).

The individual components of the double-beam optical system are the same as in the single-beam system with one marked difference. The irradiated light energy is split into two beams of almost equal intensity. One beam is called the "reference" beam and the second beam is called the "sample" beam. The two beams are then merged and passed through the monochromator and slit systems to the detector (Fig. 2.2).

Analytical Spectroscopic Techniques

The various methods that utilize the interaction between radiation and atomic, molecular components and the molecular arrangements make up the numerous methods that are available in analytical spectroscopy. They are summarized in Table 2.2.

TABLE 2.2 Analytical methods and their spectroscopic fields.

Radiant Energy	Radio Frequency	Infrared	Visible	Ultraviolet	X-ray	γ-Ray
Analytical field	Nuclear magnetic resonance	Absorption	Absorption	Absorption	Absorption	Activation analysis
	Microwave	Attenuated total reflectance	Nephelometry	Fluorescence	Fluorescence	
		Optical rotary dispersion		Phosphorescence Emission spectrography	Diffraction	Radiotracer techniques
				Flame photometry		
				Atomic absorption		
Interaction of matter	Nuclear disintegration	Vibration and rotation of molecules	Electronic excitation of atoms or molecules		Inner electrons of atoms displaced	Nuclear disintegration
					Crystal lattice diffracts lights	Stable molecules

(Source: Reprinted with permission from ref. 1, Copyright (1987), Marcel Dekker Inc.).

Nuclear Magnetic Resonance (NMR)

In analytical chemistry, NMR technique enables to study the shape and structure of molecules. Especially, it reveals the various chemical environment of different forms of hydrogen present, which provides a clue to the structures of molecules. If the type of compounds that are present in the mixture is already known, then NMR provides a means of determining their ratio. Hence, it is both a qualitative and quantitative method of analysis for organic compounds.

The NMR involves the interaction of radiowaves and the spinning nuclei of the combined atoms in a molecule. Radiowaves have the lowest energy in the order of 6.6×10^{-20} erg.sec. The energy is too small to affect the vibrational, rotational and excitational state of an atom or molecule. But it is strong enough to change the nuclear spin of the atoms of a molecule. Hence, spinning nuclei of atoms in a molecule can absorb RF (radio frequency) waves and change direction of the spinning axis. The analytical field is called Nuclear Magnetic Resonance (NMR).

Analytical Applications of NMR

Qualitatively, NMR is useful in the identification of organic compounds. The types of hydrogen present as methylene, methyl, olefins, aromatic compounds and others are indicated by the chemical shift; neighbouring groups in the molecule are shown by spin-spin splitting or multiplicity; the relative size or area of the spectral peaks is directly proportional to the number of protons involved and not the multiplicity. The peak areas provide information on how many hydrogen atoms are in each group. As an example, the ratio of the areas of methyl and methylene peak areas would be 6.2 for propane (CH_3-CH_2-CH_3) and 6.4 n.Butane (CH_3-CH_2-CH_2-CH_3).

Quantitatively, NMR provides the mole ratio of CH_3 groups to methylene or olefinic groups in a molecule. It can also provide data on the reaction rate and kinetics since appearance or disappearance of different types of hydrogens can be quantitated by NMR.

Typical applications of NMR are in the determination of structure of new organic compounds either synthesized or biologically separated. NMR can give quantitative information on the presence of one type of compound in another. They include aromatics in paraffin compounds, amines in alcohols, organic halides in other organic compounds, the number of side chains in a hydrocarbon, etc. Gases and solids are not easily amenable for analysis by NMR.

The NMR suffers from lack of sensitivity. The minimum sample volume is 0.1 mL, whereas the average volume commonly required is 0.5 mL and limit of detection is 1%. Secondly, overlap of spectra due to two different types of hydrogens absorbing at similar frequencies. The molecular weight information is not obtained in this analysis. In spite of these limitations, NMR is one of the most useful techniques for structure determination of organic chemicals including hydrogen bonding, solvation and active protonation sites in complex molecules.

Ultraviolet-Visible Absorption Spectroscopy

There are two classes of spectra, namely emission and absorption spectra; emission spectra is the light emitted by a luminous source and the absorption spectrum is obtained by the spectroscopic analysis of light transmitted by an absorbing medium placed in the path of monochromatic light.

The light absorption and consequent energy increase of the absorbing molecule is given by

$$E = h\nu = hc/\lambda \tag{2.9}$$

where h = planck's constant, ν and λ = frequency and the wavelength of the radiation respectively, and c = velocity of light. The change in energy may be in the electronic, vibrational or rotation energy of the molecule. The changes in energy in electronic levels involve relatively large quanta, followed by smaller vibrational energy changes and even smaller rotational energy changes. The electronic energy level of a molecule under normal conditions is called its ground state and the higher electronic levels are called excited levels. For each electronic level, there are ground and excited vibrational states and similarly for every vibrational level, there are ground and excited rotational states (Fig. 2.3).

Saturated organic molecules do not generally absorb light in ultraviolet (UV) or visible regions (200-800 mμ). However, the presence (or introduction) of a chromophore which is a multiple bond, causes the molecule to absorb in UV-visible region. The wavelength corresponding to maximum absorption is called λ_{max} which varies from chromophore to chromophore. The factors governing the λ_{max} of chromophores are the differences in the electronegativities of elements forming double bond and the relative ease of forming double bond. Examples are:

Compound	λ_{max} (mμ)
$H_2C=CH_2$	180
$(CH_3)_2-C=O$	277
$(CH_3)_3N=N-CH_3$	347
$(CH_3)_2-C=S$	400
$C_4H_9N=O$	665

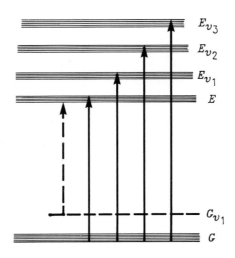

Fig. 2.3. Energy levels for a polyatomic molecule: G, ground electronic state; E, excited electronic state; V_1, V_2, V_3, different vibrational states. The closely spaced lines represent rotational levels.
(Source: Reprinted with permission from ref. 4, Copyright (1961), Butterworths).

Electrons forming single bonds are called σ electrons, the electrons of the double bonds are called π electrons and the electrons which are not shared or non-bonded in molecules such as N, O, etc. are called n electrons. The n electrons of the first rows of periodic table are called p electrons. The example, of formaldehyde is given below:

The various possible transitions giving rise to an electronic spectra are given in Table 2.3.

TABLE 2.3 Classification of electronic transitions.

Transition	Description	Region of electronic spectra
N → V	From a bonding orbital in the ground state to an orbital of higher energy	
	(a) $\sigma \rightarrow \sigma^*$ (between σ orbitals)	Vacuum ultraviolet, e.g., methane at 125 mμ
	(b) $\pi \rightarrow \pi^*$ (between π orbitals) (often called K or A or E bands in different systems)	Ultraviolet e.g., ethylene at 180 mμ or benzene at 203 mμ
N → Q	From a non-bonding atomic orbital to a high energy molecular orbital	
	(a) $n \rightarrow \pi^*$ (to π orbitals) (often called R bands)	Near ultraviolet and visible e.g., acetone at 277 mμ, nitrosobutane at 665 mμ
	(b) $n \rightarrow \sigma^*$ (to σ orbitals)	Far ultraviolet and sometimes near ultraviolet e.g., acetone at 190 mμ, methylamine at 213 mμ
N → R	From an orbital in the ground state to one of very high energy in the direction of the ionization of the molecule	Vacuum ultraviolet

(Source: Reprinted with permission from ref. 4, Copyright (1961), Butterworths).

The wavelength region for UV-visible spectrum is between 200 nm to 800 nm and the radiation has sufficient energy to excite valence electrons in atoms and molecules of a chemical. The UV region (200 to 400 nm) has relatively higher excitation energy than the visible region (400 to 800 nm). Tables 2.4 and 2.5 list the six major fields of analytical methodologies that utilize electronic excitation principle in this wavelength region.

TABLE 2.4 Atomic UV spectroscopy.

No.	Electronic Function	Analytical Area	Analytical Use
(1)	Absorption of UV radiation	Atomic Absorption	Quantitative elemental analysis
(2)	Emission of radiation	Flame Photometry	Quantitative analysis of alkali metals, alkaline earth metals and other metals
(3)	Emission of radiation	Emission Spectrography Plasma Emission	Qualitative and quantitative analysis of multielements

(Source: Reprinted with permission from ref. 1, Copyright (1987), Marcel Dekker Inc.).

TABLE 2.5 Molecular UV spectroscopy.

No.	Electronic Function	Analytical Area	Analytical Use
(1)	Absorption of UV radiation	UV absorption	Determination of aromatics, and unsaturated compounds and natural products
(2)	Emission of UV radiation	Molecular fluorescence	Detection of small amounts of (low μg) of certain aromatics and natural products
(3)	Emission of UV radiation	Molecular phosphorescence	Analysis of gels and glasses

(Source: Reprinted with permission from ref. 1, Copyright (1987), Marcel Dekker Inc.).

The three types of electrons involved in organic molecules are: (1) sigma; (σ) bond electrons that make saturated bonds between carbon and hydrogen atoms; (2) pi (π) bond electrons that make unsaturated bonds such as in olefinic and aromatic compounds; and (3) 'n' electrons that are not involved in any bonding between atoms such as the lone pair of electrons on halogens, sulfur, oxygen, nitrogen atoms substituted on organic compounds.

The UV radiation has enough energy to excite both pi bond and n electrons and not the sigma bond electrons which are relatively more stable. The molecular groups which absorb UV and visible light are called chromophores. A list of compounds and their wavelength of absorption maxima is given in Table 2.6.

TABLE 2.6 Absorption maxima of some organic moities.

Chromophore	Functional Moiety	Wavelength Corresponding Absorption Maximum (nm)
Amine	$-NH_2$	195
Ester	$R - C \overset{O}{\underset{OR}{\diagup}}$	205
Bromide	$-Br$	208
Carboxylic Acid	$R - C \overset{O}{\underset{OH}{\diagup}}$	200-210
Aldehyde	$R - C \overset{O}{\underset{H}{\diagup}}$	210
Nitro	$-NO_2$	210
Nitrite	$-ONO$	220-230
Conjugated olefins	$[-C = C]_2$	210-230
	$[-C = C]_3$	260
	$[-C = C]_5$	330
Benzene		(i) 198 (ii) 255
Naphthalene		(i) 220 (ii) 275 (iii) 314

(Source: Reprinted with permission from ref. 1, Copyright (1987), Marcel Dekker Inc.).

Optical System

Both single- and double-beam systems (as described earlier) are used in UV-visible spectroscopy. The radiation source could be either tungsten lamps or hydrogen discharge lamps. The intensity of tungsten lamp at wavelengths lower than 350 nm is small and the intensity at all wavelengths can be kept constant only when the electrical current is controlled to avoid fluctuations. But tungsten lamps are generally stable and easy to use. The hydrogen discharge lamps have hydrogen gas under high pressure and emit a continuous broad band. These lamps are used widely because they are stable and robust. Deuterium lamps are more intense at shorter wavelengths than the hydrogen lamps but more expensive.

A photomultiplier is a commonly used detector in a UV-visible optical system where photons are converted to electrons by using a metal surface. The electrons generated are multiplied by repeated strikings on an assembly of dynodes. The dynodes are operated at a steady voltage to minimize/eliminate erratic stray signal. A gain as high as 10^9 electrons per photon is possible but in practice lower gains and lower noise (background) levels may be preferable.

Applications

The UV-visible spectroscopic techniques can be used to analyze polynuclear aromatic hydrocarbons, dye stuff, natural products like chlorophyll, steroid, etc. It is also used to study the kinetics of chemical reactions. Its applications also include the analysis of enzymes, hormones, alkaloids and vitamins and water quality parameters such as phosphate, nitrate, fluoride, iodide, silica and sulfate.

Turbidimetry and Nephelometry

Turbidity involves the measurement of light transmitted by a suspension of particles (turbid solution) and nephelometry measures the intensity of light scattered by a suspension. Turbidimetry thus measures the drop in light intensity after its passage through the turbid solution. In this respect, it is somewhat similar to absorption spectrophotometry, although the actual mechanism is totally different. Nephelometry measures scattered light at right angle to the light path.

Nephelometric Method to Measure Turbidity

This method compares the intensities of the scattered light by the sample against that of a standard reference suspension under defined conditions. The higher the intensity of the scattered light, the higher the turbidity.

Formazin polymer is used as the reference turbidity standard suspension. The nephelometric turbidity units based on formazin preparation will approximate the units derived from the candle turbidimeter, but will not be identical to them.

To minimize the differences in measured values for turbidity due to the use of different turbidimeter designs, the following design criteria should be observed (ref. 5):

1. Light source - Tungsten-filament lamp operated at a colour temperature between 2200 and 3000°K.

2. Distance traversed by incident light and scattered light within the sample tube - Total not to exceed 10 cm.

3. Angle of light acceptance by detector - Centered at 90°C to the incident light path and not to exceed ± 30° from 90°. The detector, and filter system if used, shall have a spectral peak response between 400 and 600 nm.

b. Sample tubes, clear colourless glass. Keep tubes scrupulously clean, both inside and out, and discard when they become scratched or etched. Never handle them where the light strikes them. Use tubes with sufficient extra length, or with a protective case, so that they may be handled properly. Fill tubes with samples and standards that have been agitated thoroughly and allow sufficient time for bubbles to escape.

UV Fluorescence Method

When an atom absorbs radiation, it can emit monochromatic radiations called fluorescence, due to electronic transitions. The electrons in an atom in the ground state are assumed to be in definite energy levels which are known as shells, subshells, and orbitals. The shells are designated by numbers and subshells by letter (s,p,d,f) and the number of electrons present in a subshell by a superscript on the letter. For example, sodium would be designated by $3s^1$ and the complete electronic structure is $1s^2$, $2s^2$, $2p^6$, $3s^1$. Each of these energy levels have vibrational sublevels where electrons can reside. Figure 2.4 shows the electronic transitions involved in the fluorescence of sodium atom where the valence electron is excited from the 3s shell to 3p shell. On return of the electron to 3s level, the absorbed energy is emitted as orange light at 589 nm. If excitation is stronger, the electron is raised to 3d level which in turn falls back in two steps; first to 3p shell by emitting photons at 819 nm, followed by return to 3s shell with another emission at 589 nm photons.

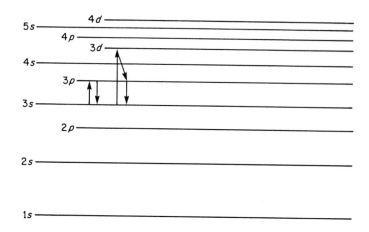

Fig. 2.4. Simplified electronic transition levels involved in fluorescence.

Molecules also have vibrational and rotational energy sublevels. Each vibrational sublevel may have several rotational sublevels. Therefore, there are a large number of energy levels which differ only slightly in their energies. Fig. 2.5 illustrates the excitation of an electron to higher level of energy, loss of vibrational energy during its descent, followed by fluorescence emission at a longer wavelength, such as visible spectrum. They finally return to the ground energy level. When the immediate emission of photon is in the wavelength same as absorption, then the phenomenon is called resonance fluorescence. This resonance is generally the most sensitive line. In solution, it is likely that part of the energy will be lost as heat and the remainder emitted at longer wavelength which is a typical fluorescence spectrum of many organic and inorganic compounds. The excited electron moves into one of numerous vibration levels (singlets) from the lowest excited electron state (Fig. 2.5). The excess energy could be lost rapidly due to collisions and energy transfer to other modes of molecular rotation and vibration. The molecule can then return to one of the excited vibratory levels of its ground electron state. The vertical bars represent the energy difference between states.

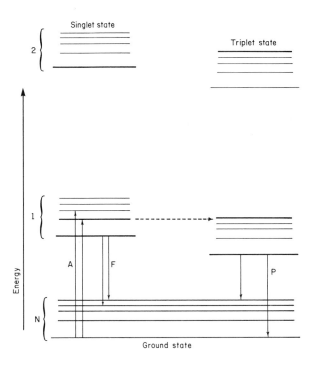

Fig. 2.5. Electronic transitions in a molecule on UV excitation. N = vibration levels; I = first excitation state; 2 = second excitation state; A = absorption transitions; F = fluorescence transition; P = phosphorescence transition. (Source: Reprinted with permission from ref. 6, Copyright (1978), Butterworths).

In certain molecules, a second series of excited states called triplet states exist, whose energies are similar to singlet levels. The excited electron can change in spin direction and enters the triplet state in a radiationless process. This is indicated by dotted line in Fig. 2.5. Transitions with energy emission or absorption between singlet and triplet states are forbidden. The phosphorescence transition P between the ground vibrational state of the triplet level to one of those of the single-line level has a time delay whose duration ranges from 10^{-2} seconds to several seconds. Since there are numerous vibration levels, the fluorescence and phosphorescence spectra have broad band spectrums. Possible loss of energy due to collision with other molecules is called quenching and is common with both fluorescence and phosphorescence. But with proper manipulation quenching of fluorescence can be eliminated but not with phosphorescence.

Atomic fluorescence is very sensitive and concentration levels as low as 10^{-10} g/mL can be detected easily (Table 2.7).

TABLE 2.7 Analytical capability of atomic fluorescence spectroscopy.

	LIMIT OF DETECTION (g)	MAXIMAL DETERMINABLE AMOUNT (g)
Ag	1×10^{-12}	2×10^{-9}
Bi	1×10^{-11}	1×10^{-8}
Co	2×10^{-11}	6×10^{-9}
Cu	1×10^{-12}	4×10^{-9}
Ga	5×10^{-11}	1×10^{-8}
Mg	1×10^{-12}	1×10^{-9}
Mn	5×10^{-12}	2×10^{-9}
Ni	5×10^{-12}	5×10^{-9}
Pb	1×10^{-11}	1.5×10^{-7}
Sb	1×10^{-9}	3×10^{-8}
Tl	5×10^{-11}	2×10^{-9}
Zn	2×10^{-14}	4×10^{-10}

(Source: Reprinted with permission from ref. 6, Copyright (1978), Butterworths).

The types of samples analyzed include vitamins, thymine, phenols, aromatic amines, alkaloids, estrogens, and flavins. Also, fluorescence indicators are commonly used in environmental tracing and analysis. The biological media are most commonly analyzed, followed by water, plants, environmental media, sediments, oils and chemical products. Fluorescence is used in multi-elemental analysis and in this respect, superior to atomic absorption spectroscopy in analyzing multi-elements in a single sample of natural water and seawater.

Interferences in Analytical Applications

Other compounds that fluoresce should be eliminated by column chromatography to improve the sensitivity of the analysis. Fluorescence quenching can be eliminated by successive dilutions. Dissolved oxygen is a powerful quenching agent and hence must be removed by bubbling nitrogen through the sample. The colder temperature of the sample reduces deactivation of fluorescence by molecular collisions with solvents. The changes in pH might change the chemical structure and cause fluorescence changes, and hence pH change must be controlled (ref. 1).

Atomic Absorption Spectroscopy

This is a measurement of the absorption of incident radiation by neutral atoms which is given by

$$A = \log \frac{I_o}{I}$$

(2.10)

where I_0 = intensity of the incident radiation; I = intensity of emitted radiation and A = absorbance. In this process, the atom changes from a low energy state to a higher energy state, without any accompanying vibrational or rotational energy changes. Thus, atomic absorption spectrum of an element has very few narrow absorption lines. There are usually three to four UV spectral lines available for each element and could be less for some elements.

The principle of atomic absorption spectroscopy is similar to other absorption spectroscopic techniques (Fig. 2.6).

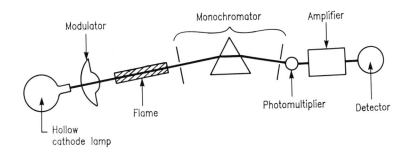

Fig. 2.6. Units of an atomic absorption spectrophotometer.
(Reprinted with permission from ref. 6, Copyright (1978), Butterworths).

Radiation Source

The hollow cathode lamps are commonly used because they emit resonance lines of sufficiently fine structure of the element to be analyzed. The interior of a lamp bulb contains an anode and a cathode in the form of a hollow cylinder consisting of an alloy containing the metal to be analyzed. When a suitable potential difference is applied, atoms of the filler gas (argon or helium) get ionized at the anode and accelerate towards the cathode. The fast moving ions strike the cathode surface and displace the metal atoms which get excited. Since the partial pressure of the cathodic gas is low as is the temperature, the lines emitted by the hollow cathodes are of very narrow widths. These narrow lines are almost completely absorbed by the absorption lines of the atoms in the sample and the atomic absorption can easily be detected and measured. A separate hollow cathode lamp has to be used which emits the spectral lines of the atom to be analyzed in the sample.

The life of a hollow cathode lamp depends on the nature of the metallic alloy which forms the cathode. The lamps with alkali metals, which are volatile elements, have relatively shorter life (few dozen to few hundred hours). This deficiency is remedied by developing electrodeless discharge lamps. It consists of a quartz tube containing the volatile compound of the metal of interest at low pressure. The tube is filled with argon, sealed off and placed in a microwave discharge cavity. Under these conditions, the argon becomes a plasma and excite the metal inside the tube. The emission produced is the resonance line of high intensity of the metal vapour. These electrode-less lamps are also recommended for atomic fluorescence spectrometry.

Atomizer

The sample has to be reduced to the atomic state in order to achieve atomic absorption of the incident light. This is carried out by the atomizer which is the flame in the flame photometry. The aspirator introduces the sample into the base of the flame as droplets which reduces the sample element into atoms. The common oxidants used are oxygen, air, and nitrous oxide and the fuel gases are acetylene and hydrogen. The maximum temperatures reached by these mixtures are given in Table 2.8.

TABLE 2.8 Maximum temperatures (^{o}C) reached by various mixtures.

| | OXIDANT | | |
FUEL	AIR	OXYGEN	NITROUS OXIDE
H_2	2100	2900	2900
Acetylene	2200	3100	3200
Propane	1900	2800	
Butane	1900	2800	

(Source: Reprinted with permission from ref. 1, Copyright (1987), Marcel Dekker Inc.).

When a sample is introduced in the form of a spray, a series of physical and chemical reactions take place, leading to atomization. These reactions involve fusion, volatilization, dissociation or decomposition, yielding free atoms and recombinations especially with the combustion products. A general scheme of reactions is illustrated in Fig. 2.7. After free atoms are formed, they are rapidly oxidized in the hostile environment of the hot flame. The signal starts off low at the base of the flame, increases to a maximum in the re-action zone of the flame, and then falls to zero (Fig. 2.8). The rate of atomization depends on the flame temperature and on the chemical form of the element in the sample. If the element exists in a stable chemical form, the atomization efficiency is decreased. The rate of loss of free atoms also depends on the stability of the chemical form of the element of analysis. If the oxide is very stable, then the free atoms will rapidly move away from the atomic state to the oxide form. This is the case with aluminum, molybdenum, tungsten, and vanadium. The absorption maximum is proportional to the atomic population in the sample, which in turn depends on the original concentration of the element in the sample and atomization efficiency. The variation of

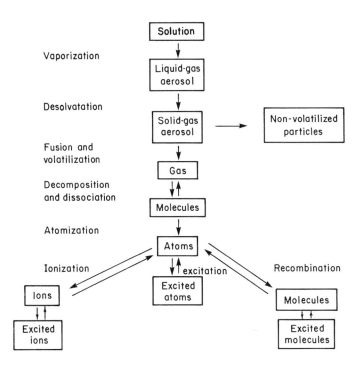

Fig. 2.7. Flow diagram of processes in atomization process.
(Source: Reprinted with permission from ref. 6, Copyright (1978),
Butterworths).

atomization efficiency with the chemical form of the element is called the
'chemical interference'. This can be circumvented by complexing the element
with strong ligands such as EDTA, and phosphate which can be atomized with
relative ease in the flame.

The monochromator separates the absorption line from other lines in the
spectrum emitted by the hollow cathode lamp source. The prisms and gratings
are most commonly used in high-dispersion monochromators. Photomultipliers are
widely used as detectors. The use of lens and slits is intended to reduce the
loss of light signal by focussing the light beam along the flame. Quartz
lenses are commonly used. The entrance slits eliminate stray light from
entering the light path and exit slit isolates the absorption line chosen from
the rest of lines emitted from the source. Thus, this sytem of slits and
monochromators enables the analyst to choose the wavelength of choice to reach
the flame.

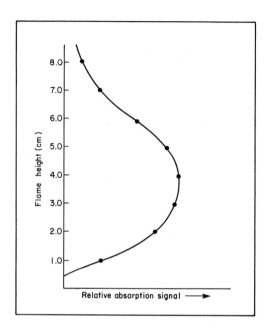

Fig. 2.8. Relative absorption versus flame height: flame profile for nickel 341.4 nm line.
(Source: Reprinted with permission from ref. 1, Copyright (1987), Marcel Dekker Inc.).

Background Correction

The background absorption may arise from molecular absorption due to hydroxyl ions from moisture in the flame, residual organic solvents, refractory metaloxides, etc. The ways of measuring the background absorption and correcting for it include:

1. Use of blank sample;

2. Use of the deuterium or hydrogen lamp as background corrector. The hydrogen lamp measures all the molecular absorption with negligible atomic absorption and thus can be used to correct for background molecular absorption. The advantages are: background is measured at exactly the same wavelength as the resonance line and the system can be automated. This is a common feature in many carbon atomizers.

3. Measuring background using the absorption of a nearby non-resonance line. This is very convenient, needs no change in the lamp source even though it could be slightly less accurate.

Atomic absorption provides a relatively rapid and sensitive analysis of many elements. The method suffers from only a very few interferences, but is more accurate than many other analytical techniques.

Carbon atomizers are several times more sensitive than flame atomizers. In the atomizer process, a low volume sample $(2-30\,\mu L)$ is loaded into an atomizer and then gently warmed to vaporize the solvent. The temperature is increased on ramp mode in stages to ash the sample to remove organics present and finally to atomize rapidly the sample at very high temperature. In this process, a small amount of organic residue is invariably present which generates a high and variable background absorption. Since the background varies significantly between sample and the blank, the use of blanks is not a solution. Automatic background correctors have been developed to correct for the background absorption and to give a computer-generated read out of the net absorption. Although the technique is not totally free from errors that could creep in due to inefficient or faulty atomization sequence, carbon atomizer has expanded the analytical capability of this technique. Biological-medical samples which are low in sample size can be analyzed. Small sample sizes and associated sensitivities in the analysis are given in Table 2.9.

The precision of the carbon atomizer has been improved by the use of the L'vov carbon platform, which is inserted into the standard atomizer. The platform stays cooler than the furnace, thereby condensing metal atoms on itself during the ashing and atomization steps. After a short delay, the temperature increases due to inside radiation, and the metal atoms are revaporized entering the light path. At this time, the background absorption has dropped considerably, increasing the accuracy of the platform method.

Zeeman Background Corrector

When the atomizer is placed in a very intense magnetic field, the orbiting electrons are influenced by the field and split to 2s + 1 energy states where s is the total spin angular momentum of the atom. This is particularly important to optical electron. Due to the different energy levels, atomic absorption does not take place, but background absorption is still measured (Fig. 2.9).

When no magnetic field is present, the detector measures the total absorption plus the background absorption. The difference between the two measurements is the net atomic absorption. The Zeeman corrector follows the same light path through the atomizer for both background correction and for total atomic absorption measurement. Another salient point is that the background is measured close to the atomic resonance lines and wavelength shift will cause negligible change in background absorption.

TABLE 2.9 Sample size and associated sensitivities (1% absorption) in the
graphite tube atomizer.

ELEMENT	ABSOLUTE SENSITIVITY $(g \times 10^{-12})$	20 μL SOLUTION $(\mu g/mL)$
Al	150	0.007
As	160	0.008
Be	3.4	0.0002
Bi	280	0.014
Ca	3.1	0.05
Cd	0.8	0.00004
Co	120	0.006
Cr	18	0.01
Cs	71	0.004
Cu	45	0.02
Ga	1,200	0.06
Hg	15,000	1.5
Mn	7	0.01
Ni	330	0.10
Pb	23	0.001
Pd	250	0.013
Pt	740	0.02
Rb	41	0.002
Sb	510	0.15
Si	24	0.10
Sn	5,500	0.2
Sr	31	0.0015
Ti	280	0.5
Tl	90	0.1
V	320	0.2
Z	2.1	0.0001

(Source: Reprinted with permission from ref. 1, Copyright (1987), Marcel Dekker, Inc.).

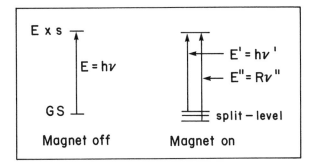

Fig. 2.9. Zeeman background correction; energy levels of valence electrons in and out of a magnetic field.
(Source: Reprinted with permission from ref. 1, Copyright (1987), Marcel Dekker, Inc.).

Heifje-Smith Corrector

This method corrects the background by increasing the voltage of the hollow cathode lamp to a high level when only the background absorption is measured because the centre is self absorbed. When the lamp is underrun (normal voltage), normal resonance lines are emitted leading to normal atomic absorption only. The difference between the two measurements is the net atomic absorption of the element.

Emission Spectrography

When the atom gets excited by an external source, its electrons and especially the valence electrons shift from a low-energy orbital to higher-energy orbital. This process is followed immediately by the return of the electron to a lower energy orbital with release of energy. The emitted radiation from the excited atom is the basis of emission spectrography. There are numerous forms of excitation sources available, but the use of plasma to excite atoms and plasma emission spectrography has become a very important instrument in analytical chemistry.

The principle of the method is as follows: An electrical discharge source is produced at a steady rate between the electrode and the counter electrode. The sample is introduced into the discharge via the electrode, where it is vapourized and excited. The emitted radiation follows on, which is detected and quantitatively measured by the detector system.

An atomic absorption technique measures the absorption by ground-state atoms whereas emission methods rely upon the number of excited atoms formed.

Both methods rely on the concentration in the original sample, efficiency of atomization (and the ability to excite the atoms in emission spectroscopy). Practical applications which includes analysis of: (1) natural minerals; (2) water; (3) plant and biological media; (4) atmospheric aerosols; and (5) chemical and industrial products are discussed in detail in ref. 6. The interference from background radiation, temperature changes, sample matrix and solvent makes emission spectroscopy less precise than the atomic absorption spectroscopy. However, emission spectroscopic methods are valuable in multi-elemental analysis. The inductively coupled plasma (ICP) method has an extensive analytical range which is superior to all methods mentioned above in simultaneous multi-element quantitative analysis. Optimum ranges of various analytical techniques including spectroscopic techniques are given in Table 2.10.

Infrared Absorption Method

When some part of a molecule vibrates at a frequency same as the incident radiation energy, then the energy is absorbed by the molecule. The absorbed energy increases the amplitude of vibration of the molecules. The rate at which these components of atom vibrate is characteristic of the atom and occurs only at well-defined frequencies. These frequencies are quantitated and are termed "finger prints" of the molecule. The following conditions have to be satisfied before the absorption of infrared energy (range 0.780-40 μm):

1. The frequency of vibration of the molecule must be equal to the frequency of the incident radiation.
2. The equation $E=h\nu$ must be satisfied by the frequency of radiation where E is the energy difference between the relevant vibrational states.
3. The change in vibration must induce changes in the dipole moments of the molecule.
4. The degree of absorption should be proportional to the square of the rate of change of dipole during excitation.
5. The energy difference in transition can be modified by rotational energy changes in the molecule (ref. 1).

Applications

Typical applications are the identification of functional groups such as carboxylic acids, ketones, etc. Common uses of this technique include identification and determination of paraffins, aromatics, olefins, aldehydes,

TABLE 2.10 Optimum concentration ranges of various analytical techniques.*

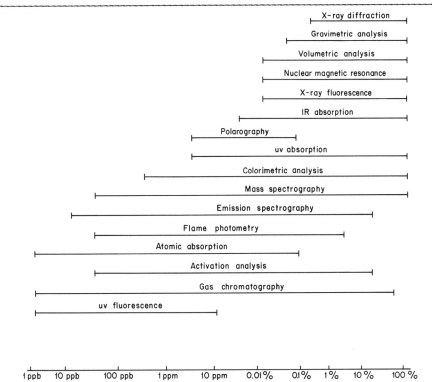

* Ranges quoted are for untreated or unconcentrated samples. Sensitivity of all methods can be extended by proper preanalytical preparation of samples. (Source: Reprinted with permission from ref. 1, Copyright (1987), Marcel Dekker, Inc.).

carboxylic acid, ketones, phenols, esters, amines and many other organic compounds.

The IR spectrum can: (1) identify the odour and taste components of food; (2) distinguish chemicals from each other; (3) determine the composition of organic additives in paints; (4) identify varnishes, pigments used in paintings in detecting the age of paintings, automobiles, etc.; (5) used in checking the identity of the research materials. The IR techniques are used in quality control of routinely produced industrial products and other numerous uses.

2.1.3 Elution and Size Separation

Under specified conditions, a solution containing a mixture of compounds can be separated by pouring it through a column of a stationary phase (finely divided solid coated with a thin layer of a liquid). The components of the mixture are adsorbed which then elute at different rates when a mobile phase (liquid or gas) moves across the stationary phase. The different rates of elution render the compounds to separate and this technique is called chromatography. This process of separation forms the basis of all branches of chromatography. Chromatography is the resolution of mixtures of compounds by differential migration from a narrow zone in porous media, the migration caused by the flow of gas or liquid. Chromatography is probably the most important single analytical technique currently in use and will remain in the forefront for the forseeable future. It was developed initially as a separation method followed by separate methods of identification and quantification. Nowadays, instrumentation and techniques are available that couple chromatography with other analytical tools such as infrared and mass spectrometry and atomic absorption spectroscopy. This tandem of methods allow automated qualitative and quantitative analysis of the fractions separated.

(i) Liquid-Solid Chromatography. A mixture of compounds in a liquid phase can be separated by eluting over a solid stationary phase. An inert liquid is used as the mobile phase and the separation efficiency of compounds depends among other factors on their partition between the two phases. The distribution is governed by the solubility of compounds in the mobile phase and their absorption on the surface of the solid stationary phase. Solubility varies greatly among solvents and this property can be used to choose a mobile phase that will meet the required rate of progression of sample compounds along the column.

The active sites on the stationary phase are the centres which attract the molecules of compounds in the liquid mixture. The better the stereospecific fit between the crystal lattice site and the compound molecule (analyte molecule), greater will be the adsorption strength. But the active sites also attract solvent molecules, thus creating a competition between sorbing molecules of the analyte and solvent. Because of the vast excess of solvent molecules present, the solvent molecules displace analyte molecules from active sites. Solvents of low affinity have slower displacement rate whereas those of higher affinity displace analyte molecules rapidly which flow down the column quickly. Hence, proper choice of solvent and solid substrate is important in the operation of liquid-solid chromatography. The active sites could irreversibly adsorb impurities from the solvent, thereby reducing the total exchangeable sites available for column chromatography.

Applications

Liquid-solid chromatography is very useful in the separation of high molecular weight compounds such as high molecular weight esters, acids, olefins, paraffins, vitamins and compounds of biological origin such as proteins. The important branches of liquid-solid chromatography are described below:

1. Thin-Layer Chromatography (TLC)

Thin-layer chromatography is similar to column adsorption chromatography except that a glass plate coated with a thin (0.025 mm) layer of some inert material is used as the solid phase. A slurry of inert materials such as Al_2O_3, MgO, or SiO_2 in a suitable inert solvent is spread evenly over a glass plate and dried. The use of inert materials which are resistant to strong chemicals such as acids and solvents eliminates the problem of substrate damage as encountered in paper chromatography.

For compounds which are not coloured and thus cannot be detected visually, reagents which form coloured compounds with the analyte are used for identification and quantitation. Reagents such as dithizone,1,10-phenanthraline are commonly used. Silica-gel thin layer chromatographic sheets are also used in thin-layer chromatographic analysis of chemical species. Fig. 2.10 illustrates an example of TLC separation of methylmercury and inorganic mercury using dithizone in benzene. A good separation was achieved and a quantitative (100%) recovery of the added mercury was also observed in that study (ref. 7) (Fig. 2.10).

Fluorescent reagents are used in the identification and quantitation of compounds which fluoresce under UV radiation. For compounds which do not fluoresce, the indirect technique of impregnating the entire TLC plate with a fluorescent material is used. Under the UV lamp the whole plate fluoresces excepting the sample spots which appear as dark spots. The commonly used fluorescent reagent is ninhydrin, which is 1,2,3-nidantrione monohydrate. Chemical reagents usually called "spray agents" locate solutes by forming coloured reaction products with one or more types of functional groups. However, most reagents are fairly specific and a few of the common reagents and their applications are listed in Table 2.11 (ref. 8). A fairly complete list of reagents (about 266), methods of preparation for use and treatments after application is provided in ref. 9.

38

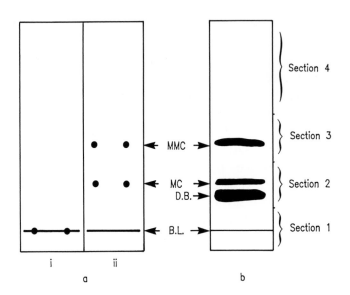

Fig. 2.10. TLC separation of methylmercury and inorganic mercury in standards
(a) and in samples (b). a(i) Dots represent a mixture of standard methylmercury and inorganic mercury dithizonates before developing; a(ii) After
developing with a mixture of benzene-hexane; B.L. = baseline; D.B. = dithizone band; MC = inorganic mercury; MMC = methylmercury.
(Source: Reprinted with permission from ref. 7, Copyright (1982),
Springer-Verlag).

TABLE 2.11 Some common TLC spray reagents.

Aniline phthalate	Reducing sugars
Bromcresol Green	Acids and bases
Bromthymol Blue	Lipids
Dichlorofluoresceine	Lipids
4-Dimethylaminobenzaldehyde	Amino sugars, indols, alkaloids, urea, and others
Ninhydrin	Amino acids, amines
Phosphomolybdic acid	Reducible compounds
Rhodamine B	General fluorescent indicator

(Source: Reprinted with permission from ref. 8, Copyright (1983), from Marcel
Dekker, Inc.).

Applications

The TLC is used widely for the quantitative determination of high molecular weight compounds of pharmaceutical and biological origin. The quantitative identification is made using the rate of flow of the compound along the TLC plate, 'R_f value' which is a ratio of flow rate of the sample over that of the solvent. R_f is a constant value for a compound at a given temperature, for a given solvent and substrate. R_f value of an unknown compound is compared with R_f values from databanks for positive identification. The quantitative determination is carried out by removing the sample spot from the TLC plate, dissolving it in a suitable solvent and analyzing it by UV, IR, or any other applicable analytical methods. The TLC methods are used for semiquantitative and rapid separation of pesticides in crops, soils and water. The separated pesticides are identified by a cholinesterase-inhibition method, using fluorometric detection. The substrate N-methyl indoxyl acetate, normally cleaved by cholinesterase to the highly green fluorescent N-methyl indoxyl. The pesticides inhibit cholinesterase and hence appear as white spots on a green fluorescent background.

TLC is commonly used to provide chemical class separations to simplify subsequent analysis. TLC-gas chromatography (GC) method is used for the analysis of PAHs, derivatives of PAHs, and other miscellaneous compounds such as isocyanates, triethylamine and benacyl in air. Details on different TLC plates used, developing solvents and procedures are given in ref. 10. Application of TLC in the analysis of aquatic pollutants (ref. 11), in soil chemistry (ref. 12) and in chemical wastes (ref. 13) are described in the literature.

2. Column Chromatography

The solid phase such as Al_2O_3, MgO, SiO_2, $CaCO_3$, or resins is packed into a column of usually 90 cm x 1.25 cm in size. Sample which is dissolved in a suitable solvent is placed on top of the solid phase in the column. The fractionation of compounds is achieved by eluting the column with more solvent at a slow and steady rate. The fractions can be collected by a fraction collector based on time or volume mode and each fraction can be analyzed. Alternatively, the effluent from the column is monitored prior to fractionation by UV absorption or refractive indices and then split into portions. Typical solvents used are alcohol, benzene, ether, heptane, and esters.

Mixtures of compounds are separated by successive elution using different solvents one after the other. For example, successive elution with heptane, followed by benzene, diethyl ether would remove paraffins first, then aromatics, followed by specific organic compounds. In general, the sequence of solvents with increasing dielectric constant would elute organic compounds of increasing polarity. A sudden change of solvents may lead to problems such as overrun of compounds into more than one fraction especially at the interface of solvent change. This has been overcome by using a gradient elution technique where pairs of solvents which are miscible with each other are used as eluants. A solvent of lower polarity is used first, followed shortly by the second solvent. This provides a phased increase in solvent polarity which leads to progressive solubility of the components of the mixture in the sample. Commonly used solvent pairs are water-methanol, water-acetonitrile, etc. The retention times are used to identify compounds with further confirmation by eluting the sample with different columns at different analytical conditions. The assumption here is that it is very unlikely that two compounds will have the same retention time under different analytical conditions.

The properties commonly used in the detection systems are the refractive index and UV absorption of the compounds in the sample. The former property can be used for any solvent with a detection limit of about 0.1 μg/mL. Whereas, the UV detectors can reach 0.1 ng/mL but limited to solvents which do not absorb UV radiation. Another difference is that refractive index detectors cannot be used with gradient elution whereas, UV system can be used. Fluorescence detectors, electrochemical detectors, conductivity detectors and Fourier-Transformed-Infra-Red (FTIR) detectors are also used with liquid chromatography.

Liquid chromatography (LC) has several advantages for the analysis of organic compounds in water. Most of the organic carbon in water and waste-waters is present as "non-volatile compounds" that can be handled by LC but not by GC. Examples include humic materials, polar organic compounds such as carbohydrates, alkyl benzene sulfonates, and aromatic and heterocyclic amines (products of coal and shale retorting). Several kinds of stationary phases such as polar, non-polar, ionic (ion-exchange resins), non-ionic phases are available. Almost any kind of selectivity can be obtained by choosing the proper mobile phase. Solvent gradients and selective detectors can be used to increase the sensitivity of detection. Application of LC in the analysis of water pollutants (ref. 14), to soil chemistry (ref. 15), to chemical wastes (ref. 16) are discussed in the literature.

3. Gel Permeation Chromatography

This technique uses a porous material with definite size pores (5-300 nm) to separate molecules according to their size. This technique is also known as gel filtration or exclusion chromatography. Small molecules enter the pores more rapidly than large molecules which are excluded by the pores. The porous material which is usually a three-dimensional network capable of acting like a "molecular sieve". This results in a differential rate of molecular movement down the column, smaller molecules moving faster than the larger molecules. By controlling the extent of cross-linking and thus the amount of swelling of the gel beads, the pore size can be controlled so that several different size ranges are available.

There are basically two types of packing materials: (1) porous glasses or silicas; and (2) porous cross-linked organic gels such as dextrans, hydroxy-ethyl cellulose gels, methacrylate-based gels, and polyvinyl alcohol-based gels. The UV fluorescence, UV absorption, refractive index detectors are commonly used.

Applications

The gel-permeation chromatography is employed in the separation, fractiona-tion, and purification of a variety of compounds including proteins, lipids, carbohydrates and polymers. Also, compounds such as hormones, vitamins, enzymes, antigens, nucleic acids, and fatty acid esters are routinely separated by this technique. It can be scaled up or down to cope with large volumes in commercial operations or small volumes in research laboratories. The columns can be refrigerated to avoid decomposition of biological compounds or breakdown of high molecular weight compounds. This technique is routinely carried out at room temperatures without any loss in biological activity of the compounds separated.

(ii) Liquid-Liquid Chromatography. This methodology is based on the two immiscible liquids as the mobile and stationary phase. The stationary phase is present as a thin layer adsorbed on the surface of a substrate. The following chromatographic techniques follow the liquid-liquid chromatographic principle:

1. Reverse-phase chromatography.

In this technique, the polarity of phases are reversed. The stationary phase is organic (organic material coated on a glass or silica surface) and the polar mobile phase can be aqueous or any solvent with high dielectric constant. The common stationary phases used are silicate esters on silica gel, and chemically-bonded organochlorosilanes on silica gel.

Applications

This technique is used widely in the separation and analysis of body fluids such as urine, saliva, blood which are essentially either aqueous in nature or organic compounds dissolved in water/saline water. The development of the reverse-phase chromatography provided a major breakthrough in the analysis of above sample types.

2. High Performance Liquid Chromatography

The conventional liquid chromatograph (LC) consumes excessive time because it uses gravity feed. This problem has been overcome with the advent of high pressure liquid chromatography (HPLC). In this technique, pressure is applied through a pump to the column, making the mobile phase to move faster. The earlier problems in pumping action which resulted in poor resolution have been resolved and the modern pumps used with LC offer good resolution. Pressures in the range of 30 to 200 atmospheres are normally applied, depending on the type of column used. The use of HPLC linked to graphite furnace atomic absorption spectrophotometer or inductively coupled plasma spectrometer as detection systems in the analysis of molecular species of trace elements and estimation of physicochemical and biological properties has been recently reported (ref. 17).

3. Capillary Column Chromatography

This method uses glass capillary columns coated with reversed-phase substrates and thus able to reach very high resolution which is encountered in capillary gas chromatography. A pump is used to force the mobile phase through the capillary column, thus allowing the separation to be completed in a reasonable time. This technique is used in the characterization of body fluids, proteins, peptides and polynucleotides.

4. Ion-exchange and Ion Chromatography

Ion exchange is the exchange of ions of same electrical sign between solution and a solid substrate in contact with it. Many naturally occurring substances such as clays, humic acids, and some artificial resins are good ion-exchangers. Synthetic ion-exchange materials are mostly derived from cross-linked polystyrene which is prepared by copolymerizing styrene and divinyl benzene. The two types of ion-exchangers in use are, the cationic and anionic exchangers. They both have the same resin backbone but have different functional groups (Fig. 2.11).

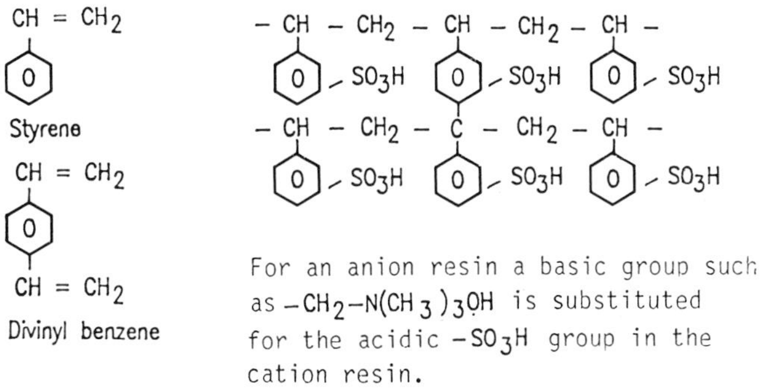

CH $=$ CH$_2$

Styrene

CH $=$ CH$_2$

CH $=$ CH$_2$

Divinyl benzene

$-$ CH $-$ CH$_2$ $-$ CH $-$ CH$_2$ $-$ CH $-$

$-$ SO$_3$H $-$ SO$_3$H $-$ SO$_3$H

$-$ CH $-$ CH$_2$ $-$ C $-$ CH$_2$ $-$ CH $-$

$-$ SO$_3$H $-$ SO$_3$H $-$ SO$_3$H

For an anion resin a basic group such as $-$CH$_2$$-$N(CH$_3$)$_3$OH is substituted for the acidic $-$SO$_3$H group in the cation resin.

Fig. 2.11. Structure of an ion-exchange resin.

The rate of ion exchange is controlled by the law of mass action selectivity rules. There are some general rules which may be used to predict the behaviour of resins in presence of ionic solutions. The ions with highest charge have the greatest affinity:

1. Na$^+$ $<$ Ca^{2+} $<$ Al^{3+}

   Mono valent ions   divalent ions   trivalent ions

2. Among ions of the same valence group, the smaller the hydrated ion, the stronger is the binding to the resin. It should be noted that it is the diameter of the hydrated ion that is critical in binding to resin and not the crystalline diameter of the bare ion. Elements with lower atomic number bind more water molecules and thus actually are larger than the elements with higher atomic number.

$$Li^+ < Na^+ < K^+ < Cs^+ < Be^{2+} < Mg^{2+} < Cu^{2+} < Sn^{2+}$$

The weak acid cation exchanger binds hydrogen much more strongly than other cations and weak base anion exchangers bind hydroxyl more strongly than the other anions. The above generalizations apply to both cationic and anionic exchangers. The newer chelating resins with iminodiacetate or other chelating functional groups offer greater specificity than the conventional ion exchangers.

In recent years, "Ion chromatography", a technique of high resolution chromatographic separation coupled with electrical conductivity detectors has become much used in environmental analysis, particularly for anions. Because it is very sensitive, many samples of water and wastewater can be analyzed without preconcentration, but on-line-enrichment may be used, if required. The main use of this ion-chromatographic technique is the preconcentration of metal ions subsequently analyzed by x-ray fluorescence or atomic absorption spectroscopy methods.

(iii) <u>Gas-Liquid Chromatography</u>. This technique is similar to column chromatography except that a gas is used as the mobile phase instead of a liquid. Gas chromatography is a technique of separation in which the gaseous or vapourized components to be separated are distributed between a stationary liquid phase of large surface area and a moving gas phase. The liquid phase is coated on an inert solid support. There are three different approaches to achieve the separation; the elution method, the frontal method and the displacement method. The elution method is by far the most common and discussion will be restricted to that method and also to gas-liquid chromatography since gas-solid chromatography is seldom used.

The gas phase moves along the solid particles coated with the liquid phase held in a glass or stainless steel column. When a sample mixture is injected into a gas stream, the components move through the column at rates depending upon the vapourization rates and strength of interaction with the stationary liquid phase. At appropriate conditions, each component of the sample emerges from the column well separated in time from other components.

The GC equipment is basically composed of a sample inlet port at one end of a column packed with stationary phase material, with a detector at the other end. Fig. 2.12 is a block diagram of a gas chromatograph.

The column is the heart of the chromatograph. The interaction between the sample components and the liquid substrate is the basis of chromatographic separation. The substrate must be chemically inert even at high temperatures and its vapour pressure must be very low over the entire temperature range of operation. Table 2.12 shows typical examples of liquid substrates and many more are commercially available. The substrates are essentially high boiling liquids of varying degrees of polarity. The inert solid support is usually derived from diatomaceous earth.

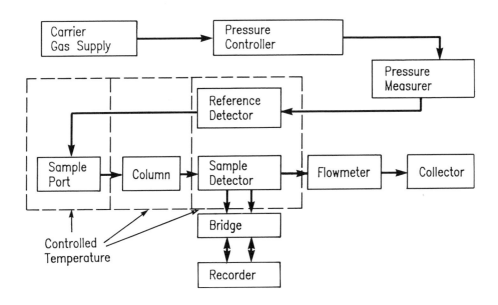

Fig. 2.12. Block diagram of a gas chromatograph.
(Source: Reprinted with permission from ref. 18, Copyright (1970), Marcel Dekker, Inc.).

TABLE 2.12 Common liquid substrates used in GC columns.

MATERIAL	MAXIMUM TEMPERATURE (^{o}C)
Squalane	150
Apiezon-L grease	300
Methyl silicone gum (SE 30)	350
Polyalkylene glycol (Ucon L. B550x)	200
Methyl silicone oil (DC 200)	200
Carbowax 20 M	250
Diethylene glycol adipate	200

(Source: Reprinted with permission from ref. 1, Copyright (1987), Marcel Dekker, Inc.).

Column substrates are chosen depending upon the type of sample to be analyzed. Technical information is available from the manufacturers which is reliable in choosing the proper column. Table 2.13 lists the commonly used liquid stationary phases and their analytical applications. The significant feature of GC which has contributed to its widespread applications, is the availability of several detectors intended for dedicated analysis. Table 2.14 lists the various detectors, their sensitivities, and range of applications. The quantitation requires peak height or peak area and a standard curve. Compounds are identified by either retention time or more accurately using spikes of standard reference compounds.

TABLE 2.13 Some commonly used liquid-stationary phases and their analytical applications.

CLASS	STATIONARY PHASES
Acids	FFAP, SE-52, Apiezon L, SE-30, Porapak Q
Alcohols	OV-1, Porapak Q, DEGS, Carbowax 20M, Chromsorb 102
Aldehydes	Porapak Q, DC-550, Ucon 280X, Carbowax 20M
Amides	Versamid 900, Apiezon L
Amines	Chromosorb 103, Porapak R, DC-550, THEED, Dowfax 9N9/KOH
Aromatics	TCEPE, Ucon LB 550-X, dibutyltetrachlorophthalate
Essential oils	Carbowax 20M, FFAP
Esters	Porapak Q, dinonyl phthalate, EGS, SE-30
Ethers	Carbowax 20 M, β, β'-oxdipropionitrile
Glycols	Porapak Q
Halogens	SE-52, DC-550, triphenyl phosphate, Carbowax 20 M
Ketones	Porapak Q, DC-550, Carbowax 20M, Lexan
Nitriles	Carbowax 400, TCEPE, XF-1150
Olefins	AgNO$_3$/ethylene glycol, tricresyl phosphate, squalane
Paraffins	Squalane, SE-30, Carbowax 400, tricresyl phosphate
Phenols	SP-2110, dinonyl phthalate, XE-60, OV-101
Steroids	OV-17, OV-210, QF-1, SE-30, XE-60, Epon 1001, SP-2100
Sugars	Carbowax 6000, PEG 4000, SE-52, DEGS, QF1, SP-2330
Sulfur	Porapak QS, Apiezon M, Carbowax 1500, Supelcoport S
Water	Porapak Q

(Source: Reprinted with permission from ref. 8, Copyright (1983), Marcel Dekker, Inc.).

TABLE 2.14 Sensitivity of GC Detectors

DETECTOR	SENSITIVITY (g)	LINEAR RANGE	COMMENTS
Thermal conductivity	10^{-8}	10^4	Universal sensitivity; non-destructive
Flame ionization	10^{-11}	10^6	Detects all organic compounds; the most widely used GC detector; destructive
Electron capture	10^{-13}	10^2	Detects halo-, nitro-, and phosphorus compounds; response varies significantly; non-destructive
Flame emission	10^{-11}	10^3	Sulfur and phosphorus compounds; response varies widely with compound: destructive
Gas density balance	10^{-6}	10^5	Universal; low sensitivity; nondestructive
Argon ionization	10^{-12}	10^5	Universal; argon carrier gas necessary; nondestructive
Cross section	10^{-6}	10^5	Universal; detects major components

(Source: Reprinted with permission from ref. 1, Copyright (1987), Marcel Dekker, Inc.).

(iv) Gas Chromatography-Mass Spectrometry (GC-MS). Mass spectrometry is relatively fast and reliable technique for obtaining qualitative and quantitative information of the molecular structure of compounds based on their mass. In this technique, the atoms and the ions are separated by the difference in their masses. The molecules or atoms are bombarded by electrons and the ions produced are then accelerated by an applied voltage. The accelerated charged particles then enter a magnetic field and move in a circle. When the attractive force of the magnet equals the centrifugal force, the particle travels uniformly around the circular path. When the applied voltage and the magnetic field are kept constant, the radius of the circular path depends on the mass of the ionized molecule. This relationship between the mass, radius, applied voltage, and magnetic field is the basis of the separation of particles based on their mass. In modern mass spectroscopy, the applied voltage is varied while keeping the magnetic field constant, thus scanning the mass range of the sample ions.

The degree of usefulness of a mass spectrometer depends on its power of resolution of mass, which is given by

$$\text{resolution} = \frac{\text{average mass}}{\text{difference in mass}}$$

This means, a resolution of 700 provides the ability to distinguish particles in the 700 mass number range. It can distinguish between particles of mass 699 and 700. The higher the solution, the easier it is to distinguish between particles in that higher mass range. The commonly used MS instruments can handle compounds up to molecular weight 2000. Special equipments can have resolution between 10,000 and 20,000, all capable of handling higher molecular weight compounds. However, there is a challenge to handle the molecules from fragmenting during the process.

In recent years, the time taken to obtain a mass spectrum of a single compound has been reduced to about 1 sec, which made the interfacing with GC a reality. Emerging compounds are fed directly into the mass spectrometer, provided there is a 1 sec retention time difference between compounds. High speed scanning is performed for qualitative purposes with some loss in resolution. Quadrupole mass spectrometer (non-magnetic: instead of a heavy magnet, it uses four electromagnetic poles) is capable of accepting samples over a wide range unlike the magnetic mass spectrometers. But the quadrupole mass spectrometers do not have the accuracy and precision of magnetic mass spectrometers. But it can provide a spectrum in a few seconds and has a wide angle acceptance which compensates for its lesser degree of accuracy. With the use of computers, the spectra can be deposited in the memory bank and the computer can search for the most likely compounds in the sample by matching its spectrum with spectra in the memory bank. Often, it will show several possibilities when a direct and complete match is not possible. It is still important to interpret the spectra from the first principles. A high resolution MS can identify the empirical formulas of fragments of large chemical molecules, such as natural products, proteins, synthetic organic compounds, etc.

TABLE 2.15 Analytical techniques, their applicable areas, and sensitivities.

ANALYTICAL TECHNIQUE	SENSITIVITY (g)	COMMENTS
Gas chromatography	10^{-8}-10^{-14}	Depends on the type of detector
Thin-layer chromatography Fluorescence	10^{-9} 10^{-9}	Nondestructive technique
Mass spectrometry	10^{-12}	Detects all elements and most volatile compounds

Liquid chromatography
  Refractive index detector
  Ultraviolet/visible detector
	
	10^{-6}
	10^{-9}
		
		Limited to absorbing compounds

Neutron activation analysis	10^{-12}	Variable sensitivity in response

Atomic absorption spectroscopy
  Flame
  Thermal
	
	10^{-9}
	10^{-14}
		Detects metals and metalloids

Atomic emission spectroscopy	10^{-9}	Rapid multi-element analysis with high sensitivity
Inductively coupled plasma technique		Ideal for screening analysis
Infrared spectroscopy Standard techniques (pure samples)	 10^{-6}	Sensitiviy fair; detects organic functional groups
Fourier transform infrared	10^{-9}	
X-ray fluorescence	10^{-7}	Used for elements with atomic numbers above 11
Optical microscopy	10^{-12}	Simple, rapid method for particulate analysis
Anodic stripping voltammetry	10^{-8}	Can analyze from 10 to 20 elements; best for Cu, Pb, Zn, Cd and their species

Surface analysis
  ESCA
  Ion scattering spectroscopy
  Auger
  Secondary ion mass
   spectrometry
	
	10^{-10}
	10^{-10}
	10^{-10}
	10^{-15}
		Detects and identifies atoms in first several atomic layers of a surface; among the most sensitive methods known

Polarography
  DC polarography
  Pulsed polarography
  Stripping voltammetry
	
	10^{-8}
	10^{-10}
	10^{-11}
		Detects most metallic elements and compounds; also organics

Ion-selective electrodes	10^{-15}	Sensitivity shown is for detection of Cu; otherwise, sensitivities vary, depending on element and electrode

Continued . . .

TABLE 2.15 Concluded.

ANALYTICAL TECHNIQUE	SENSITIVITY (g)	COMMENTS
GC/UV-photoelectron spectroscopy	10^{-5}	Using a direct-coupled GC, spectra can be obtained in less than 1 min on 10^{-5} g quantities
Proton NMR Continuous wave (single scan) Fourier transform ($\sim$10,000 scans)	10^{-4} 10^{-6}	Detects all organic and dia-magnetic organometallic com-pounds that contain hydrogen atoms; instrument costs range from moderate to expensive; NMR offers additional ability to give structure and identity for compounds
UV absorption	10^{-7}	Best for unsaturated and aro-matic samples
Combination method GC-MS GC-Fourier transform infrared GC-UV	10^{-12} 10^{-9} 10^{-6}	Quantitative analysis based on peak area and qualitative analy-sis based on data obtained by instrument linked to GC; compu-ter interfacing greatly extends potential and speed of method

(Source: Reprinted with permission from ref. 1, Copyright (1987), Marcel Dekker, Inc.).

Applications

The technique of GC-MS is useful in the analysis of molecular structures, isomeric analysis, and quantitation of organic compounds, environmental contaminants such as dioxins, PAHs, PCBs, etc., even in the presence of impurities. It is used in the analysis of hydrocarbon fractions and chemicals and impurities present in individual fractions. It is used in the quantitative analysis of components in natural products in the presence of each other such as steroids.

2.2 TOXICITY ASSESSMENT

Every chemical has various effects on human beings, the environment and its components. The effects of chemicals may be assessed by: (1) the nature of the chemical; (2) the exposure period of the receptor; and (3) the dose of the chemical. For example, exposure to a high concentration of a contaminant for a relatively short period would result in noticeable effects that are experienced promptly; this type of an exposure is classified as "acute". On the other hand, exposure to a low concentration of a chemical over a considerable period of time, will show effect after a long latent period. These types of effects are classified as "chronic".

In recent times, through the expansion of knowledge, the effects of various chemicals have been understood to a greater extent. Chemicals have been linked to the induction of cancer, promotion of cancer, degeneration of various organs in the human body, and the changes of both physiological and behavioural patterns. Studies have also revealed that the effects of certain chemicals through mutagenesis and teratogenesis, could alter cellular structure that control the processing of genetic information. These subtle alterations would have detrimental effects upon the various evolutionary protective systems that have been developed by biological species over time.

The major factors that determine the toxicity of a chemical to biological species is dependent upon the quantity of the substance. The words of Ottoboni (ref. 19) "the dose makes the poison" have clarified this aspect of toxicity vividly. Thus, exposure to certain chemicals in large quantities would produce adverse effects; however, when administered in lesser amounts or regulated quantities, the same chemicals such as magnesium, selenium, iron, copper, and certain vitamins (A&E) become necessary for life itself.

Another important variable that determines the magnitude of the toxic effects of the chemical is the duration of exposure. If a large amount of a chemical is administered in a single dose, the consequences would be disastrous and it might even result in the death of the specimen. On the other hand, the effects might not be noticeable if the same dose was administered over a longer period of time. In both cases, the specimen would have produced various forms of defense mechanisms; however, these would have been effective in preventing serious effects in the case of a long time exposure only. This type of defense mechanism is present in all biological systems, and it has evolved over time as a protective mechanism that allows the species to survive.

A chemical itself could have varied toxicological effects depending upon its form at the time of exposure. Taking mercury as an example, the toxic potential and the targetted organs of the compound will vary regarding the valence state of the metal and its speciation. Organomercury compounds are very toxic, with methylmercury being several orders of magnitude higher in toxicity than inorganic mercury. Within the organic group of mercury compounds itself, toxicity varies. Aliphatic mercury compounds are much more toxic to biological systems than aromatic compounds. It is evident that toxicity of a chemical is dependent upon the speciation of the chemical itself, and will vary substantially even within compounds of the same basic group.

There is no single approach to evaluating toxicity. There are a number of variables that may have different effects on a chemical, on a combination of chemicals, and on a biological system. However, tests should reflect the level of exposure to the chemical that is expected to be present in the environment, the possible effects and consequences of this chemical, and the concentration that is likely to produce adverse effects. Toxicity testing must be developed in such a way that it could incorporate new advances and changes regarding previous findings. Pretesting is an important step in the design and development of an appropriate battery of tests. Toxicity testing should not be utilized to provide absolute answers or considered to be the final step in the prevention of toxic effects but it should lead towards the provision of information that allows for the development of appropriate degree of safety.

2.2.1 Acute Toxicity

(i) Oral. Acute oral toxicity has often been defined as systemic damage produced by a substance as a result of a one-time exposure of relatively short term. The test is usually conducted on animals through the administration of a specific concentration of a compound on a single occasion. The purpose of the test is to determine the symptomology consequent to administration of the compound, and to determine the order of lethality of the compound (ref. 20).

All initial toxicity testings are usually performed on rats and mice because of their reasonable costs, their ease of availability and their homogeneity thus providing large number of animals for replication and studies at various concentrations. Also large amounts of toxicological data are available for various chemicals from the scientific community utilizing these species. Several toxicity tests have been performed using various other species, such as rabbits, guineapigs, dogs, hamsters, etc. The procedure, in every case, has been very similar to that carried out with rats and mice, and the results indicate an estimation of the order of lethal toxicity for the specific species used in the test. The response of rat to acute oral doses of some chemicals differs from the response of the human because of one particular difference that the rat cannot vomit. Therefore, it may be instructive also to assess the acute oral toxicity of a substance using the dog or some other species that is capable of vomiting (ref. 21). In every case, the selected species must be in a state of good health and should be under observation in a certified laboratory or central animal care unit for a period of time which will vary depending upon the animal that was used for the acute test.

In order to determine the acute toxicity of a new compound, a series of experiments are designed and executed utilizing the chosen test animals. Basically, there are three groups of studies.

The initial series of experiments are designed in order to obtain information on how much of the compound is required to be acutely toxic. The doses used for these studies are estimates, which are obtained from reviewing the chemical structure and properties of the compound and published information on the toxicity of similar benchmark chemicals. This information will enable to assess the structure-activity relationship of the chemical and estimate the range of acute toxicity.

Further studies are designed and carried out to approximately determine the lethal dose of the chemical in question, which may vary slightly among studies. By using logarithms of the doses (ref. 20), a range of doses that would produce mortality versus no effects or minimal effects is experimentally determined. The doses are basically selected that would allow the estimation of the lethal dose for 50% (LD_{50}) of the group of experimental animals. A second series of experiments are designed in order to obtain a range of concentrations that would produce some mortalities to the animals treated with the high concentrations, to no mortalities in the group treated at the lowest concentration, but instead display symptoms of adverse effect by the animals.

After the data from the previous experiments are analyzed, final experiments are designed and executed. Animals chosen for the experiments must be of similar body weight and age. The same sex and/or equal numbers from both sexes are selected and placed randomly into tests and control groups. Test groups are administered different doses of the chemical that had been previously estimated to produce between 10 to 90% mortality. All animals are observed very closely for the duration of the experiment and accurate records are taken for both mortality and post-recovery period. Observation of animals is continued until all signs of toxicity disappear in survivors, then gross pathological examinations are carried out.

(ii) <u>Inhalation</u>. Human beings are exposed to numerous chemicals through inhalation, at work, home, and in the environment. As a result, acute inhalation toxicity studies have been important in identifying inhalation as one of the exposure pathways. Quantification of exposure determines its place in the estimation of the total integrated exposure among other exposure routes of a chemical.

Inhalation toxicity test is measured in a similar manner to that used for acute oral toxicity. However, in this exposure instead of recording a lethal dose, a lethal concentration, which is required to produce mortality to 50% of the animals, is determined. The duration of exposure is always kept constant during the test. The exposure period of these types of experiments is very variable and is depended upon the toxicants, the species utilized, and the exposure facilities. Short-time exposure could range from as little as a few minutes or up to eight hours, and in all cases the LCT_{50} (lethal concentration time) is determined. The LCT_{50} for these tests is defined as the concentration of the chemical which is required to kill 50% of the test animals during or after the exposure period. Animals are usually observed for 14 d after the exposure.

The exposure of animals through inhalation route requires elaborate laboratory equipment and preparation, and therefore, it might be classified as one of the most expensive and time-consuming methods of testing. It is important that considerable planning and experimental flexibility be incorporated to ensure that results are relevant, and scientifically valid.

Another factor to consider in inhalation toxicology is the variation in physical and chemical properties among compounds that are tested. In such cases, specific protocols might be required for the different toxicants, and considerable experience and judgement might be needed to ensure that utilized procedures are appropriate.

An inhaled toxicant could exert either a systemic effect or other effects to the respiratory system itself. The former effect could be determined by other easier and less expensive studies instead of inhalation toxicity experiments. If systemic effects are produced by other routes it is usually safe to assume that inhalation at similar doses would produce, at least, as great an effect; therefore, it might be wise to perform the inhalation test last, although inhalation might be the most likely route of exposure. It is quite possible to base a "no-go" decision for a chemical likely to be inhaled on results of exposure by routes other than inhalation (ref. 22).

Inhalation toxicity experiments will provide information on the respiratory system itself. The types of effects could be short term direct chemical irritation, irreversible damage, and death. In most cases, acute effects are usually reversible, unless severe damage produces pulmonary edema, or extensive inflammation which could result in the lung being non-functional. In acute studies, it is quite possible that damage could have occurred but it might not have been recorded because the animal might have survived the toxicity-testing session. These types of effects are easily detectable by an adjunctive study through the introduction of bacteria into the animals' lungs following inhalation exposure to the pollutant. It is quite likely that some might regard this exercise as a test of the mechanism of action of a toxic chemical; the fact remains that exposure to chemicals by animals with affected areas of the pulmonary systems could consequently be more susceptible to infection.

Another effect occasionally seen in the respiratory tract is an asthmatic type sensitization, which would not be manifested for some time after the first or possibly multiple exposures. This is apparently a rare phenomenon, but the effects produced can be extremely serious. Animal models have been of limited use for predicting this type of inhalation sensitivity, although it has been adequately demonstrated in humans as a result of industrial exposure; for example, exposure to toluene diisocyanate and also to cotton dust result in such effects. There is, therefore, great risk of missing this type of toxic manifestation when examining the effects of new materials on animals (ref. 22).

When using aerosols as a toxicant in inhalation toxicity tests, it is critical that the equipment must simulate actual human exposure conditions especially regarding particle size (ref. 22). Inhalation data on aerosol are difficult to characterize because these pollutants may be solid or liquid and effects will vary depending upon air currents and the level of uniformity of experimental design. This aspect is critical because if smaller respirable particles do not receive the appropriate treatment, it is quite likely that the deeper penetrative effects of these particles will not be included in the toxicity assessment.

Because of the difficulty and limited ability of some volatile liquids to evaporate at a given temperature, the upper fractions of saturated vapour might not be obtained for exposure purposes. This will not produce true effects of the tested toxicant during an experiment.

Although, offensive and unpleasant odours could create serious problems for humans during various activities, it is not possible to analyze for this type of an effect through inhalation experiments. Even if it is likely that the odours might be detected by the test animals, it is impossible to statistically or scientifically analyze the results.

(iii) Aquatic. Acute aquatic effects are those that occur rapidly in the aquatic organisms as a result of short-term exposures to a chemical. The period of exposure might extend from a few hours to a few days. The target organisms are usually fish, aquatic mammals, plants, invertebrates, and/or algae; although, in recent years, some species of amphibians have been utilized (ref. 23). Acute aquatic effects are usually severe in the exposed organisms resulting in mortality. The chemical would be considered to be acutely toxic if it had directly resulted in killing 50% or more of the test species exposed for a relatively short period, such as 48 h to 14 d (ref. 24).

The objective of an acute aquatic toxicity test is to determine the concentration of a test material (e.g., a chemical or effluent) or the level of a parameter (e.g., temperature or pH) that produces a deleterious effect to a group of test organisms during a short-term exposure under controlled conditions (ref. 25). Basically, acute aquatic toxicity tests are carried out by the exposure of organisms to various concentrations of a chemical which is mixed into the treated water for a measured period of time. The acute lethality of the substance is determined by measuring the percentage of organisms that died within the time during which the test was run.

Experimentally, a 50% response is the most reproducible measurement of toxicity of a test material and 96 h (or less) is the standard exposure time because it usually covers the period of acute lethal action (ref. 25). As a result, the most frequently used measurement of acute toxicity in aquatic toxicology for biota is the 96-h median lethal concentration (96-h LC_{50}).

Acute toxicity tests are usually carried out in a laboratory where conditions are controllable and various natural situations could be simulated through the use of different combinations of variables. The variables that affect the type of response are as follows:

1. the concentration of the chemical that is being used;
2. the duration of the test/exposure;
3. the species of the test organism;
4. the variation in exposure apparatus (static, recirculation, renewal, flow through); and
5. the test conditions.

(a) The test chemical. The test chemical could be pure in nature or could be a mixture of chemicals as present in an effluent. The test compound used should be representative of either the chemical or effluent entering the aquatic environment. If the effluent's composition is relatively constant, then sample quantities could be taken at any time period. On the other hand, if the effluent has a variable composition, mixing of more than one sample is not recommended, and samples that are collected at different times should be kept separately.

All concentrations needed for a batch of toxicity test should be prepared from the same sample material. Care should be taken to simulate as close as possible the environmental condition. Solvents, surfactants, or other dispersants/carriers should not be included unless these do exist in the environmental situation. In certain instances where use of solvents might be necessary, they should be kept at minimum concentration, and solvents such as triethylene glycol (TEG) should be used because of its low volatility, ability to dissolve many organics, and its low toxicity to most aquatic organisms.

However, this technique of mixing external solvent is rarely used for regulatory assessments of industrial chemicals.

(b) Test duration. The test commences as soon as the test species are placed into the treatment and control solutions. The duration of the test is variable, however, and is dependent upon the species utilized. The normal duration of the acute toxicity is 96 h but for some species of organisms the exposure time is 48 h. In these cases, longer exposure periods could result in measuring toxicity at various stages in the animals' developmental process that is not considered under acute toxicity testing protocol.

(c) Test species. Table 2.16 lists some of the most utilized species in acute aquatic toxicity test. Animals should be collected, handled and transported in such a manner so as to minimize stress and physical injury. They should be representative of the native or standard test species populations and should not be collected by electrofishing or chemical intoxication. Transportation in round or elyptical containers are recommended so as to prevent crowding or damage as a result of battering against the walls of the container.

In the laboratory, test animals are held for a specific period of time in uncontaminated water under stable conditions of temperature and water quality, in a flow-through system changing at least three water volumes/day. Fish are maintained and observed for 7 to 14 d prior to treatment and invertebrates for about 2 to 4 d. In preparation for treatment, test organisms are transferred to acclimation tanks in appropriate number and size. Water in tanks are gradually changed to 100% dilution water and the appropriate test temperature is slowly reached over 24 h. Animals are kept in the facility for 2 d prior to toxicity tests. Longer periods of acclimation are usually required for fish species but are seldom necessary for invertebrates (ref. 26).

It is important to ensure that all animals are healthy and not under unnecessary stress before treatment. All diseased animals should be removed and discarded unless they could be effectively treated. Because of the importance of eliminating bias regarding diseased organisms, it would be advisable not to initiate treatment if more than 10% of the population is lost during the acclimation period.

(d) Exposure variation. There are basically two types of acute tests that are carried out in aquatic toxicity: these are static and dynamic. Static acute tests have three variations; these could either be totally static, recirculating, or treatment liquid renewal design systems. The water baths should be maintained at a controlled temperature and should be constructed of material that is inert or non-leaching, and unable to absorb or change the test solution.

TABLE 2.16 Species commonly used in acute aquatic toxicity tests.

Fish - Freshwater

Rainbow trout (Salmo gairdneri)
Brook trout (Salvelinus fontinalis)
Channel catfish (Ictalurus punctatus)
Fathead minnow (Pimephales promelas)
American flagfish
Goldfish (Carassius auratus)
Bluegill (Lepomis macrochirus)

Fish - Saltwater

Sheephead minnos (Cyprinodon variegatus)
Threespine stickleback (Gasterosteus aculeatus)
Mummichog (Fundulus heteroclitus)
Longnose killifish (Fundulus similis)
Silverside (Menidia sp.)
Pinfish (Lagondon rhomboides)
Sanddab (Citharichthys stigmaeus)
Spot (Leiostomus xanthurus)

Invertebrates - Freshwater

Daphnids	Daphnia magna
	Daphnia pules
	Daphnia pulicaria
Amphipods	Gammarus laustris
	Gammarus fasciatus
	Gammarus pseudolimnaeus
Crayfish	Oreonectes sp.
	Cambarus sp.
	Procambarus sp.
Midges	Chironomus sp.
Snails	Physa integra
Insects	Plecoptera
	Ephemeroptera
	Trichoptera
	Diptera

Invertebrates-Saltwater

Copepods	Acartia tonsa
	Acartia clausi
Polychaetes	Capitella capitata
	Neanthes sp.
Crab	Callinectes sapidus
	Uca sp.
Shrimp	Penaeus setiferus
	Penaeus duorarum
	Penaeus aztecus
Grass shrimp	Palaemontes pugio
	Palaemontes vulgaris
Sand shrimp	Crangon septemspinosa
Mysid shrimp	Mysidopsis bahia
Oyster	Crassostrea virginica
	Crassostrea gigas

Continued . . .

TABLE 2.16 Concluded.

Other

Amphibians	Xenopus laevis
	Ambystoma mexicanum
Bacteria	Pseudomonas putida
	Microcystis aeruginosa
	Salmonella typhimurium
	Photobacterium phosphoreum

Dynamic or flow through acute test systems should have basically the same properties regarding material makeup and temperature. Figure 2.13 shows a continuous flow mini-diluter (ref. 27). It is divided into four major units as illustrated; these include toxicant and water cell, dilution cell, flow booster cell and flow splitter cell. Flow rates through the test chambers should be at least five volumes every 24 h. This is dependent, however, upon the size of the test animal, size of the test chamber, and the ratio of test animals biomass to the total volume of the test water in the chamber. The operation of the entire unit should be continually checked during a test run.

Acute toxicity test is a basic tool available to toxicologists that permits quick and relatively inexpensive evaluation of the toxic effects of a test chemical. It is useful in screening many chemicals by comparing their LC_{50} values for different species of the test organism. Acute toxicity test provides only a median lethal concentration result and does not evaluate cumulative, chronic, or sublethal effects of a chemical.

2.2.2 Subchronic and Chronic Toxicity

(i) Subchronic toxicity. Subchronic toxicity procedures are generally designed to evaluate the adverse effects of chemicals administered to biological organisms during repeated exposures on a daily basis from a period of a few days to about three to four months. In many instances, subchronic exposures are also classified as prolonged exposure and the tests are usually designed to incorporate the effects that are expected to manifest in humans. The effective doses of subchronic exposures are also lower than that of acute toxicity studies; these doses are developed for prolonged experiments and lethal effects are not the expected end results.

In order to develop a battery of subchronic toxicity tests, it is usually necessary to experiment with several short-term dose finding pilot studies. These preliminary tests provide information regarding body weight, target organs, organ damage, behavioural changes, biochemistry, hematology, and toxicological and physiological responses. Based on the information on target

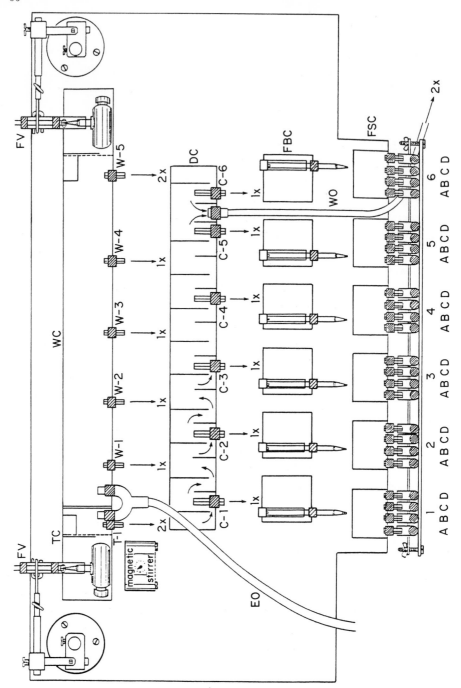

Fig. 2.13. A continuous flow mini-diluter system for toxicity testing. (Source: Reprinted with permission from ref. 27, Copyright (1981), Pergamon Press Inc.).

organ, critical concentration and associated effects, administration of the test chemical to the animal must be designed prior to the commencement of the exposure studies. It is recommended to perform an autopsy on all the animals at the end of the pilot study, noting all lesions, and histological and patho-logical changes.

The test chemical is usually administered orally for subchronic tests. In certain instances, however, if there is reason to believe that the test animal's food could alter the toxicity of the test chemical, the chemical should be administered separately through a tube inserted through the mouth and into the stomach of the test animal. Other dosing practices such as the use of hypodermic needles intravenously are not commonly used.

Subchronic oral toxicity results are utilized also to investigate systemic effects as a result of cumulative exposure. The choice of animal for the study is dependent on variables such as the physical and chemical properties of the test substance, length of exposure, laboratory treatment facilities, and similarity or metabolic pathway of the animal to that of human beings. The study period varies between 21 to 30 d, with an increase of dose level at the end of the period and continuation of the treatment for an additional period, if the effects are questionable. The dose range is made up of several levels, commencing at a no observed effect level and concluding with maximum tolerable levels. During the entire study gross observations are continually recorded in order to ensure that toxicity signs are not missed.

(ii) _Chronic toxicity_. Chronic toxicity usually occurs as a result of repeated or prolonged exposures to chemicals which might result in deleterious effects to the exposed organism. The observed toxic response of a chemical during a chronic exposure could result from the following causes: (i) direct effect of the chemical; (ii) altered form of the chemical; (iii) redistribu-tion of the metabolites in the animal body; and (iv) continued aggravation of target organs, enzyme systems, and hormonal systems by the chemical. Table 2.17 summarizes the type of analytical and functional tests that are commonly involved in chronic toxicity tests. Samples are required from the test animals periodically throughout the experiment; it is important to take samples without inflicting harm or causing excessive stress to the animals. In many instances, for the purposes of comparison, two different species are used, one of which is not a rodent.

TABLE 2.17 Analytical and functional tests employed in chronic toxicity tests.

Hematology	Erythrocyte count Total leucocyte count Differential leucocyte count Reticulocyte count Heinz bodies search Prothrombin time	hermatocrit hemoglobin
Blood Chemistry	Sodium Potassium Chloride Calcium Carbon dioxide Serum glutamate-pyruvate transaminase* Serum glutamate-oxalacetic transaminase+ Serum alkaline phosphatase* Serum protein electrophoresis	fasting blood sugar blood urea nitrogen total serum protein total serum bilirubin serum albumin
Urine Analyses and Renal Function Studies	pH Specific gravity Total protein Microscopic examination of sediment Clearance studies	glucose ketones bilirubin
Special Function Tests	Bromsulphalein retention* Thymol turbidity* Indocyanine green clearance*	
Lung Function Studies	Resistance studies Compliance studies	
Central Nervous System Responses	Electroencephalogram Central nervous system effects Neurophysiology	

* liver function tests
+ test for injured tissue cells
(Source: Reprinted with permission from ref. 20, Copyright (1978), Lea & Febieger).

At the end of a chronic exposure, all animals are evaluated for gross pathological and histological effects. Also, any animals that might have died during the experiment are completely autopsyed and all of their respective organs are examined and analyzed. Table 2.18 summarizes the physical, pathological, and histological examinations that are performed.

It is imperative that the scientist obtain necessary information regarding the purity, and the nature and amounts of impurities of the test substance. If an effluent is used, it is beneficial to attempt a characterization of the mixture as accurately as possible. This information assists in understanding some of the effects that could be observed as a result of chemicals that are present in the effluent. Synergistic and antagonistic effects should not be ruled out. When samples of industrial effluents are used for chronic studies, information should be obtained regarding process changes, addition of new chemicals and newly-adopted treatment procedures.

TABLE 2.18 Pathologic and histologic examinations commonly performed in chronic toxicity tests.

Weights	body thyroid heart liver	spleen kidneys adrenals testes with epididymis
Histologic Examinations	adrenals heart liver large intestine small intestine spleen ovary mesenteric lymp nodes all tissue lesions	pituitary thyroid kidneys stomach pancreas urinary bladder testes
Food Consumption	quantity type	
Appearance	fatigue colour	

(Source: modified from ref. 20).

Chronic studies must be designed in such a way so as to include various levels of exposure. Experiments should range from exposures at levels that would be expected to produce no adverse effects to those that might be expected to cause deleterious or harmful effect to the test organisms. This allows for a wide range of adverse effects to be observed and thus should enable a thorough evaluation of the test chemical under investigation.

It is important that clinical evaluations of the biological species under test, be carried out prior to the commencement of the study. This should be continued daily during the initial stages of the study and at least bi-weekly during the rest of the experiment. Both symptomatic responses and behaviour should be continually followed throughout the study period. Other measurements such as weight, food and water consumption and appropriate biochemistry of blood and urine should be performed at routine intervals throughout the study.

Eventually, all animals of the exposed and control groups are subjected to a complete pathological and histological evaluation.

Generally, chronic toxicity tests are carried out in order to evaluate the effects of a chemical ultimately on the human beings. As a result, the species selected and tested under controlled experimental conditions should produce information that would indicate absorption rate, metabolic pathways, time taken to react, target organs effects, etc. similar to that in the human being.

Knowledge of nutritional requirements, metabolic differences, life history stages, frequency and exposure to various diseases, and housing requirements are other considerations in ensuring that the chosen species are adequately suited. When rats are used as test species, the duration is usually less than a year, and in certain cases, it could be extended to two years or beyond for purposes of evaluation of carcinogenicity.

Aquatic Chronic Toxicity

Chronic toxicity in the aquatic environment is also used for the purpose of evaluating the potential hazards of a chemical. It verifies what concentations affect the life cycle activities (development, growth and reproduction) of an aquatic organism. In the aquatic environment, however, the amount of chemical utilized is measured through its concentration in water into which the test species are placed. Test species utilized are aquatic organisms whose physiological and life cycle responses have been thoroughly understood. The most commonly utilized species are outlined in Table 2.19.

Chronic toxicity testing with fish outlined in Table 2.19 requires a minimum exposure period of 6 to 12 months or more while the use of invertebrates could require about three to four weeks or more.

Similar to mammalian type chronic toxicological studies, aquatic assays provide information that permits the evaluation of the potential adverse effects of chemicals to test organisms that have been carefully exposed under stringently controlled conditions. Chronic studies of this nature are laboratory based and, as such, results obtained should not be extrapolated directly to either the terrestrial or aquatic environment. There are several other variables such as distribution, bioavailability, fate processes, antagonism and synergism, etc. that could alter the chemical, its residence time in a given medium and its effects to biological organisms in the environment.

Short-term Chronic Tests

Developments in toxicity testing procedures during the last decade have resulted in the availability of several methods that permit the detection of low-level adverse effects of mainly effluents to certain organisms in eight days or less. The U.S. Environmental Protection Agency (U.S. EPA) supports these short-term tests through their policy for the Development of Water Quality-Based Permit Limitation for Toxic Pollutants (ref. 28). This policy proposes the use of toxicity test to assess and control the discharge of toxic substances into the aquatic environment.

There are four short-term tests that are normally utilized to assess chronic toxicity. These include:

1. Fathead Minnow (<u>Pimephales</u> <u>promelas</u>) Larval Survival and Growth Test (refs. 29,30);

2. Fathead Minnow (<u>Pimephales</u> <u>promelas</u>) Embryo Larval Survival and Teratogenicity Test (refs. 29,30);

3. Ceridaphnia Survival and Reproduction Test (ref. 31); and

4. Algal (<u>Selanastrum</u> <u>capricornutum</u>) Growth Test (ref. 32).

These tests have been developed to further reduce the length of initially designed tests without compromising their predictive values. They have been very popular because they provide a more direct estimate of the safe concentration of effluents in receiving waters than what was produced from acute toxicity tests, at a slightly increased level of effort, compared to that required by the fish full life-cycle chronic (ref. 33) and 8-week early life stages tests (ref. 34) and the 21- to 28-d Cladocern tests (refs. 35).

TABLE 2.19 Commonly-used species for chronic toxicity studies in the aquatic environment.

SPECIES	REFERENCES
Vertebrates	
Fathead Minnow (<u>Pimephales promelas</u>)	(34)
Sheepshead Minnow (<u>Cyprinodon variegatus</u>)	(36)
Flagfish (<u>Jordanella fluridae</u>)	(37)
Bluegill sunfish (<u>Lepomis macrochirus</u>)	(38)
Brook trout (<u>Salvelinus fontinalis</u>)	(33)
Invertebrates	
Daphnia (<u>Daphnia magna</u>)	(39)
(<u>Daphnia pulex</u>)	(40)
Amphipod (<u>Gammarus pseudolimnaeus</u>)	(41)
Midges (<u>Chironomus tentans</u>)	(42)
(<u>Tanytarsus dissimilis</u>)	(43)
Mysid shrimp (<u>Mysidopis bahia</u>)	(44)
Grass shrimp (<u>Palaemonetes pugio</u>)	(45)
Copepod (<u>Acartia tonsa</u>)	(46)
Annelids (<u>Neanthes arenaceodentata</u>)	(47)
(<u>Capitella capitata</u>)	(48)

2.2.3 Genotoxicity

(i) Carcinogenicity. Biological systems are exposed daily to variety of chemicals in different combinations through air, water, food and soil. Some of these chemicals have been shown to induce malignant tumours in experimental animals. Most known human carcinogens, with the exception of a few such as arsenic and alcohol, cause cancer in animals (ref. 49). For many of the identified carcinogens in animals, it is difficult to predict whether they will cause cancer in humans, because of difficulty in studying human populations and obtaining data regarding exposure to low concentration levels encountered in the ambient medium. On the other hand, for some known human carcinogens (benzo-a-pyrene, diethylstilbestrol, vinyl chloride, mustard gas, etc.), the first evidence was identified through animal bioassays. It has not been established, however, whether these factors worked synergistically with bacteria or viruses or whether they act alone. Although, the link of chemicals to cancer has been tenuous, there is definite support that it is a disease correlated to certain environmental chemicals. The aspects of threshold versus non-threshold hazards, uncertainties in low-dose extrapolation of data, interspecies extrapolation of data, guidelines for testing, and risk assessment methodologies are discussed in later chapters. The step towards minimizing the risk of cancer should commence by determining which chemicals in the environment are carcinogens, and then follow by the establishment of appropriate measures in order to eliminate or reduce human exposure to such carcinogens.

Short-term tests (STTs) for the purpose of evaluating chemicals to predict carcinogenicity have been reviewed in the literature (refs. 50,51). The duration, costs, and concerns over the choice of test species have been main factors in influencing the details in various studies. Nevertheless, evaluation must determine that the substance is indisputably carcinogenic under the condition of an experimental exposure, giving positive results in appropriately performed animal carcinogenic exposures. In certain cases, however, a rodent bioassay might identify a chemical to be carcinogenic, but a battery of genotoxic bioassays might fail to predict its carcinogenicity due to the limitations of STTs as evidenced in the literature. Therefore, there is a definite need that chemicals must be assessed on a case-by-case basis along with the structure-activity data for the purpose of hazard identification.

Testing Procedures

Because of their similarity of the genetic assembly to humans, mammalian species have been utilized as test organisms for many years. Aquatic species, on the other hand, have been used to assess potential environmental effects.

When cancerous tumours have been known to develop in aquatic organisms (ref. 52) the toxicant is further tested using mammalian species.

In mammalian species, small rodents (rats, mice, rabbits, and hamsters) are generally used, and test substances are usually assayed by the following methods:

1. Feeding - substance introduced to the animals' diet, dissolved into drinking water, or administered directly into stomach by feeding tube.

2. Skin painting - The hair of the animal is shaved and the test substance is introduced by means of a brush onto its skin.

3. Subcutaneous - The test substance is introduced subcutaneously by means of a hypodermic needle.

4. Inhalation - The test substance is introduced into the trachea by means of a special tube or the animal is exposed to the substance in an aerosol form or as gas in an inhalation chamber.

At the end of the testing period, all animals are killed and completely autopsied. Tissues are fixed and histophathological examinations are then carried out. Arcos (ref. 53) outlined five principles that should be considered regarding the final results of a bioassay. They are as follows:

1. A positive result, i.e., a chemical agent is found to be carcinogenic, carries a much greater weight than a negative result. This is because it can never be excluded that a compound, found inactive (negative result) under certain experimental conditions, may prove to be carcinogenic when tested in another species by different routes and ways of administration, and under different dietary conditions.

2. It is a general consensus among investigators of chemical carcinogenesis that for any testing experiment to be meaningful at all, it must be carried out for a minimum of 1 year, unless a statistically significant tumour incidence manifests earlier.

3. No chemical compound may be stated safely to be devoid of carcinogenic activity toward man unless it has been found inactive when tested in several mammalian species and by several routes of administration for a length of time corresponding to one half (or even better, the whole) life span of each species. This statement is based on these frequent findings: A carcinogen that is inactive in one species may be highly active in another; the susceptibility of a speices to a given carcinogen also depends on the genetic strain, sex, and dietary conditions; the detectability of carcinogenic activity often depends on the route of administration. Moreover, it is well established that the incidence of

cancer in humans increases with the age group, and the tumour, if its origin can be traced to a single or repeated exposures to a carcinogenic agent, will often appear only decades after exposure. Hence, the preference for using short-lived test species and to test for the entire life span can be understood.

4. A chemical agent that would induce a 1% net tumour incidence over that of a control group, even though statistically significant, would not be regarded as really meaningfully carcinogenic from the standpoint of laboratory experimentation. It is evident, however, that a chemical agent would be regarded as a major health hazard if it were known with certainty to produce 1,000 cancer patients per 100,000 population.

5. The latter considerations lead us to examine the statistical limitation of any bioassay procedure. To illustrate the point, consider that a chemical is being evaluated in 200 rats or mice, a good size group. It is evident that in this group the limit of detectable tumour incidence is 0.5%, which is one animal. However, should the chemical be a marginally carcinogenic agent, inducing tumours at a given dose level at the rate of 0.3%, it will most probably escape detection in a group of 200 animals. Moreover, the tumour incidence represented by even one tumour-bearing animal in a group of 200 would be far below statistical significance. This means that, should the compound be carcinogenic to humans to the same degree as to rats, testing in 200 rodents does not by far represent an adequate safety evaluation.

Short-term Tests

Short-term tests (STTs) permit the screening of a large number of chemicals for their genotoxic potential in a short period of time at a fraction of the cost. They are usually not considered to be as authoritative as the long-term rodent carcinogenic bioassays. They can be used in support of existing animal data or as surrogates if such chronic studies have not been carried out. In certain cases, short-term tests could call into question adequately conducted long-term animal studies, but this can occur only if short-term tests are consistently and clearly positive and long-term findings are negative. In this case, short-term tests are taken as suggestive evidence of hazard until further long-term testing resolves the discrepancy (ref. 54).

Genetic Alterations

Beginning over a decade ago, in vitro tests for genetic changes were developed and rapidly applied to the practical problem of carcinogen identification. This approach was spurred on by the belief that genetic alteration in somatic cells is closely linked to one or more of the stages of carcinogenesis, and by the early results which showed that the coupling of metabolic activation to relatively simple bacterial assays for mutation gave results highly correlated with the carcinogenicity of certain groups of chemicals (ref. 55).

Over 100 tests of this nature are available. They involve the use of many organisms ranging from prokaryotes to human cells and they can be performed under various conditions ranging from studies of isolated DNA to observation of cells in vivo and in vitro. They can be grouped into three general categories:

1. Tests for DNA damage including adduct formation, strand breakage, induction and DNA repair.
2. Tests for mutagenicity, including forward and reverse mutation as evidenced by alteration of DNA, gene products, or cellular behaviour.
3. Tests for chromosomal effects, in isolated cells or whole organisms, including aneuploidy, structural aberration, micronuclei, sister chromatid exchange and lost, broken, or disarranged chromosomes.

The effectiveness of short-term tests (STTs) are limited because no single test is capable of detecting all chemicals that are positive in animal cancer tests. These false negatives could be minimized when a battery of tests are implemented for the purpose of identifying the genetic effects of toxins (ref. 56). The use of microorganisms are quite valid and popular in short-term tests, and in certain cases, when negative findings occur, it is possible that they might be offset by a positive one. The initial high correlation observed between genetic changes (STTs) and carcinogenicity has decreased with the enlargement of the set of chemicals tested and with the separation of test development from test deployment. Estimates of correlations between findings in STTs, and determination of carcinogenicity in vivo varies, depending on the chemical class, test type, and laboratory. At present, the overall performance of STTs, as judged by the proportion of correct results for chemicals classified by carcinogen bioassay is in the range of 50 to 70 percent. Although, often significantly better than chance, these results are not adequate to allow reliance in short-term tests alone in the determination of carcinogenicity (ref. 55).

The following recommendations are suggested regarding short-term tests:

1. Research should be continued along the line of bioassays improvements, particularly regarding standards and metabolic activation.
2. The use of cell transformation methodology for the purpose of identifying chemical carcinogens has not been successful as predictive tools. However, research should be continued to elucidate some aspects of cancer causation.
3. Bioassays should be developed to respond to more classes of chemicals.
4. Early tissue changes as a predictive tool for carcinogenicity is far from being consistent and accurate. Short-term tests that are capable of identifying preneoplastic lesions or markers of neoplastic transformation should be pursued.

Predictability

There is a great interest in the ability of short-term test to be capable of predicting rodent carcinogenicity. This type of study has been of particular interest to researchers since long-term rodent studies are expensive (about $2 million) and time consuming. On the other hand, a battery of short-term test would cost approximately $10,000.00. Tennant et al. (ref. 57) examined the results of the rodent test and genetic toxicity tests of 73 compounds recently tested by the National Cancer Institute and concluded that of the four short-term tests examined, only a single test, the Ames Salmonella-microsome test, was 60% concordant with the rodent test. A rearrangement of the results by Young (ref. 54) in Table 2.20 shows a good correlation between the number of short-term test positives and the probability of a positive rodent result. When all four short-term tests were positive, the rodent test was positive about 80% of the time. In only three instances were all short-term tests positive and the rodent test negative.

Data on acute toxicity of certain chemicals could be used to make a preliminary estimate of carcinogenic risk and also could give an estimate of the uncertainty (ref. 58). Fig. 2.14 outlines the scheme for deciding the path that a potential chemical carcinogen would follow in order to arrive at an estimated risk. If at the end of the test calculation the estimated number indicates a risk, then exposure must be reduced, the use of this application limited, further studies made, or some combination of these actions taken.

TABLE 2.20 Summary of genetic toxicity STTs and rodent tests, positive and tested. Cochrane-Armitage linear trend test, P <0.007.

STTs POSITIVE/ TESTED	RODENT	
	POSITIVE TESTED	POSITIVE (%)
4/4	14/17	82.3
3/4	10/15	66.7
2/4	7/14	50.0
1/4	7/11	63.6
0/4	6/16	37.5
Total	44/73	60.3

(Source: Reprinted with permission from ref. 54, Copyright (1988), the Amer. Assn. of Advancement of Science, (AAAS), U.S.A.).

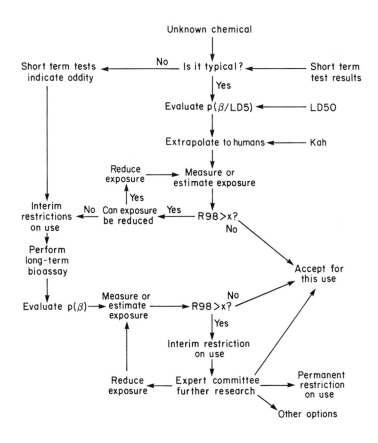

Fig. 2.14. Decision scheme to arrive at an estimated risk.
(Source: Reprinted with permission from ref. 58, Copyright (1983), from Plenum Publishing Corp.).

Long-term Tests

Conventional long-term animal studies provide useful information about chemical carcinogenicity. If an increase in incidence of one or more types of malignant or benign neoplasms (or a combination of both) occur in treated animals as compared to control, under identical conditions, with the exception of exposure to the test compound, carcinogenicity can be said to be established (ref. 59). In certain cases, however, it is not uncommon for some of the control rodents to develop incindences of even up to 100 percent of neoplasms of a particular kind. But if control animals develop, say 50 percent of a certain kind of neoplasm and this incidence is significantly increased in treated animals, or if there is a decrease latency period for the occurrence of such tumour, this is usually classified as evidence of carcinogenesis (ref. 55). In these instances, such experiments require full evaluation using a high level of statistical significance, and if possible, an analysis of the incidence in historical controls would strengthen the conclusion.

Laboratory animal bioassays for the purpose of identifying chemical carcinogenesis have been widely used; in recent years, these tests have been generally accepted as a result of standardization. The recommended design by several authoritative groups (refs. 59,60) for carrying out bioassay of a chemical for the purpose of identifying tumourogenesis includes the following:

1. Two species of test animals (usually rats and mice of both sexes) tested at two, or preferably three, dose levels: a high dose level (roughly the estimated maximum tolerated dose [MTD]) and a lower dose level (roughly one-half the MTD) as determined in a 90-day subactue toxicity study;
2. Dosing and observation for most of the animals' natural lifetime, usually 104 weeks for rodents;
3. Adequate numbers of animals (at least 50 per sex) in each test group;
4. Adequate concurrent controls;
5. Detailed pathologic examination of tissues; and
6. Appropriate statistical evaluation of results (dose-response relationships, etc.).

Evidence that can lead to a conclusion of carcinogenicity from animal experiments includes (ref. 61):

1. Statistically significant increases in malignant tumours relative to the controls at one or more of the dose levels tested;
2. A statistically significant dose-related increase in malignant tumours in an analysis that makes appropriate use of data on the times at which tumours were detected;

3. An increase in the occurrence of rare malignant tumours (those having a zero or low spontaneous incidence rate among historical controls); and/or

4. Early appearance of cancer in the treated animals.

Concerns

1. Animal cancer bioassays are relatively insensitive (ref. 61)

   The limitation of 50 animals per sex per group means that the test cannot reliably detect an increase in cancer incidence of less than about 15%. Thus, weak carcinogens may be very difficult to detect especially if high actue toxicity severely limits the maximum dose that can be administered to the test animal.

2. Negative results from shortened animal exposure do not rule out the possibility of carcinogenicity that might have occurred during a normal life span exposure. In human beings, about one-half of all forms of cancer occur after the age of 65.

3. Bioassay animals will die of toxic effects if treated with doses that are too high to provide good dose-response relationship, before cancerous effects could have been established. It is, therefore, important to ensure that the maximum tolerated dose is used for testing carcinogenicity.

4. The use of in-bred strains of test animals could result in the underestimation of carcinogenic risks regarding a heterogenous human population. The choice of animals should be from healthy, heterogeneous population chosen randomly for both controls and treatments. (Note -- tests should be carried out in two species).

5. The route of administration used in a bioassay should be similar to that expected for humans. Other routes might result in significant differences in absorption, metabolism, distribution, and execution of the chemical that is being tested.

6. When a negative result is obtained after the analysis of bioassay tests, it only implies that there is a low probability that the chemical is carcinogenic under the test conditions. Such results are not conclusive as proof of non-carcinogenicity and the issue could re-surface if new evidence is recorded in other studies.

Epidemiologic Studies

Epidemiology is the study of the relationships between the frequency and distribution of disease in human populations and various factors that may influence observed occurrences. These types of studies are likely to provide evidence that a substance is a human carcinogen through the demonstration of an increase in cancer in a population exposed to a specific agent, as compared with a population without such exposure.

When these studies are properly conducted, they may offer direct evidence of the risk of cancer to humans. Unfortunately, the link is difficult to establish because of genetic and environmental biases in the human population. Considering the life span of the average human being, and the long latency period of cancer onset in humans, these studies cannot adequately warn or protect people from the risk of exposure to carcinogens.

Epidemiologic studies do not provide information on cause and effect relationship as do animal exposure studies. This is due to the enormous difficulties in attempting to collect reliable information on length of exposure, levels of exposure, and the initiation of cancer in humans. However, epidemiological studies have successfully identified several determinants of both lifestyle cancer risks (cigarette, alcohol, etc.) and important chemical carcinogens (benzene, arsenic, asbestos, vinyl chloride, etc.) (ref. 61).

These are two types of analytical epidemiologic studies that are commonly used, these include cohort studies and case control studies. Cohort studies involve the comparison of two groups of people; one that has been exposed to an agent or chemical, and the second is a control group that was not exposed. Apart from the exposure, the groups should be otherwise similar. Cohort studies could either be prospective or historical.

Case control studies identify and compare a group of people that are presently suffering from a disease to an otherwise similar control group that is normal and not suffering. Past experiences are also included in this type of study.

Criteria for the adequacy of epidemiologic studies include factors such as the proper selection and characterization of exposed and control groups, the adequacy of duration and quality of follow up, the proper identification and characterization of compounding factors and bias, the appropriate consideration of latency effects, the valid ascertainment of the causes of morbidity and death, and the ability to detect specific effects. Where it can be used, the statistical power to detect an appropriate outcome should be included in the assessment (ref. 62).

The selection of the appropriate population to identify a health problem is difficult. Most populations are usually exposed to a wide variety of chemicals at varying exposure levels and not a single chemical at a known level of concentration. Because the former situation is prevalent and also due to the poor records of exposure, it becomes an almost impossible task for epidemiologist to clearly identify the effects of any single chemical/agent on a specific population. There is also a problem regarding which segment of the population should be sampled. Studies on industrially exposed population are carried out on healthy males at working age (20 to 65 years old). It is very doubtful to apply findings using data from this sector to women, older persons, chronically ill or disabled from the same population.

It should be recognized that epidemiologic studies are inherently capable of detecting only comparatively large increases in the relative risk of cancer. Negative results from such studies cannot prove the absence of carcinogenic action; however, negative results from a well-designed and well-conducted epidemiologic study that contains usable exposure data can serve to define upper limits of risks; these are useful if animal evidence indicates that the agent is potentially carcinogenic in humans.

2.2.4 Ecotoxicity

Ecotoxicology in direct contrast to classic toxicology deals with the multi-causal simultaneous effects of all chemicals, no matter how little in the environment and all its components. Any assessment of the ultimate effect of an environmental pollutant must take into account, in a quantitative way, each of the distinct processes involved (ref. 63). First, a chemical is released into the environment; the amounts, forms, and sites of such releases must be known if its subsequent environmental fate is to be understood. Secondly, the chemical is transported geographically and into different biota, and perhaps chemically transformed, giving rise to compounds which have quite different environmental behavioural patterns and toxic properties. The nature of such processes is unknown for the majority of environmental contaminants, and the dangers arising from ignorance of the ultimate fate of certain chemicals have been well documented in recent years. The third part of the process is the exposure of one or more target organisms. To assess this process, one must first identify the nature of the target (man, livestock, or similar sources, etc.) and the type of the exposure that is to be examined. Finally, one has to assess the response of the individual organism, population or community to the specified (perhaps transformed) pollutant over the appropriate time scale.

Ecotoxicology involves a toxicological assessment that includes the combination of the above four steps in a quantitative and integrated way (ref. 64).

The Scientific Committee on Problems of the Environment (SCOPE) outlines an approach that uses results, values, and estimations from classic toxicology and incorporates them into studies of ecosystem (ref. 65). The SCOPE approach focussed on the living processes of the environment and its objective was to develop six procedures that could integrate the total sum of environmental effects:

1. Basic features of biological responses to toxic agents, including tissues, reproduction, growth, immune system, life span, synergism of agents.
2. Animals: how sublethal effects on individuals may affect population.
3. Aquatic animals: they are especially useful for integrating the effects of environmental contamination by virtue of the fact that all contaminants tend to be transferred eventually to water.
4. Plants: effects on normal community dynamics. Search for species that are particularly sensitive, e.g., lichens.
5. Microorganisms: in particular, study of soil organisms.
6. Geophysical systems: study of ozone, weather changes, global transport of pollutants.

Because most information is generated retrospectively, some change will have to occur to the environment and/or its components before such influences could be recorded. Nevertheless, the above procedures are vital towards the establishment of a broad approach to ecotoxicity.

Testing Methods

The environment, as it is known, consists of various types of ecosystems; these include: air, water (freshwater or marine), soil/sediments, and various forms of biota. The effects of any chemical on such a diverse system are further influenced by various factors, such as chemical, physical, biological, geological, climatic, and socioeconomic and their interrelationships. An attempt to investigate the toxic effects to such a multi-faceted system is further complicated by changes that might occur as a result of adaptation, the range of differences in the responses that might be observed by components, and the diversity of the components within any one of the ecosystems.

In broad terms, the choice of test methods not only should balance considerations of costs, precision, and accuracy but it should take into account also the fate and transport that are influencing the chemical in the environment. One must know how the chemical is distributed within the ecosystem, and how it may affect the population utilizing that specific ecosystem. Also, the original state of the chemical might be modified with other chemicals or biological components as it is transported through any one ecosystem to produce new forms that might have totally different effects, thus developing new and different concerns.

For example, the increasing acidity of atmospheric deposition has been recognized as a widespread phenomenon in Scandinavia, the Canadian Shield, and the eastern United States. Early studies, utilizing simple aquatic bioassays consisting of fish and invertebrates, showed that measurable effects on physiological processes and mortality occurred at pH values below 4.5 (Fig. 2.15) in the natural environment. However, acid deposition and the resultant acidification of aquatic ecosystems produced mortality effects on similar aquatic biota at higher pH values (range 4.5-5.5). Additional research on natural ecosystems (refs. 66,67), revealed the cause: as a result of acid deposition, aluminum was mobilized from soils into the aquatic environment. The mobilized aluminum was adsorbed onto fish gills, leading to mortality at pH levels that were not themselves directly toxic to the fish. Simplified laboratory bioassays failed to predict the indirect terrestrial effect of aluminum toxicity on aquatic biota because they ignored the biogeochemical linkages between the terrestrial and aquatic ecosystems and the resultant

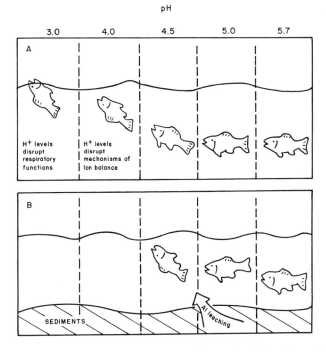

Fig. 2.15. Differences in mortality as determined by pH and the availability of aluminum in the environment. Trout succumb at a lower pH under laboratory conditions without sediments (A), compared with field conditions (B) where toxic levels of aluminum can be leached from watershed soils and lake sediments.
(Source: Reprinted with permission from ref. 68, Copyright (1984), from Springer-verlag).

complexity of the natural environment. Only ecosystem-level fate and transport studies could have led to appropriate testing regimes; without them, the laboratory tests led to an underestimation of effects (ref. 68).

Single-Species Testing

The single-species acute tests are relatively rapid, simple and inexpensive. They are easily replicated and offer a fair degree of precision within statistical limits. They usually provide much information on the concentration and duration of exposure to chemicals that might cause changes in survival patterns, reproduction, physiology, biochemistry and behaviour of individuals within particular species, but results from such tests cannot predict or be used to evaluate aspects of chemical impacts beyond this level of biological organization (ref. 69).

Single-species tests also could incorporate highly designed chronic effects studies. Observations under these tests could include long-term survival and growth rates; changes in reproduction, pharmacokinetic responses, and mechanisms of toxicity; biochemical, pathological, and physiological changes, and genotoxic effects. Most of the single-species tests that are carried out, however, do not venture much beyond growth, reproduction, and survival rates. Apart from being exceedingly complex, chronic toxicity tests are usually very expensive, requiring qualified personnel, and very specific laboratory facilities. Nevertheless, the data generated from chronic tests reveal detailed effects of chemicals on biota from various ecosystems.

Single-species testing are considered not realistic regarding both the ecosystem and the fate of the pollutant. The test represents the effect of a pollutant on one species, and in most cases, in a closed environment, most likely carried out under laboratory conditions. A study on long-term effects of toxic substances in aquatic plants indicated that acute toxicity results were not adequate for making realistic predictions about the effects of pollutants on natural systems. Extrapolation to natural systems is prevented mainly by their high complexity due to their abiotic and biotic interactions, and because the characteristics of populations are fundamentally different from those of communities and ecosystems (ref. 70). Similarly, expensive and sophisticated chronic, single-species tests could lead to incorrect conclusions regarding the potential impact of a chemical because of unrealistic application of the results to environmental ecosystems.

One of the objectives of testing is to try to identify and use the most sensitive species in an ecosystem. This is not an easy task unless detailed chronic toxicity test were carried out on all species within that particular ecosystem. A multi-species model of an ecosystem might permit identification of the more sensitive species, depending on inclusion of several factors in the model such as: a significant number of species representing the degree of diversity found into the ecosystem, detailed observations on physiological and behavioural responses for individual species, and a time period similar to the duration of expected chemical exposure in the ecosystem (ref. 69). As the number of the species increases the size and complexity of the test also increases, resulting in an impractical approach. On the other hand, comparative toxicity analyses using several multi-species systems could produce information regarding the most sensitive species within any single ecosystem.

Because natural stresses such as predation and competition are not included in laboratory single-species tests, the test organism cannot be expected to respond to a test chemical in the same manner as it would in its natural habitat (ref. 69). Concentrations of 1 μg/kg of PCBs or 10 μg/kg of DDT do not produce any effects on pure cultures of Thalassiosira pseudonana; but when tested in mixed cultures with Dunaliella tertiolecta, the competitive success of T. pseudonana is decreased (ref. 71).

The indirect effects resulting from population or species interactions cannot be observed using single-species tests. For example, the chemical might not directly affect a test species, however, it might be transformed and the new product might have various effects regarding the interaction of the test species with other organisms in the ecosystem. An example of this indirect effect of a chemical is shown by the ability of sublethal doses of 2,4-D on ragwort producing increased sugar levels in the plant and making a normally toxic plant more palatable to grazing cattle (ref. 72).

Realistically, single-species test, cannot provide the data that is needed to adequately assess chemical effects on populations or multiple components of an ecosystem (ref. 73). In some cases, however, it might be possible to extrapolate some results depending on the similarity of the species within a systematic group. In general, ecosystems are complex having various components and processes that exhibit specific properties that are particular to only that specific ecosystem. Therefore, it is not possible to characterize the response of any system to general or specific perturbations solely from the knowledge of the response of a few or single component.

Multi-Species Tests

A multi-species toxicity test may be defined as any test at a level of biological organization higher than a single species. Under this definition, microcosms, mesocosms, and macrocosms can be classified as multi-species tests. Microcosms are those systems which are 10 L in volume. Mesocosms are all test systems with a volume greater than 10 L but less than 1000 L, and macrocosms are all test systems greater than 1000 L in volume (ref. 74).

Multi-species test have many advantages over single-species test; the most important being the identification of effects beyond the level of single-species study. These tests, especially microcosms and mesocosms, are relatively compact and they are able to reasonably maintain some standard environmental conditions, making them easy to permit replication and standardization. Different physical, chemical, and biological variables can be tested with minimal effort and with no greater expense than that associated with well designed single-species tests (ref. 69). These systems also permit the testing of potentially dangerous chemicals without fear of environmental contamination because they are closed systems that will allow proper disposal of toxic materials after any study.

There are also limitations regarding multi-species testing. Because they are designed as simplified models of a natural ecosystem, they can not undergo changes in the various biological, chemical, and physical variables that are encountered in the natural environment. Therefore, results gathered from these systems cannot reliably be extrapolated to those expected in nature.

Ecological reality is further reduced when small-sized microcosms are used in multi-species tests. These problems are most apparent in aquatic systems. The shallow depths of most aquatic microcosms result in unrealistic influences by benthic compartments on nutrient fluxes and decomposition activities. Shallow depth also distort the vertical migration patterns of zooplankton and the loss of phytoplankton as they move from the water column to the sediment layer (ref. 75).

Multi-species testing is a middle way that bridges the gap between the ecological and industrial points of view and will improve our understanding of the impacts of toxic material until we can device community- or ecosystem-level testing programs (ref. 75).

Models

Mathematical models not only serve as predictive tools, but they could provide a link between actual recorded observations and predictions. Models for time varying processes are concepts of basic differential equations, which relate the rate of change of the concentration of each component of the system to some function of the state of the system, time and external parameters. The components of the system may include species abundances and chemical concentrations, the parameters of the system include thermal variations and level of nutrients and toxins (ref. 22). They help in the organization and testing of ideas, hypothesis, and the identification of gaps in existing knowledge and data. Properly used, models may also permit identification of those aspects of a complex ecosystem that are most sensitive or are most critical to analyze (ref. 68).

In toxicological investigations, modelling can be used to in several ways such as attempting to assemble chemical and environmental information into a mathematical form in order to interpret the behaviour of chemicals in aquatic ecosystems. Initially, estimates of a chemical compound is supplied to the model, together with variable such as water chemistry and physical measurements of the watercourse (length, width, velocity, etc.). Then through the use of a computer, several scenarios may be developed indicating exposure concentrations, magnitudes of the fate processes, and persistence of the chemical can be estimated in a quantitative systematic framework. The reliability of any strategy, however, depends on an accurate prediction of the fate of a chemical from its point of release to points of biological impact and subsequent movement to other systems (ref. 69).

If a quantitative model is developed and verified to provide short-term predictions about a specific system, it is questionable whether or not this particular model might be applicable to another system. These models are usually insensitive to many details that are important in simulation-type models, and the resulting predictions might only be qualitative and applicable to a specific system.

In many applications, when one model provide favourable results, a second is usually applied in order to verify the outcome. If favourable results are obtained by the second application, the confidence in the prediction is enhanced. On the other hand, if dissimilar models predicted different impacts, further investigations and verification are usually required.

If a correlation is obtained between an experimental study and a model prediction for the same system, the estimates will be strengthened for the identified points of impact. If the results were not compatable with scientific tests identifying biological responses, it might be concluded that the model could require further investigation.

REFERENCES

1 J.W. Robinson, Undergraduate Instrumental Analysis, 4th Edition, Marcel Dekker Inc., New York, U.S.A., 1987, 640 p.
2 S. Ramamoorthy and D.J. Kushner, Microbial Ecology, 2 (1975) 162-176; Nature, 256 (1975) 399-401.
3 CRC Handbook Series in Organic Electrochemistry, in L. Meites, P. Zuman, and E.B. Rupp (Editors), Vols. 1-5, CRC Press Inc., Boca Raton, 1982.
4 C.N.R. Rao, Ultraviolet and Visible Spectroscopy - Chemical Applications, Butterworths & Co. Publishers Ltd., 1961, 164 p.
5 A.E. Greenberg, R.R. Trussell, and L.S. Clesceri (Editors), Standard Methods for the Examination of Water and Wastewater - 16th Edition, American Public Health Association (AWWA and WPCF), Washington, D.C., U.S.A., 1985, p. 135.
6 M. Pinta, Modern Methods for Trace Element Analysis, Ann Arbor Science, Ann Arbor, Michigan, U.S.A., 1978, 492 p.
7 S. Ramamoorthy, T.C. Cheng, and D.J. Kushner, Bull. Environ. Contam. Toxicol., 29 (1982) 167-173.
8a R.L. Grob (Editor), Chromatographic Analysis of the Environment - 2nd Edition, Marcel Dekker, Inc., New York, 1983.
8b T.G. Bunting, in R.L. Grob (Editor), Chromatographic Analysis of the Environment, Marcel Dekker, Inc., New York, 1983, pp. 3-83.
9 E. Stahl (Editor), Thin Layer Chromatography - A Laboratory Handbook (translated by M.R.F. Ashworth), Springer-verlag, New York, 1969, 86 p.
10 S.G. Zelenski and G.T. Hunt, in R.L. Grob (Editor), Chromatographic Analysis of the Environment, Marcel Dekker, Inc., New York, 1983, pp. 175-191.
11 G.T. Hunt, in R.L. Grob (Editor), Chromatographic Analysis of the Environment, Marcel Dekker, Inc., New York, 1983, pp. 297-344.
12 W.E. Thornsburg, in R.L. Grob (Editor), Chromatographic Analysis of the Environment, Marcel Dekker, Inc., New York, 1983, pp. 499-511.
13 E.J. McGonigle, in R.L. Grob (Editor), Chromatographic Analysis of the Environment, Marcel Dekker, Inc., New York, 1983, pp. 585-623.
14 H.F. Walton, in R.L. Grob (Editor), Chromatographic Analysis of the Environment, Marcel Dekker, Inc., New York, 1983, pp. 263-296.
15 D.A. Graetz and B.G. Volk, in R.L. Grob (Editor), Chromatographic Analysis of the Environment, Marcel Dekker, Inc., New York, 1983, pp. 423-497.
16 D.N. Armentrout, in R.L. Grob (Editor), Chromatographic Analysis of the Environment, Marcel Dekker, Inc., New York, 1983, pp. 555-583.
17 K.J. Irgolic and F.E. Brinckman, in M. Bernhard, F.E. Brinckman, and P.J. Sadler (Editors), The Importance of Chemical "Speciation" in Environmental Processes, Springer-Verlag, Berlin, 1986, pp. 667-684.
18 G.G. Guibault and L.G. Hargis, Instrumental Analysis Manual-Modern Experiments for the Laboratory, Marcel Dekker, Inc., New York, 1970.
19 M.A. Ottoboni, The Dose Makes the Poison Third Edition, Published by Bacchus Press, California, U.S.A., 1986, 222 p.
20 T.A. Loomis, Essentials of Toxicology, Published by Lea & Febiger, Philadelphia, U.S.A., 1978, 245 p.
21 L.W. Beck, A.W. Maki, N.R. Artman, and E.R. Wilson, Outline and Criteria for Evaluating the Safety of New Chemicals, Reg. Toxicol. and Pharmacol., 1 (1981) 19-58.
22 EPA, Principles for Evaluating Chemicals in the Environment, A Report of the Committee for the Working Conference on Principles of Protocols for Evaluating Chemicals in the Environment, National Academy of Sciences, Washington, D.C., U.S.A., 1975, 453 p.
23 D. De Zwart and W. Sloof, Aquatic Toxicol. 4 (1983) pp. 129-138.
24 M.H. Roberts, Jr., in A.L. Buikema, Jr. and John Cairns, Jr. (Editors), Aquatic Invertebrate Bioassays, ASTM STP 715, American Society of Testing and Materials, 1980, pp. 131-139.

25 P.R. Parrish, in G.M. Rand and S.R. Petrocelli (Editors), Fundamentals of Aquatic Toxicology, Hemisphere Publishing Corporation, Washington, D.C., U.S.A., 1985, pp. 31-58.

26 H.E. Tatem, J.W. Anderson, J.M. Neff, Bull. Environ. Contam. Toxicol., 16 (1976) 368-375.

27 D.A. Benoit, V.R. Mattson, and D.L. Olson, Water Res., 16 (1981) 457-464.

28 USEPA, Policy for the Development of Water Quality-Based Permit Limitations for Toxic Pollutants, Fed. Reg., 49 (1985) 48 p.

29 D.I. Mount and T.J. Norberg, Environ. Toxicol. Chem., 3 (1984) 425-434.

30 T.J. Norberg and D.I. Mount, Environ. Toxicol. Chem., 4 (1985) 711-718.

31 W.I. Birge and J.A. Black, In Situ Acute/Chronic Toxicological Monitoring of Industrial Effluents of the NPDES Biomonitoring Program using Fish and Amphibian Embryo/Larval Stages as Test Organisms, Office of Water Enforcements and Permits, U.S. Environmental Protection Agency, Washington, D.C., OWEP-82-001, 1981.

32 W.E. Miller, J.C. Greene, and T. Shiroyama, The Selenastrum capricornutum Printz Algal Assay Bottle Test, Environmental Research Laboratory, U.S. Environmental Protection Agency, Corvallis, OR, U.S.A.. 1978.

33 J.M. McKim, D.A. Benoit, J. Fish. Res.Bd. Can., 22 (1971) 655-662.

34 D.A. Benoit, Users Guide for Conducting Life-cycle Chronic Toxicity Tests with Fatheat Minnow (Pimephales promelas), U.S. Environmental Protection Agency, Environmental Research Laboratory, Duluth, Minnesota, U.S.A., 1982, 17 p.

35 K.J. Macek, K.S. Buxton, S.K. Derr, J.W. Dean, S. Sauter, Chronic toxicity of Lindane to Selected Aquatic Invertebrates and Fishes, Ecological Research Series EPA-600/3-76-046, U.S. Environmental Protection Agency, Washington, D.C., 1976.

36 D.J. Hanson and P.R. Parrish, in F.L. Mayer and J.L. Hamelink (Editors), Subtability of Sheephead Minnows (Cyprinodon variegatus) for Life-Cyle Toxicity Test, Aquatic Toxicology and Hazard Evaluation, ASTM STP 634, Philadelphia, U.S.A., 1977, pp. 117-126.

37 W.E. Smith, J. Fish. Res. Bd. Can., 39 (1974) 329-330.

38 J.G. Eaton, Water Res., 4 (1970) 673-684.

39 K.E. Biesinger and G.M. Christensen, J. Fish. Res. Bd. Can., 29 (1972) 1691-1700.

40 A.L. Buikema, Jr., J.G. Geiger, and D.R. Lee, in A.L. Buikema, Jr. and J. Cairns, Jr. (Editors), Aquatic Invertebrates Bioassays, ASTM STP 715, American Society of Testing and Materials, 1980, pp. 48-69.

41 J.W. Arthur, Water Res., 4 (1970) 251-257.

42 S.K. Derr and M.J. Zabik, Bull. Environ. Contam. Toxicol., 7 (1972) 366-368.

43 A.V. Nebeker, J. Kans. Entomol., Soc., 45 (1973) 160-165.

44 D.R. Nimmo, L.H. Bahner, R.A. Rigby, J.M. Sheppard, A.J. Wilson, Jr., in F.L. Mayer and J.L. Hamelink (Editors), Aquatic Toxicology and Hazard Evaluation, ASTM STP 634, Philadelphia, U.S.A., ASTM, 1977, pp. 109-116.

45 D.B. Tyler-Schroeder, in L.L. Marking and R.A. Kimerle (Editors), Aquatic Toxicology, ASTM STP 667, Philadelphia, ASTM, 1979, pp. 159-170.

46 S.L. Sosnowski and J.H. Gentile, J. Fish. Res. Bd. Can., 35 (1978) 1366-1369.

47 D.J. Reish, Rev. Int. Oceanogr. Med., 33 (1974) 1-8.

48 D.J. Reish, F. Piltz, J.M. Martin, and J.Q. Word, Water Res., 10 (1976) 299-302.

49 International Agency for Research on Cancer, An Evaluation of Chemicals and Industrial Processes Associated with Cancer in Humans Based on Human and Animal Data, IARC Monographs, Vols. 1-20, Report on an IARC Working Group, Cancer Res., 40 (1980) 1-12.

50 R.W. Tennant, J.W. Spalding, S. Stasiewicz, W.D. Caspary, J.M. Mason, and M.A. Resnick, Comparative Evaluation of Genetic Toxicity Patterns of Carcinogens and Non-carcinogens: Strategies for Predictive Use of Short-term Assay, 1987.

51 National Academy of Sciences/National Research Council Report on Toxicity Testing Strategies to Determine Needs and Priorities, National Academy Press, Washington, D.C.

52 J.J. Black, M. Holmes, P.P. Dymerski, W.F. Zapisek, in B.K. Afghan, D. Mackay (Editors), Fish Tumour Pathology and Aromatic Hydrocarbon Pollution in a Great Lake Estuary, in Hydrocarbon and Halogenated Hydrocarbons in the Aquatic Environment, New York Plenum, 1980, pp. 559-566.

53 J.C. Arcos, American Laboratory, 6 (1978) 65-74.

54 S.S. Young, Science, 241 (1988) 1232-1233.

55 Interdisciplinary Panel on Carcinogenicity, Science 225 (1984) 682-687.

56 M. Holstein, J. McCann, F.A. Angelosante, and W.W. Nichols, Mutat. Res., 1979, pp. 133-226.

57 R.W. Tennant, B.H. Margolin, M.D. Shelby, E. Zeiger, J.K. Haseman, J. Spalding, W. Caspary, M. Resnick, S. Stasiewicz, B. Anderson, and R. Minor, Science 236 (1987) 933-941.

58 L. Zeise, R. Wilson, and E. Crouch, Risk Analysis, 4(3) 187-199, 1983.

59 J.M. Sontag, N.P. Page, and U. Saffiotti, Guideline for Carcinogenic Bioassay in Small Rodents, U.S. National Cancer, Institute, Bethesda, MD, U.S.A., 1976.

60 International Agency for Research on Cancer, Long-term and Short-term Screening Assays for Carcinogens: A Critical Appraisal, IARC Monographs, Suppl. 2, Lyon, France, 1980.

61 California Department of Health Services, Guidelines for Chemical Carcinogens Risk Assessments and Their Scientific Rationale, Epidemiological Studies and Surveillance Section, Berkely, CA, U.S.A., 1985.

62 USEPA, 1986 Federal Register, Guidelines for Carcinogen Risk, Environmental Protection Agency, Washington, D.C., U.S.A., 51 (1985) 33992-34003.

63 R. Truhaut, A.D. McIntyre and C.F. Mills (Editors), Ecotoxicology - A New Branch of Toxicology, in Ecological Toxicology Research, Proc. NATO Science Comm. Conf. Mt. Gabriel, Plenum Press, Quebec, Canada, May 6-10, 1974, 323 p.

64 D.R. Millar, G.C. Butler (Editor), Environmental Behaviour of Pollutants: General Considerations, in Principles of Ecotoxicology, Published by John Wiley and Sons on behalf of the Scientific Committee on Problems of the Environment (SCOPE) of the International Council of Scientific Unions (ICSU), 1978, pp. 3-9.

65 Environmental Issues, Scientific Committee on Problems of the Environment (SCOPE) of the International Council of Scientific Unions (ICSU), 1976.

66 C.S. Cronan and C.L. Schofield, Science, 204 (1979) 304-306.

67 C.L. Schofield and J.R. Trojnar, Environ. Sci. Res., 17 (1980) 341-366.

68 S.A. Levin, in K.D. Kimball (Editor), Environmental Management, 8 (1984) 375-442.

69 National Research Council, Testing for Effects of Chemicals on Ecosystems, A Report by the Committee to Review Methods for Ecotoxicology, National Academy Press, Washington, D.C., U.S.A., 1981, 103 p.

70 C. Hunding and R. Lange, in E.C. Butler (Editor), Ecotoxicology of Aquatic Plant Communities, Principles of Ecotoxicology, John Wiley and Sons, Chichester, England, 1978, pp. 239-255.

71 J.L. Mosser, N.S. Fisher, and C.F. Wurster, Science, 176 (1972) 533-535.

72 J.E. Boldgett, Ecosystem Effects of Environmentally Dispersed Pollutants, in Effects of Chronic Exposure to Low Level Pollutants in the Environment, Committee on Science and Technology, U.S. House of Representatives, 94th Congress, Government Printing House, Washington, D.C., U.S.A., 1975.

73 R. Schneider, Classes of Ecotoxicological Tests: Their Advantages and Disadvantages for Regulation, In Working Papers for the Committee to Review Methods of Ecotoxicology, Environmental Studies Board, Commission of Natural Resources, National Academy Press, Washington, D.C., U.S.A., 1980.

74 J.P. Giesy and P.M. Allred, in J. Cairns, Jr. (Editor), Replicability of Aquatic Multi-species Test Sytems, in Multispecies Toxicity Testing, Pergamon Press Inc., New York, U.S.A., 1985, pp. 245-253.

75 L.B. Tebo, Technical Considerations Related to the Regulatory Use of Multispecies Toxicity Tests, Assessment of Optimum Microcosm Design for Pollution Impact Studies, Final report prepared for Electric Power Research Institute, Palo Alto, CA, U.S.A., 1980.

Chapter 3

QUALITY OF ANALYTICAL DATA

High quality environmental analytical data are essential in the protection of ecosystem and human health from deterioration due to exposure to toxic chemicals in the environment. These data are used to estimate accurately the level of exposure of a given chemical to calculate the hazard and eventually the risk posed to human health and other biological species. Regulatory agencies rely heavily on the monitoring data for the development of both source and ambient standards for the toxic chemicals to be regulated. The data are also essential in environmental monitoring to ensure that the set standards are complied with by the industries, as well as, to detect any changes in the trend. In addition, environmental regulatory agencies at all levels (federal, state [or provincial] and municipal) are moving towards increased monitoring programs to establish long-term trends, both in terms of the fate of the chemicals in the environment and in terms of assessing the chronic effects on the biota, including humans. Unfortunately, the data collected in many monitoring studies are typically compromised in one or more aspects of monitoring and hence offer only limited use or specific application. Common causes associated with such databases include: (1) inappropriate analytical protocol, or outdated protocol, or no protocol at all; (2) limited financial or human resources; (3) improper sampling techniques; and (4) choice of detection limit. But the basic problem is the misconception of goal for which these data are collected. Instead, environmental monitoring often becomes a goal in itself (ref. 1). This chapter will deal with the factors which determine the level of quality, detection limit, methodology to be chosen, etc.

3.1 DETERMINANTS OF QUALITY

3.1.1 End-use of Data

The environmental analytical data are gathered for a broad range of applications and a variety of decision-making processes. The varying needs for the environmental measurements may require differing ranges of analytical certainty. The objectives of any monitoring program will certainly determine the data quality requirements and also dictate the extent of quality control and quality assurance activities essential to reach the expected quality level of the data. For example, environmental data of high quality is required to develop standards, or to reinforce an enforcement action, or to support health impact studies. Whereas, data of lesser quality may be acceptable for environmental trend analysis. Program managers are responsible for setting monitoring objectives since they are the ultimate users of the collected data. Data collected without set end-use will be of unknown quality. Problems also arise when monitoring data collected for one specific objective are used by other groups or agencies with entirely different objective, ignoring the importance of the required quality of data. Data needed for the development of health-based standards require measurements of very high quality in terms of both precision and accuracy, as well as lowest detection limit possible. In addition, instead of the whole group of compounds being analyzed, it is essential that the toxic compound is quantitatively analyzed with positive identification. Examples are: (1) in the analysis of polychlorinated dibenzo dioxins (PCDDs) and polychlorinated dibenzo furans (PCDFs) in environmental samples, it is important to analyze for the most toxic compounds, the 2,3,7,8-tetrachlorodibenzo-p-dioxin (TCDD) and 2,3,7,8-tetrachlorodibenzofuran (TCDF). When requesting for analysis of the total TCDDs and TCDFs in effluents, such as pulp and paper mill effluents for regulatory compliance purposes, it is critical that quantitative analysis for 2,3,7,7-TCDD and 2,3,7,8-TCDF are included. Without information on the latter two compounds, the data will become useless becasue of the fact that the toxicity equivalency factor (TEF) cannot be arrived at. Another example is the analysis of mercury in fish in setting consumption guidelines for the general population and the sensitive population like pregnant women and children. Fish have to be analyzed for methylmercury content with QC/QA (Quality Control/Quality Assurance) set for methylmercury analysis and not the total mercury analysis. This is because of the fact that methylmercury is 10,000 times more toxic than the inorganic mercury.

Retrospective analysis of historical data has to be conducted carefully because of the difficulty in estimating the quality of the data in the absence of accompanying proper quality assurance data. The end-user should be suspicious of any monitoring data if proper QA activities were not part of the data-gathering process. Often data of unknown quality is worse than no data at all, since very expensive compliance programs could possibly be mandated unnecessarily based on erroneous decisions. Most of these problems have occurred in the past due to the lack of a nationally or even internationally accepted uniform quality assurance programs.

With changing time and due to the awareness of the data users, proper and deserving attention is being paid to the QC/QA portion of the environmental data gathering activities. Several regulatory agencies (refs. 2-6) have set guidelines or criteria for collecting monitoring data, both analytical and effect (toxicity including genotoxicity) data. These agencies have also published pollution monitoring, data reporting, and quality assurance regulations or guidelines. For example, in 1979, United States Environmental Protection Agency (U.S. EPA) has in addition to publishing these regulations also adopted a policy to include a mandatory quality assurance program in all U.S. EPA research and monitoring activities (ref. 7). Even if resources are limited, it is important to produce data with known quality, even if it is less in volume than more data with unknown or questionable quality. Data of unknown quality does eventually become suspect, and it is often discarded and the monitoring effort never gets reported. As a result, additional resources have to be found to repeat the monitoring studies, if necessary.

3.1.2 Methodologies

Another important factor in the production of compromised monitoring database arises from a failure or resistance to select an appropriate analytical protocol. Many regulatory agencies (motivated largely by the desire to retain historical continuity) mandate or use inappropriate/inadequate and outmoded analytical methodologies. In some cases, the choice of methods are dictated by regulation or resource (both human and financial) limitations.

Measurement method is the most critical part of chemical analysis. Analytical instrumentation has changed dramatically in the last 30 y from simple electro-analytical and spectrophotometric devices to extremely sophisticated precision instruments, such as menu-driven atomic absorption/ emission spectrophotometers, inductively coupled plasma emission instruments, gas chromatographs (GC), GC-mass spectrometers (MS), MS-MS, etc. These changes reflect a change from the measurement of properties of the element or the chemical moiety to the actual determination of extremely low concentrations of a specific chemical structure or an element. The change in terms of analytical methodology, is transition from milligrams to pico or even femtograms (10^{-12} (pg) or 10^{-15} (fg)), from dissolved oxygen and pH to mass units of a pesticide or dioxin has been a tremendous challenge to the analytical chemist, especially in the clean up of samples since the analyte to be measured is present in a matrix containing large number of background molecules interfering in the analysis.

Regulatory agencies recognize the fact that uniformity of methodology eliminates a significant variable in assessing data from multiple sources such as industrial laboratories, state (or provincial) laboratories, and consulting laboratories. Analytical chemistry, particularly in the environmental field is very dynamic with new methods being continually developed, which improve specificity, limit of detection, precision, and accuracy. In order to assure that laboratory testing methods are adequate for monitoring purposes, the regulatory agencies insisted on standardization of available analytical methodologies. In spite of the rapidly changing instrumentation and analytical methodologies, the standardizing agencies, such as the Association of Official Analytical Chemists (AOAC, U.S.A), U.S. EPA Office of the Environmental Monitoring and Support Laboratory (EMSL), Environment Canada, provincial laboratories, etc. have provision in their process for regular updating of the approved methodologies.

(i) Improved Methodologies. The early scrutiny and adoption of improved methodologies through standardization process eliminates the continued use of a less efficient technique. But many laboratories have a tendency to adhere to a traditional methodology and postpone the acquisition of a new analytical system and learning new techniques, which may adversely affect the volume throughput, quality, and cost of analysis.

Lack of uniform analytical testing procedures will likely introduce difficulties in enforcement and litigation in environmental management. When data collected using differing analytical methodologies are introduced by the litigants, then the expert witness is asked to testify on the validity of the methodologies, and not the dataset. Traditionally, courts will be reluctant to make any judgement, since the case then rests on the qualifications of the witness rather than the validity of the data introduced. The solution to this situation is simple, which is, to use the same or approved equivalent laboratory methods. The attention of the court is then directed to the signficance of the data and not how the data was obtained. In U.S. EPA, for example, the responsibility for the selection of test procedures and recommendations to EPA programs lies with one of its regional offices (EMSL). The criteria used in selecting methods for promulgation are (ref. 8):

- The method should measure the required property or constituent with precision, accuracy, and specificity sufficient to meet the data needs of EPA in the presence of interfering materials usually encountered in water and wastewater samples.

- In consideration of economic requirements, the procedure should utilize equipment and skills normally available in modern environmental laboratories, or the use of specialized instrumentation must be justified by the analytical needs.
- The selected method should be established by common use in many laboratories or sufficiently tested to establish its validity.
- The method should be rapid enough to permit routine use for the examination of large number of samples.
- Often the staff of EMSL, must strike a balance between the need for highly accurate procedures with good precision, and the economic burden placed upon the reporting laboratory. Such cost considerations may preclude the use of some instrumental methodologies. The requirement for unambiguous determination of specific chemical structures at ultra trace concentrations, however, justifies the use of instruments such as GC/MS, MS/MS, etc.

(ii) Available Methods. Methods used by the U.S. EPA for measuring pollutants in water are published in special manuals. Procedures for groups of organic contaminants, such as chlorinated hydrocarbons, polynuclear aromatics, nitrosoamines, trihalomethanes, and organochlorine pesticides, are given in special publications. The EMSL laboratory conducts an active in-house and extramural research programs to develop and validate new analytical methodologies and improve traditional methodologies as and when necessary. To assure that the test procedure will meet the criteria for an approved method, the candidate procedure is subjected to rigorous examination for interference and applicability in different matrices by a research scientist.

After selection, the method is further evaluated through formal validation studies involving interlaboratory comparisons for precision and accuracy. To utilize contributions from other agencies and standardization groups, the proposed test procedures are selected from sources such as: (i) EPA manuals; (ii) standard methods of water and wastewater; (iii) ASTM annual book of standards; (iv) U.S. geological survey methods for collection and analysis of water samples for dissolved minerals and gases; and (v) other pertinent literature. The specific methods are cited in each publication to ensure uniformity.

In addition to approved test methods, the regulations permit the use of approved alternative test methodologies. The process for obtaining approval are listed in publications from regulatory agencies, for example, U.S. Federal

Register. Application for an alternate test methodology may be for selected use in a specific area or for nationwide use.

One of the recent studies conducted in the Chesapeake Bay (ref. 1), provided an account of problems encountered in their program, which were also met with by other monitoring programs but not reported explicitly. The above study was published in the open literature to draw attention to deficiencies in the monitoring concept and to scrutinize and update standard methods employed. Generic causes of inadequate quantitative measurement for a broad range of environmental analytes included: (i) a weak conceptual framework; (ii) lack of an explicit statement of goals; (iii) only minor consideration given to the choice of analytical methods without fully appraising the limitations of different methods and the implications thereof; (iv) not specifying the intended use of the data; and (v) not explicitly specifying the complementing process-oriented scientific studies.

EPA's standard protocols (ref. 7) were chosen for the Chesapeake Bay monitoring program without realizing the fact that EPA's methods are oriented toward legal standards of the pollutant set at concentrations relatively higher than the receiving water levels. Thus, in this study, the EPA's methods would not have been suitable for estuarine samples where low environmental concentrations or unusual sample matrices usually prevail. Sections 308 and 106 of the U.S. Clean Water Act are meant to differentiate between methodologies required for legal and research purposes with some leniency for the latter analyses. Although, the Chesapeake Bay samples qualified for Section 106 type of analyses, many laboratories who perform both types of analyses prefer to analyze the samples by the mandated methods under Section 308. Usually the source of the samples is disregarded and attention is paid to use fewest possible procedures and costly analytical instruments.

After concerns were raised, the EPA-Chesapeake Bay Liaison Office conducted a comparison of methods before permitting a change to "non-standard methods." This study reported and discussed elsewhere (refs. 9-11) showed that data quality improved by changeover from EPA's methods to methods used by oceanographic scientific community. Thus, this study illustrated problems with standard EPA's methodologies when sample matrix changes. The problems cited include: (i) right method, but wrong sensitivity range for many parameters; (ii) wrong method for some parameters such as elemental analysis for particulate-carbon (PC), particulate-nitrogen (PN), and particulate-phosphorus (PP); (iii) no satisfactory methods available for dissolved organic carbon (DOC) or dissolved organic nitrogen (DON), which are critical measurements of many aquatic monitoring programs. The recommendations drawn from the Chesapeake study (ref. 1) are given below and must be taken into account seriously because a substantial portion of the limited fiscal resources is now diverted to monitoring programs.

1. Review standard methods in the context of ambient concentrations of analytes in environmental matrices and distinguish clearly between methods developed for source discharges and methods used for ambient media, such as receiving waters or ambient air.

2. Establish a national system of regional centres of analytical expertise capable of providing expert information on current analytical techniques, conduct interlaboratory quality control studies, develop reference standards, train analysts and perform specialty analyses.

3. Begin to bridge the gap between service laboratories conducting routine analyses and academic research community for the benefit of both groups as well as users.

4. Encourage research into new methods and investigating existing methodologies by ensuring adequate funding.

5. Establish guidelines or criteria for reporting analytical measurements to eliminate ambiguity or misleading statements, e.g., reporting "non-detectable".

6. Review methods used in a given monitoring program in the context of explicitly stated goals and choose appropriate methods. Avoid using bad and inappropriate standard methods to eliminate ensuing problems with data quality. Improve QA/QC plans to address specific objectives and provide rationale for making the measurements.

These recommendations are basic needs built on practical experience and certainly not novel. When the environmental concerns are so intense, we must strive to ensure that most current and appropriate methodologies are employed to build a reliable database based on which long-term progress can be made on environmental management.

3.1.3 Speciation Changes

Research in the last two decades has shown clearly that toxicity of many trace elements and some organic compounds is a function of their chemical form. The following are some typical examples for measuring the right chemical form in a health-based monitoring survey.

(i) Methylmercury. A typical example of the toxic group of alkylated metal compounds. Methylmercuric compounds, $CH_3 - Hg^+ - X^-$ (where X = halide or acetate) are ampiphilic, i.e., soluble in both lipid and water due to their chemical structure. The methyl group (CH_3) is attached to the mercury atom (Hg) by a strong covalent bond, whereas, the anions such as halide or acetate ions are bonded by an electrovalent bond to Hg. This dual bond structure gives methylmercury its unique ability to cross cellular membranes 10,000 times faster than the inorganic mercury (Hg^{2+}) (refs. 12-14). The ease with which methylmercury crosses cellular membranes is directly correlated to its much higher toxicity than inorganic mercury (ref. 15). Any analysis for mercury in environmental matrices for health purposes should measure the methylmercury form and the total mercury but not the total mercury alone. Analysis of methylmercury in environmental substrates, such as sediments, fish, body fluids, etc. should include an appropriate preanalytical oxidative digestion procedure to extract all methylmercury from the binding sites in the matrix. Failure to take account of this aspect of methylmercury in analysis has resulted in underrecovery in many studies. Such data will tend to create a false-negative scenario in terms of human health protection. Tin, antimony, and lead are the other elements which have the potential to form toxic alkyl compounds in the environment. Any monitoring survey with a health-based objective should carefully evaluate the methods so that these chemical forms, if present, are detected in the measurement and reported.

(ii) Chromium. Hexavalent Cr(+6) and the trivalent Cr(+3) are the two important oxidation states of chromium in natural waters. In well oxygenated waters Cr(+6) is the thermodynamically stable species and is removed by reduction to Cr(+3) by dissolved sulfides, Fe(+2) and certain organic compounds with sulfhydryl (-SH) groups. The Cr(+3) is rapidly sorbed to particulates and sediments (ref. 16). Speciation studies (ref. 17) showed that chromium was principally in the particulate form (67 to 98%) in the municipal waters. The major fraction of the dissolved chromium was Cr(+3) form. The relatively more toxic Cr(+6) accounted for < 1% of the total chromium in the wastewaters. Chlorination did not increase the amount of Cr(+6), whereas the clean coastal waters contained predominantly Cr(+6); the median concentrations of Cr(+3) and Cr(+6) were 0.045 and 0.14 $\mu g.L^{-1}$, respectively (ref. 18). In contrast, subsurface seawater samples, characterized by incoming high waste-water plumes containing large amounts of particulates, also contained particulate-bound Cr(+3) and control levels of Cr(+6). In summary, the municipal waste discharge does not increase the levels of the toxic Cr(+6) in seawater. In freshwaters, the anthropogenically derived Cr(+6) is reduced to Cr(+3) and removed by sorption to particulates and sediments (ref. 16). The domestic waste input into the rivers reduced the dissolved oxygen content with hydrogen sulfide formation. This reduced Cr(+6) from 87% to 34% of the total chromium in solution.

Chromium is transported in rivers primarily in the solid phase; 51-36% of the total chromium in the Iowa river (ref. 19) and 85% in the Amazon and Yukon rivers (ref. 20). The proportion of Cr(+3) in the dissolved fraction may range from 34 to 65% (ref. 21) and 44 to 95% (ref. 19).

Studies on the speciation of chromium in the Pacific Ocean and Japan Sea (ref. 22) reported the distribution of chromium species as follows: 10 to 20% inorganic Cr(+3), 25 to 40% Cr(+6), and 45 to 65% organic-chromium species. The difference in the vertical profile of Cr(+6) at a depth of ≥ 1000 m in the two seas was attributed to the abundance of highly oxidizing manganese dioxide at considerable depth in the Pacific Ocean and lack of it in the Japan Sea. Based on these results of interconversions, it is desirable that all species are analyzed and water quality standards are based on total chromium rather than Cr(+6).

(iii) Elevated levels of aluminum (Al) may have serious effects on aquatic organisms, particularly fish under acidic stress. Dissolved Al, mobilized from sediments and suspended matter at increased acidities, was implicated in fish deaths in waters of pH 4.5-6.0 (refs. 23-25). It is known that complexation modifies the distribution and toxicity of trace metals (refs. 26,27). Organic sequestration with citrate and humic matter was reported to reduce Al toxicity (ref. 28). A recent study (ref. 29) on the effect of pH on speciation and toxicity of Al from alum sludge to rainbow trout (Salmo gairdneri) reported fish mortalities at pHs 4.5, 6.0 and at 10.0. At pH 7-9, Al in water present essentially as filterable non-exchangeable Al (FNEX-Al) species, was not lethal to fish. Fig. 3.1 shows the speciation of Al at different pHs.

It is evident that the toxicity of Al to fish depends upon the speciation which is a function of pH. Hence, monitoring study on Al in natural waters to determine its toxic impact on fish should determine the speciation and not the total extractable Al.

(iv) Although aquatic bioassays provide only a gross assessment of the toxicity of whole and diluted portions of wastewater, they are used by several regulatory agencies in the enforcement of Environmental Acts. Often the agencies find the bioassay data ineffective for litigation purposes in environmental disputes. This is not because of failure to prove the effect (fish mortality), but because of inability to identify the agent(s) causing the effect. Ramamoorthy and Morgan (ref. 30) reported a physicochemical speciation scheme in tandem with bioassays, for identifying toxic fractions of wastewaters. Wastewater from a base metal refining and fertilizer complex was chosen for the study. The toxic fractions were identified to be whole effluent, leachates from suspended solids, purgeables, and bound cations of the dissolved fraction. About 91 to 97% of zinc, cobalt, and nickel were bound

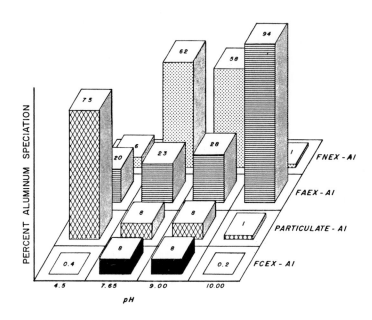

Fig. 3.1. Three-dimensional plot of Al species in water and their concentra-
tions as a function of pH at 12 h (units = percentage concentrations).
FCEX-Al= filterable cation-exchangeable Al species; particulate-Al=particulate
matter bound Al species; FAEX-Al=filterable anion-exchangeable Al species and
FNEX-Al=filterable nonexchangeable Al species.
(Source: Reprinted with permission from ref. 29, Copyright (1988), Can. J.
Fish. Aquat. Sci.).

to macrosolutes of molecular weight (M_r) > 30,000, whereas chromium and
surfactants were substantially bound to microsolutes of M_r < 1500. Weak or
strong cation and anion resins removed 95 to 99% of Cd, Zn, Co, Ni, and Pb.
The removal of metals by anion-exchange resin suggests that the metals were
ligand bound in the wastewater. The presence of total chromium and surfactants
as strongly bound species is evidenced by their removal only by the strong
anion-exchange resin.

The scheme used for the physicochemical fractionation of the industrial
wastewater is given in Fig. 3.2.

(v) In the past decade, the detection limit has been improved by more than
six orders of magnitude for analyses of both inorganic elements and organic
compounds. Both the instruments and analytical methods have become more
sophisticated. With the ultra-trace analyses in use, it is hoped that there
will be very few "chemical surprises" in the 1990s. However, the increased
ability to detect compounds has resulted in the "List Syndrome". The clients
request the analysis of every compound in the list without realizing either

the complexity of the resulting database, or limitations in the identification or quantification of compounds in the absence of proper standards. In addition, the interpretation becomes convoluted with respect to toxicity data when the mass balance, if at all performed, shows that the compounds analyzed constitute only a small fraction of the total dissolved organic matter.

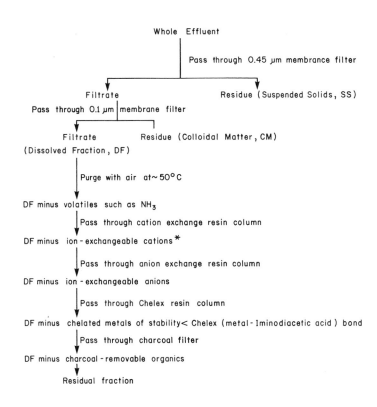

*Ion-exchangeable cations include free metal ions and metal ions from labile metal complexes.

Fig. 3.2. Scheme for physico-chemical fractionation of industrial wastewaters. (Source: Reprinted with permission from ref. 30, Copyright (1983), Academic Press, Inc.).

This analytical development has created a dilemma about the way we conduct environmental monitoring and impact assessment. The two scenarios currently operating are, firstly, the analyst after having detected a new chemical in an environmental sample, initiates an extensive monitoring program, followed by toxicological studies to assess the impact. Secondly, the field biologist observes an impact and transmits a request to the chemist to search for the cause through diagnostic services. The question which emerges is which scenario should be followed in order to be cost-effective in environmental protection. For example, the discovery of Mirex hiding beneath a PCB peak was a brilliant piece of analytical sleuthing (refs. 31,32), but subsequent toxicological testings were not convincing that Mirex was of any toxicological significance critical to the biology of Lake Ontario (ref. 32). However, this turn of events did divert scarce resources away from the search for the chick edema factor during the late 1970s. To be cost-effective, we have to keep our eyes on the critical compounds.

(vi) Halogenated aliphatic organic compounds are frequently-detected contaminants in groundwater and also in hazardous wastes and landfill leachates. These compounds undergo abiotic transformations excluding photo-lysis which does not contribute significantly to the transformation process. Most abiotic transformations are slow, but they can still be significant within the time scales usually associated with the groundwater movement (ref. 33). Whereas, biotic transformations aided by viable microbial population, can proceed much faster than the abiotic transformations. A summary of half-lives for several chlorinated and brominated aliphatic compounds in aqueous solution is given in Table 3.1. In general, monohalogenated alkanes have a hydrolytic half-lives of about one month at $25^{\circ}C$.

The half-life of transformation and end-product data should be taken into account in deciding the types of compounds to be analyzed and the periodicity of environmental monitoring survey. In addition, the knowledge of the physico-chemical properties of the organic chemicals, such as vapour pressure, aqueous solubility, and solubility in octanol-water mixture will provide an excellent indication of the chemical's ability to transmigrate among the environmental media, such as water, air, sediments, and biota. This will help to identify the types of samples to collect and set the levels of detection needed for interpretation.

Ignoring transformation data could lead to false-negative trend in environ-mental monitoring of a given pollutant. For example, monitoring of Mirex in the Niagara peninsula over a period of time led to believe that Mirex residue levels were going down. In fact, Mirex was photolytically converted to

TABLE 3.1 Environmental half-lives and products from abiotic transformations at 20°C.

COMPOUND	HALF-LIFE (Years)	PRODUCT(s)
Methanes		
Dichloromethane	1.5, 704	
Trichloromethane	1.3, 3500	
Tetrachloromethane	7000	
Bromomethane	0.10	
Dibromomethane	183	
Tribromomethane	686	
Bromochloromethane	44	
Bromodichloromethane	137	
Dibromochloromethane	274	
Ethanes		
Chloroethane	0.12	Ethanol
1,2-Dichloroethane	50	
1,1,1-Trichloroethane	0.5, 1.7	Acetic acid
	0.8[a], 2.5[b]	1,1-Dichloroethylene
1,1,2-Trichloroethane	170	1,1-Dichloroethene
1,1,1,2-Tetrachloroethane	384	Trichloroethene
1,1,2,2,-Tetrachloroethane	0.8	Trichloroethene
1,1,2,2,2-Pentachloroethane	0.01	Tetrachloroethene
Bromoethane	0.08	
1,2-Dibromoethane	2.5	Bromoethene
	2.5	Ethylene glycol
Ethenes		
Trichloroethene	0.9, 2.5[a]	
Tetrachloroethene	0.7, 6[a]	
Propanes		
1-Bromopropane	0.07	
1,2-Dibromopropane	0.88	Bromopropene
1,3-Dibromopropane	0.13	Bromopropanol
1,2-Dibromo-3-chloropropane	35	Bromochloropropene

[a] At 10°C in sea water.

[b] At 20°C.

Cross-references are cited in ref. 33.

(Source: Reprinted with permission from ref. 33, Copyright (1987), American Chemical Society).

photo Mirex, which was equally or more toxic than the parent compound Mirex, went undetected until the analysts realized the possible transformation of Mirex to photo Mirex (ref. 34). Mirex was used as a fire retardant in plastic polymers and as an insecticide for fire ant control (refs. 34,35).

(vii) Polychlorinated dibenzo-para-dioxins (PCDDs) and dibenzofurans (PCDFs), often called dioxins and furans, comprise of 210 different chemical compounds of which twelve - "the dirty dozen" are especially toxic. During the late 1970s and early 1980s, analytical chemists achieved the capability of quantifying the presence of PCDDs and PCDFs, in addition to the long- and well-studied 2,3,7,8-TCDD.

Detection and quantification of a variety of dioxins and furans in environmental samples is a testimony to the innovation, and skill of analytical chemists in different countries. But these findings also pose an enormous challenge to toxicologists and regulators who have to interpret and act upon the significant findings of the analytical data. Since the toxicity information on PCDDs and PCDFs, other than 2,3,7,8-TCDD, is very limited, the traditional approaches to ascribe a rigorous level of concern to these additional compounds are not generally applicable. In order to make best use of these analytical data, several schemes have been proposed to assess the toxicological significance of the complex mixtures of PCDDs and PCDFs. The latest scheme proposed by the International Toxicity Equivalences Factor (I-TEF) Group, of the NATO Committee on the Challenges of Modern Society (ref. 36) seems to have been accepted by many countries until more definitive methods can be developed.

In developing the I-TEFs, the Group used the following guiding principles:

" - The scheme should be as simple as practicable. A complex scheme suggests greater precision and sophistication than can be scientifically supported.

- The focus should be on the PCDD and PCDF congeners that are preferentially accumulated in mammalian tissue. These are principally the congeners that are substituted at the 2,3,7 and 8 positions and which are the more toxic forms.

- The TEFs should reflect the relative toxicity exhibited by the various congeners in a variety of toxicological endpoints.

The I-TEFs adopted by this pilot study are given in Table 3.2.

Ideally, isomer-specific data on dioxins and furans should be generated for toxicological assessment of the sample. Increasingly, isomer-specific data are being reported from analytical laboratory. Then, the toxicity of the mixture is assessed by summing up individual TEFs of the 2,3,7,8-substituted congeners.

TABLE 3.2   International toxicity equivalency factors (I-TEFs) of congeners of
            concern and their proportion in a homologous group.

CONGENER OF CONCERN	I-TEF	CONGENERS OF CONCERN IN A HOMOLOGOUS GROUP
2,3,7,8-TCDD	1	1 out of 22 (5%)
1,2,3,7,8-PeCDD	0.5	1 out of 14 (7%)
1,2,3,4,7,8,-HxCDD 1,2,3,7,8,9-HxCDD 1,2,3,6,7,8-HxCDD	0.1	3 out of 10 (30%)
1,2,3,4,6,7,8,-HpCDD	0.01	1 out of 2 (50%)
OCDD	0.001	1 out of 1 (100%)
2,3,7,8-TCDF	0.1	1 out of 38 (3%)
2,3,4,7,8-PeCDF	0.5	1 out of 28 (4%)
1,2,3,7,8-PeCDF	0.01	1 out of 28 (4%)
1,2,3,4,7,8-HxCDF 1,2,3,7,8,9-HxCDF 1,2,3,6,7,8-HxCDF 2,3,4,6,7,8-HxCDF	0.1	4 out of 16 (25%)
1,2,3,4,6,7,8-HpCDF 1,2,3,4,7,8,9-HpCDF	0.01	2 out of 4 (50%)
OCDF	0.001	1 out of 1 (100%)

DD = Dibenzodioxin; DF = Dibenzofuran; TC = Tetrachloro; PeC=Pentachloro;
HxC = Hexachloro; HpC = Heptachloro; and OC = Octachloro.
(Source: Reprinted from ref. 36).

RELEVANCE OF THE I-TEFs TO ANALYTICAL MEASUREMENTS

Many laboratories still generate homologue-specific data on dioxins and
furans due to either limited resources or difficult-to-analyze matrices.
Homologue-specific data refers to the measurement of the total amount of TCDDs
present without identifying the isomers. In these cases toxicity estimates can
be made based only on assumptions about the quantity of the 2,3,7,8-isomers.
In most cases, this will produce an overestimate of toxicity.

3.1.4 Sampling Techniques

Sample integrity is another important determinant of the quality of
analytical data. Analysis begins in the field when the sample is collected.
Analytical quality is only as good as the sample itself and a poorly collected

sample limits the accuracy and precision of the analytical measurement. Unfortunately, not enough attention is directed toward quality sampling and storage prior to analysis.

(i) Planning. Since the quality of the analytical data is critically dependent on the validity of the sample, proper planning is required prior to commencement of the sampling program. The sample should adequately represent the larger population or bulk material from which the sample was drawn. Otherwise, the extrapolation of analytical results of the sample to the source of the sample will be uncertain or even impossible to interpret. All aspects of the sampling program, including sampling protocol, sample storage, preservation and preanalytical treatment of the sample, should be planned and documented in detail (ref. 37).

A sampling program should address the following:
(a) choosing sampling locations and individual sites
(b) access to the sampling sites
(c) transport of samples to the analytical laboratory
(d) timing of sample collections
(e) setting limits of fluctuations arising from heterogeneity of the sampling medium
(f) sampling methodology
(g) sampling equipment
(h) labelling
(i) container preparation
(j) sample storage
(k) preanalytical sample treatment methods
(l) chain of custody of samples and
(m) training of personnel in the sampling techniques and procedures specified

Fig. 3.3 illustrates, in simple terms, the determinant role of sampling in the overall analytical quality of any environmental monitoring program (ref. 38).

Careful consideration should be paid to:
(1) choice of the container
(2) sampling implements
(3) methods of cleaning
(4) sampling

Literature shows evidence for contamination during sampling and storage when rubber, neoprene, vycor, polyvinyl chloride, polystyrene, ordinary glass, and linear polyethylene are used (ref. 39). FEP Teflon, ultrapure quartz,

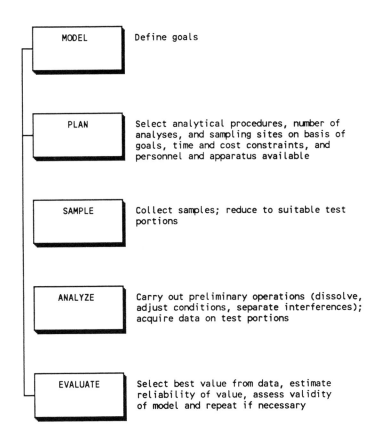

MODEL	Define goals
PLAN	Select analytical procedures, number of analyses, and sampling sites on basis of goals, time and cost constraints, and personnel and apparatus available
SAMPLE	Collect samples; reduce to suitable test portions
ANALYZE	Carry out preliminary operations (dissolve, adjust conditions, separate interferences); acquire data on test portions
EVALUATE	Select best value from data, estimate reliability of value, assess validity of model and repeat if necessary

Fig. 3.3. Role of sampling in environmental analysis.
(Source: Reprinted with permission from ref. 38a, Copyright (1981), American Chemical Society).

conventional cross-linked polyethylene or TEF Teflon containers are recommended for contamination-free sampling and storage.

Most of the sources of analytical error can be traced to and controlled by proper use of blanks, reagents, standards and reference materials. However, an invalid sample poses a problem which cannot be corrected by checking on analytical train. Thus, sampling uncertainty has to be treated separately from analytical uncertainties. It has been shown (ref. 40) that once the analytical uncertainty is reduced to a third or less of the sampling uncertainty further drop in analytical uncertainty is of little or no significance in improving quality further. If the sampling uncertainty is large and cannot be improved, a rapid and approximate analytical method may be sufficient to provide the dataset. Further refinement in analytical measurement may not improve the quality of the overall results. In fact, by using a rapid method of low precision, more samples can be analyzed, thereby improving the average value of the bulk material under examination. Fig. 3.4 shows the relative errors associated with three operations of sampling, subsampling and analysis in testing peanuts for the highly toxic aflatoxins. The analytical procedure is the solvent extraction followed by thin-layer chromatography and measurement of the fluorescent aflatoxin spots. As can be seen from Fig. 3.4, sampling error is the largest source of uncertainty in this analysis.

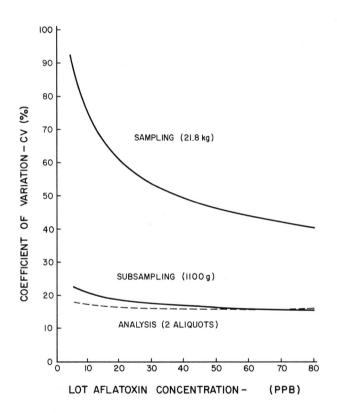

Fig. 3.4. Relative percent standard deviation for the three distinct steps in the analysis of aflatoxins in peanuts.
(Source: Reprinted with permission from ref. 41, Copyright (1977), Pergamon Press, Inc.).

Hence, any sampling protocol should include details on sampling sites, periodicity of sampling, sampling implements, on-site criteria for collection of a valid sample, type of containers, cleaning procedures and protection from contamination before and after sampling, sample preservation (both physical methods and chemical additives) and field blanks and/or field-spiked samples.

Types of Samples

Random Samples

In environmental monitoring studies, it is ordinarily generalized from a small body of data to a larger body of population or medium. If the samples are biased, then any inferences drawn from them will likewise be biased. In statistical terms, the results of samples from a parent population are extrapolated to a target population. These two populations are rarely identical in characteristics, although the differences may be small. Random sampling minimizes these differences, since each population has an equal chance of being represented.

A haphazard selection is not random sampling. Whereas, samples selected by a set protocol are likely to be biased. Also, it is not easy to convince an untrained sampler that an apparently unsystematic collection pattern has to be followed to obtain valid samples. The bulk environmental medium, such as a water body or soil, is divided into either real or imaginary segments both horizontally and vertically. Each cell in this grid is assigned a number and the starting point is chosen arbitrarily on the random number table and proceeding according to a predecided pattern. Choice could be made among alternate, adjacent or n'th entries and those cells whose numbers have been picked are sampled.

The results of random sampling survey should be analyzed to detect any possible systematic trends of biases that might exist. If so, plans should be devised to identify and minimize such biases. If simple random sampling, like sampling at regular spaced intervals, is used, the results must be closely scrutinized to eliminate errors from periodicity (ref. 42).

Systematic Samples

Samples are collected in a systematic manner to confirm an anticipated correlation between a property of the environmental medium and one of the several environmental variables, such as time, temperature, spatial location etc. Such samples are called systematic samples as they represent a select and discrete population under the existing conditions. However, the data should be tested for random events or properties, which might occur especially when the systematic process is not well understood and/or followed.

Representative Samples

Environment is truly heterogeneous and it is almost impossible to obtain a truly representative sample, unless the process and efforts to obtain such a sample is justified. For example, seven protocols which are specified in the U.S. Hazardous Waste Monitoring System for obtaining samples of most kinds of wastes "will be considered by EPA to be representative of the waste" (ref. 43). An example for a truly homogeneous material is a pharmaceutical product.

Because of difficulties in producing a "representative sample" and also the fact that analytical results of that sample will not have the high quality status of the valid random samples, this concept has been discouraged (ref. 42).

Composite Samples

A composite sample is a practical alternative to a representative sample. Compositing is based on the assumption that average composition is the desired sample matrix. Such averages may include bulk averages, time-weighted averages and flow-proportional averages. Detailed procedures are available for producing homogenized composite samples (ref. 42).

Compositing can best be used when the matrix homogeneity or within-sample variability is not a significant problem or is not of great importance. Compositing generally saves analytical time and costs. But compositing should not be adopted when there is a chance that an undetected single unit of sample could pose a threat to public health. Compositing can also hide an individual unit of sample which might have violated environmental compliance because of matrix dilution.

Youden (ref. 44) noted that "many materials are notoriously difficult to sample. Often the variability among samples is the controlling factor in the confidence placed in the analytical results". It is a common practice to composite several individual samples. The problem with the composited sample is that it conceals the between-sample variation and hence gives the analyst the dubious satisfaction that the analytical quality is in control and the results are in close agreement in terms of accuracy and precision. Users may have enormous confidence in the results. What is being forgotten here is that only the analytical error was verified on the homogenate and between-sample variability was not addressed at all. Youden remarked "it should be mandatory to run the samples individually, for only by doing so will anybody be in a position to make any statistical statement about the results, no matter how good the analytical procedure" (ref. 44). Analysis of a number of individual samples allows determination of the average and the distribution of samples within the population (between-sample variability). This might involve additional costs due to some extra analytical effort. But all this information is vital when composite samples are used in collaborative tests and as reference materials. The information will help to evaluate the apparent differences in analytical results from participating laboratories.

A somewhat similar view of sampling for analysis is expressed in a paper published in Chemical and Engineering News (ref. 45) by an Ad Hoc Subcommittee of the American Chemical Society for "Dealing with the Scientific Aspects of Regulatory Measurements." This report observes, "the number of samples to be analyzed in a given situation usually is limited by the resources available for the collection of the samples or for their analysis. However, the reliability of the result generally increases with the square root of the number of samples analyzed. For this reason, analyses of multiple samples always are preferred over single samples since single samples give no information on the homogeneity of the lot that was sampled. In addition, for single samples, the sampling error is also confounded with the analytical error. As a result, if the total number of determinations must be fixed, multiple independent single samples are preferred over replicate aliquots from a single sample. If only a single analysis is possible, a composite sample is preferred over a single random sample. In any case, the sampling decision should be an a priori decision and should be based on the question at issue."

It is essential that the sample or samples be prepared to achieve homogeneity and not treated drastically so as to prevent alteration from the original composition. Obviously, failure to prepare homogeneous samples at this point will affect the results of the analysis regardless of the method used.

The monitoring agencies should be cognizant of the fact that only limited information is available by a composite sample and full consideration should be given to the information on quality before deciding between composite sampling and the analysis of individual samples.

Subsampling

Often test portions are taken in the laboratory from the main sample for analysis of different parameters or for replicate measurements on the same parameter. Obviously, such portions should be sufficiently similar so that the results are comparable. If the main sample is of acceptable homogeneity, further efforts to improve homogeneity need not be undertaken. The rule applicable here is that subsampling standard deviation should not exceed one-third of the sampling standard deviation. It is a waste of time and effort to reduce the uncertainty any further (ref. 42). When the main sample is of acceptable homogeneity, subsampling should be done carefully to avoid introducing segregation. Analysts in their own interest, should have adequate knowledge of sampling theory in order to subsample properly. Analysts should be given the available information on the homogeneity of the main sample.

Whenever possible, the analyst should supervise the sampling operation to know the origin of sample and how they were collected.

When the characteristics of the test materials are unknown, a good approach is to collect a small number of samples making them as representative as possible from previous experience. From the results, using the following equation:

$$\mu = \bar{x} \pm tS_s/\sqrt{n} \tag{3.1}$$

where S = standard deviation, m = true mean value of the population, $\bar{x}$ = average of the analytical measurements, t = value from statistical tables for n measurements (n-1 degrees of freedom) at the desired level of confidence.

From these preliminary results, a more refined sampling plan can be devised as described later in this chapter. After one or two cycles, the confidence levels of the parameters are known, the optimum size and number of samples can be arrived at with a high degree of confidence. This process saves considerable amount of time and analytical costs (ref. 42).

Sample Size for Incremental Analysis

The samples size taken for a given increment should not increase the sample uncertainty beyond the preset level. Although there are several methods developed, the approach using sampling Ingamells' constant (ref. 46) used by the U.S. National Bureau of Standards (NBS) will be discussed below.

The between-sample standard deviations, given in equation 3.1 decreases as the sample size increases. Ingamells developed an equation (3.2),

$$WR^2 = K_s \tag{3.2}$$

W = weight of sample analyzed; R = relative standard deviation (in percent) of sample composition; and K_s = sampling constant corresponding to sample weight required to limit sampling uncertainty to 1% at 68% confidence level.

Using the equation 3.2, the magnitude of K_s may be determined by estimating s from a series of measurements of samples of weight W. Once K_s is evaluated for a given sample, the minimum weight W required for a maximum relative standard deviation R percent can be calculated. A tested example is the study on human liver sample in the National Environmental Specimen Bank pilot program at NBS in conjunction with U.S. EPA (ref. 47). Evaluation of specimen storage under different conditions was one of the major goals of the study. The requirement is that the test material should be small in weight and sufficiently homogeneous that between-sample variability will not mask small variations in composition arising from changes during storage. The homogeneity was assessed by a radio-tracer technique. Fig. 3.5 shows that the weight of

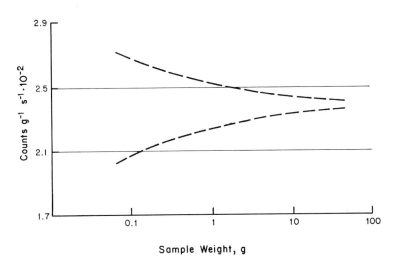

Sample Weight, g

Fig. 3.5. Sampling profile of sodium-24 in human liver homogenate.
(Source: Reprinted with permission from ref. 38a, Copyright (1981), American
Chemical Society).

the sample required to produce 1% (± 2.4 counts g^{-1}.s^{-1}) is about 35 g. For
a subsample of 1 g liver, a sample uncertainty of 5% can be expected.

Sample Number for Incremental Analysis

When the bulk material is not homogeneous or when a representative sample
is not mandated for analysis, then sufficient replicate samples (increments)
have to be analyzed. The sampling variance has to be set, either from previous
information on the bulk material or fresh measurements on samples. Equation 3.3 provides a relation from which the number of samples required to
reach a given level of confidence can be estimated.

$$n = \frac{t^2 S_s^2}{R^2 \bar{x}^2} \tag{3.3}$$

where t = student's t-table value for the level of confidence desired; s^2
and $\bar{x}$ are estimated from preliminary results and R = relative percent standard
deviation acceptable. Initially, t is set at 1.96 for 95% confidence limits
and preliminary n value is calculated. The t value for this n value is then
substituted and the process is reiterated to a constant n. This expression is
applicable for a gaussian distribution of the component. Such distributions
are characterized by having an average μ which is larger that the
variance σ_s^2 (values of σ_s and S_s) may depend on the size of the
individual samples.

The other kind of distribution of the component is a random one, called poisson distribution. In this situation;

$$n = \frac{t^2}{R^2 \bar{x}}$$
(3.4)

The other type of distribution is when the analyte occurs in spots and patches and $\sigma^2 s$ is larger that μ. (called negative binominal distribution) Usually this situation is encountered in the spread of contaminants from point sources. For this situation, equation 3.5 provides an estimate of n number of samples

$$n = \frac{t^2}{R^2} \left\{ \frac{1}{\bar{x}} + \frac{1}{k} \right\}$$
(3.5)

Sampling Stratified Bulk Materials

This is applicable to samples where settling is caused by differences in particle size and density. The procedure for obtaining a valid sample of a stratified material is described in an ASTM manual and reproduced in a recent article (ref. 42). For details on sampling of various types of bulk materials including particle-size sampling in particulate mixtures, discrete units, etc. readers are referred to review articles (refs. 42,48,50).

Valid sampling depends on the previous knowledge of certain parameters (such as $\bar{x}$, s, k_s, etc.) which provide an estimate of the sampling uncertainty. Then the number and size of the samples to be collected for quality analytical results can be determined. But, more than normal, these numbers are at the worst only approximate estimates and do not exist at all. The preliminary samples and measurements performed on them provide for more precise sampling protocols. These protocols, when implemented properly, will ultimately produce a sampling strategy that optimizes the quality of the analytical results while holding down the time and resources.

3.1.5 Quality Assurance/Quality Control (QA/QC) Programs

Due to increased activity in the environmental monitoring area, analytical data are being generated by several laboratories including, federal, provincial (or state), academic, private and industrial. Reports are being released from different groups at much faster rates than before.

On the one hand, it is encouraging to see the intensity of environmental activity particularly in the monitoring area where public want to know how much they are exposed to a given chemical and from which component of the environment. On the other hand, the intense activity is also a matter of real concern for many regulatory agencies regarding the validity of analytical data generated at trace and ultra-trace levels. The main reason for such concern comes from methodology differences, non-adherence to established protocols, lack of documentation procedures, and varying QA/QC procedures used in various laboratories.

Quality assurance and quality control (QA/QC) programs are in effect in environmental analysis for the last 15 years or so. In early years, the QA/QC activities were construed as policing action on the analysts and resulted in resistance to implementation of QA/QC programs as part of their analytical measurements. With continuing education and conductance of several inter-laboratory studies on a variety of environmental parameters, personnel in analytical laboratories view QA/QC programs as validation of their analytical performance. In addition, the procedures also point out any systematic and random errors that may be causing problems in the quality of the output data. Presently, some analytical laboratories especially private consulting laboratories do include 15 to 20% of the total analytical efforts to QA/QC activities without any additional cost to clients.

Analytical sensitivity has increased by more than a million-fold in the last decade and has reached detection limits as low as few femtograms (10^{-15}g) for a few environmental contaminants such as chlorinated dioxins and furans. Problems associated with the low level detections are the variances between laboratories, poor precision within a laboratory, etc. Many datasets reported lack the level of confidence associated with the data. Unfortunately, these numbers are taken as absolute concentrations and used to predict loadings, estimate exposure levels and also to make regulatory and control decisions. Media often rely on these analytical results in their coverage on environmental matters and indirectly lead to increased public concerns.

It is important that an analytical laboratory should set the production of high quality analytical data as one of its cherished objectives. Controlling and ensuring the quality of analytical data of a laboratory requires dedica-tion by management and, support, clear understanding, adherence to the set guidelines and a total dedication by all staff. Management must be willing to set aside personnel and time for quality assurance activities with the realization that productivity may decrease slightly during the designing and implementation of the program. The reward is the improved morale, confidence and performance by the staff once the program is working. These returns alone make the investment in QA/QC programs worth the effort.

The level of commitment to QA/QC programs will depend upon the size of the analytical operation and end-use of the data. Laboratories which perform analyses for regulatory agencies require a high level of dedication to the QA/QC programs. Similarly, contractual analyses performed for federal and state agencies also have to insist on a high level of QA/QC activities in generating analytical data. Whereas, small laboratories with a low volume of operation can manage with a minimal but well managed program to produce quality results.

For multi-disciplinary environmental laboratories, lines of authority must be well established with written guidelines, standard operating procedures (SOPs) and a quality assurance coordinator appointed to oversee the entire activity and manage the programs. Most importantly, qualified and well-trained personnel are always the critical components of QA/QC program in any laboratory (ref. 48).

Definitions

The following definitions for frequently used terms in QA/QC activities are taken from contemporary publications.

Quality Assurance (QA)

Quality assurance is defined as a planned system of verification activities whose purpose is to provide data users assurance that preset standards of quality at predetermined level of confidence have been met in generating the analytical data. The two elements involved in QA are the Quality Control (QC) and Quality Assessment (QAS).

Quality Control (QC)

Quality control is the overall system of guidelines, procedures and practices which have been developed to control the quality of the end-product with reference to previously established performance criteria.

Quality Assessment (QAS)

Quality assessment is the mechanism to verify that the system is operating within acceptable limits. This is carried out immediately after QC and involves evaluation and auditing of QC data to ensure the effectiveness of the QC program.

Analytical Measurement System

Fig. 3.6 illustrates the various steps in the analytical measurement process, and it is expected that a thorough understanding of the system is essential in generating data of highest quality possible.

(i) Sample. Sampling methodology and its importance in controlling the quality of the analytical data have been discussed earlier in this chapter.

(ii) Measurement Methodologies. The role of measurement methodologies has also been discussed earlier. The following information is vital before accepting a given method suitable for routine analysis to generate data for regulatory decision making purposes (ref. 42).

(a) adequate sensitivity

(b) selectivity

(c) accuracy and precision

(d) wide measurement range

(e) ease of analytical operation

(f) multi-analyte capability

(g) cost-effective

(h) ruggedness to moderate variables

(i) forms of analyte determined

(j) limit of detection

(k) bases and interferences

(l) operational skills needed to operate

(m) multi-matrix applicability

In choosing a suitable method, all of the above characteristics have to be assessed in terms of the measurement requirements. A trial measurement to validate the applicability of the chosen method to the measurement needs is recommended. If more than one method is available then unit cost analysis will help to decide on a particular method. Once a method is chosen, standard operating procedures (SOPs) with quality assurance objective should be prepared, detailing every step of the method. Once a method is adopted, it should be followed faithfully and consistently, without making any changes, even if it is a minor change.

(iii) Calibration. Analytical instruments differ in the way they detect the analyte which depends upon the property of the analyte. The property whose signal is detected could be ultraviolet-visible spectra, elution pattern, mass spectra, nuclear properties, electrical charge, etc. Any instrument which is involved in the analysis (routine or specialty analysis) of elements or chemical moities have to be calibrated to establish its analytical function. Calibration requires the analysis of reputable standard containing the analyte

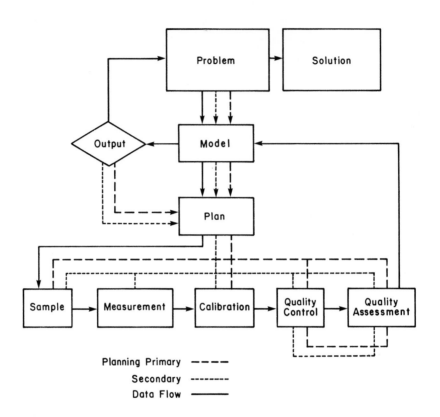

Fig. 3.6. QA/QC in the analytical measurement system.
(Source: Reprinted with permission from ref. 38b, Copyright (1981), American Chemical Society).

in question at a known concentration. This is called a primary reference standard which means that it is a homogeneous matter whose specific properties, such as identity, purity, and potency have been measured and certified by a qualified and recognized organization. Primary reference standards are available from the U.S. National Bureau of Standards (NBS), the U.S. Pharmacopeial Convention (USP), the American Society for Testing Materials (ASTM), and the U.S. Environmental Protection Agency (U.S. EPA). The primary reference standards are used to calibrate analytical systems to validate the specificity of the measurement technique and assure the reliability of the methodology.

Most laboratories prepare their own primary standards which contain the analyte at reasonably high concentration in order to avoid losses during storage. These primary standards have a longer shelf life than the working standards or secondary standards, which are solutions prepared by proper dilution of the primary standard. The working standards contain the analyte at a concentration which is in the measuring range of the instrument. Often, primary reference standards, when available, are used to "calibrate" the laboratory primary standard. The working standard is used in day-to-day analyses for calibrating the instrument before sample analysis.

The preparation and standardization of in-house standard solutions should be well monitored and proper records should be maintained in a log book for each solution. The information should include name of the solution, strength, method of preparation, standardization calculations, periodic assay of their strength and cross-check by a second analyst. Working solutions have to be made on a daily basis.

A calibration curve is prepared by analyzing graded solutions of working standard to cover as wide a range as possible and also to detect the non-linear response range of the instrument for the analyte. Results of concentrations of the analyte and the scale reading of the instrument are plotted on the x and y axis, respectively. The curve-fitting should preferably done by least squares method to avoid human error. Theoretically, the curve should go through zero on both scales. An intercept on the y-axis denotes background problem to which the instrument is responding. An intercept on the x-axis refers to "non-detectable range".

NBS has in stock about 900 primary reference standards, which are really "standard reference materials (SRMs)" in 70 major categories. Most do not have direct application in the routine operation of an analytical laboratory. SRMs are useful in method development and interlaboratory quality control studies.

Quality Control Program

Quality control pervades all areas in the analytical measurement process to insist that a quality output is the objective. It is important to identify the program elements. Laboratory design or laboratory safety procedures may not be listed, but they are called "hygenic" elements which influence morale, dedication to the job, efficiency of operations and achievement of set objectives.

The U.S. National Institute of Occupational Safety and Health (NIOSH) has developed a document entitled "Industrial Hygiene Laboratory Quality Program Requirements". The following elements which must be addressed in a quality control program are listed (ref. 49):

- Objectives statement
- Policy statement
- Organization
- Quality planning
- Standard operating procedures (SOPs)
- Record keeping
- Chain of custody protocols
- Corrective action
- Quality first-hand training - not serial
- Document control
- Instrument preventive maintenance
- Calibration of the instrument
- Reagents and reference standards
- Instrument procurement and control
- Sample receiving, identification and control
- Laboratory analysis
- Control charts
- Interlaboratory and intralaboratory testing programs
- Sample handling, storage and delivery
- Statistical quality control
- Data validation
- System audits

Selection of element from this list for a QA program depends on the size of the laboratory, end-use of the data and the management's commitment to a desired level of quality. Protocols are essential components of QC program in any laboratory. Protocols are needed for:

- Good laboratory practices (GLPs)
- Validation of analytical methods
- Approval of new methodology
- Delisting an approved method
- Modifications to an existing valid method.

Quality control procedures provide the analysts a standardized set of guidelines for minimizing or eliminating analytical errors and to produce highest quality data possible in terms of precision and accuracy. This can be achieved by adhering to good quality control practices, detect and eliminate errors resulting from contamination, matrix effects, systematic errors arising from methodology, instrument and human biases, random errors, and variable analytical sensitivity.

All analysts should consult GLPs before they start to implement any QA/QC programs. The GLPs cover all aspects of the analytical train including: (1) laboratory facilities and safety; (2) staff relations and work environment;

(3) chemicals, reagents and standards; (4) apparatus; (5) methodologies; and (6) data handling. The GLPs and protocols should be developed collaboratively by all those involved in the monitoring program. Analysts must be their own critics in their aim to produce highest quality data possible. However, provision must be in the QC program for external inspection, periodic and unannounced audits to evaluate the level of routine analytical performance of the laboratory.

Inter-laboratory Quality Control Program

For every batch of sample analysis, the following steps should be followed:

1. The analytical standard should be double-checked with another standard for its purity and analytical quality.

2. Background noise should be checked out by running deionized-distilled water blank or pure solvent blank as the case may be.

3. Reagent blank should be run to check for any possible contamination.

4. Every tenth sample should be spiked with standards of concentration close to that found in the natural sample. This step will identify any matrix interference and will determine the recovery efficiency.

5. If matrix interference is confirmed, the method of "standard additions" should be used to calculate the "true" concentration of the analyte.

   a. Standard Additions Method

   This method is used to estimate the loss in recovery of the analyte due to interference from sample matrix. In this method, several aliquots of the unknown sample is spiked with a known standard at different concentration levels of the analyte (usually a blank and 3 more spikes). Thus, the spikes are subjected to similar matrix effects. Care should be taken to keep the additional volume as small as possible to avoid correcting for dilution factor. The unspiked solution should also be corrected for equal volume increase as for the spikes to keep the dilution factor constant. The analytical results are plotted and the straight line is extended through the concentration points of the spikes to intersect the abscissa. The intersection point on the abscissa is the concentration of the unknown sample (Fig. 3.7).

   In using standard addition method to estimate percent recovery, attention must be paid to two critical points. They are: (1) the spike and the analyte must be the same species of the chemical. For example, in analyzing for methylmercury in fish, the spikes should be methylmercury and not the inorganic mercury; and (2) enough time should be allowed for the spike to become part of the matrix similar

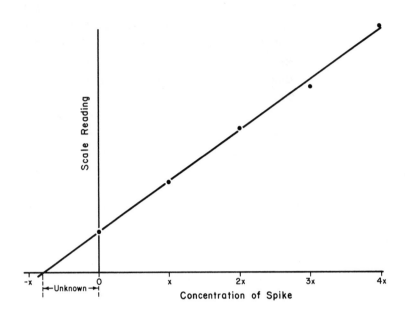

Fig. 3.7. Analysis by standard addition method.

to the analyte being an integral part of the natural matrix which is causing the recovery problem. Most laboratories do not pay attention to the second point and thus do not really address the unavailable portion of the analyte, which has become part of the matrix. If drastic chemical digestion and extraction cannot release the matrix-bound analyte, then it may not be bioavailable and becomes irrelevant from the toxicity point of view. Also, the response of the spikes should be linear and in the same response range as that of the analyte.

6. To continue monitoring the sensitivity of the measurement, mid standard (or a standard close to the analyte concentration) should be included in the sample train at one every tenth sample.

7. Duplicates should be run every tenth sample to monitor the within-the-run precision.

8. If available, certified Standard Reference Materials (SRMs) should be run one in a batch of samples to check the accuracy of the method.

9. House reference standards (control samples) should be analyzed in a run to check on recovery. This information will be used in generating control charts.

10. Quality control charts should be prepared and posted in the laboratory to maintain control of the analytical system. These charts are important to detect: (1) fluctuations of analytical quality; (2) random and systematic errors; and (3) deterioration and eventual out-of-control measurements.

Control Charts

Control on analytical performance can be visually demonstrated by the use of control charts. The theory of control charts was developed in 1920s by Dr. Walter A. Shewart of Bell Telephone Laboratories Inc. as a basic method for evaluating the quality of products from manufacturing processes. In industrial operations, separate control charts are recommended for each product, each machine, and each operator. Comparable system variables in an environmental laboratory are the parameter, the instrument, and the analyst. However, environmental analytical laboratories have to routinely contend with a variable that has no counterpart in industrial operations - the true concentration level of the analyte which may vary considerably among environmental samples. The solution to this problem of variation in the true concentration of the analyte is the use of a statistical method which is not sensitive to the variation.

Control charts are used in routine analysis of a given analyte in many samples over a period of time. Statistical control is defined as follows (ref. 50):

"A measurement process may be said to be in a state of statistical control if the significant assignable causes of variation have been removed or corrected for, so that a finite set of n measurements from the process can be used to: (a) predict limits of variation for the measurements; and (b) assign a level of confidence that future measurements will lie within these limits."

Measurements must be made only when the analytical methodology and the whole process is in control, which means that all possible sources of error have been identified and rectified and the methodology has been sufficiently validated so that the system generates results of acceptable quality. Whenever a new method is undertaken, control charts should not be set up until all "bugs" in the system have been eliminated and quality results begin to generate from the measurement system.

To set up a control chart, the standard deviation of a single measurement of a homogeneous and stable control sample should be determined. The measurements should consist of 2 to 5 determinations per run carried out numerous times over a set period. This provides data on precision and accuracy over a period of time which includes all sources of random errors. Usually, 25 measurements are necessary to establish control charts, however, fewer measurements may suffice as long as they are not very close to each other in time. The mean of all means for each set of measurements is calculated and next, the standard deviation is computed. The control limits are set using the value of the standard deviation of the measurement; 2σ limit represents the range between +2 and -2 standard deviations of the mean $\bar{x}$, where measured means will fall 95.5% of the time. This limit is called the warning limit and departures from this limit are warnings of possible analytical problem. The 3σ level is the rejection limit and mean values outside this limit indicate serious problems which need corrective measures before further sample analysis can proceed (Fig. 3.8).

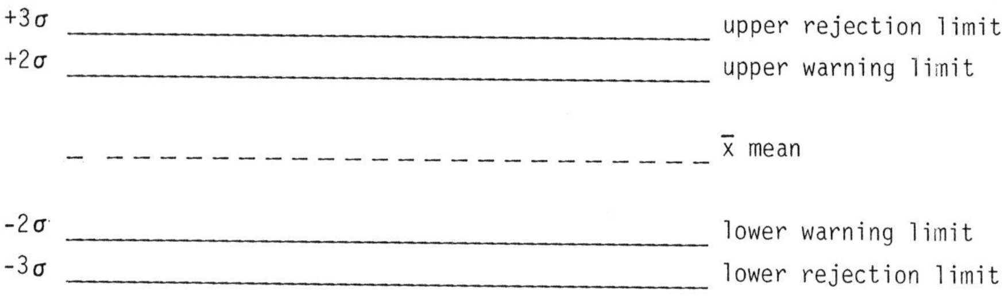

$+3\sigma$ _____ upper rejection limit
$+2\sigma$ _____ upper warning limit

— $\bar{x}$ mean

-2σ _____ lower warning limit
-3σ _____ lower rejection limit

Fig. 3.8. Control chart in environmental analysis.

In the use of control charts, the following two conditions would indicate an out-of-control situation:

1. Any point beyond rejection (control) limits; and
2. Seven successive points on the same side of the central line (mean value, $\bar{x}$) or seven consecutive points decreasing or increasing.

When an out-of control situation occurs, routine analyses must be discontinued until the problem has been identified and rectified. After which sample analysis can begin and the quality checks should be performed at more frequent intervals. The problem and its solution must be documented and all analyses since the last in-control point should be repeated or discarded.

Analytical laboratories now allot 15 to 20% extra effort ordinarily required to QA/QC programs without any additional cost to the clients. This is a small price to pay for the quality assurance it provides to the data. Laboratories that perform duplicate measurements on routine analysis at regular intervals in any given run, can use the control chart results to detect systematic errors, deterioration of detectors, and other analytical problems.

Table 3.3 illustrates the problem seen in control charts and possible causes.

TABLE 3.3 Problems detected in control charts and possible causes.

Type of problem	Possible Cause of Problem
1. Shift in the mean value	(i) Incorrect preparation of standard and reagents (ii) Sample contamination (iii) Incorrect calibration of instrument (iv) Analyst error
2. Upward trend of mean	(i) Deterioration of standard (ii) Deterioration of reagents
3. Downward trend of mean	(i) Concentrated standard due to evaporation of solvent or water. (ii) Deterioration of reagents
4. Variability widening	(i) Related to analyst's performance such as choice of poor technique, non-adherance to set procedure, lack of training and concentration.

(Source: F.M. Garfield (1984)).

The following examples will illustrate the use of control charts (ref. 50).

Example 1. Food samples were analyzed for lead and each batch contained two samples of NBS bovine liver which has a certified lead concentration of 0.34 μg/g. Each batch required one week for analysis. The data generated are given below.

Week	Observed		Mean	Range
		Lead Level, ppm		
1	0.287	0.334	0.310	0.047
2	0.280	0.280	0.280	0.000
3	0.324	0.347	0.336	0.023
4	0.311	0.313	0.312	0.002
5	0.320	0.296	0.308	0.024
6	0.327	0.324	0.326	0.003
7	0.353	0.330	0.342	0.023
8	0.278	0.305	0.292	0.027
9	0.408	0.372	0.390	0.036
10	0.317	0.313	0.315	0.004
11	0.357	0.327	0.342	0.030
12	0.324	0.351	0.338	0.027
13	0.332	0.354	0.343	0.022

From these data, the following parameters were calculated:

Overall mean $\overline{X}$ = 0.326

Average range value $\overline{R}$ = 0.020

Standard deviation of the mean $\overline{S}_x$ = 0.0278

Rejection limits (mean) = 0.326 $\pm$ 3(0.0278) = 0.243 to 0.409

Warning limits (mean) = 0.326 $\pm$ 2(0.0278) = 0.270 to 0.382

Upper rejection limit (range) = 3.267(0.020) = 0.065

Lower rejection limit (range) = 0(0.020) = 0

Upper warning limit (range) = 2.512(0.020) = 0.050

Lower warning limit (range) = 0(0.020) = 0

These values were used to set up the following control charts:

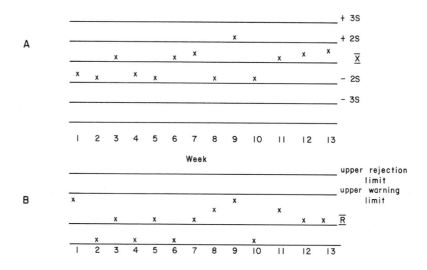

Fig. 3.8. Control charts for the analysis of lead in food samples.

The control data pattern showed a small negative bias (A) but the entire data were within the certified range (B).

Quality Assessment

Internal procedures for quality assessment include precision estimates, recovery data on internal reference standards and use of control charts to monitor the overall performance of the measurement system, comparison of results obtained as a function of variables operating in the system, such as change of analysts, equipment, change of suppliers of chemicals used (potency of some chemicals, e.g., oxidizing and reducing agents vary among name brands), can validate the state of operational stability, adjustment time and also can identify the malfunctions of the system.

External quality assessment is carried out through participation in inter-laboratory quality control studies, sample exchange programs and participation in ongoing round-robin studies using certified reference materials or well-characterized reference materials, such as mercury in fish standards. Partici-pation in external quality assessment procedures should be done under normal and routine operational mode rather than under specialized performance mode.

Interlaboratory Quality Control Studies

Interlaboratory Quality Control Studies provide a valuable assessment of data compatibility and analytical performance of the participating labora-tories through statistical examination of the data for systematic and random errors. Analytical problems associated with blank determinations, recovery from synthetic and natural samples, effect of matrices on the extraction and analytical procedures, calibration at low and high range, sample holding time prior to analysis and the detection limit are identified from the analysis of the data. Such data analyses should prove useful in individual method assess-ment and upgrading of applied analytical techniques by the participating laboratories. With more laboratories participating in this continuing program of Interlaboratory Quality Control Studies, the quality and compatibility of the analytical data reported will be improved.

Data Evaluation - The Ranking Test for Laboratories

The presence of a pronounced systematic error in a laboratory's data can be revealed by the ranking test as described by Youden and Steiner (ref. 40). Laboratories' results are ranked in order giving a score of 1 to the labora-tory with the highest measurement and numerically progressing until the laboratory with the lowest result receives the highest score. The ranking criteria is utilized to determine whether or not a laboratory's results should be excluded from further data evaluation, based on its total rank score. The acceptable rank range for laboratories 6 to 35 and samples 3 to 6 at the 95% confidence level is available in literature (ref. 40). The laboratory whose total rank score exceeds the upper limit is flagged "a" indicating a high rank score with consistent low values. Similarly, a laboratory is flagged "b" for consistent high values scoring a rank total below the lower limit at the acceptable rank range. Extrapolated values for limits from literature are used in cases where actual values are not available.

Elimination of Outliers

Further to rejecting data by the ranking test, which identifies laboratories with consistently low or high bias, outlying results or a result which
differ significantly from the normal distribution of data, are evaluated. The
rejection of outlier(s) from the data set is performed using Dixon's Method
(ref. 51), which compares the difference between the suspected outlier and the
next closest result to the range of all the results.

Values reported "less than" a certain value and N.I. (Not Included) values
are also excluded from further data analysis if actual numbers cannot be
obtained from the participating laboratories.

Paired Analysis by Two-Sample Chart (Youden Plot)

The analytical results for paired samples, which are identical duplicates
of a high synthetic standard, are graphically presented in two-sample charts
for each analyte.

Each laboratory's data are paired for the duplicate samples and plotted in
order to provide detection of systematic and random errors.

Systematic errors are identified by paired results that fall in the +,+
(upper right) or -,- (lower left) quadrant, which indicate that a laboratory's
results are consistently high or consistently low compared to the mean or
design level. It means that when a laboratory gets a result that is high (in
reference to the design level or mean) for one sample, it is almost certain to
get high result for the other sample (++ quadrant). So is the case with low
results (-- quadrant). The points form an elliptical pattern with the major
axis of the ellipse running diagonally at an angle of 45 degrees to the
x-axis. The points found far out along this diagonal away from the elliptical
cluster clearly demonstrate the presence of relatively large systematic errors
in the analyses.

Presence of random errors will be shown by the scatter of points divided
equally among the four quadrants away from the elliptical axis. An estimate of
the magnitude of random errors is given by the lengths of the perpendicular
drawn from the points to the diagonal axis.

Case Study
Study Design

The eight samples provided in this study (ref. 52) consist of: (1) blank;
(2) one synthetic low standard of metal nitrate in deionized water; (3) a pair
of synthetic high standard of metal nitrate in deionized water; (4) unfiltered
effluent of industrial and municipal origin unspiked and spiked; (5) filtered
effluent of industrial and municipal origin, unspiked and spiked. Samples were

preserved by the addition of 5 mL of 1:1 HNO_3 in a litre of sample. The internal precision of a laboratory was evaluated from their results for the identical pair of synthetic high standards.

Each participating laboratory was requested to analyze each sample for cadmium, copper, iron, lead, nickel, chromium (total), and zinc on a routine basis. Results were to be reported in mg/L only for those metals that a laboratory routinely analyzes.

A questionnaire was sent along with the samples on which information about instrumentation, methods of analysis, normal detection level, required dilutions, date of analysis, normal preservation techniques, and if any comments could be provided.

The design levels for samples 1, 3, 5, and 7 are known (Table 3.4a). For samples 2, 4, 6, and 8, assumed design levels were calculated from the means obtained, since these samples were composited effluents of industrial and municipal origin of unknown concentrations for the study parameters.

Participating laboratories are identified only by an assigned number for this Interlaboratory Quality Control Study. The true identity of the participating laboratories is kept strictly confidential.

Discussion of Results

Cadmium

Laboratories 2 (consistent low values), 6, and 20 (consistent high values) were eliminated by the ranking test. The two-sample chart (Fig. 3.9) confirmed the presence of large systematic errors in the data produced by these laboratories. Laboratory 22, although not rejected by the ranking test, is very close to the lower limit of acceptability (Table 3.4b). The presence of large systematic error in Laboratory 20 was confirmed by: (1) the point lying far out along the elliptical pattern (Fig. 3.9); and (2) consistent higher recovery of the spikes.

Excepting laboratories 2, 6, 16, and 20, the percent recovery of spikes from filtered and unfiltered matrices was very good.

All laboratories excepting Laboratory 20 demonstrated good internal precision as shown by the results for cadmium for the identical pair of samples 5 and 7.

The coefficient of variation for synthetic samples 5 and 7 was 10.02% and 18.67% for a design level of 0.1943 mg/L. The coefficient of variation of a low and high standard were 18.29% and 10.02% for design levels of cadmium, 0.0298, and 0.1943 mg/L, respectively.

126

The means obtained for synthetic samples 1 and 5 compared well with the design levels. The design and mean levels of cadmium for samples 1 and 5 were 0.0298 and 0.0291; 0.1943 and 0.1881 mg/L, respectively.

Laboratories 4, 8, 9, and 18 performed very well, scoring a rank total close to ideal rank score (Table 3.4b) and achieving excellent recoveries in 5 out of 5 determinations.

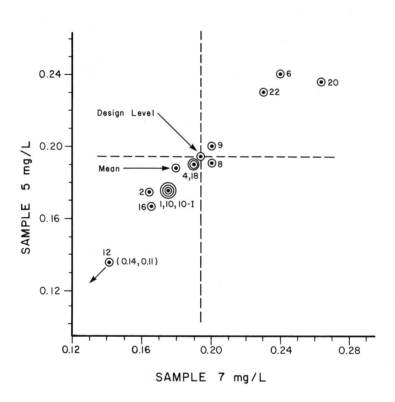

Fig. 3.9. Two-sample chart for cadmium analysis (samples 5 and 7).

TABLE 3.4a Interlaboratory Quality Control Study. Ranking of Cadmium Data.

Laboratory Number	Results in mg/L Sample Number							
	1	2	3	4	5	6	7	8
1	0.02	0.055	<0.01	0.105	0.175	0.045	0.175	0.105
2	0.012	0.020	<0.0001	0.1222	0.175	0.022	0.164	0.089
4	0.030	0.068	<0.001	0.13	0.19	0.06	0.19	0.12
6	0.05	0.09	<0.02	0.17	0.24	0.08	0.24	0.14
8	0.03	0.07	<0.01	0.13	0.19	0.06	0.20	0.12
9	0.030	0.069	<0.001	0.14	0.20	0.063	0.20	0.13
10	0.030	0.062	<0.001	0.107	0.176	0.058	0.176	0.102
10-I	0.025	0.058	<0.001	0.109	0.175	0.053	0.174	0.107
12	0.0	0.1	0.0	0.1	0.1	0.1	0.1	0.1
16	0.027	0.061	≤0.012	0.115	0.167	0.059	0.166	0.106
18	0.03	0.07	<0.01	0.13	0.19	0.06	0.19	0.12
20	0.0474	0.1002	0.0210	0.1661	0.2363	0.0987	0.2631	0.1777
22	0.04	0.08	<0.02	0.15	0.23	0.08	0.23	0.15
D.L.*	0.0298	A	Blank	A+0.0643	0.1943	B	0.1943	B+0.0637
Mean	0.0291	0.0693		0.1216	0.1881	0.0638	0.1801	0.116
SD	0.0053	0.0130		0.0167	0.0189	0.0154	0.0336	0.0155

TABLE 3.4b

Laboratory Number	Ranked Results Sample Number								Total Lab. Rank Score	Average Rank Score
	1	2	3	4	5	6	7	8		
1	11	12	-	12	10	12	9	10	76	10.9
2	12	13	-	8	10	13	11	13	80[a]	11.4
4	6	8	-	6	6	7	6.5	6	45.5	6.5
6	1	3	-	1	1	3.5	2	3	14.5[b]	2.1
8	6	5.5	-	6	6	7	4.5	6	41	5.9
9	6	7	-	4	4	5	4.5	4	34.5	4.9
10	6	9	-	11	8	10	8	11	63	9.0
10-I	10	11	-	10	10	11	10	8	70	10.0
12	13	2	-	13	13	1	13	12	67	9.6
16	9	10	-	9	12	9	12	9	70	10.0
18	6	5.5	-	6	6	7	6.5	6	43	6.1
20	2	1	-	2	2	2	1	1	11[b]	1.6
22	3	4	-	3	3	3.5	3	2	21.5	3.1
Ideal Rank Score									42.0	7.0

No. of labs = 13
No. of samples = 7
Lower limit = 21[+]
Higher limit = 77[+]

[a] = high rank score, consistent low values
[b] = low rank score, consistent high values
< = less than
≤ = equal to or less than
*D.L. = Detection limit; SD=Standard deviation; A=Unfiltered effluent; B=Filtered effluent

[+] Table B, Criterion for rejecting a low or high ranking laboratory score with a 1 in 20 probability of a wrong decision, p. 85 (ref. 40).

Lead

Laboratories 1 and 12 (consistent high values) and Laboratory 6 (consistent low values) were flagged for large systematic errors by ranking test. This is confirmed by the corresponding Youden Plot (Fig. 3.10). Laboratory 12 exhibited a very large systematic error. Analysis of individual results from this laboratory revealed a significant blank problem, poor precision and recovery problems. Laboratory 20, close to being rejected by ranking test, had a blank problem which contributed to consistently high results. Laboratories 4 and 10 reported relatively lower results, and it is recommended that these laboratories search their method for the under-recovery problem.

Seven out of thirteen laboratories over-recovered spiked lead from unfiltered effluent. Laboratory 6 showed a significant under-recovery problem.

All laboratories excluding 2, 12, and 20 had a good internal precision for synthetic duplicates 5 and 7. The coefficients of variation for samples 5 and 7 were 15.48% and 13.46% at a design level of 0.2242 mg/L of lead. This shows

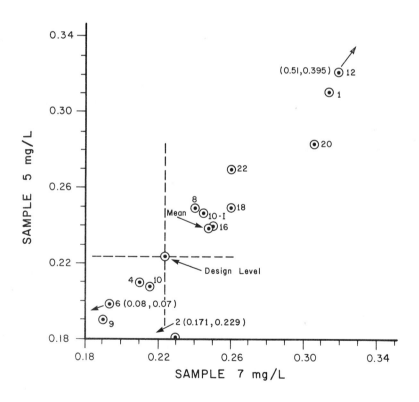

Fig. 3.10. Two-sample chart for lead analysis (samples 5 and 7).

a reasonably good precision of the method at high concentration. Whereas, at the low level of 0.0418 mg/L of lead, the coefficient of variation was 29.24%, revealing the degree of relative inaccuracy of the method.

Laboratories 4, 8, 10, and 18 performed well considering both ranking and recovery efficiencies.

Nickel

Laboratories 10 and 20 were flagged for consistent low and high values, respectively. Youden Plot (Fig. 3.11) confirms the elimination of these laboratories for systematic errors. Laboratory 20 possesses a blank problem. Absence of pronounced systematic error is indicated by the short elliptical

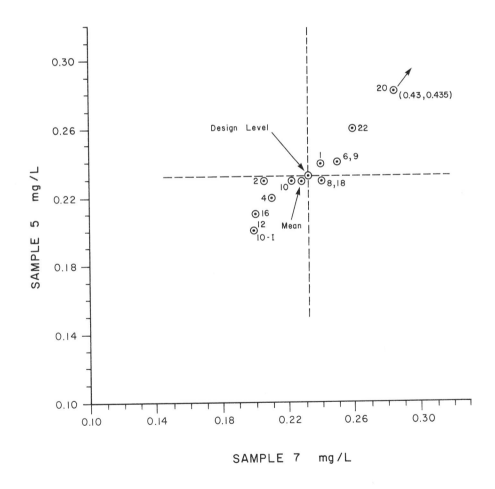

Fig. 3.11. Two-sample chart for nickel analysis (samples 5 and 7).

pattern of the Youden Plot (Fig. 3.11). Laboratories 2 and 12 have random errors in their data. Laboratory 12 by chance (three high and four low individual sample ranking) scored an acceptable rank total. These laboratories should eliminate their random errors by providing matching analytical conditions. Laboratories 6 and 22 were nearly rejected because of their relatively large blank problems.

Systematic Errors

Systematic errors arise from sources, such as faulty operations, use of erroneous constants, incorrect calculation methods, improper units of measurement or reporting of data and non-rectifiable matrix effect. Some of these can be rectified by adopting correction procedures or modification of the adopted analytical technique. Others may originate from fundamental characteristics of the measurement process. Another important source of systematic error is the continuous use of questionable calibrating standards.

Analytical data can be released only when all aspects of data quality have been evaluated. Guidelines for data evaluation, applicable to most environmental analytical laboratories are available in literature (ref. 48,62). Data released should be accompanied by the limits of uncertainty and accompanied by certification of the data by a professional analytical chemist.

3.6   LIMITS OF DETECTION, QUANTITATION, AND REPORTING

Limit of Detection (LOD) is the lowest concentration of an analyte that can reliably be detected by an analytical process, statistically different from the blank signal.

LOD, in most instrumental analyses, is based on the relationship between the gross analyte signal S_t, the field blank signal S_B, and the variability in the field blank signal σ_b (ref. 49). The LOD is defined by the extent to which the analyte signal exceeds the blank signal (Equation 3.6).

$$S_t - S_b \geq K_d \sigma \qquad (3.6)$$

If field blanks are unavailable or the analysis involves only one small with no field blank data, then LOD is based on the peak to peak noise measured from the closest baseline signal. The guideline stipulates that LOD should be $\geq 3\sigma$ above gross blank signal, S_b (Fig. 3.12)

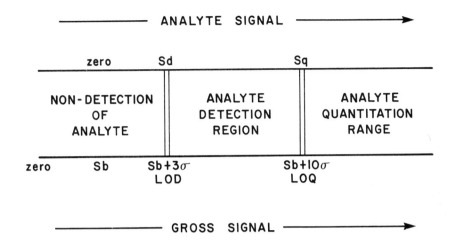

Fig. 3.12. Minimal criteria for limit of detection (LOD) and limit of quantitation (LOQ) with respect to blank signal.
(Source: Reprinted with permission from ref. 37, Copyright (1980), American Chemical Society).

A K_d value of 3 is minimal requirement and hence associated with definite false-positive (reporting analyte as present when it is absent) and false-negative (reporting analyte as absent when it is present) results up to 7% of the values. The question of risk levels associated with different K_d values has been reviewed by Kaiser (ref. 53) and Currie (ref. 54). Precision between replicate analyses above LOD increases the likelihood of actual detection of the analyte. The actual presence of the analyte has to be validated by other independent methods of analysis. The reliability or accuracy of σ increases with increasing number of replicated analyses. LOD may be represented by instrument detection limit (IDL), method detection limit (MDL), and practical detection limit (PDL) as discussed below:

Instrument Detection Limit (IDL)

The instrument detection limit is the lowest concentration of analyte that an analytical instrument can detect and which is statistically different from the background instrumental noise.

The IDL is established by adding the analyte in reagent (blank) water or appropriate organic solvent to give a final concentration within five times the estimated IDL and calculating standard deviation by analyzing the solution to obtain seven or more replicate measurements. The IDL at 95% confidence level is calculated as follows:

$$IDL = t_{(n-1)} \times S.D. \text{ for } n = 7 \text{ or more} \qquad (3.7)$$

where $t_{(n-1)}$ is the value for a one-sided student's t-distribution for n - 1 degrees of freedom.

The IDL should be used to indicate absolute sensitivity of the analytical technique and/or instrument.

Method Detection Limit (MDL)

The method detection limit (MDL) is the lowest concentration of analyte in an organic solvent or distilled water that a method can detect at a level which is statistically different from the blank response using the complete method, including the entire preanalytical preparation steps.

The MDL is calculated using the equation:

$$MDL = S_b + t_{(n-1)}S.D. \qquad (3.8)$$

where S_b is the average signal for the blanks, S.D. is the standard deviation of replicate measurements and $t_{(n-1)}$ is the student's t-distribution for n - 1 degrees of freedom at a confidence level of 95%.

If the repeated analysis of method blanks do not show a positive response for the analyte, MDL can be calculated by spiking reagent to water or the samples, to give a final concentration within five times the estimated IDL and by calculating MDL using standard deviation (n = 7 or more) and 95% confidence level.

For methods requiring concentration and pretreatment MDL is determined by selecting a standard sample size (e.g., 1 L in case of water), volume of final aliquot (e.g., 1 mL prior to analysis by HPLC, GC, GC/MS), and volume required for analysis (e.g., 2 μL for GC).

Practical Detection Limit (PDL)

The practical detection limit is the lowest concentration of analyte in a real sample-matrix that a method can detect at a level which is statistically different from the blank response using the complete method. It is calculated in the same manner as MDL.

For a specified method and analyte, PDL will vary with sample matrices, since these may affect reproducibility, blanks, and interference levels.

PDL is always equal to or greater than MDL, but will never be less than MDL.

Limit of Quantitation (LOQ)

The criterion for quantitation is that its region should be well above the limit of detection. The chosen criterion should be consistent with the end-use of the data, such as synoptic survey, screening, mandatory monitoring, enforcement, etc. The limit of quantitation (LOQ) is located above the measured average blank signal S_b according to the equation:

$$S_t - S_b \geq K_q \sigma \qquad (3.9)$$

where the recommended minimum value for K_q is 10, which is illustrated in Fig. 3.12. Where the analyte concentration is given as gross signal $\geq S_b$ + 10 and as the analyte signal, $S_x \geq 10\sigma$. The corresponding concentration term is obtained from the calibration function. For gas chromatographic (GC) or coupled mass spectrometric (MS) measurements, the level of replication should be high to reduce the level of error since σ_t increases proportionally with the gross signal (S_t).

Reporting of Results

Signals below 3σ should be reported as not detected (ND) with the limit of detection given in parentheses. Signals obtained in the region of detection should be measured and reported as actual numbers with the limit of detection included in parentheses. Reporting data in a region between LOD and LOQ as Tr (trace) should be abandoned since it does not refer to any specific level of certainty (ref. 48).

Reporting Analyte Concentrations

Analyte Signal (S_x)	Recommended Reporting
$<3\sigma$	Analyte not detected
3σ to 10σ	Region of analyte detection
$>10\sigma$	Region of analyte quantitation

If the field blank (actual or simulated) is not properly defined in the protocol, then the results are invalid. Also, the quantitative results, however precise they may be, are unconfirmed until one or more independent methods provide confirmation to the identity of the measured analyte in the sample. For example, one GC/MS (gas chromatographic/mass spectrometric) method may be validated by another GC/MS method which differs in chromatographic set of conditions, methods of ionization and/or detection (ref. 48). In other words, the confirmation procedure should be highly specific and should be selective to an unambiguous specific property of the analyte.

The significance of the measured number is indicated by the reporting method which provides the level of uncertainty. Expressed numbers (results) should include the average measured value, and the uncertainty associated in obtaining the value. The number of measurements and the standard deviation should be reported along with the results. The data on individual samples should also include results on blanks, percent recovery, variabilities, and relative standard deviation. The average value should include the standard deviation of the mean value and details on the averaging process, to clearly indicate the degree of heterogeneity in samples. Scientifically based assessment of the bounds of systematic error in the analytical methodology should be explicitly stated in the report. Any new methodology should be described in detail, including test results of validation. Existing methodologies should be identified by literature references. The calculation methods, complete raw data (including sample specification, sample weights, extraction volume, final weight, and volume analyzed, details on instrument response), data on blanks, control and "spikes" should be provided. All laboratory records or appropriate copies should be archived for future reference. Any interferences in the analytical measurement process and their effect on the analyte identification and quantification should be reported.

REFERENCES

1　C.F. D'Elia, J.G. Sanders and D.G. Capone, Environ. Sci. Technol., 23 (1989) 768-774.
2　U.S. Environmental Protection Agency, Handbook for Analytical Quality Control in Water and Wastewater Laboratories, Environmental Monitoring and Support Laboratory (EMSL), Cincinnati, Ohio, U.S.A., 1979.
3　Health and Welfare Canada/Environment Canada, Guidelines on the Use of Mutagenicity Tests in the Toxicological Evaluation of Chemicals, DNH&W/DOE Environmental Contaminants Advisory Committee on Mutagenesis, Ottawa, Canada, 1986.
4　U.S. Environmental Protection Agency, Calculation of Precision, Bias, and Method Detection Limit for Chemical and Physical Measurements, Quality Assurance Management Staff Guidance Document, Office of Research and Development, U.S. EPA, Washington, D.C., U.S.A., 1984.
5　U.S. Environmental Protection Agency, Part II of VI, Five Guidelines for Assessing the Health Risks of Environmental Pollutants, USEPA, Washington, D.C., Federal Register, 51 (1986) No. 185, pp. 33992-34003; 34006-34012; 34014-34025; 34028-34040; 34042-34054.
6　U.S. Environmental Protection Agency, Methods of Chemical Analysis of Water and Wastes, EPA-600/4-79-020, Cincinnati, Ohio, U.S.A., 1979.
7　T.R. Hauser, Part I. Special Report, Quality Assurance Update, Environ. Sci. Technol., 13 (1979) 1356-1361.
8　D.G. Ballinger, Part II, Special Report, Quality Assurance Update, Environ. Sci. Technol., 13 (1979) 1362-1366.
9　C.F. D'Elia, Nitrogen and Phosphorus Determinations in Estuarine Waters: A Comparison of Methods Used in Chesapeake Bay Monitoring, Final Report, Chesapeake Program, Region III, U.S. Environmental Protection Agency, U.S. Govt. Printing Office, Washington, D.C., U.S.A., 1987.

10 R.E. Magnien and C.F. D'Elia, in Proc. of the Special Symp. on U.S. Natl. Monitoring Strategies, Oceans '86 Conference, Washington, D.C., U.S.A., 1986, pp. 1010-1016.

11 C.F. D'Elia and J.G. Sanders, Mar. Poll. Bull., 18 (1987) 429-434.

12 U.S. Panel on Mercury, An Assessment of Mercury in the Environment, National Academy of Sciences, Washington, D.C., U.S.A., ISBN-0-309-02736-5, 1978, 185 pp.

13 Y. Takizawa, in J. Nriagu (Editor), The Biogeochemistry of Mercury in the Environment, Elsevier-North Holland Biomedical Press, Amsterdam, The Netherlands, 1979, pp. 325-365.

14 T. Suzuki, in J.O. Nriagu (Editor), The Biogeochemistry of Mercury in the Environment, Elsevier-North Holland Biomedical Press, Amsterdam, The Netherlands, 1979, pp. 399-431.

15 J.K. Miettinen, in M.W. Miller and T.W. Clarkson (Editors), Mercury, Mercurials, and Mercaptans, Plenum Press, New York, U.S.A., 1973, pp. 233-343.

16 W.C. Pfeiffer, M. Fiszman, and N. Carbonell, Environ. Pollut. (Series B), 1 (1980) 117-126.

17 T.K. Jan and D.R. Young, J. Wat. Pollut. Control., Fed., 50 (1978) 2327-2336.

18 J.W. Moore and S. Ramamoorthy, Heavy Metals in Natural Waters: Applied Monitoring and Impact Assessment, Springer-Verlag, New York, U.S.A., 1983, p. 63.

19 M.S. Shuman and J.H. Dempsey, J. Wat. Pollut. Control., Fed., 49 (1977) 2000-2006.

20 R.J. Gibbs, Geol. Soc. of Amer. Bull., 88 (1977) 829-843.

21 J.F. Pankow and others, The Sci. Total. Environ. 7 (1977) 17-26.

22 E.H. Nakayama, T. Tokoro, T. Kuwamoto and T. Fujihaga, Nature, 290 (1981) 768-770.

23 W.C. Burrows, Aquatic Aluminum: Chemistry, Toxicology, and Environmental Prevalence, CRC Crit. Rev. Environ. Control., 7 (1977) 167-216.

24 C.L. Schofield and T.R. Trojnar, in T. Toribara, M. Miller and P. Morrow (Editors), Polluted Rain, Plenum Press, New York, U.S.A, 1980, pp. 341-366.

25 J.R. Hutchinson and J.B. Sprague, Can. J. Fish. Aquat. Sci., 43 (1986) 647-655.

26 G.K. Pagenkopf, R.C. Ruso and K.V. Thurston, J. Fish. Res. Board. Can., 31 (1974) 462-465.

27 J.P. Giesey, G.J. Leversee and D.R. Williams, Water Res., 11 (1977) 1013-1020.

28 C.T. Driscoll, J. Baka, J. Bisogni and C. Shofield, Nature, 284 (1980) 161-164.

29 S. Ramamoorthy, Can. J. Fish. Aquat. Sci., 45 (1988) 633-642.

30 S. Ramamoorthy and K. Morgan, Reg. Toxicol. & Pharmacol., 3 (1983) 172-177.

31 K.L.E. Kaiser, Science, 185 (1974) 523-525.

32 M. Gilbertson, Can. J. Fish. Aquat. Sci., 42 (1985) 1681-1692.

33 T.M. Vogel, C.S. Criddle and P.L. McCarty, Environ. Sci. Technol. 23 (1987) 722-736.

34 The Joint Department of Environment and National Health and Welfare Committee on Environmental Contaminants, Mirex in Canada, A Report of the Task Force on Mirex (April 1977) Technical Report 77-1, Ottawa, Ontario, Canada.

35 G. Gilbertson, A Review of Hexachlorocyclopentadiene Adducts Intended for Use as Flame Retardants, Environment Canada, Economic and Technical Review Report, EPS-3-EC-82-4, Ottawa, Ontario, Canada, 1982.

36 NATO/CCMS Pilot Study, International Toxicity Equivalency Factor (I-TEF) Method of Risk Assessment for Complex Mixtures of Dioxins and Related Compounds, North-Atlantic Treaty Organization/Committee on the Challenges of Modern Society, U.S. EPA/Versar Inc., U.S.A, Report #176, 1988.

37 American Chemical Society Subcommittee on Environmental Analytical Chemistry, Anal. Chem. 52 (1980) 2242-2249.

38a B. Kratochvil and J.K. Taylor, Anal. Chem., 53 (1981) 924A-938A.
38b J.K. Taylor, Anal. Chem., 53 (1981) 1588A-1596A.
39   E.J. Maienthal and D.A. Becker, A Survey of Current Literature on Sampling, Sample Handling, and Long-Term Storage for Environmental Materials, National Bureau of Standards, Washington, D.C., U.S.A, Tech. Note 929, 1976, 40 p.
40   W.J. Youden, J. Assoc. Off. Anal. Chem., 50 (1967), pp. 1007-1013.
41   T.B. Whittaker, Pure and Appl. Chem., 49 (1977) 1709-1717.
42   B.G. Kratochvil and J.K. Taylor, A Survey of Recent Literature on Sampling for Chemical Analysis, National Bureau of Standards Technical Note 1153, U.S. Gov't. Printing Office, Washington, D.C., U.S.A., 1982, 27 p.
43   Hazardous Waste Monitoring System, General Fed. Regist., 45 (1980) 33075-33127.
44   W.J. Youden, in W.J. Youden and E.H. Steiner, Statistical Manual of the Association of Official Analytical Chemists, AOAC Publication, Arlington, VA, U.S.A., 1975, pp. 1-63.
45   Ad Hoc Subcommittee of the American Chemical Society, Chem. Eng. News, 60 (1982) p. 47.
46   C.O. Ingamells, Talanta, 21 (1974) 141-155; 23 (1976) 263-264.
47   S.H. Harrison and R. Zeisler, in C.W. Reiman, R.A. Velapoldi, L.B. Hagan and J.K. Taylor (Editors), NBS Internal Report 80-2164, U.S. National Bureau of Standards, Washington, D.C., U.S.A., 1980, 66 p.
48   Environment Canada, Quality Assurance in the National Water Quality Laboratory, Canada Centre for Inland Waters, Burlington, Ontario, Canada, 1986, 98 p.
49   NIOSH, Specification for Industrial Hygiene Laboratory Quality Program Requirements, National Institute of Occupational Safety and Health, Cincinnati, OH, U.S.A., 1976.
50   G. Wernimont, Mat. Res. Stdu., 9 (1969) 8-21.
51   F.M. Garfield, Quality Assurance Principles for Analytical Laboratories, AOAC, Arlington, VA., U.S.A., 1984, 212 p.
52   S. Ramamoorthy, Interlaboratory Quality Control Study No. 7, Metals, Alberta Environmental Centre, Vegreville, Alberta, Canada, Report. No. AECV81-A7, 1981, 47 p.
53   H. Kaiser, Anal. Chem., 42 (1970) 26A-59A.
54   L.A. Currie, Anal. Chem., 40 (1968) 586-593.

Chapter 4

QUALITY OF BIOLOGICAL DATA

4.1 DETERMINANTS OF QUALITY
4.1.1 Effects of Fate Processes on Toxicity Assessment

In order to determine the fate of pollutants and to assess their effects on toxicity, it is imperative to be aware of the physico-chemical processes of the ecosystem, and the physical and chemical properties of the compound. Any contaminant that is released into the environment is likely to be transported through water, sediment/soil, and air. It is also taken up and displaced by biological systems (Fig. 4.1).

The physico-chemical processes of the ecosystem would include the properties of the aquatic environment such as temperature, salinity, pH, conductivity, surface area to volume relationship, dissolved and suspended solids, sediment particle size, and organic content of the water column and sediment control parameters. The mass flow of the water column determines the rate of transport of the chemical discharged into surface water. The type (whether associated with suspended solids, or sediment or as dissolved fraction in water) and the mass of the chemical transported are dependent upon the hydrogeological parameters. Removal mechanisms specific to chemical structure greatly influence the dispersal of toxicants in aquatic systems. Flocculation, volatilization, hydrolysis, coprecipitation, complexation with natural organics, in addition to solubility characteristics of a chemical, all may determine how long a toxicant remains within a component of an aquatic ecosystem (ref. 1). Similarly with the biological components of the system, the distribution of the chemical is dependent upon the bioaccumulative capacity of the organisms.

Chemical that ultimately reaches the atmosphere depends upon the various atmospheric currents for movement. In this medium, meteorological and climatological processes determine the speed and direction of movement of the chemical. The mass and particle size of the particular contaminant also influence its final destination. Chemicals that approach the density of air are subjected to Brownian movements, while heavier pollutants are deposited more quickly. Deposition of a discharged chemical from a point source follows a gradient with decreasing quantities of a pollutant being deposited with increasing distances from the source. For example, the gradient of lead concentration in soils along the edges of a highway has been well

138

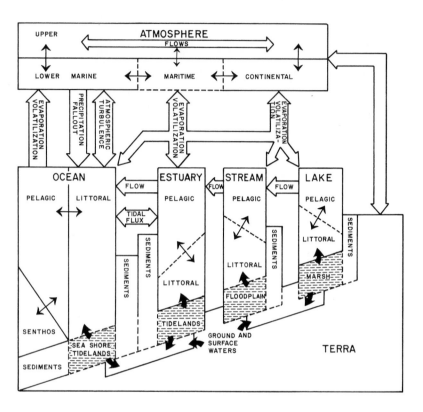

Fig. 4.1. The movement of pollutants released into the environment through transport and transformation pathways.
(Source: Reprinted with permission from ref. 2, Copyright (1974), USEPA).

documented (refs. 3,4). Lighter particles could remain aloft and travel long distances. Anthropogenic lead has been found in remote valleys of the high Sierra Mountains and in snow at elevations of 2134 m in the Wastch Mountains of Utah (refs. 5,6).

Movement of chemicals in the soil takes place in the medium itself or together with particles from that medium. In the former instance, chemical movement occurs by diffusion or mass transport. While in the latter case, soil particles moving in the air (dust) or water (suspended solids) may have chemicals absorbed to them. Obviously, the movement of the dust particles and suspended solids are governed by the factors affecting the medium in which they are travelling. Nevertheless, the physical constraints of the medium itself determine the duration of the chemical within the medium. Important factors include: pH, temperature, redox, calcium carbonate content, cation exchange capacity, and organic matter and clay content for the aqueous medium and photochemical stability, moisture, and air currents for the atmospheric medium.

(a) Fate Processes on Toxicity Testing

When a chemical is tested for toxic effects, it may undergo one or more fate processes (Fig. 4.2) that change, or influence the form of the chemical during the test period. For aquatic toxicity test, the process include sorption-desorption, volatilization, and biological and chemical transformation. Solubility, vapour pressure, and partitioning into biotic and abiotic substrates determine the aqueous residence time of the chemical and its fate processes.

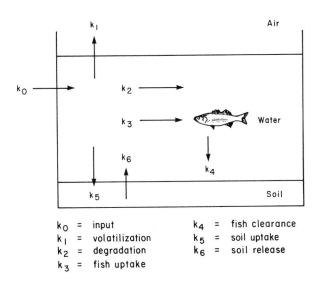

k_0 = input

k_1 = volatilization

k_2 = degradation

k_3 = fish uptake

k_4 = fish clearance

k_5 = soil uptake

k_6 = soil release

Fig 4.2. Dynamics of a chemical in an aquatic ecosystem. (Source: Reprinted from ref. 7).

(i) Sorption-Desorption. Sorption is the process by which a chemical is bound to a surface by either covalent, or electrovalent bonds or molecular forces. When these chemicals are attached to the dermis of aquatic biota, they are not only contributing to the total body burden of the animals but they could have substantial effects on various physiological processes that take place on the skin or epithelial surfaces. For instance, zinc sorbed onto diatoms is transported by diffusion into the cytoplasm (ref. 8).

A chemical can be sorbed onto an abiotic solid substrate or onto the epidermal tissue of biota. Apart from having toxicological effects in the exposed biota, the concentration of the chemical in the dissolved phase in the aquatic medium is reduced as a result of sorption.

Sorption can be expressed in terms of the equation:

$$C_s = K_p \, C_w^{1/n} \tag{4.1}$$

where C_s and C_w are the concentrations of the chemical in solid and water phases, respectively,

K_p is the partition coefficient for sorption, and

1/n is the exponential factor.

At environmentally significant concentrations that are low compared with the sorption capacities of the surface components, the term 1/n approximates unity. It should be emphasized that in the measurement of K_p, sufficient time must be allowed for the equilibration between phases to be established. This time could vary from a few minutes to several days depending on the organic compound. For neutral organic compounds, the sorption was shown to correspond to the organic content of the particulates (ref. 9). K_{oc} (K_p/fraction of organic carbon) was shown to correlate well with water solubility and K_{ow} (K for octanol/water mixture). However, the relationship between K_p and K_{oc} has limited predictability since many neutral organic compounds are also sorbed by materials with little or no organic content (ref. 10).

Another method that is used for expressing sorption is the purely empirical relationship, namely, Freundlich Isotherm which is expressed as follows:

$$\frac{x}{m} = KC^{1/n} \tag{4.2}$$

where x/m is the mass of the chemical sorbed per mg of sorbent

C is the equilibrium constant of the material in solution

K is the Freundlich adsorption constant

1/n represents the degree of non-linearity or the slope of the isotherm.

The slope of the isotherm could be obtained by plotting log X/m against log C for various concentrations. The higher the value of log K the greater the sorption; and the larger the slope the greater the efficiency of sorption. Freundlich isotherm assumes a constant ratio of sorbent to water. Higher sorbent concentration tend to produce proportionately less sorption. A good example of a Freundlich relationship is illustrated in Fig. 4.3 by the uptake of 2,4,5,2',5'-pentachlorobiphenyl by phytoplankton (ref. 11). The amount of sorbed PCB (x/m) decreased in a linear fashion with increasing algal density (D) when logarithmically plotted.

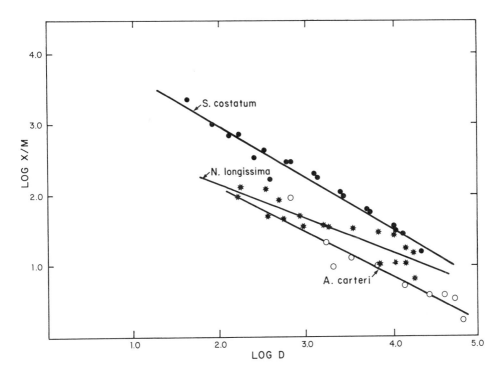

Fig. 4.3. Relationships between cell density as log D (micrograms of cell carbon per litre) and equilibrium concentration of 2,4,5,2',5'-pentachloro-biphenyl (PCB) in phytoplankton as log x/m (micrograms of PCB per gram of cell carbon). Suspensions of Skeletonema costatum, Nitzschia longissima, and Amphidinium carteri were incubated at 12°C with an initial PCB concentration of 0.31 μg/L.
(Source: Reprinted with permission from ref. 11, Copyright (1978), Springer-Verlag).

(ii) Volatilization. The route of exposure of a chemical can be modified by its ability to move from liquid to vapour phase then into the atmosphere. This process or movement is called volatilization and it is an important fate process for chemicals with high vapour pressures or low solubilities. The loss of a chemicals from the aqueous environment is a kinetic function and involves additional factors such as diffusion, vapour pressure, dispersion of emulsions, solubility, and temperature.

The volatilization rate of a chemical can be calculated (ref. 10) using:

$$R_v = -\frac{d[c_w]}{dt} = k_v[C_w]$$

where

$$k_v = \frac{1}{L}\left[\frac{1}{k_\ell} + \frac{RT}{H_c k_g}\right]^{-1}$$

and R_v = volatilization rate of a chemical C (moles $L^{-1}hr^{-1}$)

C_w = aqueous concentration of C (moles $L^{-1}(=M)$)

k_v = volatilization rate constant (hr^{-1})

L = depth (cm)

k_ℓ = mass transfer coefficient in the liquid phase (cm hr^{-1})

H_c = Henry's law constant (torr M^{-1})

k_g = transfer coefficient in the gas phase (cm hr^{-1})'

R = gas constant (litre-atm-mole^{-1} degree^{-1})

T = absolute temperature (degrees Kelvin)

In both phases,

$$k_\ell = D_\ell/\partial\ell \quad \text{and} \quad k_g = D_g/\partial g$$

where D = diffusion coefficient

∂ = boundary layer thickness

   In general, volatilization is a first-order kinetic process(refs. 12,13). For highly volatile compounds and for Henry's law constant H_c >3000 torr M^{-1}, volatilization rate is determined by the diffusion through the liquid-phase boundary layer. In cases where H_c < 10 torr M^{-1}, the diffusion through the gas-phase boundary layer limits the volatilization rate. For conditions between 3000 and 10 torr M^{-1}, both liquid and gas phase are significant. In these cases, the mass transport coefficients of the chemical in the water column are estimated from representative values of mass transport coefficient for oxygen reaeration and water where liquid-phase resistance and gas-phase resistance are controlled, respectively (ref. 10).

   (iii) <u>Biotic influences on fate</u>. Biological systems could affect the distribution of chemicals in an ecosystem by: (1) accumulating chemicals in their tissue to quantities that are above ambient levels; and (2) by transforming the chemical from one form to another, such as changing inorganic mercury to methylmercury by methylation, or transforming various xenobiotic compounds to compounds of modified toxicity through oxidation catalyzed by microsomal enzymes.

   The characteristics of a chemical will determine its ability to bioaccumulate, however, the conditions of the ecosystem and the differences in biota will provide contributing factors that will influence both uptake and depuration. Volatile chemicals may not persist long enough to cause significant accumulation in biological systems (ref. 14). On the other hand, non-polar lipophilic compounds of low vapour pressures have relatively higher potential to concentrate in biological species (ref. 15). The ratio of a chemical's solubility in a mixture of n-octanol and water at equilibrium, is used to estimate the propensity of a chemical to bioconcentrate in aquatic organisms. This quotient is called the octanol-water partition coefficient and it is a rough measure of the lipophilicity of a compound.

Bioaccumulation occurs only if the rate of uptake of a chemical exceeds the rate of depuration. Uptake is dependent upon the concentration of a chemical in food, water, air, and the various uptake sites and mechanisms in aquatic biota. The three main processes of uptake are diffusion, mediated transport and sorption. Depuration or the process of elimination is a function of the organism's ability to transform, metabolize and/or to eliminate the compound, and generally increases exponentially with the concentration of toxicant in the organism (ref. 1). Table 4.1 outlines some of the routes that are commonly used for depuration in some aquatic biota.

TABLE 4.1 Routes that are commonly used for depuration in aquatic biota.

BIOTA	ROUTES OF ELIMINATION
Fish, Amphibians, Reptiles	respiratory surfaces integumentary system gallbladder bile through kidney in urine digestive system excretory system egg deposition
Arthropods and Invertebrates	process of molting

Biotransformation may be defined as the biological alteration or conversion of one chemical form into another. It can be distinguished from other chemical conversions because in many cases it requires biological catalysts called enzymes. The new products may have chemical and physical properties that are different from the parent compound, and therefore, may behave differently within the biological system. Parameters that may be affected include: bioaccumulation, biological half-life, tissue distribution, and excretion. It is also possible that the transformed product may have different pharmacokinetic and toxicokinetic properties.

Biodegradation tend to make lipid-soluble compounds more water-soluble and thus more easily excreted by intact organisms. Some reactions may do the opposite, and convert a chemical into a more lipid-soluble form, which will increase its retention in the organism ((ref. 16). The production of metabolites that are more toxic than the parent compound have been experimentally demonstrated (ref. 17). Biodegradation, however, within most aquatic organisms, with the exception of bacteria, rarely, leads to complete degradation of chemicals to carbon dioxide and water. In many instances, biodegraded products are excreted from organisms as relatively intact molecules that may or may not be degraded further by other components of an ecosystem (ref. 16).

(iv) <u>Chemical influences on fate</u>. Chemical alteration of a compound in the environment could arise from one or more of the following reactions: (1) redox changes; (2) hydrolysis; (3) halogenation-dehalogenation; and (4) photo-chemical breakdown. The extent to which a chemical breaks down to simple molecules will determine its degree of persistence and toxicity. Studies have shown that some of these transformation processes can convert a compound into a derivative that may be substantially more hazardous and persistent. Examples are the photochemical degradation of hydrocarbons and nitrogen oxides to produce a smog that has more direct and active effect on the environment and humans. Thus, transformations may magnify the environmental effects of organic compounds. Halogenation of aromatic compounds and aliphatic hydrocarbons are environmentally significant. Many active systems affecting such transforma-tions occur in the biota owing to their catalytic enzymes and abundant bioenergy (ref. 10).

(v) <u>Solubility</u>. Solubility is the extent to which a chemical substance mixes with a liquid to form a homogeneous phase (ref. 18). Water solubility is an intrinsic property of a chemical and is a determinant of its potential fate in the aquatic environment. Precise determination of solubility data remain elusive for many organic compounds because of their extremely low aqueous solubility. In fact, some of the data on aqueous solubility are no more than estimates.

The solubility change of a test chemical during a bioassay will influence its toxicity assessment. Water-soluble (hydrophilic) chemicals are more available to aquatic biota than many organic hydrophobic compounds which have water solubilities in the parts per billion range. Thus, the concentration of the chemical could decrease dramatically during the course of the bioassay, due to combination of fate processes such as volatilization and sorption to container walls. This will lead to reduced exposure concentration of the chemical in the system, resulting in false-positive or false-negative assessment depending on the adverse effects at the residual exposure level.

Other factors such as pH and temperature could significantly influence the behaviour of a chemical in aqueous solution. Solubility generally increases with temperature, while pH of a solution may influence the stability of some forms of the test chemical.

(vi) <u>Vapour pressure</u>. Vapour pressure is the partitioning of a chemical into air from the liquid phase due to differential phase resistances at a given temperature. For some organic compounds, the solids possess a finite vapour pressure that should also be considered in the evaluation of its behaviour during a test situation or in the environment; this is particularly important for compounds of low solubility (ref. 10).

Precautions should be taken when dealing with hydrophobic substances whose aqueous solubilities are in the parts per billion range. These substances tend to evaporate simultaneously with water (ref. 19). This coevaporation has been observed with DDT in water (ref. 20).

The vapour presssure of a chemical can give a good estimate of volatility as long as the chemical is in free state or is deposited on an inert surface. However, when the chemical is bound to soil, the vapour pressure cannot be used as a measure of volatility. Factors affecting the rate of vapourization from soil include binding to organic matter, temperature, moisture, bacterial activity, and pH (ref. 19).

(vii) Partition coefficient. The partition coefficient is the ratio of a concentration of a chemical in two immiscible phases at equilibrium. Partition coefficients are commonly measured between n-octanol and water. These are valuable during an assessment of the environmental behaviour of a compound. Since partition coefficients are additive in nature, value for a complex compound could be estimated from the values of the parent compound and those of the substituents.

4.1.2 Multi-Tier Toxicity Testing

The objective of the test program is to screen chemicals for adverse effects on the environment and human health, using a procedure of sequential testing referred to as multi-tier testing. The process includes decision points where positive or negative results allow the test substances to proceed to different levels of testing before acceptance or rejection is made. The multi-tier testing procedures for mutagenicity and aquatic hazards evaluation procedures are outlined below:

(a) Mutagenic Screening

Multi-tier toxicity testing (Fig. 4.4) for mutagenic screening has also been referred to as phased testing and usually involves three tiers (ref. 21). This three-tier protocol is designed for the detection of mutagens as well as for the evaluation and control of hazardous chemicals.

The extent of testing at each tier is determined by the degree of hazard indicated from the previous tier, compared with that predicted by factors such as production volume, projected human exposure and the known toxicity of related benchmark chemicals. Consideration of this information will dictate the level of testing required for the protection of human health in proportion to the anticipated risk involved (ref. 21).

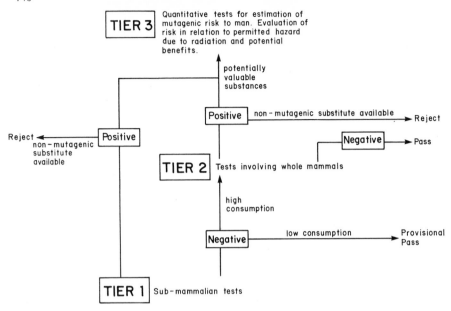

Fig. 4.4. Three-tier framework for mutagenicity screening.
(Source: Reprinted with permission from ref. 22, Copyright (1974), Elsevier
Science Publishers, B.V.).

The first tier consists of inexpensive and sensitive short-term screening
tests which will detect gene mutation or chromosomal damage. It utilizes lower
organisms such as Salmonella, E. coli, or yeast, and mammalian activation
systems (rat liver enzymes). Some of the tests that belong to this tier
include: Ames test, yeast forward and reverse assays, in vitro cytogenetics,
HGPRT, TK, and Na/K-ATPase assays, sister chromatid exchange, and unscheduled
DNA synthesis. Those initial tests should include mammalian cells that will
provide metabolic activities similar to the human system. The first tier could
include an in vitro testing with eukaryotic or prokaryotic cellular systems
(ref. 23). Positive results that are obtained from the short-term first tier
tests are taken as suggestive evidence of a hazard, and further conclusions
are not warranted unless second and third tier tests resolve any discrepancy.

These short-term tests evaluate the ability of a chemical to damage the
genetic material of a cell. Because the basic structure of DNA is the same in
all organisms, a chemical that affects or alters the DNA of a cell in an
organism could have similar effects on cells of the human systems. However,
the amount and complexity of DNA varies according to the differences in the
organism. Therefore, the more complex the test organism, the more likely that
form of DNA organization will approximate the response in human systems. As a
result, mammalian cells tend to be better models than bacterial systems for
relating the effects to humans.

The main purpose of the second tier of tests is to detect substances that might not necessarily be directly mutagenic in vitro but their metabolites could be mutagenic in vivo. Some of the tests that belong to this level include: the dominant lethal test, host-mediated assay, in vivo cytogenetic tests, heritable translocation assay, and clonal and/or focus transformation assays. Similar to the first tier, chemicals that yield positive results in at least one test would automatically proceed to the third level.

The use of in vitro procedures and sub-mammalian tiers in mutagenicity testing has been questioned on the grounds that these tests do not take into account activation or detoxication mechanisms that occur in intact animals as opposed to microbial systems (ref. 24). It is likely that the above statement could have resulted because of a misunderstanding of the justification for the use of tier one only for some compounds and also due to an underestimation of the importance of in vitro tests even when accompanied by in vivo tests. Sub-mammalian or in vitro tests are important event when mammalian tests are also going to be carried out because of the relative insensitivity of the latter. A mutagen active in sub-mammalian systems may not be detected in vivo even if it is not detoxified (ref. 25).

The tests in the third tier are different from those in the initial tiers in that they carry out an evaluation of the test chemicals, and ultimately an estimation of the mutational risk to humans. Some of these include tumor formation tests such as skin tumorigenesis, mouse pulmonary adenoma and rat trachea transplant, and chromosomal effects in whole organisms such as in vivo cytogenetics, micronucleus tests, non-disjunction assay, and heritable translocation assay.

Certain chemicals, in spite of their passing both the first and second tier, testing, may not be approved for use due to their other undesirable properties. It is also possible that chemicals which are tested positive in both the tiers and are unlikely to be approved for use by the sensitive population, might be allowed for restricted use by the general population. Restricted use of a chemical could be possibly due to higher risk by the alternative choice or due to lack of an alternative choice.

The success of multi-tier testing protocol will ultimately depend upon the ability of the assessors to choose the right tests within the different tiers. In case of ambiguity, further tests should be carried out within a tier in order to arrive at an accurate decision, possibly before proceeding to the next level.

(b) Aquatic Hazard Evaluation

Multi-tier testing is also used in aquatic toxicology for estimating the hazard of new chemicals to aquatic life towards developing criteria (ref. 26). Although, the objective of any such testing program would be to screen chemicals for their adverse effects, it should be accurate so that results would not limit utilization of new and useful chemical. Procedures of sequential environmental testing should include points in the process to choose the appropriate testings for filling the data gaps which will assist in decision-making for the approval or disapproval of the chemical for use.

The typical sequence of data required and the associated testings for a hazard assessment is shown in Fig. 4.5. The special tasks that are performed are dependent upon the nature of the chemical being assessed and the objectives of the assessment. Information on the pollutant, including the conditions under which they might be released into the environment, plus chemical, physical, and biological data of the receiving system should be obtained in order to assess the possible fate of the pollutant and also for the purpose of designing a comprehensive toxicological investigation. If there is insufficient information to assess the chemical, then studies must be designed to gather such information.

Following the environmental fate and aquatic field studies, a multi-tier toxicity assessment is carried out in order to determine the toxicity of the chemical to selected biological systems. Each of the tiers is located within a particular phase and data obtained from the tiers are utilized towards the final decisions regarding the use of the compound (Fig. 4.6). The initial tests for the first tier includes static toxicity bioassays and the objective is to obtain preliminary estimate of the effect of the chemical on various species of aquatic life. Although the objectives of the first tier could vary greatly, it is possible to attempt to obtain answers for the following:

1. Relative toxicity to fish, invertebrates, and algae;
2. Relative toxicity to various life stages of fish;
3. Effects of temperature, pH, and hardness on the toxicity to fish;
4. Persistence of the toxicological characteristics of the toxicant; and
5. Potential for fish flesh tainting and bioaccumulation. All toxicity tests conducted during this phase employ static procedures over a wide range of nominal concentration (ref. 25).

When the first tier is completed, results obtained are assessed and a decision is made regarding whether or not sufficient information has been obtained. Data from the first tier should provide information towards the following:

1. The relative sensitivity of the aquatic organism;
2. The relative toxicity of the test chemical (LC_{50}s and EC_{50}s 1000 mg/L);

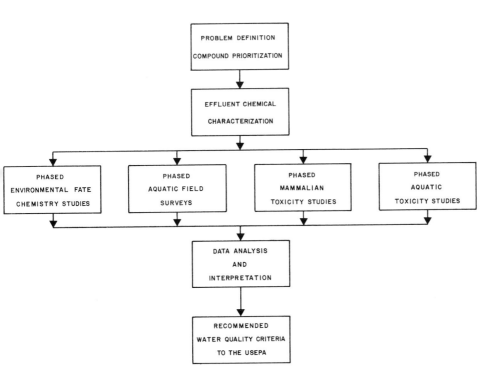

Fig. 4.5. Hazard assessment strategy.
(Source: Reprinted with permission from ref. 26, Copyright (1977), ASTM).

3. The effects of environmental factors on the chemical (toxicity increased or decreased by parameters such as volatility, sorption, solubility, degradation, etc.);

4. The potential of the chemical for bioconcentration (extrapolation from bioconcentration tests, BCF >100);

5. Effects on various life stages of fish; and

6. Assessment of potential environmental effects from previous studies (this will be a literature review to determine effect from studies on mammals and environmental fate/chemistry).

The second tier of the toxicity testing information program is designed to obtain more definitive data on acute toxicity and initial estimates on chronic toxicity through acute flow-through toxicity tests. Particulars regarding different types of tests and their various procedures are discussed elsewhere (refs. 28,29). However, the tests that are utilized in Tier II must be designed to provide the following answers:

150

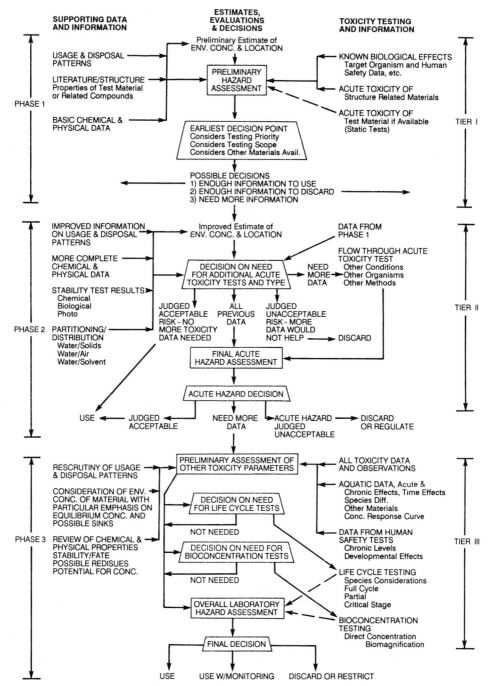

Fig. 4.6. Aquatic hazard assessment-evaluation scheme; Phases I, II, and III; and Tiers I, II, and III.
(Source: Reprinted with permission from ref. 27, Copyright (1977), ASTM).

1. Relative toxicity to various species of aquatic organisms;

2. Further investigations regarding the effects of environmental fate parameters on toxicity;

3. Effects on various life stages of fish (embryo-larval toxicity tests, etc.)

4. Bioconcentration details (relative estimates of uptake and depuration rates; and

5. Preliminary evaluation of the subchronic toxicity of the test chemical.

Completion of Tier II testing should provide evidence to determine if the chemical has the potential to be chronically toxic. Data obtained to this stage should also allow for the assessment of the acute hazard of the test chemical. The key factor in the decision on whether a chemical can be utilized with appropriate acute risk level is determined by the ratio of concentrations found to be toxic for test species to the concentration expected in the environment. Hazard has no direct relationship to the absolute level of toxicity but it is a function of the chemical exposure. Exposure as indicated in the evaluation scheme, depends on usage patterns plus a variety of chemical and physical factors (ref. 27). If the decision at the end of the second tier is to continue testing (Fig. 4.6) because data to date did not clearly indicate discarding or approving the test chemical, a third tier of tests is followed. All studies within this tier are conducted under flow-through conditions, using analytically measured concentrations of toxicant for predetermined exposure periods. Particulars of the various tests are outlined elsewhere (refs. 30,31); however, the following are outlines of some of the possible tests that could be carried out:

1. Daphnia chronic tests;

2. Midge-larvae chronic tests;

3. Fathead minnow chronic tests;

4. Life cycle or partial life cycle tests (rainbow trout, brook trout, etc.); and

5. Food chain biomagnification tests.

At the end of the multi-tier tests, it is likely that questions regarding the toxicity of the test material will be answered; however, it is possible that a certain level of uncertainty might still remain.

4.1.3 False-Positive and False-Negative Data

In addition to precise positive and negative data, toxicity testing could generate erroneous results called false-positive and false-negative information. False-positive information is when a chemical is identified as a toxicant but it is actually not; while false-negative information is identifying a toxicant as a non-toxicant.

False-negatives are of great concern in short-term testing particularly when these tests are used as early warning systems. For this reason, it is tempting to suggest the inclusion of tests which are likely to yield false-positive results in the first tier of the multi-tier testing protocol. This type of bias might minimize the chances of a hazardous chemical not being detected, and therefore, eliminated from further test verifications. In designing tests for the second tier, however, tests could be used that are less likely to produce false-positive results in order to minimize the chances of a relatively harmless chemical being sent to the third tier in which the average test is substantially more expensive. With results indicating false-negative, however, a toxic compound might not be examined in long-term tests before significant human or environmental damage has occurred. On the other hand, with false-positive results, it is quite likely that the incorrect classification will be corrected before too long by follow-up testing. In general, false-positives present a cost rather than a public health concern.

There are various factors that influence the toxicity of a chemical. These include: (i) biological, (ii) chemical, (iii) pharmacokinetic and (iv) the route of administration of the toxicant. These factors could influence the results of toxicity tests by altering the speciation of the chemicals either rendering them inactive or more toxic than the original chemical. The chemical could also reach the wrong critical organ (depending upon the route of administration) or could reach the right critical organ with much less reduced chemical concentration to cause any detectable effects. This could possibly yield erroneous toxicity profile for the administered chemical.

(i) Biological. In complex organisms, the chemical must reach the target organ for manifesting its toxic effect upon the organism. The chemical must effectively travel through a series of protective biological barriers using processes such as sorption and active and passive transport. After a chemical has entered a test organism, it is subjected to various competing biological and pharmaco-kinetic processes that could result in transformation or translocation within the organism itself or metabolized by the detoxifying enzymes such as mixed function oxidases and eliminated from the body via urine and feces.

The organs of certain mammals including humans might have the ability to operate "normally" with less than 100% of the original tissue content. For example, approximately 50% of the liver of the dog can be damaged or even surgically removed and the remaining intact liver will carry on adequately to support at least the minimal requirements of the animal. Likewise, half the lung tissue in the rat may be removed without seriously endangering the life of the rodent (ref. 32).

(ii) Chemical. The properties of a chemical that would influence the results of toxicity tests are its initial concentration, transport and transformation properties and metabolism. In mammalian studies, the chemical which is administered to the test species through various routes stays structurally intact and reaches the critical organs. However, the chemical could possibly be altered by cellular or enzymatic reactions which could lead to the formation of different forms of the chemical to which the organism might be exposed. The altered forms of the chemical could be less or more toxic than the parent chemical.

Water hardness could have significant influence on the results of toxicity tests. Fig. 4.7 shows the relationship between total hardness and the 48-h LC_{50} concentrations to rainbow trout for nickel, lead, zinc, cadmium, and copper. It can be seen that for almost every metal (except lead) illustrated on the figure, increases in water hardness resulted in the heavy metals becoming less toxic. This is an example of alteration of heavy metal toxicities by sequesteration of chemical species.

Although some chemicals such as phenols (ref. 34) and alkyl benzene-sulfonate (ref. 35) are not affected greatly by changes in pH, the same is not true for all organics. For instance, when the pH changes from 6.9 to 8, the toxicity of 2-secondary-butyl-4,6-dinitrophenol increases by about five times for rainbow trout and blacknose dace (ref. 36). On the other hand, 2,4-dichlorophenol becomes less toxic to fathead minnow at higher pH values (ref. 37). Actually, these are examples of the effect of pH on the speciation of chemicals and their toxicities.

Suspended and dissolved materials in test waters could alter the toxicity of test chemicals. One such example is complexation of copper with natural inorganic ions such as carbonate, orthophosphate and pyrophosphate to produce non-toxic copper compounds (refs. 38,39).

(iii) Genetic. Metabolic transformation of a toxicant within biological systems is dependent upon the involvement of enzymes which exist according to the genetic templates characteristic of each member of a population of organisms. Therefore, genetic defects in members of a species may result in a deficiency or complete lack of certain enzymes. Such genetic defects have been shown to be responsible for some specific types of toxicities from chemicals (ref. 36). If animals are selected from such a genetic pool for toxicity testing purposes, it is possible that the results could produce either false-negative or false-positive trends.

154

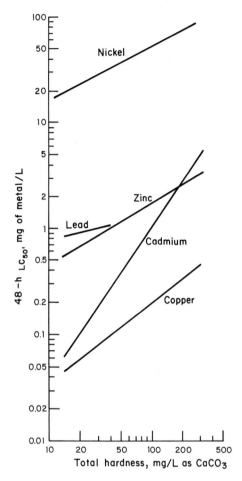

Fig. 4.7. Relation between total hardness of water and 48-h LC_{50} to rainbow trout of nickel, lead, zinc, cadmium, and copper.
(Source: Reprinted with permission from ref. 33, Copyright (1968), Pergamon Press Plc.).

Accumulation of certain chemicals could also result due to genetically deficient or absent metabolic mechanism. This condition could readily occur in experiments where regular dosing is repeated throughout the experimental period. Because of the inability of these animals to transform or metabolize the test chemical, the end data would show this bias and could be interpreted as false-positive results. However, if interpreted correctly, these results would illustrate the existence of variable levels of detoxification among biological species in dealing with toxic chemicals.

(iv) <u>Routes of administration</u>. Although a chemical can be administered to a test organism by a variety of routes, however, the selection of the route is dependent upon the physico-chemical properties of the chemical, and its ability to reach the critical target organ. There are four main routes of administration of a test chemical; these include oral, inhalation, percutaneous and peritoneal routes. The exposure of human beings to a chemical usually takes place through the surface of the body, or through natural body orifices, such as the mouth, eyes, and the respiratory systems. With test animal, natural methods of exposure are not always possible and therefore the use of peritoneal techniques are commonly used when test species are not willing receptors. In carrying out toxicity tests, every effort possible should be attempted to expose the test animal from the same manner by which, humans and/or other biological systems will be exposed in order to eliminate non-comparable results.

4.1.4 Single versus Battery of Tests

In recent years, toxicity testing has been extensively used to determine the effects of toxic chemicals on ecosystems and human health. In order to do this, researchers have conducted various kinds of tests using different species of mammals, invertebrates, reptiles, fishes, plants, bacteria, and both human and animal tissue cultures. Most of these tests are carried out using one or more of the same species; and, as such, they have been referred to also as single species tests.

In order to eliminate these artifacts such as false-positive and false-negatives, a battery of tests should be developed to suit the level of concern of the chemical. This would ensure that the toxicity assessment of a test chemical accurately reflect the degree of concern for the compound.

(a) Acute 96-h Static Bioassay

The acute aquatic toxicity test has been designed to determine the concentration of a test chemical that will produce lethal effects to a group of test organisms during a short-term exposure. The test chemical is added directly into the water column at various concentrations in different test chambers and the concentration at which a 50% mortality is observed for a standard exposure of 96-h is classified as the median lethal concentration (96-h LC_{50}).

There are four methods that are used to expose the test organisms to the test chemical; these include static, recirculation, renewal and flowthrough. Static exposure technique is described below.

Methodology

The test species for this acute 96-h static bioassay is the rainbow trout (<u>Oncorhynchus</u> <u>mykiss</u>); they should be obtained from certified disease-free hatchery stock. Individual fish should weigh between 0.3 and 5 g (refs. 40,41) and the length of the largest fish should not exceed twice the length of the smallest. The test species should not be fed for 12 hours prior to, or during the bioassay.

Especially for static bioassay, fish loading densities in each of the test and control vessels should not exceed 0.5 g/L for the 4-d test period (ref. 40). The minimum number of fish exposed to each treatment and control should be 10, however, this number is dependent upon the volume of each test chamber.

The temperature of the tests is maintained at $15 \pm 1^{o}C$ and lighting condition is similar to that during acclimation; gentle aeration supplied to each test and control chamber during exposure.

Records of alive and dead fish are taken through out the experimental period at the following times: 0h, 0.25h, 0.5h, 1h, 2h, 4h, 24h, 48h, 72h, and 96h, frequency of checks may be increased depending upon response of test species. Finally, the 96-h LC_{50} is then calculated.

Daphnia

<u>Daphnia</u> has been used in toxicity testing for acute lethality of complex effluents, industrial discharges, and newly developed chemicals, such as pesticides and industrial chemicals. Because of the relatively high sensitivity compared to other aquatic species, <u>Daphnia</u> has been used on many occasions as test species for setting water quality criteria (ref. 42,43). <u>Daphnia</u> is used in toxicity tests for industries to screen their discharges and assess the effectiveness of waste treatment facilities (ref. 44).

Methodology

There are basically four different types of studies that are carried out using <u>Daphnia</u>, which include: acute lethality tests (ref. 45), 21- to 28-d subchronic studies (ref. 46), life history studies (ref. 47) and chronic toxicity studies (ref. 48). The acute lethality tests are usually conducted under static conditions while the other types of studies are carried out using a continuous flow system. In some cases, however, static conditions are used but the test solutions are renewed daily or every other day.

The species of Daphnia chosen for the toxicity study is dependent upon location, water quality criteria, and water chemistry. Daphnia pulex is widely distributed covering much of the North American continent, while D. magna has a more limited distribution and tends to be further restricted to hard water habitats. Although D. magna might be preferred because of its size, available toxicity data appear to support that D. pulex is as sensitive as D. magna (ref. 49).

For static test, between 200 to 300 mL of test solutions are used with about 10 animals per beaker. The solution and animals are placed in 400 to 500 mL beakers and exposed from 1 to 2 d depending upon the study requirements. Dynamic or continuous flow systems are used for subchronic, chronic, and life history studies.

Toxicity data is analyzed in many ways, usually for 24-h or 48-h, LC_{50}, values are generally calculated by the moving average-angle method (ref. 50). Calculations using the log-concentration plotted against the percent survival are also applicable. The precision of the tests are based on the relative standard deviation, commonly referred to as percent coefficient of variation (CV), where CV = (Standard deviation x 100)/mean; group observations are compared using students' "t", after testing the data for homogeneity of variance (ref. 51).

The feeding of Daphnia during a toxicity study is variable. For short-term chronic toxicity tests, the animal is usually not fed during the testing period. For subchronic, chronic, and life history studies, however, feeding is important for the animal's survival, especially when dealing with neonates.

Other factors that could have an effect on the study include: test organism's age, acclimation, temperature, pH, dissolved oxygen, light, size of air bubbles, degree of aeration, and osmotic and ionic balance. Details of the variables that could have an effect on toxicity tests using Daphnia can be found in the literature (refs. 45,48,49,51). The information summarized in Table 4.2 is reasonably complete and offers guidance to possible users, however, it may not incorporate all the details that might be required for certain specialized work.

Although Daphnia has been widely used for the purpose of aquatic toxicity testing, it still requires more research in order to clarify uncertainties such as the effects of various foods in the production of the animal and the sensitivity of the offspring to toxicants. There is also an uncertainty regarding temperature-photoperiod interactions because the reproductive cycles are dependent upon photoperiods, and temperature, and therefore they (the parameters) could have an effect on the sensitivity of this species during toxicity tests.

TABLE 4.2 Suggested guidelines for using <u>Daphnia</u> in toxicity testing and evaluation of chemicals.

| | Test Need | | | |
Experimental Design Option	Screening-Pure or Mixed Compounds, Effluents Process Waters, etc.	Hazard Evaluation Pure Compounds	Mixed Compounds	Compliance Needs- Effluents
Species				
Sensitive	⋆	⋆	⋆	⋆a
Indigenous	⋆			⋆a
Most practical	⋆			⋆a
Age or size of organism				
Neonate (24 ± 12h)		⋆	⋆	⋆a
Adult (7 + days)	⋆			⋆a
Test setup				
Static[b]	⋆			⋆a
Static with renewal	⋆			⋆
Continuous flow		⋆	⋆	⋆
Test type				
Acute (adult)				
48-h, 20 to 25°C	⋆	⋆	⋆	⋆
72-h, 15 to 10°C	⋆	⋆	⋆	⋆
96 to 144 h, <15°C				
Chronic				
Six-brood minimum	⋆	⋆a	⋆a	⋆
Lifetime		⋆a	⋆a	
Multigeneration		⋆a	⋆a	
Environment-organism interaction				
Hard water (≥120 ppm)				
D. <u>magna</u>		⋆		⋆
D. <u>pulex</u>	⋆	⋆c	⋆c	⋆
Other species				⋆d
Soft water				
D. <u>pulex</u>	⋆	⋆	⋆	⋆
Other species	⋆			⋆d
Other test conditions				
Light intensity				
≤300 lux (≤28 footcandles)		⋆	⋆	⋆
540 to 1615 lux (50 to 150 footcandles)	⋆			
Photoperiod				
16L:8D; high temperature		⋆	⋆	⋆e
8L:16D; low temperature				⋆e
8 to 16L; room temperature	⋆			
Fluorescent bulb type[f]				
CRI >90		⋆	⋆	⋆a
CRI <90	⋆			⋆a

Continued . . . .

TABLE 4.2 Concluded.

Experimental Design Option	Test Need			
	Screening-Pure or Mixed Compounds, Effluents Process Waters, etc.	Hazard Evaluation		Compliance Needs- Effluents
		Pure Compounds	Mixed Compounds	
Acclimation				
24 to 48 h ($\sim$20°C)	★			★a
Three or more broods		★	★	★a
Food type				
Trout chow plus	★			★
Algae		★	★	

a   This depends on requirements of the regulatory agency.
b   If the simple acute test is satisfactory, there is no need for more expensive tests.
c   Daphnia pulex may be more sensitive than D. magna because of its smaller size.
d   One may need to look at other species if the regulatory agency requires resident species.
e   This depends on the time of year.
f   CRI refers to Colour Rendering Index.

(Source: Reprinted with permission from ref. 49, Copyright (1980), ASTM).

Algal

Toxicity tests with unicellular algae have been widely used for the purpose of screening toxic chemicals, especially herbicides or chemicals that have the potential to deleteriously affect plant life. Although these are classified as short-term test because of the length of the exposure (4 to 5 d), they ideally represent a chronic exposure period for the algae family, because algae growth rates and cellular densities have probably reached its maximum within the test period. Hence, for practical purposes, algal short-term test is based on a life cycle of the test species.

Methodology

The purpose of this test is to obtain information on the toxicity of various chemicals to specific species of algae in vitro. Toxicity responses in algae are usually measured through effects to growth (minor or major) to the death of the cell itself.

The following species are commonly used for algal toxicity tests.

Freshwater green algae   Selenastrum capricornutum Printz
Freshwater blue-green algae Microcystis aeruginosa kutz. enend
                            Elenkin (Anacystis cyanea) Drouet and Daily

Freshwater diatom   _Navicula seminulum_ var. husteditii

Marine green flagellate   _Dunaliella tertiolecta_ Butcher

The methodology used for culturing freshwater and marine algae are detailed in USEPA's Algal, Assay Procedures: Bottle test and USEPA's Marine Algal Assay Procedures: Bottle test (ref. 52). These test organisms vary in response depending upon the nature of toxicant. For example, _Selenastrum capricornutum_ is sensitive and consistent in response to a wide range of nutrients (refs. 53,54), while _Microcystis aeruginosa_ is very sensitive to trace metals (ref. 55), and on the other hand, _Navicula seminulum_ has a nutrient requirement for silicon.

Concentrations of test chemicals are selected to elicit a range of responses; these include no effect, inhibitry, algistatic and algicidal. In some cases, however, it is necessary to initiate a series of pilot experiments in order to find a concentration range that could be used in a definitive study, especially when work is being carried out on chemicals that are relatively new or have no prior toxicity information or assessment data.

The actual algal assay entails the inoculation of the chosen species of algae into various flasks that contain the test chemical at different concentrations. The flasks are then incubated under standard conditions for five days. The biomass of each flask is then determined and comparisons are made with control flasks. Although only a Day 5 biomass measurement is required for statistical generation of the algistatic response, more frequent measurements (daily) would provide a more accurate determination of toxicity responses. For example, the degradation of some chemicals under test could change the chemical from being toxic initially to a non-toxic state or sequesteration by algal exeluates or binding to algal surfaces will allow the resumption of normal algal growth. Measurements of biomass are usually determined either by cell counts or in vivo chlorophyll $\underline{a}$ flouorescence (ref. 52). In some instances, additional information may be obtained through the use of both types of measurements. For example, some toxic chemicals appear to inhibit cellular division but allow growth and chlorophyll $\underline{a}$ production to continue for at least a few days, while other compounds may cause a reduction in chlorophyll $\underline{a}$ but allow continued cellular division (ref. 55).

In certain cases, it might be beneficial to investigate if there is a possible period of recovery following the test exposure period. This activity confirms an algistatic response. Therefore, populations that displayed a decline in biomass or remained basically the same (algistatic) are transferred into fresh media and matched with appropriate number of controls. These flasks are incubated for a period of nine days during which measurements of biomass are taken.

The results of each tests are recorded and expressed as a no observed effect, inhibitory effects, algistatic responses or algicidal effects. The algistatic concentration level indicates that a meaningful toxicity threshold has been established.

In vitro Cytogenetic Assay

In biological systems, the chromosomes are the carriers of the genetic material which, in turn, controls all functions of the individual cells that make up an organism. Thus, a small change in the genetic material could have severe consequences on both the organism and its offspring.

Chromosomal aberration or alteration, due to exposure to a test chemical, appear as visible changes to the chromosome through a microscope. These types of changes include: chromosomal breaks, nondisjunctions, translocation, disagreement, or possible loss or gain of an entire chromosome. Chromosomal alterations result in major heritable diseases, some of which have been related to cancer.

Methodology

Chromosomal damage from exposure to a chemical could be detected using growing mammalian cell cultures. The Chinese hamster ovary (CHO) cell has been used for this chromosomal test because of its easy availability, short-generation time (12 to 14 h) and low chromosomal number (20 to 22). The CHO cells are seeded onto coverslips and placed in petrie dishes. These are then fed minimal essential medium (MEM) supplemented with 15% Foetal Bovine Serum (FBS) and antibiotics. Cultures are then incubated in an environment of carbon dioxide and air (19:1 ratio).

Aqueous test samples are prepared differently from non-aqueous samples; aqueous are diluted directly with MEM while non-aqueous samples are prepared using acetone, hexane, and MEM supplemented with FBS before adding to cell cultures. Treated cells are then arrested at metaphase prepared for cytological investigations, fixed and mounted.

For each dose level, a minimum of 100 well-spread metaphase plates are analyzed. Chromosomal damages are scored and classified according to the methods used by Savage (ref. 56).

The Ames Test

The Salmonella/microsome assay which is also referred to as the Ames Test or the Ames/Salmonella assay has been widely used for the purpose of evaluating chemicals that might have potential adverse effects on humans. The development of this assay was targeted towards identification of chemical carcinogens; however, it is also applicable (probably more directly applicable) to the identification of potential mutagenic agents (ref. 57).

Methodology

Plate assay

The strains used for genetic testing are outlined in Table 4.3. Considerable efforts have been spent over a period of years towards the improvement of sensitivity and reliability of the Salmonella/microsome test. This has resulted in the development of additional strains that are more sensitive to certain mutagens.

Upon receiving a bacterial strain it should be cultured, inoculated and grown-up; it should then be checked for the following:

- histidine requirement
- crystal violet sensitivity;
- the presence of the ampicillin resistant factor, especially for newer strains with R factors;
- the presence of uvrB deletion; and
- the spontaneous reversion rate.

The different strains are prepared and stored for use as specified by Ames et al. (ref. 58).

After the agar plates are prepared, the following are added in order:

- Molten agar at 45°C;
- overnight nutrient broth culture of the bacterial test strain; and
- the sample to be tested.

The plates are then left to harden. Within an hour (the use of S-9 mix is recommended for general mutagenesis screening; details regarding its preparation are outlined in Ames et al. (ref. 58)), the plates are placed in an incubator and left for two days, after which plates are analyzed.

A positive or questionable result should be confirmed by demonstrating a dose-response effect using a narrower range of concentrations. Finally, dose-response curves are developed from the results.

Spot Test

The Ames spot test is also a simple method for testing chemicals for mutagenicity. It is also easily adopted for screening large numbers of chemicals in a short period of time. It does not entail the preparation of various solutions of the test chemicals, instead a small amount can be placed directly in the surface of the agar preparation. The spot test allows for a preliminary indication of the toxicity of the chemical toward the bacterial strain by the size of the zone of inhibition of the background lawn of

TABLE 4.3 Genotype of the TA strains used for mutagen testing.

HISTIDINE MUTATION			ADDITIONAL MUTATIONS			USE
hisG46	hisC3076	hisD3052	LPS	REPAIR	R FACTOR	
TA1535	TA1537**	TA1538	rfa	ΔuvrB		Standard tester strains and R factor strains; recommended for general mutagenesis screening
TA100		TA98	rfa	ΔuvrB	+R	
(TA1975)	(TA1977)	TA1978	rfa		–	Used in combination with the standard tester strains in the repair test***
hisG46	hisC3076	hisD3052				Additional related strains available
TA92		TA2420			+R	
TA1950	TA1952	TA1534		ΔuvrB	–	
TA2410				ΔuvrB	+R	
TA1530	TA1532	TA1964	Agal	ΔuvrB	–	
TA2631		TA2641	Agal	ΔuvrB	+R	
	TA2637		rfa	ΔuvrB	+R	

*   All strains were originally derived from S. typhimurium LT2. Wild-type genes are indicated by a +. The deletion (Δ) through uvrB also includes the nitrate reductase (chl) and biotin (bio) genes. The Δgal strains (and the rfa uvrB strains) have a single deletion through gal chl bio uvrB. The rfa, repair+ strains have a mutation in galE R - pkM101. The standard tester strain TA1536, originally included in the tester set and all other strains containing the histidine mutation hisC207 have been deleted as they are reverted by only very few mutagens and these can be detected well by the other tester strains.

** A new tester strain is under development which will, with its R factor derivative, replace TA1537.

*** The TA1538Δ1978 pair is recommended.

(Source: Reprinted with permission from ref. 58, Copyright (1975), Elsevier Science Publishers, B.V.).

bacterial growth around the spot and an indication whether the previously mentioned S-9 mix is necessary for mutagenicity and in the case of a positive result, which tester strain should be used for the dose-response curve (ref. 58).

The spot is basically a qualitative test, and has definite limitations regarding the assessment of water insoluble chemicals. It is also less sensitive than the previously described plate assay. Positive results regarding mutagenicity when using the spot test should be confirmed by the standard plate test.

Microtox Test

The use of microorganisms for the purpose of evaluating toxicological concerns has been an accepted methodology because of its relative accuracy, speed and ease of conducting the test and low costs. Other biological methods and assays that use target species such as algae, fish, protozoas, insects, etc. (ref. 59), are relatively long (48-h to several months), require extensive planning and preparation, and are expensive.

The rationale for the use of bacteria in toxicity testing is that they:
- Possess the majority of the same biochemical pathway present in higher organisms (ref. 60);
- Exhibit a significant degree of organization in membrane structure (ref. 60);
- Generally, elicit toxic response to many chemicals through mechanisms similar to that of higher organisms (ref. 60);
- Represent the lowest common denominator in the food chains of both marine, and freshwater systems (refs. 61);
- Grow using standard techniques and cost less to maintain; and
- Require small sample volumes, and offer an advantage regarding statistical analysis because of their large numbers when compared to other live biological organisms.

A simple inexpensive rapid bioassay for determining toxicity in aquatic systems was described earlier by Bulech and Associates (ref. 62); it utilizes a luminiscent bacterium (Photobacterium phosphoreum). This test which is designated as Microtox^{TM*}, records changes in luminous activity when the bacterium is exposed to a toxicant. The toxicity at the end of the exposure is measured as the effective concentration of the test sample that causes a 50% reduction in bacterial light production (EC_{50}).

Methodology

Bioassays are performed using the Microtox Model 2055 Toxicity Analyzer System and the analyzers are equipped with a temperature controlled incubator and a reaction chamber both of which are maintained at $15 \pm 0.1^{\circ}C$. Luminous activity is measured and recorded either on a chart recorder or a digital display system.

The luminescent bacterium (Photobacterium phosphoreum) and osmotic adjustment solution are available commercially. The osmotic adjustment solution is specially purified water containing 22% sodium chloride and it is used to osmotically adjust samples to 2% sodium chloride.

The test procedures are similar to those of Bulich et al. (ref. 62), however, detailed procedures are outlined in Operating Manuals. Basically, the procedure entails the following:

- Adjustment of test samples using osmotic adjustment solution;
- Further dilution of test samples using Microtox diluent;
- Calibration and adjustment of treatments and controls to $15 \pm 0.1^{o}C$;
- Preparation of luminescent bacterial reagent;
- Addition of test samples (0.5 mL) and controls to bacteria; and
- Record light measurements at 5, 10, 15, 20, and 30 minutes after addition of toxicants to bacterial systems.

Factors such as sample pH, age of bacterial agent, and the assaying of bioassay mixtures could have significant effects on the final outcome of Microtox results. Alteration of pH for instance, may cause precipitation of certain toxicants creating problems in data interpretation. Similarly, the age of the bacterial reagent after reconstitution may have an effect on the light production by increasing the sensitivity and producing false-positive results (ref. 60).

Battery of Tests

There are large numbers of tests that are available, therefore it is necessary to choose the particular ones that will provide the result that will assist in assessing a specific test chemical. Each test has been developed to elicit information towards a particular end-point such as non-genetic toxicity or mutagenicity, but the relevance of this end-point towards providing data that is required for final assessment is the main concern.

In certain cases, a test might be quite reasonable to carry out, however, its relevance towards the end-point might be questionable. For example, the Salmonella/mammalian microsome test (Ames Test) is relatively quick and inexpensive; it has a reasonable degree of association with carcinogenicity, but it is not definitive in term of extrapolation to man (ref. 63). In other cases, a test could indicate positive or negative results which could be false. Other factors that determine the extent of toxicity testing are chemical structures of the compounds and their relations to other known toxicants, and available chemical and toxicological information. If a test chemical is related structurally to known toxicants, then it is possible that the test chemical could have similar toxic effects and similar pharmaco-kinetic pathway. In order to eliminate biases and misinterpretations a battery of tests using different test substrates designed to provide information on adverse effects that will assist in assessing the test chemical. The design of a battery of test is dependent upon the level of concern for a test chemical. Health and Welfare Canada (ref. 63) suggests three levels of concern, each corresponding to a different battery to suit the level of concern. These batteries indicate the extent of testing deemed sufficient to conclude that if negative, a chemical has no significant mutagenic or toxic potential for each level of concern. Basically, a compound cannot be assigned to the lowest battery until it has been tested and found to be non-mutagenic after an appropriate number of assays.

If a chemical whose molecular structure is not related to known mutagens or carcinogens (structure-activity relationship) and is of low toxicity, then it should require only the least amount of testing. Similarly, if the test chemical is classified at either the intermediate or high level of concern from considerations of its toxicity and exposure potentials, it should be subjected to more rigorous testing than that carried out at the lower level of concern. Usually a battery of four single short-term tests is chosen to screen chemicals which fall either into the intermediate or high level of concern. Fig. 4.8 modified from Health and Welfare Canada illustrates the use of a battery of tests to delineate mutagenic or carcinogenic compounds.

In conclusion, no single test is capable of providing information that would permit the evaluation of a test chemical, i.e., no single test can stand alone. A single test must be used in conjunction with other developed assays in order to accurately evaluate the effects of any test chemical. Such well-developed toxicity testing programs will help to prioritize chemicals through screening for toxic and genotoxic effects. This, in turn, will provide a focus for monitoring programs to assess their exposure potential in the ambient environment.

4.1.5 Boundary of Information

In order to assess the hazards of a chemical, information on its hazards and exposure levels in the environment must be sufficient to develop valid and defensible criteria and standards in order to adequately protect both environmental and human health. Decisions regarding a particular chemical must be based on accurate, up-to-date scientific information. Criteria development and prediction models must be supported by sufficient technical, scientific, and monitoring data.

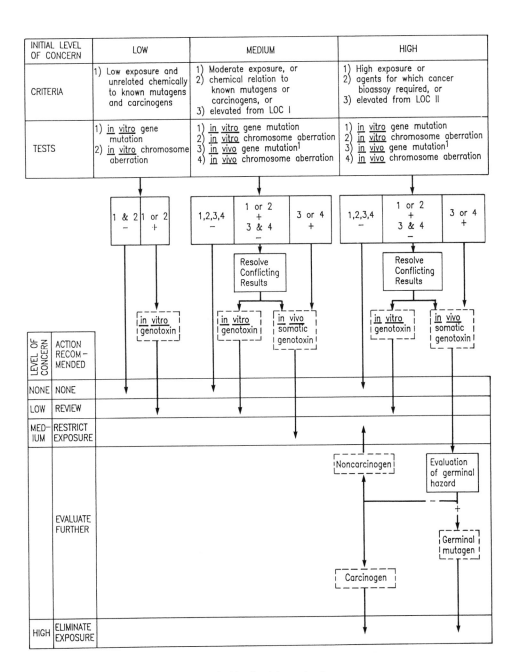

Fig. 4.8. Comprehensive mutagenicity testing strategy.
(Source: Reprinted with permission from ref. 63a, D.S.S. Canada).

1. Mammalian somatic in vivo indicated tests can be substituted until
appropriate in vivo tests for somatic gene mutation are available.

Laboratory Data

Substantial laboratory data are used to assess a test chemical, and in many instances, there are several concerns about the quality of the information. There are many variables that could have an effect on the quality of the data that are generated from toxicity experiments; these include biotic and abiotic factors, influences by other chemical and methodology differences. The determinants of analytical quality of data have been described in detail in Chapter 3.

The choice of species used in any bioassay (both short term and long term) is critical in the applicability of the results to the natural environment. The species should be representative of the particular environment where the chemical is to be used. The choices of tests used for the assessment must provide information that is relevant to all sections of the exposed population. For example, if sensitive life stages of a population might be exposed, then embryo-larval and egg-fry studies (or gene mutation analysis for mutagens) should be incorporated. These tests are less expensive than full chronic studies and they also can be performed rapidly providing reasonably reliable data.

Although field data on various terrestrial and aquatic organisms can be valuable, it is difficult to control all the variables that operate in the natural environment; therefore, in many instances, laboratory studies in controlled environment might produce more consistent results and their relevance to natural environment depends on how many of the critical variables have been taken into account in the studies. Epidemiological studies might result in interesting information also, but like field research these are very specific, difficult delineate cause and effect relationship, and expensive. In every case, however, it is necessary to ensure that the information obtained is sufficient, applicable and capable of assisting in proper assessment.

Data on Chemical

It is necesary to ensure that sufficient information on the chemical has been collected in order to carry out a proper assessment. This includes data on the volume, use pattern of the chemical, and its physical properties for assessing its behaviour in the environment and its possible effects on biological systems.

Table 4.4 outlines some of the basic data requirements that are necessary for the evaluation of a test chemical. More detailed information on the data requirements outlined in this table can be obtained in other chapters of this book.

The assessment of a chemical requires an evaluation of its fate after it enters the environment. It should include the resident compartment of environment, and biological systems that would be exposed. The possible

TABLE 4.4 Basic data requirement for the evaluation of chemicals to ensure
necessary boundary of information for toxicological assessment.

DATA REQUIREMENTS	DETAILS
Usage/Release Human exposure	Quantities Location How used Method of transportation
Physico-chemical factors	Structure Melting point Boiling point Density Viscosity Solubility Vapour Pressure Adsorption Dissociation Surface Tension Spectra Octanol/Water Partition Coefficient Purity

Bioaccumulation Potential	Persistence
	Tests Results
	1/2 Life - Water
	         - Soil
	         - Air
	Bioavailability
	Adsorption
	Octanol/Water Partition Coefficient
	Bioconcentration Factor
	Model Prediction

Degradation/Potential	Stability Thermal Stability Biotic/Abiotic Factors
Transformation Potential	Hydrolysis Reduction Oxydation Conjugation Seasonal Effects Temperature Photoperiod
Disposal	Disposal Techniques
Testing	Mutagenic Potential Toxicity Potential Media Use

degradation, transformation and bioaccumulation potential of the chemical should also be evaluated. The above information, together with the results obtained from a well developed battery of tests will assist in setting the necessary boundary of information.

REFERENCES

1 S.A. Levin and K.D. Kimball. Environmental Management 8 (1984) 375-442.
2 J.W. Gillett, J. Hill, A.W. Jarviner, and W.D. Schnoor, A Conceptual Model for the Movement of Pesticides through the Environment, U.S. Environmental Protection Agency, Corvallis, Oregon, EPA 660/3-74-024, 1974.
3 T.C. Hutchinson, The Occurrence of Pb, Cd, Ni, V, and Cl in Soils and Vegetation of Toronto in Relation to Traffic Density IES University of Toronto Publication EH-2, 1972, 27 p.
4 A.C. Page and T.J. Gange, Environ. Sci. Technol., 4 (1970) 140-142.
5 Y. Hirano and C.C. Patterson. Science 184 (1974) 989-992.
6 H. Ashmead, J. Appl. Nutr., 24 (1972) 8-17.
7 W.B. Neely, in K.L. Dickson, A.W. Maki, and J. Cairns, Jr. (Editors), Analyzing the Hazard Evaluation Process, Proceedings of a Workshop, Waterville Valley, New Hampshire, American Fisheries Society, Washington, D.C., U.S.A., 1979, pp. 74-82.
8 A.G. Davis, Radioactive Contamination of the Marine Environment, Vienna International Atomic Energy Agency, 1973, pp. 403-420.
9 E.E. Kenaga and C.A.I. Goring, in J.G. Eaton, P.R. Parrish, and A.C. Hendricks (Editors), Proceedings of the 3rd Symposium on Aquatic Toxicology, American Society of Testing and Materials, Philadelphia, U.S.A., 1980, pp. 78-115.
10 J.W. Moore and S. Ramamoorthy, Organic Chemicals in Natural Waters, Springer-Verlag, New York, U.S.A., 1984, 289 p.
11 L.W. Harding, Jr. and J.H. Phillips, Jr., Mar. Biol., 49 (1978) 103-111.
12 P.S. Liss and P.G. Slater, Nature 247 (1974) 181-184.
13 D. Mackay and P.J. Leinonen, Environ. Sci. Technol., 9 (1975) 1178-1180.
14 D. Mackay, W.Y. Shiu, and R.J. Sutherland, in R. Haque (Editor), Exposure, and Hazard Assessment of Toxic Chemicals, ACS Symposium, Ann Arbor Science, Ann Arbor, Michigan, U.S.A., 1980.
15 W.B. Neely, D.R. Branson, and G.E. Blau, Environ. Sci. Technol., 8 (1974) 1113-1115.
16 J.J. Lech and M.J. Vodicnik, in G.M. Rand and S.R. Petrocelli (Editors), Fundamentals of Aquatic Toxicology, Hemisphere Publishing Company, Washington, D.C., U.S.A., 1985, pp. 526-667.
17 W.B. Jakoby (Editor), Enzymatic Basis for Detoxification, Vols. 1 & 2, New York, Academic, 1980.
18 J. Thibodeaux, Chemodynamics, John Wiley & Sons, New York, U.S.A., 1979.
19 National Research Council, Principles of Evaluating Chemicals in the Environment, National Academy of Sciences, Washington, D.C., U.S.A., 1975, 453 p.
20 F. Acree Jr., M. Beroza, and M. Bowman, J. Agric. Food. Chem., 11 (1963) 278-280.
21 USEPA, Short-term Tests for Carcinogens, Mutagens, and Other Genotoxic Agents, United States Environmental Protection Agency, Health Effects Research Laboratory, Research Triangle Park, 1979, pp. 1-29.
22 B.A. Bridges, Mutation Res., 26 (1974) 335-340.
23 B.A. Bridges, Env. Health Persp., 6 (1974) 221-227.
24 M.S. Legator, The Inadequacies of Sub-mammalian Tests for Mutagenicity, in Molecular Aspects of Mutagenesis, Thomas, Springfield, 1974.
25 J.G. Pearson and J.P. Glennon, in K.L. Dickson, A.W. Maki, and J. Cairns, Jr. (Editors), Analyzing the Hazard Evaluation Process, American Fisheries Society, Washington, D.C., U.S.A., 1977, pp. 30-49.

26 J.A. Pearson, J.P. Glennon, J.J. Barkley, J.W. Highhill, in L.L. Markin and R.A. Kimerle (Editors), Aquatic Toxicology, ASTM STP 667, American Society for Testing and Materials, 1977, pp. 284-301.

27 J.R. Duthie, F.L. Mayer and J.L. Hamelink (Editors), Aquatic Toxicology and Hazard Evaluation, American Society of Testing Material, ASTM STP 634, 1977, pp. 17-35.

28 American Society of Testing and Materials, Standard Practice for Conducting Toxicity Tests with Fish, Macroinvertebrates, and Amphibians, ASTM, Philadelphia, U.S.A., ASTM E 729-80, 1980.

29 American Society for Testing and Materials, Proposed Standard Practice for Conducting Toxicity Tests with Freshwater and Saltwater Algae, ASTM, Philadelphia, U.S.A., ASTM E 47.01, 1981.

30 K.E. Biesinger, Tentative Procedure for Daphnia magna Chronic Tests in a Flowing System, Fed. Reg. 40 (1975) 26902-26903.

31 K.J. Macek and B.H. Sleight III, in F.L. Mayer and J.L. Hamelink (Editors), Aquatic Toxicity and Hazard Evaluation, American Society of Testing and Materials, Philadelphia, ASTM STP 634, 1977, pp. 137-146.

32 T.A. Loomis, Essentials of Toxicology, Lea and Feliger, Philadelphia, U.S.A., 3rd Edition, 1978, 245 p.

33 V.M. Brown, Water. Res., 2 (1968) 723-733.

34 EIFAC (European Inland Fisheries Advisory Commission), Water Res., 7 (1973) 929-941.

35 R. Marchetti, Critical Review of the Effects of Synthetic Detergents on Aquatic Life, Stud. Rev. FAO Gen. Fish. Counc. Mediterranean No. 26, 1965.

36 M. Lipschuetz and A.L. Cooper, Toxicity of 2-secondary-butyl-4,6-dinitrophenol to Blacknose Dase and Rainbow Trout, New York Fish Game J., 8 (1961) 110-121.

37 G.W. Holcombe, J.T. Fiandt, and G.L. Phipps, Water. Res., 14 (1980) 1073-1077.

38 G.K. Pagenkopf, R.C. Russo, and R.V. Thurston, J. Fish. Res. Bd. Can., 31 (1974) 461-465.

39 R.W. Andrew, K.E. Biesinger, and G.E. Glass, Water Res., 11 (1977) 309-315.

40 J.B. Sprague, The abc's of Pollutant Bioassay using Fish, in Biological Methods for the Assessment of Water Quality, ASTM STP 528, American Society for Testing and Materials, 1973, pp. 6-30.

41 American Public Health Association, Standard Methods for the Examination of Water and Wastewater, 16th Edition, American Public Health Association, Washington, D.C., U.S.A., 1985, 1268 p.

42 APHA, Standard Methods for the Examination of Water and Wastewater. 14th Edition, American Public Health Association, Washington, D.C., U.S.A., 1976.

43 National Academy of Sciences, Water Quality Criteria, USEPA Research Series, U.S. Environmental Protection Agency, Washington, D.C., U.S.A., 1973.

44 A.L. Buikema Jr., D.R. Lee, and J. Cairns Jr., Journal of Testing and Evaluation, 4 (1976) 119-125.

45 W.J. Adams and B.B. Heidolph, R.D. Cardwell, R. Purdy, R.C. Bahmer (Editors), Aquatic Toxicology and Hazard Assessment: Seventh Symposium, ASTM STP 854, American Society for Testing and Materials, Philadelphia, U.S.A., 1985, pp. 87-103.

46 K.E. Biesinger and G.M. Christensen, Journal of the Fisheries Research Board of Canada, 29(12) (1972) 1691-1700.

47 R.W. Winner and M.P. Farrell, Journal of the Fisheries Research Board of Canada, 33(8) (1976) 1685-1691.

48 K.J. Macek, K.S. Burton, S.K. Derr, J.W. Dean, and S. Sauter, Ecological Research Series, EPA-600/3-76-046, U.S. Environmental Protection Agency, Duluth, Minnesota, U.S.A., 1976.

49 A.L. Buikema Jr., J.G. Geiger, and D.R. Lee, in A.L. Buikema Jr. and J. Cairns (Editors), Aquatic Invertebrates Bioassays, ASTM STP 715, American Society for Testing and Materials, 1980, pp. 48-69.

50 E.K. Harris, Biometrics, 15 (1959) 424-432.

51 P.A. Lewis and C.I. Weber, in R.D. Cardwell, R. Purdy, and R.C. Bahner (Editors), Aautic Toxicology and Hazard Assessment: Seventh Symposium, ASTM STP 854, American Society for Testing and Materials, Philadelphia, U.S.A, 1975, pp. 73-86.

52 U.S. EPA, Algal Assay procedure: Bottle Test; Marine Algal Assay Procedure: Bottle Test, U.S. Environmental Protection Agency, National Environmental Research Centre, Corvallis, Oregon, U.S.A., 1971; 1974.

53 A.G. Payne, Water Research, 9(4) (1975) 437-445.

54 J.C. Green, W.E. Millar, T. Shiroyama, and T.E. Maloney, Water, Air and Soil Protection, 4 (1975) 415-434.

55 A.G. Payne and R.H. Hall, in L.L. Marking and R.A. Kimerle (Editors), Aquatic Toxicology, American Society of Testing and Materials, ASTM STP 667, 1979, pp. 171-180.

56 J.R.K. Savage, J. Med. Genet., 12 (1975) 103-122.

57 L.D. Kier, Reg. Toxicol. and Pharmacol., 5 (1985) 59-64.

58 B.N. Ames, V. McCann, and E. Yamasaki, Mutation Research, 31 (1975) 347-364.

59 G. Bringmann and R. Kuhn, Water Res., 14 (1980) 231-241.

60 A.A. Qureshi, R.N. Coleman, and J.H. Paran, in D. Liu and B.J. Butka (Editors), Toxicity Screening Procedures using Bacterial Systems, Marcel Dekker Inc., New York and Basel, 1984, pp. 1-22.

61 E.A. Laws, Food Chain Theory, In Aquat. Pollution, John Wiley & Sons, New York, U.S.A., 1981, pp. 1-12.

62 A.A. Bulich, Use of Luminiscent Bacteria for the Rapid Detection of Toxic Substances in Water, Abstracts of the Annual Meeting, American Society of Microbiology, 1979, p. 225.

63a Health and Welfare Canada, Guidelines on the Use of Mutagenicity Tests in the Toxicological Evaluation of Chemicals, DNH & W/DOE Environmental Contaminants Advisory Committee on Mutagenesis, Ottawa, Canada, 1986, 84 p.

63b R.H. Haynes et. al. Environ. Molecular Mut., 11 (1988) 261-304.

64 D.I. Mount, in K.L. Dickson, A.W. Maki, J. Cairns (Editors), Adequacy of Laboratory Data for Protecting Aquatic Communities, Analyzing the Hazard Evaluation Process, Water Quality Section, American Fishereis Society, Washington, D.C., U.S.A., 1979, pp. 112-118.

Chapter 5

SCREENING OF TOXIC CHEMICALS

5.1 ENVIRONMENTAL DISTRIBUTION

The total number of existing chemicals is enormous and the global use of synthetic organic chemicals is increasing annually in number and diversity. Among the five million entities listed by the Chemical Abstracts Service Registry, more than 80,000 chemicals are produced commercially (ref. 1). This creates a need to assess the potential environmental exposure of these chemicals, including those which have not been tested adequately. The basic component in any chemical hazard evaluation is the assessment of its total environmental exposure levels. The environmental exposure level is determined by the physico-chemical properties of the chemical, volume used, and its use pattern.

The environmental persistence and fate of a large number of chemicals cannot possibly be assessed by actual monitoring of all environmental compartments and conducting all conceivable tests because of the prohibitive cost. Hence, screening protocols have been evolving in the last 15 y to accurately estimate the extent of dispersion of a chemical among the different environmental media, such as air, water, soil, and biota. This process helps to distinguish between single-medium-, and multi-media contaminants, which in turn, identifies the medium (or media) of concern in environmental monitoring of a given chemical. It is essential to decide how closely models or protocols should simulate the natural environment. Too many descriptive details can hinder their use in identifying a pollutant's fate pathways (ref. 2). Mathematical models can potentially be used to predict the fate of a chemical if the environmental situation is well characterized. Screening models are limited by an optimum point beyond which any increase in the complexity of the model does not increase the usefulness of its predictions as basic indicators of environmental fate patterns (ref. 3). Complex models can sometime mask some very basic problems inherent in the data base. The fundamental danger in this situation is that we may create complex table of numbers without the accompanying confidence levels (ref. 3). Hence, in many cases, a less-detailed but more practical model is preferable so that the user can identify easily the limitations and make scientific adjustments accordingly. Some typical examples of protocols and models used in screening chemicals for their environmental distribution are discussed below.

5.1.1 WMS-Scoring System

This system developed by the Directorate General for Environmental Protection, The Netherlands, (ref. 4) is intended for use in the preparation of a policy on existing chemicals to be implemented within the framework of The Netherlands's Chemical Substances Act (in Dutch: Wet Milieugevsarlijke Stoffen, WMS). This system recommends systematic approaches for selecting a manageable number of chemicals from a large number, using readily available data sources and expert judgement. The WMS scoring system incorporates the salient points of other systems including those developed for the U.S. Environmental Protection Agency and follows the guidelines set by the OECD system.

The system considers the steady-state distribution conditions for evaluating the exposure levels and four scenarios are taken into account, relating releases of chemicals to their production and use:

1. contamination of air;
2. contamination of soil/water;
3. contamination of aquatic biota;
4. in products.

The scoring system does not include occupational environment nor the point source exposures.

The following parameters are chosen to assess (1) the environmental exposure and (2) product exposure to chemicals:

1. Environmental exposure
1a - Use volume
1b - percentage release to the environment
1c1 - degradation in air
1c2 - degradation in soil/water
1d1 - relative occurrence in air
1d2 - relative occurrence in soil/water
1e - bioconcentration
2   - exposure via products
2a - use pattern
2b - exposure frequency
2c - intensity of exposure

EXPOSURE

Since reliable data on the magnitude of exposure are not frequently available, it seems possible to identify a set of variables for which the product is proportional to the actual exposure. For example, the actual concentration of a chemical in surface water will depend on the variables

A_1-A_n such as use volume, fraction released and degradation rate. This is expressed mathematically as follows:

$$E_x = K_{ex} A_1 . A_2 ..... A_n \qquad (5.1)$$

where k_{ex} = system parameter with appropriate dimensions reflecting the receiving environment; and
$A_1 . . . . A_n$ = variables which influence the level of exposure

On substituting A_n by 10^{An}, the equation 5.1 becomes:

$$E_x = K_{ex} 10^{a_1} . 10^{a_2} ..... 10^{a_n} \qquad (5.2)$$

in which $a_1 . . . a_n$, express the magnitude of the exposure variables

The nature and size of the receiving ambient environment and the magnitude of the parameter K_{ex} will depend on the particular mode and site of chemical production, its use and properties. For this exercise, K_{ex} is assumed to be consistent for a given target system. For scoring purposes, the combination of parameters a_1 - a_n is chosen in such a way they represent the major elements which determine parameters such as volume, release, distribution, and degradation.

Scoring

Fundamental prerequisite in a scoring system is reducing the available information to numbers and scores. For each parameter, criteria are given for scoring (ref. 4). The absence of information which is common for many chemicals leads to estimating the score instead of assigning actual numbers and also makes the scoring criteria slightly flexible. Scientific expert judgement is required to assign appropriate scores.

"To assure the quality of the scoring, at least two independent scores are made by different experts in nine different fields of expertise. In case of significant differences between both scores (two or more points, see scoring scales below), the final score is determined in a discussion between the experts. Minor (1 point) differences are solved by taking the average of both estimates.

Experts are provided with readily available information on the criteria to be scored and some general physical chemical information which is useful for scoring. This information is collected from computerized databanks, handbooks, etc. They are not expected to perform additional data collection. Of course, they are allowed to include other information available to them (e.g., own unpublished experimental results). With this information, the experts should be able to score one parameter for one chemical within 5 minutes. Moreover, they can add to the attributed scores remarks adding additional considerations or explaining a deviation from the criteria scales." (Reprinted from ref. 4 with permission from Pergamon Press Plc.).

Processing Scoring Results

I. Integration of Exposure Parameters

The following combinations of exposure parameters are considered to be useful. The maximum values of the scores are also given (for production volume one extra point can be added to the maximum score at the discretion of the scorer).

1. Exposure via air

When exposure via air occurs, the following scores can be integrated:
- production volume (1a, maximum 6)
- percentage release (1b, maximum 3)
- degradation in air (1c1, maximum 3)
- relative occurrence in air (1d1, maximum 3)

The integration can be described as:

A = 1a - 1b - 1c1 - 1d1 (maximum 6)

2. Exposure via soil/water

When exposure via soil/water occurs, the following scores can be integrated:
- production volume (1a, maximum 6)
- percentage release (1b, maximum 3)
- degradation in soil/water (1c2, maximum 3)
- relative occurrence in soil/water (1d2, maximum 3)

The integration can be described as:

B = 1a - 1b - 1c2 - 1d2 (maximum 6)

3. Indirect exposure of terrestrial organisms via water

For the exposure of terrestrial organisms (including man) indirectly via water (with predation), the following scores can be integrated:
- production volume (1a, maximum 6)
- percentage release (1b, maximum 3)
- degradation in soil/water (1c2, maximum 3)
- relative occurrence in soil/water (1d2, maximum 3)
- bioconcentration (1e, maximum 2)

The integration can be described as:

C = 1a - 1b - 1c2 - 1d2 + 1e (maximum 8)

4. Exposure via products

When exposure via products occurs, the following scores can be integrated:

- use pattern (2a, maximum 3)
- exposure frequency (2b, maximum 3)
- intensity of exposure (2c, maximum 2)

The integration can be described as:

D = 2a + 2b + 2c (maximum 8)

In combining the exposure parameters, the principle used was that the scores of factors which diminish the exposure originating from the use volume, are subtracted (% release, biodegradation, distribution among compartments of the environment) and that scores of factors which increase the exposure or effect, are added (e.g., bioconcentration). This means that negative total exposure scores can be obtained, but this is no problem in further processing of the scores.

II. Combination of Exposure and Effects

For all chemicals, the effect score is combined with the relevant exposure score. In that way, 10 different combinations were considered useful:

Exposure via air (A)	and	- general toxicity for mammals (3)
		- mutagenicity (4a)
		- carcinogenicity (4b)
Exposure via soil/water (B)	and	- toxicity for aquatic organisms (5)
Indirect exposure via water (C)	and	- general toxicity for mammals (3)
		- mutagenicity (4a)
		- carcinogenicity (4b)
Exposure via products (D)	and	- general toxicity for mammals (3)
		- mutagenicity (4a)
		- carcinogenicity (4b)

For each given combination, the scores are added. The 10 resulting combinations can have differing maximum combined effect-exposure scores. The maxima are:

Combination	Maximum
A-3	6 + 3 = 9
A-4a	6 + 3 = 9
A-4b	6 + 3 = 9
B-5	6 + 3 = 9

C-3	8 + 3 = 11
C-4a	8 + 3 = 11
C-4b	8 + 3 = 11
D-3	8 + 3 = 11
D-4a	8 + 3 = 11
D-4b	8 + 3 = 11

III. Scoring Profile

"The scoring profiles will be the principal tool for the priority setting. But in addition to this, still three other items will be used as check up.

1. All chemicals with a score of 3 for one of the effects or for biodegradation will be checked separately, even when the safety margin is large, to see if they can be hazardous in special circumstances.
2. Chemicals with low endscores, but for which the effect scores are 0, will be checked separately to see if there are any special considerations with respect to exposure which could not be expressed in the scores.
3. The remarks made by the scorers in addition to the scores will be taken into account.

These check up points are introduced to make sure that aspects which may not be covered adequately in the scoring, are not simply neglected. When a chemical is given high priority based on one or more of these check up points, however, a good justification is needed." (taken from ref. 4 with permission from Pergamon Press, Plc.)

Final Selection

1. Environmental Exposure

1a. Use Volume

Score	Criteria	
5	Use volume	$>10^4$ ton/year
4	Use volume	10^3-10^4 ton/year
3	Use volume	10^2-10^3 ton/year
2	Use volume	10-10^2 ton/year
1	Use volume	1-10 ton/year
0	Use volume	<1 ton/year

Note: When it is known or estimated that more than 30% of the production or processing of the total amount of the compound takes place at one location, one extra point has to be added to the score by the scorer.

1b. Percentage release to the environment

Score	Criteria	Indication
3	Use in chemical industry in closed systems	< 0.3%
2	Use in chemical industry in open system; use in general industry	0.3-3%
1	Some disperse use, by a number of specific consumer categories	3-30%
0	Largely disperse use; widely spread use by consumers	> 30%

1c. Degradation in air

Score	Criteria
3	halflife < 1 week
1	halflife 1 week - 1 year
0	halflife > 1 year

Note: Information on (bio)degradation in soil/water is often only semi-quantitative in nature. Frequently occurring classifications are "readily biodegradable" and "inherently biodegradable". The first class is assumed to have half-lives of less than 1 week, the second one between 1 week and 1 year. Due to the greater uncertainty in the latter class, there is a difference of 2.

1d. Distribution in air (d1) and soil/water (d2)

Score	Criteria	
3	In compartment considered	<0.3% of the total quantity of the compound
2	In compartment considered	0.3-3% of the total quantity of the compound
1	In compartment considered	3-30% of the total quantity of the compound
0	In compartment considered	> 30% of the total quantity of the compound

Two scores are given: d1 - score for compartment air
d2 - score for compartment soil/water

Note: The distribution is calculated according to ref. 5.

1e. Bioconcentration

Score	Criteria	
	Organic compounds	Inorganic compounds and organometals
2	log P > 4	log BCF > 3
1	2 < log P < 4	1.5 < log BCF < 3
0	log P < 2	log BCF < 1.5

Note: If significant dissociation occurs (pK < 7 for acids or > 7 for bases) lower scores can be assigned to take into account the diminishing influence of dissociation on bioconcentration.

2. Exposure via Products

2a. Use pattern

Score	Criteria	Examples
3	Compounds in products generally used in household, buildings, vehicles, etc.	Clothes, furniture, upholstering, detergents, cleaning agents, frequently used types of dyes, disinfectants, plasticizers, synthetic materials, motor fuels, packing material, etc.
2	Compounds in products less generally used	Hobby and do-it-yourself materials, special types of dyes, glues, inks, tools, etc.
1	Compounds in products not frequently used	Photographic material, maintenance material for pieces of apparatus, etc.
0	Compounds in products which are rarely used but not occupationally	Industrial raw materials, solvents, additives, etc.

2b. Exposure frequency

Score	Criteria	Examples
3	Exposure frequency > once per week	Clothes, furniture, upholstering, household products like detergents and cleaning agents, printing ink, paints, pigments, etc.
2	Exposure frequency: once per week - once per month	Hobby materials, household products like shoe polish, polishing agents, motorfuel, etc.

| 1 | Exposure frequency: once per month - once per year | Solvents, maintenance materials for furniture and cars, specific cleaning agents, gardening chemicals, etc. |
| 0 | Exposure frequency < once per year | Solvents in paints, maintenance materials for house or floor-covering, etc. |

2c. Intensity of exposure

Score	Criteria	Examples
2	High	Solvents used indoors, sprays, fluids, which are frequently used and come in contact with the skin, dusts, etc.
1	Moderate	Solvents used outdoors, textile additives, compounds in solutions in low concentrations, not volatile fluids, etc.
0	Low	Polymers, including the monomers and plasticizers contained, metal products, etc.

Note to 2a, b, c: parameter 2a is reflecting the number of people potentially exposed, 2b indicates the frequency of exposure and parameters 2c the degree of exposure to a chemical. These three parameters are considered to be independent variables indicating the total exposure of man to consumer products (Reprinted from ref. 4 with permission from Pergamon Press Plc.).

This first step in WMS-Scoring System produced a prioritized list of 378 chemicals from a list of approximately 80,000 existing chemicals (ref. 6).

5.1.2 Vector Scoring System

The Vector Scoring System for the prioritization of environmental contaminants was developed for the Ontario Ministry of Environment, Ontario, Canada, in 1988 (ref. 7).

In this system, chemicals are given numerical scores for several parameters (called vector elements) which describe their environmental behaviour, exposure potential, and adverse effects on biota in the environment, including humans. If no information is available on a chemical, an asterisk is substituted for the score for that vector element. In addition, various element score modifiers can be applied under specific circumstances. For example, a question mark placed on element score indicates questionable data; an exclamation mark denotes worst-case scenario value. Individual elements scores can be combined in specific ways to give a priority ranking for groups of chemicals. The methods of combining element scores can be adjusted to meet the needs of specific users of the scoring system (ref. 8).

The scoring system consists of three phases. Each phase requires more specific information about a chemical than the previous phase. Chemicals are ranked in each phase and passed into the next phase according to their priority ranking. Phase 1 of the Vector Scoring System simply determines which chemicals that may be present in a given environment, are actually considered in the scoring system.

Phase 2 of the Vector Scoring System contains the following nine elements, divided into three broad groupings:

1. Elements describing exposure ("E" elements):

   P2E1   - Sources
   P2E2   - Releases
   P2E3   - Environmental Distribution
   P2E4   - Environmental Transport
   P2E5   - Environmental Persistence
   P2E6   - Bioaccumulation

2. Elements describing adverse effects ("T" elements):

   P2E7   - Acute Lethality
   P2E8   - Other Toxicity

3. Element describing aesthetic properties:

   P2E9   - Undesirable Aesthetic Properties

"Scores from zero to three are assigned for each element based on increasing severity of specific criteria. The criteria for Phase 2 elements rely heavily on chemical/physical properties and adverse effect indicators of chemicals that are readily available from summary-type data sources such as books and review articles (Table 5.1).

Once scores are generated for each element based on available information, the chemical is placed into a high, medium, or low priority list, or lists indicating a lack of information or chemicals with undesirable aesthetic properties. Those chemicals on the high priority list enter Phase 3 of the scoring system first, followed by those on the medium priority list. Those on the undesirable aesthetic properties list are automatic candidates for regulatory assessment in Phase 3.

Phase 3 of the scoring system is made up of the following 15 elements in 3 broad categories:

1. Elements describing exposure parameters ("E" elements):

   P3E1 - Environmental Concentrations - Air

   P3E2 - Environmental Concentrations - Water

   P3E3 - Environmental Concentrations - Soil

   P3E4 - Environmental Concentrations - Sediment

   P3E5 - Environmental Concentrations - Animals

   P3E6 - Environmental Concentrations - Plants

   P3E7 - Frequency of Dispersion

2. Elements describing adverse effects ("T" elements):

   P3E8 - Acute Lethality

   P3E9 - Sub-lethal Effects on Non-mammalian Animals

   P3E10 - Sub-lethal Effects on Plants

   P3E11 - Sub-lethal Effects on Mammals

   P3E12 - Teratogenicity

   P3E13 - Genotoxicity/Mutagenicity

   P3E14 - Carcinogenicity

3. Element describing undesirable properties

   P3E15 - Undesirable Aesthetic Properties

More effort and resources are needed to acquire information for this phase than for Phase 2 (i.e., primary reference sources from a variety of databases provide the main information sources). Phase 3 element scores range from 0 to 10 (Table 5.2). Once scores are generated, the chemical is placed on one of five lists: high, medium or low priority, inadequate information or undesirable aesthetic properties. Chemicals placed on the high priority list receive first assessment for regulatory consideration by the Ministry of Environment". (taken from ref. 7). A simplified version of the Vector Scoring System (ref. 8) is currently used for screening and categorizing environmental contaminants for several programs due to the limited database available for most contaminants. This makes it difficult to adequately evaluate some parameters included in the Vector Scoring System.

5.2 PREDICTIVE CAPABILITIES OF FATE PROCESSES

5.2.1 Volatilization

Volatilizational loss of chemicals from water to air is an important fate process for chemicals with low aqueous solubility and low polarity. Many chemicals, despite their low vapour pressure, can volatilize rapidly owing to their high activity coefficients in solution. Volatilizational loss from surfaces is a significant transport process. Volatilization of organic chemicals from the soil surface is complicated by other variables. There is no

TABLE 5.1 Scoring Criteria for Phase 2 Vector Elements (taken from ref. 7).

ELEMENT NUMBER	UNITS	SCORING CRITERIA 0	1	2	3
P2E1	kg/yr	<5	5 to 300	300 to 10,000	>10,000
P2E2	% release narrative	0 not used or imported in Ontario	0 to 3 used in closed systems with no routine releases	3 to 30 Most converted to another product, OR largely restricted to industrial uses, OR very slowly released, OR shipped in large batches	>30 Most released directly into the environment, or used in an open, dispersive manner
P2E3	Measurement basis Release basis	Not yet detected in Ontario No known release sites in Ontario	Infrequently detected at specific locations Few release sites concentrated in a few locations	Frequently detected but only at specific sites Relatively few release sites, but not concentrated in a few locations	Frequently detected over much of Ontario Many release sites throughout Ontario
P2E4	Narrative	<5% of releases partitions into other media, OR vapour pressure ≤1 kPa, solubility ≤100 g/m³	≥ one media other than receiving medium containing 5-10% of the amount released, OR vapour pressure ≤1 kPa solubility ≤100 g/m³	≥ one medium other than receiving medium containing 10-20% of the amount released, OR vapour pressure >1 kPa solubility >100 g/m³	>two media other than receiving medium containing more than 20% of the amount released OR vapour pressure >1 kPa, OR solubility >100g/m³, most is associated with fine particles when released into the environment
P2E5	$t_{1/2}$ (day) narrative	<10 designated not persistent	10 to <50 slightly persistent	50 to <100 moderately persistent	>100 very persistent
P2E6	BCF Log K_{ow}	≤20 ≤2.0	20 to 500 2.0 to 4.0	500 to 15,000 4.0 to 6.0	>15,000 >6.00

TABLE 5.2 Scoring Criteria for Phase 3 Vector Elements.

ELEMENT NUMBER*	UNITS	0	2	4	6	8	10
P3E1	μg/m3	<0.03	0.03-0.3	0.3-3	3-30	30-300	300
P3E2	μg/L	<0.3	0.3-3	3-30	30-300	300-3000	300
P3E3	μg/kg with						
	K_{ow} <1	<0.6	0.6-6	6-60	60-600	600-6000	>6000
	K_{ow} 1-3	<6	6-60	60-600	600-6000	6000-60000	>60000
	K_{ow} 3-5	<60	60-600	600-6000	6000-60000	60000-600000	>600000
	K_{ow} >5	<600	600-6000	6000-60000	60000-600000	600000-6000000	>6000000
P3E4	μg/kg	<5	5-50	50-500	500-5000	5000-50000	>50000
P3E5	μg/kg	<0.6	0.6-6	6-60	60-600	600-6000	>6000
P3E6	μg/kg	<0.6	0.6-6	6-60	60-600	600-6000	>6000
P3E7	release	<1	1-10	10-50	50-150	150-300	>300

* P3E1   Concentrations in air
   P3E2   Concentrations in water
   P3E3   Concentrations in soils
   P3E4   Concentrations in sediments
   P3E5   Concentrations in plants
   P3E6   Concentrations in animals
   P3E7   Frequency of dispersion

186

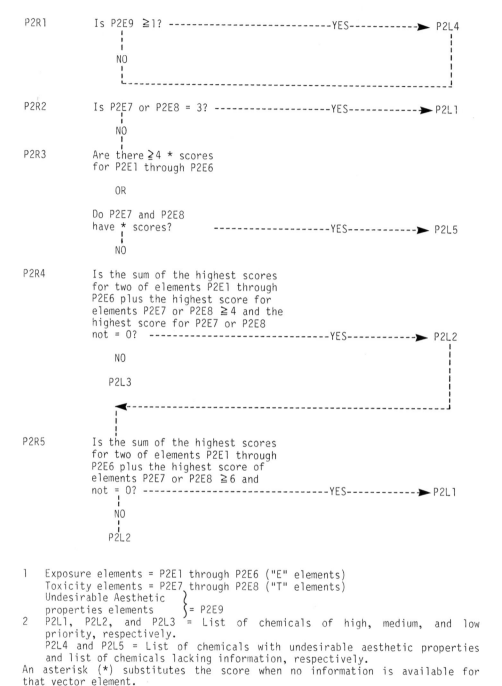

P2R1   Is P2E9 ≥1? ----------------------------------YES----------▶ P2L4

        NO

P2R2   Is P2E7 or P2E8 = 3? --------------------YES-----------▶ P2L1

        NO

P2R3   Are there ≥4 * scores
        for P2E1 through P2E6

           OR

        Do P2E7 and P2E8
        have * scores?   --------------------YES-----------▶ P2L5

        NO

P2R4   Is the sum of the highest scores
        for two of elements P2E1 through
        P2E6 plus the highest score for
        elements P2E7 or P2E8 ≥4 and the
        highest score for P2E7 or P2E8
        not = 0? ----------------------------YES-----------▶ P2L2

           NO

           P2L3

P2R5   Is the sum of the highest scores
        for two of elements P2E1 through
        P2E6 plus the highest score of
        elements P2E7 or P2E8 ≥6 and
        not = 0? ----------------------------------YES-----------▶ P2L1

        NO

        P2L2

1   Exposure elements = P2E1 through P2E6 ("E" elements)
    Toxicity elements = P2E7 through P2E8 ("T" elements)
    Undesirable Aesthetic
    properties elements   } = P2E9
2   P2L1, P2L2, and P2L3 = List of chemicals of high, medium, and low
    priority, respectively.
    P2L4 and P2L5 = List of chemicals with undesirable aesthetic properties
    and list of chemicals lacking information, respectively.
An asterisk (*) substitutes the score when no information is available for
that vector element.

Fig. 5.1. Combining rules for Phase 2 (P2R).
(Source: Reprinted from ref. 7).

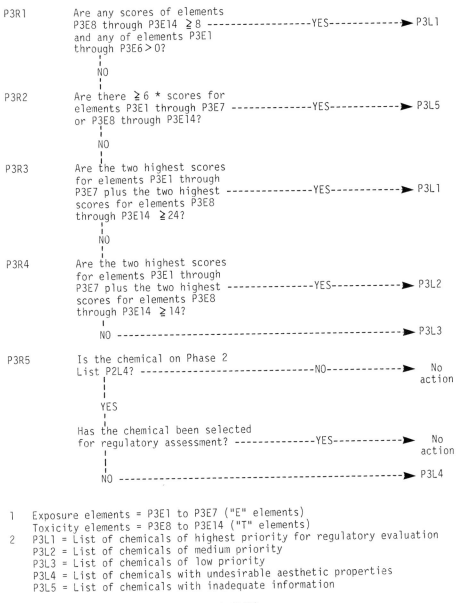

P3R1   Are any scores of elements
P3E8 through P3E14 ≥ 8 ------------------YES------------▶ P3L1
and any of elements P3E1
through P3E6 > 0?

                NO

P3R2   Are there ≥ 6 * scores for
elements P3E1 through P3E7 --------------YES------------▶ P3L5
or P3E8 through P3E14?

                NO

P3R3   Are the two highest scores
for elements P3E1 through
P3E7 plus the two highest ----------------YES------------▶ P3L1
scores for elements P3E8
through P3E14 ≥ 24?

                NO

P3R4   Are the two highest scores
for elements P3E1 through
P3E7 plus the two highest ----------------YES------------▶ P3L2
scores for elements P3E8
through P3E14 ≥ 14?

                NO --▶ P3L3

P3R5   Is the chemical on Phase 2
List P2L4? ----------------------------NO------------▶   No
                                            action

                YES

        Has the chemical been selected
for regulatory assessment? --------------YES------------▶   No
                                            action

                NO --▶ P3L4

1   Exposure elements = P3E1 to P3E7 ("E" elements)
    Toxicity elements = P3E8 to P3E14 ("T" elements)
2   P3L1 = List of chemicals of highest priority for regulatory evaluation
    P3L2 = List of chemicals of medium priority
    P3L3 = List of chemicals of low priority
    P3L4 = List of chemicals with undesirable aesthetic properties
    P3L5 = List of chemicals with inadequate information

Fig. 5.2. Combining rules for Phase 3 (P3R).
(Source: Reprinted from ref. 7).

simple laboratory measurement that will reliably extrapolate itself to the field for the soil situation.

Calculation of volatilization rate constant:

$$R_v = -\frac{d[C_w]}{d_t} = k_v[C_w] \qquad (5.3)$$

where

$$k_v = \frac{1}{L}\left[\frac{1}{k_\ell} + \frac{RT}{H_c k_g}\right]^{-1} \qquad (5.4)$$

and

R_v = volatilization rate of a chemical C (mole $L^{-1}hr^{-1}$)

C_w = aqueous concentration of C (mole L^{-1}(=M))

k_v = volatilization rate constant (hr^{-1})

L = depth (cm)

k_ℓ = mass transfer coefficient in the liquid phase (cm hr^{-1})

H_c = Henry's law constant (torr M^{-1})

kg = transfer coefficient in the gas phase (cm hr^{-1})

R = gas constant (litre-atm-mole^{-1} degree^{-1})

T = absolute temperature (degrees kelvin)

In both phases:

$$k_\ell = D_\ell/\partial_\ell \quad \text{and} \quad k_g = D_g/\partial_g \qquad (5.5)$$

where

D = diffusion coefficient

∂ = boundary layer thickness

Calculation of the volatilizational loss of an organic chemical

$$(k_v^c)_{env} = (k_v^c/k_v^o)_{lab}(k_v^o)_{env} \qquad (5.6)$$

where

k_v^c = volatilization rate constant for the chemical (hr^{-1}); and

k_v^o = oxygen reaeration constant (hr^{-1}) in the laboratory or environment.

The volatilizational process represents the physical transport of organic chemicals from waterbodies to the atmosphere. Theoretical concepts of volatilization of chemicals (or chemical compounds) from water to atmosphere have been presented by several researchers (refs. 9-13). A review of these theoretical approaches and their limitations have been discussed recently (ref. 14). The transport across two-layer system (ref. 15) can also be expressed on the assumption that concentrations close to either side of the interface are in equilibrium as expressed by a Henry's law constant (H).

$$F = K_L (C_L - C_S) \tag{5.7}$$
where

$$C_S = Pv/H \tag{5.8}$$

$$\frac{1}{K_L} = \frac{1}{k_L} + \frac{RT}{Hk_G} \tag{5.9}$$

in which K_L is the overall mass transfer (or liquid film) coefficient based on the liquid phase (metres/day); R = gas constant (atm.m^3/mol.K); T = temperature (in ^{O}K)(ref. 18); P_v = atmospheric partial pressure (std. atmospheric units) and C_S = Concentration in the liquid phase in equilibrium with P_v (or saturation concentration)(ref. 16)(Fig. 5.3).

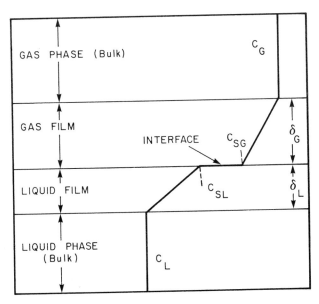

Fig. 5.3. Schematic illustration of two-film gas transfer model. (Source: Reprinted from ref. 16).

Equation 5.7 can be rewritten to express phase resistances to mass transfers:

$$\frac{r_L}{r_T} = \frac{1}{1 + (r_G/r_L)}$$ (5.10)

$$\frac{r_G}{r_T} = \frac{1}{1 + (r_L/r_G)}$$ (5.11)

where $r_L = \dfrac{1}{k_L}$ and $r_G = RT/Hk_G$

Equations 5.10 and 5.11 can be utilized to determine the relative magnitudes of mass transfer resistances in the liquid and gas phase, respectively. The smallest percent resistance can be predicted for the largest k_L and the smallest k_G. Liquid film resistance can be evaluated as a function of Henry's law constant (H) by utilizing known data on k_L, k_G, and H for organic compounds (ref. 17) (Fig. 5.3). Results show that for average conditions, more than 90% of the resistance is in the liquid film for compounds with H values of about 10^{-3} M atm.m^3/g.mole. This profile for ethylene and propane (Fig. 5.3) can be used to identify organic compounds with similar volatilization characteristics.

Equations have been developed and evaluated to predict values of k_L for streams and rivers in Ontario, Canada (ref. 16). The observed and predicted values of k_L are given in Table 5.3. Results indicate that the predictions from equations 5.12 and 5.13 seem to agree fairly with the observed values (Table 5.3).

Similarly, volatilization rates from lakes, ponds, or rivers were estimated for the 114 organic chemicals from the EPA priority pollutants list using volatilization rate constant equation (ref. 18). The results of these estimates with values selected for the parameters in the equation are given in Figs. 5.4 and 5.5. The plots suggest that H_c is the major factor in determining the magnitude of k_v^c. It should also be noted that for values of H_c greater than about 40 torr.M^{-1} (roughly corresponding to 25% liquid phase mass transfer resistance), the volatilizational half-life of the chemical will be less than 10 days.

Comparison of theoretical loss rates with the measured loss rates are given in Table 5.4 for a few pairs of pesticides (ref. 19). The theoretical values were derived from the literature values for vapour pressures (P) and molecular masses (M) and assuming that loss rate was proportional to $P\sqrt{M}$. The agreement was within a factor of 10 which was anticipated in earlier studies (ref. 20). If high melting chemicals with vapour pressure difference greater than 10 were

TABLE 5.3 Observed and computed K_L for Ontario streams.

OBSERVED K_L (m/d)	EQUATION 5.12 $\overline{K_{LC}}$ (m/d)	$\dfrac{K_{LC}}{\overline{K_L}}$	EQUATION 5.13 $\overline{K_{LC}}$ (m/d)	$\dfrac{K_{LC}}{\overline{K_L}}$
2.66	2.10	0.79	2.51	0.95
2.39	2.22	0.93	2.66	1.11
3.57	3.34	0.94	4.17	1.17
3.04	3.01	0.99	3.19	1.05
1.80	3.80	2.11	4.22	2.35
4.64	3.14	0.68	3.65	0.79
8.07	5.57	0.69	6.31	0.78
2.63	2.57	0.98	2.43	0.92
2.26	2.60	1.15	2.86	1.27
0.97	1.87	1.93	2.57	2.64
3.01	3.32	1.10	3.07	1.02
3.10	1.97	0.64	2.39	0.77
3.74	3.15	0.84	2.72	0.73
5.73	2.51	0.44	3.01	0.52
4.33	4.28	0.99	3.48	0.80
AVERAGE: 3.46	3.03	1.01	3.28	1.12

K_{LC} = Computed value; K_L = observed value; m/d = metre/day.

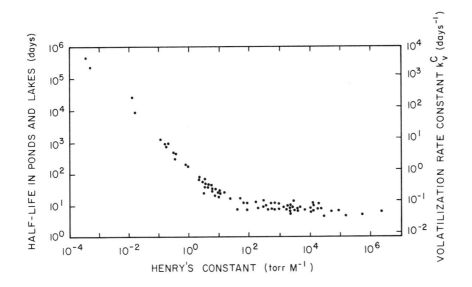

Fig. 5.4. Estimated half-lives versus Henry's Law constant for the 114 priority pollutants in lakes and ponds (Values used in equation L = 200 cm, k_ℓ^0 = 8.0 cm hr^{-1}, k_g^w = 2100 cm hr^{-1}, n = 1, m = 0.7.)

(Source: Reprinted with permission from ref. 18a, Copyright (1981), Pergamon Press, Plc.).

Footnote to Table 5.3

$$K_L = 2.70g^{0.35}\nu^{-1.85}D_m^{1.89}B^{0.4}Z^{-0.25}U^{0.26}(LS)^{0.16} \qquad (5.12)$$

$$K_L = 7.16g^{0.23}\nu^{-1.51}D_m^{1.59}Z^{0.15}U^{0.46} \qquad (5.13)$$

where K_L = liquid film coefficient
 B = channel width
 Z = average depth
 U = mean velocity
 LS = drop in height
 L = length of reach

S = bed slope
g = acceleration due to gravity
D_m = molecular diffusivity of
    organic compounds
$\nu = \mu/\rho$ = kinematic viscosity of
    water at the instream
    temperature
ρ = density of water at $T^{\circ}C$
μ = absolute viscosity of water

(Source: Reprinted from ref. 16).

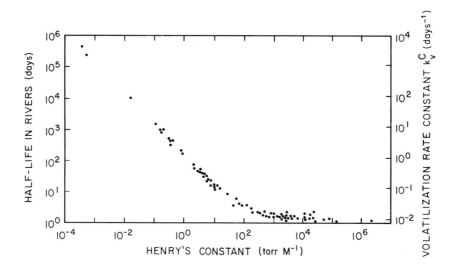

Fig. 5.5. Estimated half-lives versus Henry's law constant for the 114 priority pollutants in rivers. (Equation and values are same as given for Fig. 5.4 except k_g^0 = 8.0 cm hr^{-1} and n = m = 0.7).

(Source: Reprinted with permission from ref. 18a, Copyright (1981), Pergamon Press, Plc.).

TABLE 5.4 Theoretical loss versus measured loss for some pesticide pairs.

CHEMICALS	THEORETICAL RATIO (TR)	MEASURED RATIO (MR)	$\frac{MR}{TR}$
Parathion ethyl/Parathion methyl	0.60	0.64	1.1
Dinoseb/Dimethoate	6.2	7.7	1.2
Dibutyl phthalate/hexachlorobenzene	1.2	1.0	0.83
Hexachlorobenzene[*]/Dieldrin[*]	5.0	3.0	0.60
Trifluralin/Dieldrin	40	21.0	0.53
Atrazine+/Dieldrin	0.091	0.037	0.41
Parathion ethyl/Dieldrin	1.7	0.62	0.36
Dinoseb/Parathion methyl	5.8	2.0	0.34
Dibutyl phthalate/Dieldrin	6.0	0.74	0.12
Atrazine/di(-2 ethylhexyl) phthalate[+]	0.31	1.1	3.5
Trifluralin/Dimethoate	15	39	2.6
Atrazine[+]/Monuron[+]	0.62	1.9	3.1
Picloram[+]/Dieldrin	0.018	0.14	7.8

* Average value from two experiments
+ Only a small amount of chemical was volatilized during the experiment and the log (amount remaining) - time regression had large 95% confidence limits, therefore the loss rate ratio may be suspect.

(Source: Reprinted with permission from ref. 19, Copyright (1984), Pergamon Press, Plc.).

excluded, then the agreement was within a factor of 3, indicating the validity of the estimation method.

5.2.2 Sorption

All chemicals released into the environment are continually being transported and redistributed between the various media such as soil/sediment, water, air, and biota. Water is the medium of transport of chemicals to other media and hence the residence time of chemicals in water is a critical determinant in transport processes. The partitioning of the chemical between water and air depending on Henry's law constant and other parameters have been discussed earlier in this chapter under volatilization.

The term "sorption" used here covers both adsorption and absorption, which are difficult to distinguish in most situations. Many metals and organic chemicals sorb strongly to sediments, suspended solids and soils. This determines the fraction that is available for other fate processes.

The understanding and quantification of exchange processes occurring at the sediment/water interface is important in formulating a model for the speciation and transport of heavy metals, and organic chemicals. The sediment is a complex mixture, with four main components: silica, clays, organic matter, and oxides of iron and manganese. The term "silica", as used here, includes minerals other than clays and ferromanganese oxides; in most cases, they are silicates, commonly silica in the form of quartz. The association of chemicals with sediments can range from weak van der Waals forces to strong covalent bonding, coprecipitation with ferromanganese oxides, and incorporation within crystal lattices. The release of sorbed chemicals into the bulk water is dependent on partition coefficients, which in turn are related to sediment characteristics, the type of chemical, and other environmental parameters. Desorption may be a slow process, posing a long-term problem even after the sources of pollution are eliminated (ref. 21).

The sorption coefficient (K_{oc}) is the concentration of chemical sorbed by the sediment or soil on organic carbon basis divided by the concentration of chemical in the surrounding water column. Expressing sorption on organic carbon basis instead of a total sediment/soil basis renders a valid comparison of sorption coefficients. Residual variation still experienced could be due to: (1) inherent differences in the type of organic matter and their sorption characteristics; (2) variation in methods used to measure sorption; and (3) influence of other soil constituents. Sorption coefficients are relatively constant at low aqueous concentrations of the chemical, but tend to decrease as the concentration of the chemical in the water column is increased (ref. 22), especially for chemicals with high aqueous solubilities. However, most sorption studies are done at concentrations low enough to minimize the variation that could arise from this factor.

Another factor that could affect the sorption coefficients is the contact time between the sorbent and the sorbate. There are two sorption processes: (1) initial rapid sorption on the surface followed by (2) slow continued sorption due to slow diffusion of the chemical into the organic matrix. This two-stage sorption process would increase the time taken for desorption to reach an equilibrium. The distribution coefficients obtained from desorption data would be substantially higher than those obtained from sorption data which seems to be true from the studies reported (ref. 22).

Sorption of chemicals to organic matter depends upon the pH and the type of chemical interaction, either ionic or non-ionic. Interaction of non-ionics will not be greatly affected by changes in pH. Whereas, ionic compounds will be repelled by the sorbent surfaces at high pH values due to repulsion of like-charges of the sorbent and sorbate. Chemicals like 2,4-dichlorophenoxy acetic acid (2,4-D), 2,4,5-trichlorophenoxy acetic acid (2,4,5-T), dicamba, chloramben, and picloram behave in this manner. The sorption of these chemicals increase with decrease in pH leading to the formation of unionized surface and unionized form of the chemical. These compounds are also sorbed strongly by hydrated ion and aluminum oxides at low pH values.

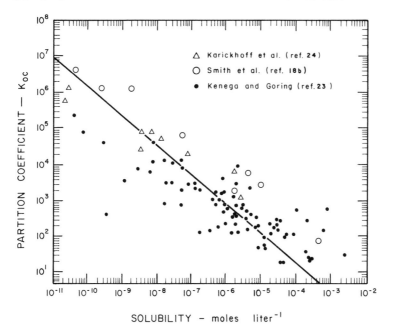

Fig. 5.6. Correlation of K_{OC} with WS (aqueous solubility). (Source: Reprinted with permission from ref. 28, Copyright (1980), Butterworths).

Sorption coefficients based on the organic carbon content of the sorbent provide a good basis for relating to other accumulation parameters such as n-octanol/water partition coefficients and bioconcentration factors for biota. Sorption coefficients also provide a measure of the leachability of chemicals which is valuable in environmental impact assessment. Compounds having a K_{oc} value equal to or greater than 1000 are quite strongly bound to organic matter of sediment/soil and are considered immobile. Chemicals with K_{oc} values below 100 are moderately to highly mobile. Thus, K_{oc} values can be useful predictors of the potential leachability of compounds through soil or from aqueous sediments.

Values of K_{oc} can be estimated using correlations with other properties of the chemical: (1) water solubility (WS); (2) n-octanol/water partition coefficient (K_{ow}); and (3) bioconcentration factor for aquatic organisms (BCF). Table 5.5 lists some of the commonly used regression equations for estimating K_{oc}.

TABLE 5.5 Estimation of K_{OC} from other related parameters.

EQUATION	No.[a]	r^{2*}	CHEMICAL CLASSES COVERED	REF.
$\log K_{OC} = -0.55 \log WS + 3.64$ (S in mg/L)	106	0.71	Wide variety, mostly pesti-cides	(23)
$\log K_{OC} = -0.54 \log WS + 0.44$ (S in mole fraction)	10	0.94	Mostly aromatic or polynuclear aromatics; two chlorinated	(24)
$\log K_{OC} = -0.557 \log WS + 4.277$ (S in μmoles/L)	15	0.99	Chlorinated hydrocarbons	(25)
$\log K_{OC} = 0.544 \log K_{OW} + 1.377$	45	0.74	Wide variety, mostly pesticides	(23)
$\log K_{OC} = 0.937 \log K_{OW} - 0.006$	19	0.95	Aromatics, polynuclear aromatics, triazines and dinitroaniline herbicides	(14)
$\log K_{OC} = 1.00 \log K_{OW} - 0.21$	10	1.00	Mostly aromatic or poly-nuclear aromatics; two chlorinated	(24)
$\log K_{OC} = 1.029 \log K_{OW} - 0.18$	13	0.91	Variety of insecticides, herbicides and fungicides	(26)
$\log K_{OC} = 0.524 \log K_{OW} + 0.855$[b]	30	0.84	Substituted phenylureas and alkyl-N-phenylcarbamates	(27)
$\log K_{OC} = 0.681 \log BCF + 1.963$	13	0.76	Wide variety, mostly pesti-cides	(23)
$\log K_{OC} = 0.681 \log BCF + 1.886$	22	0.83	Wide variety, mostly pesti-cides	(23)

[a] No. = Number of chemicals used to obtain regression equation; $*$ r^2 = correlation coefficient for regression equation; [b] = the relationship $K_{OM} = K_{OC}/1.724$ was used to rewrite the equation in terms of K_{OC}. (Source: Reprinted with permission from ref. 14).

One or more equations should be chosen based on the availability of data and chemical classes covered by the equation. In addition, the range of the input parameter and K_{OC} should be within the range covered by the dataset from which the equation was derived (Figs. 5.6 and 5.7). The following Equation 5.14 was developed by Mill (ref. 28) for predicting sorption coefficients of monocyclic aromatics:

$$\log K_{OC} = -0.782 \log [C] - 0.27 \tag{5.14}$$

where [C] = Concentration in moles litre^{-1}.

The estimate is reliable to a power of 10 for most non-polar chemicals, which is sufficiently accurate for screening purposes in most cases.

5.2.3 Bioconcentration

Bioconcentration denotes the concentration of a chemical in an organism or in the tissue of an organism and the bioconcentration factor (BCF) is the ratio of the concentration of the chemical in the organism to its concentration in surrounding water column. Three commonly used methods for measurement of BCFs are: (1) exposure of fish in an aquarium to flowing water spiked with the chemical; (2) a model ecosystem containing plant or animal organism or both in water; and (3) a terrestrial-aquatic model ecosystem containing soil and animal and plant organisms. The BCF obtained is determined by factors such as solubility, residence time in water and hydrophobicity of the chemical and

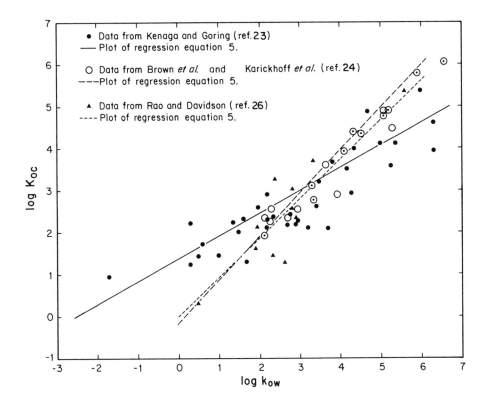

Fig. 5.7. Correlation of K_{OC} with log K_{OW}.
(Source: Reprinted with permission from ref. 14).

surface-to-volume ratio and lipid content of the organism. Lieb (ref. 29) measured the lipid content of 14-week old rainbow trout over a period of 32 weeks. The lipid content doubled in that time period from 4.4% to 8.4%; gill (9.7%), muscle (2.7%), stomach (6.5%), liver (3.5%), and whole fish (8.5%). Concentrations of chemicals that appear safe for organisms can bioconcentrate to levels that are harmful to predators. Reliable bioconcentration values can provide early warning of potential problems in aquatic media without extensive monitoring information. Examples where predators suffered the toxicity effects are DDD in California in 1950s to 1960s and more recently with organophosphates (ref. 30). In addition, some stages of fish life-cycle take up and tolerate chemicals which later either become toxic during periods of stress or passed on to produce toxic effects in more susceptible stages (ref. 31).

It is important to measure the uptake and depuration rates of the organisms or alternatively the measurements should be made over a sufficiently long period of time to ensure that equilibrium conditions exist. Flow-through bioassay systems should be used so that chemical concentrations remain relatively constant during the test.

The accumulation of organic chemicals in aquatic organisms can be predicted by several methods. The relationship between bioconcentration and other physico-chemical properties (n-octanol/water partition coefficient), K_{ow} and aqueous solubility, WS are used to predict the results of the expensive and time-consuming BCF test to provide a preliminary environmental safety assessment of the chemicals. Published correlations of BCF with WS and log K_{ow} are given in Table 5.6. Shortcomings of some of the data used and replacing with data obtained under closely defined and comparable experimental conditions have been discussed in ref. 31.

TABLE 5.6 Published regression equations between BCF and K_{ow} and WS.

EQUATION NO.	EQUATION (log BCF =)	BCF vs WS WS UNITS	r	t	n	SYSTEM	REF.
(5.15)	3.995-0.389(logWS)	ppb	-0.923	7.20	11	Static ecosystem	(32)
(5.16)	3.410-0.508(logWS)	μmol^{-1}	-0.964	9.04	8	Flow-through	(33)
(5.17)	2.791-0.564(logWS)	ppm	-0.72	6.05	36	Flow-through	(23)
(5.18)	2.183-0.629(logWS)	ppm	0.66	6.09	50	Static	(23)
(5.19)	3.710-0.316(logWS)	ppb	-0.565	3.28	25	Flow-through	(34)
(5.20)	5.09-0.85 (logWS)	ppb	0.87	5.29	11	Static	(35)
(5.21)	2.83-0.55 (logWS)	ppm	-	-	42	Flow-through	(36)

TABLE 5.6 Concluded.

		BCF vs K_{ow}				
EQUATION NO.	EQUATION (log BCF =)	r	t	n	SYSTEM	REF.
(5.22)	0.542(log K_{ow})+0.124	0.948	7.30	8	Flow-through	(37)
(5.23)	0.935(log K_{ow})-1.495	0.87	8.64	26	Flow-through	(23)
(5.24)	0.767(log K_{ow})-0.973	0.76	6.82	36	Static	(23)
(5.25)	0.85 (log K_{ow})-0.70	0.947	21.46	55	Flow-through	(38)
(5.26)	0.456(log K_{ow})+0.634	0.634	3.93	25	Flow-through	(34)
(5.27)	0.634(log K_{ow})+0.729	0.788	3.84	11	Static	(32)
(5.28)	0.74 (log K_{ow})-0.77	-	-	40	Flow-through	(36)

r = correlation coefficient; n = no. of data points and t = student's t value for regression.
(Source: Reprinted with permission from ref. 31, Copyright (1985), Pergamon Press, Plc.).

The data on BCF and WS, and log K_{ow} for selected organic chemicals have been plotted in Figs. 5.8 and 5.9, using the following regression equations:

$$log_{10}BCF = 4.358 - 0.444 \, [log_{10}WS(\, g \, L^{-1})] \tag{5.29}$$
$$r = -0.803, \, n = 29, \, and \, t = 7.00 \, (Fig. \, 5.8)$$

and
$$log_{10}BCF = 0.597 \, (log_{10}K_{ow}) + 0.188 \tag{5.30}$$
$$r = 0.748, \, n = 31, \, and \, t = 6.07 \, (Fig. \, 5.9)$$

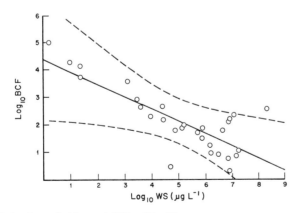

Fig. 5.8. Correlation of BCF with WS.
(Source: Reprinted with permission from ref. 31, Copyright (1985), Pergamon Press, Plc.).

Fig. 5.10 presents the correlation of BCF vs log K_{ow} of hydrocarbons and chlorohydrocarbons which restrict the range but increase the reliability of correlations. Various aspects of BCF measurements such as steady state and kinetic approaches to BCF, experimental factors, relevance of laboratory-measured BCFs to field situations (good laboratory practices, etc.) are

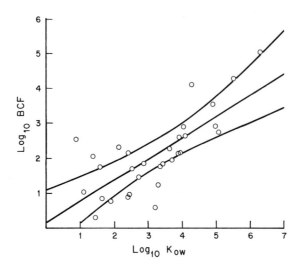

Fig. 5.9. Correlation of BCF with log K_{OW}.
(Source: Reprinted with permission from ref. 31, Copyright (1985), Pergamon Press, Plc.).

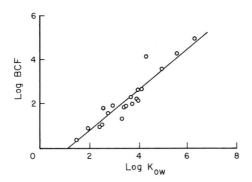

Fig. 5.10. Correlation of BCF with log K_{OW} for hydrocarbons and chlorinated hydrocarbons. (regression equation: $\log BCF = -1.30 + 0.98 \log K_{OW}$ with $r = 0.898$; $n = 20$; and $t = 8.66$) (5.31)
(Source: Reprinted with permission from ref. 31, Copyright (1985), Pergamon Press, Plc.).

discussed in detail in ref. 31. Because of the variations that occur in BCF tests and comparable variations expected in the environment, it would be illusory to expect a high level of precision in BCF tests. However, efforts are underway to make BCF tests to provide results that are consistent and widely applicable recognizing the differences in fish species and strains, together with appropriate sizes and temperatures to use in BCF tests (ref. 31).

Some recommended regression equations for estimating log BCF from laboratory flow-through studies are as follows:

Equation	n	r^2	Chemical Classes	Range of independent variable	Species Used
log BCF=0.76 log K_{ow}-0.23 (Equation 5.32)	84	0.823	wide range	7.9 to 8.1×10^6	Fathead minnow Bluegill sunfish Rainbow trout Mosquito fish
log BCF=2.791-0.564 log WS (Equation 5.33)	36	0.49	wide range	0.001 to 50,000 ppm	Brook trout Rainbow trout Bluegill sunfish Fathead minnow Carp
log BCF=1.119 log K_{oc}-1.579 (Equation 5.34)	13	0.757	wide range	<1 to 1.2×10^6	Various

n = number of chemicals used in the regression; r = correlation coefficient for regression equation.

Equation 5.32 = ref. 34; Equations 5.33 and 5.34 = ref. 23.

(Source: Reprinted with permission from ref. 14, Copyright (1982), American Chemical Society).

The comparison of estimated BCF with field observed BCF are given in Table 5.7.

5.2.4 Water Solubility

Of the various parameters which influence the fate and transport processes of chemicals in the enviironment, water solubility is one of the most important parameter. Water solubility is more important for liquids and solids and of much less environmental importance for gases. The latter is governed by Henry's law constant. Highly water-soluble chemicals have long residence time in the aquatic media and undergo the biodegradation (microbial or otherwise) photolytic, hydrolytic processes more readily. These chemicals have low sorption coefficients for soils and sediments and have relatively low BCF values. Factors such as temperature, salinity, dissolved organic matter, and pH play a significant role in the aqueous solubility of organic chemicals.

TABLE 5.7 Estimated and field evaluated BCF values.

Compound and Location	log K_{ow}	log WS (ppm)	Estimated BCF	Ambient Water Conc.	Conc. in Fish (Duration and Species)	Observed BCF	REF.
Aroclor 1016 (Hudson River)	5.88	-	17,000	Mean of 0.17 µg/L	2.6 µg/g (mean of 18 fish 3 species, 14 day exposure)	15,000	(39)
DDT (Hamilton Lake, Ontario)	5.75	-	14,000	4.5 ng/L	0.14 µg/g (Alewife) 0.23 µg/g (Smelt)	31,000 51,000	(40)
DDE (Hamilton Lake, Ontario)	5.69	-	12,000	37.4 ng/L	0.46 µg/g (Alewife) 1.36 µg/g (Smelt) 0.94 µg/g (Sculpin)	12,000 36,000 25,000	(40)
Dieldrin (Hamilton Lake, Ontario)	-	-1.66	5,300	3.1 ng/L	0.04 µg/g (Alewife)	13,000	(40)
PCB (Aroclor 1254) (Two lakes in South Dakota)	6.47	-	49,000	<0.5 µg/L	0.11 µg/g	>220	(41)
Lindane (Limestone quarry)	3.89	-	530	25-13 ng/L	~27.3-13.3 ng/g (trout, 3-7 fish per sample)	~1,090	(42)
Trifluralin	5.33	-	6,600	~1.8 µg/L	10.46 µg/g (237 sauger, residue in fat)	5,800	(43)

(Source: Reprinted with permission from ref. 14, Copyright (1982), American Chemical Society).

There are about 18 different regression equations available to correlate water solubility (WS) with n-octanol/water partition coefficient (K_{ow}) (ref. 14). It can be concluded that most equations covered two-thirds of the chemicals within a factor of 10. Many of the large errors (5 to 14% of the estimates were more than a factor of 100) were associated with the nitrogen-containing compounds and almost all were overestimated.

Equations:

$$\log 1/WS = 1.214 \log K_{ow} - 0.850 \tag{5.35}$$

where WS = mol/L, n= 140, r^2 = 0.914 covering a large variety of chemicals;

$$\log 1/WS = 1.339 \log K_{ow} - 0.978 \tag{5.36}$$

where WS = mol/L, n = 156, r^2 = 0.874 covering a large variety of chemicals; were relatively quite accurate when limited to liquids. Seventy-seven percent of the chemicals were within a factor of 10 and 93% within a factor of 100.

Fig. 5.11 presents a correlation of log K_{ow} with WS using the dataset from literature (ref. 44) for a mixed class of aromatics and chlorinated hydrocarbons. The two outliers, 1,3,5,-triazo-1,3,5,-trinitrocyclohexane and hexachloro-1,3,-butadiene, were not included in the regression to avoid increasing the errors in the estimate. Thus, correlations cover most of the chemicals but it is not universal in coverage.

5.2.5 Abiotic Transformations

A chemical in the environment could be altered by transformation processes such as: (1) ionization; (2) hydrolysis; (3) photodegradation; and (4) halogenation-dehalogenation processes. The extent to which a chemical breaks down to simple moities will determine its persistence and toxicity. The transformed derivative could be substantially more hazardous and persistent. Examples are the photochemical degradation of hydrocarbons and nitrogen oxides to produce a smog that has more direct and active effect on the environment and humans. Halogenation of aromatic compounds and aliphatic hydrocarbons are environmentally significant. Chlorinated dioxins and furans and formation of chloroform in the presence of organic matter are examples of this process. Some of the transformation processes are briefly described below.

(i) Ionization. An organic acid or base that is extensively ionized in the environment may be significantly different from the corresponding unionized neutral molecule in solubility, sorption, bioconcentration and toxic potential. For example, the ionized species have longer residence time in water, less ability to migrate into the organic or lipid part of the abiotic (such as sediment) and biotic substrates (fish), respectively, than the parent

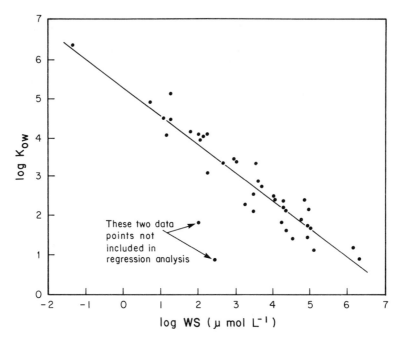

Fig. 5.11. Correlation of K_{OW} with WS for a mixed class of aromatics and chlorinated hydrocarbons using the regression equation:
log WS = -1.37 log K_{OW} + 7.26
where WS = μmol/L, n = 41 and r^2 = 0.903.
(Source: Reprinted with permission from ref. 44, Copyright (1980), American Chemical Society).

neutral unionized molecule. The equations for electron and proton changes (ionization and redox conditions, respectively) are given below:

pH = - log $[H^+]$	P_{ε} = log$[e^-]$
High pH = low H^+ activity and conversely	High P_{ε} = low ε^- activity and conversely
pH = pK_a + log $[A^-]/[HA]$	P_{ε} = $P_{\varepsilon}°$ + log $\dfrac{[oxidized]}{[reduced]}$
pH = pK_a when $[A^-]$ = $[HA]$	P_{ε}=$P_{\varepsilon}°$when [oxidized] =[reduced]
K_a= acid dissociation constant, $HA \rightleftharpoons H^+ + A^-$	$P_{\varepsilon}°$ = equilibrium potential
$[H^+]$ = Proton concn.	$[e^-]$ = Electron concn.

The dissociation constant of an organic acid or base can be estimated by using the linear free energy relationship (LFER). As applied to the estimation of acid dissociation constants, the LFER method uses a substituent-effect approach. One member of the "A" series, typically an unsubstituted prototype with dissociation constant $K_a^o(A)$, is the reference acid. A similarly unsubstituted member of the "B" series may be regarded as the parent compound of the acid whose dissociation constant $(K_a^x[B])$ is to be estimated using the following equation:

$$\log \frac{K_a^x(B)}{K_a^o(B)} = m.\log \frac{K_a^x(A)}{K_a^o(A)} \tag{5.37}$$

where

$K_a^o(A)$ = dissociation constant of reference acid in A series (e.g., benzoic acid)

$K_a^x(A)$ = dissociation constant of substituted acid in A series (e.g., p-chlorobenzoic acid)

$K_a^o(B)$ = dissociation constant of parent acid in B series (e.g., phenol)

$K_a^x(B)$ = dissociation constant of substituted acid in B series (e.g., p-chlorophenol)

m = proportionality constant (a measure of the relative sensitivity of B series to substituent changes compared to reference compounds in A series).

The choice of "A" series used in defining the substituent parameters distinguishes the different LFER systems. The Hammett relationship for aromatic compounds and Taft system for aliphatics are the widely used LFERs for estimating acid dissociation constants (ref. 14). Table 5.8 lists the measured and estimated values of dissociation constants for selected chemicals. Errors seem smaller for aromatic compounds with single acid group and errors are larger for aliphatics and for compounds with more than one acid group.

(ii) Hydrolysis. Hydrolysis is likely to be the most important reaction of organic chemicals in water and also a significant fate process for several organic chemicals. Freshwaters generally range in pH from 6.0 to 8.0. A hydrolysis reaction is one where hydrogen, hydroxyl radical, or the water molecule interacts with the organic compound depending on the pH and polarity of the site of attack on the molecule. Hydrogen ions lacking electrons are called electrophiles and essentially attack a site with a negative charge or lone pair of electrons of unsaturated compounds possessing a double bond. Typical examples are acid-catalyzed cleavage of ester linkage. On the other hand, nucleophiles, rich in electrons, interact with positive sites on the molecule being attacked.

Calculation of the rate of hydrolysis of a chemical compound

$$-\frac{dc}{dt} = k_h[C] = k_A[H^+][C] + k_B[OH^-][C] + k_N[C] \qquad (5.38)$$

where k_h = first order hydrolysis rate constant at a specific pH; k_A and k_B = second-order acid and base hydrolysis constants respectively and k_N = first-order hydrolysis rate constant for pH independent reaction.

Kinetic half-lives of chemicals

Half-lives of organic compounds are calculated from the respective rate constants and their dependence on physical parameters such as temperature.

TABLE 5.8 Measured and estimated dissociation constants for selected aromatic and aliphatic compounds.

COMPOUNDS	K_a		ERROR IN ESTIMATED VALUE
	MEASURED	ESTIMATED	(%)
AROMATIC COMPOUNDS			
p-Aminobenzoic acid			
K_1 (NH_3^+ group)	5.13×10^{-3}	2.58×10^{-3}	-49
K_2 (COOH group)	1.37×10^{-5}	1.36×10^{-5}	- 0.7
m-Aminobenzoic acid			
K_1 (NH_3^+ group)	8.51×10^{-4}	2.39×10^{-4}	- 72
K_2 (COOH group)	1.86×10^{-5}	4.32×10^{-5}	+132
p-Methoxybenzoic acid	3.38×10^{-5}	3.62×10^{-5}	+ 7
m-Phenoxybenzoic acid	1.12×10^{-4}	1.11×10^{-4}	- 0.9
m-Methylsulfonylbenzoic acid	3.02×10^{-4}	2.49×10^{-4}	- 17
p-Tolylacetic acid	4.27×10^{-5}	4.07×10^{-5}	- 5
p-Nitrophenylarsonic acid, K_1	1.27×10^{-3}	1.47×10^{-3}	+ 16
p-Cyanophenol	1.12×10^{-8}	1.31×10^{-8}	+ 17
ALIPHATIC COMPOUNDS			
Bromoacetic acid	1.25×10^{-3}	1.06×10^{-3}	- 15
Dichloroacetic acid	5.53×10^{-2}	8.22×10^{-2}	+ 49
Trifluoroacetic acid	0.59	10.35	+1600
Cyanoacetic acid	3.36×10^{-3}	2.68×10^{-3}	- 20
But-3-enoic acid	4.62×10^{-5}	2.82×10^{-5}	- 39
Chloromethylphosphonic acid	3.98×10^{-2}	6.89×10^{-2}	+ 73
Hydroxymethylphosphonic acid	1.23×10^{-2}	1.81×10^{-2}	+ 47

Values are from ref. 45.
(Source: Reprinted with permission from ref. 14).

For a first-order kinetic reaction,

A $\xrightarrow{j}$ products at a constant volume.

The rate of disappearance of A is given by:

$$-\frac{dC_A}{dt} = k_j\, C_A \tag{5.39}$$

where C_A = concentration of A in moles L^{-1}

t = time in appropriate units

k_j = reaction rate for the process j in units of inverse time, and

$-\dfrac{dC_A}{dt}$ = rate of change of C_A with time.

Integrating the equation between the limits of t_o (initial time) and t, yields:

$$k_j = \frac{1}{(t - t_o)}\ \ln\frac{(C_{A_O})}{(C_A)} \tag{5.40}$$

where C_{A_O} = initial concentrations of C_A at t_o

For $C_A = 0.5\ C_{A_O}$ the half-life is given by:

$$t_{1/2} = \frac{1}{k_j}\ \ln\frac{(2\,C_{A_O})}{(C_{A_O})} \qquad \text{or} \qquad t_{1/2} = 0.693\left(\frac{1}{k_j}\right) \tag{5.41}$$

If all the transformation processes are expressed as a first-order or pseudo first-order kinetic process, the net half-life for the chemical is given by:

$$t_{1/2} = \frac{\ln 2}{\sum\limits_j k_j} \tag{5.42}$$

The use of hydrolysis data in calculating the hydrolytic half-lives has been reviewed by Mabey and Mill (ref. 46). The hydrolytic half-lives of a variety of organic compounds are presented in Fig. 5.12 and Table 5.9.

Organic Functional Groups that are
Generally Resistant to Hydrolysis[a]

Alkanes	Aromatic nitro compounds
Alkenes	Aromatic amines
Alkynes	Alcohols
Benzenes/biphenyls	Phenols
Polycyclic aromatic hydrocarbons	Glycols
Heterocyclic polycyclic	Ethers
aromatic hydrocarbons	Aldehydes
Halogenated aromatics/PCBs	Ketones
Dieldrin/aldrin and related	Carboxylic acids
halogenated hydrocarbon pesticides	Sulfonic acids

[a] May be reactive if a hydrolyzable group is present.
(Source: Reprinted with permission from ref. 14).

Organic Functional Groups that are
Potentially Susceptible to Hydrolysis

Alkyl halides	Nitriles
Amides	Phosphonic acid esters
Amines	Phosphoric acid esters
Carbamates	Sulfonic acid esters
Carboxylic acid esters	
Epoxides	Sulfuric acid esters

(Source: Reprinted with permission from ref. 14).

(iii) Photolytic processes. It is well recognized that photochemical processes may be important in determining the fate of organic pollutants in the environment.

Structural changes of a molecule induced by electromagnetic radiation in the near ultraviolet-visible light range (240 to 700 nm) are called photochemical reactions. However, ionizing radiation is not present in a concentrated form to inflict any molecular alterations. Photochemical reactions could take place either by: (1) direct absorption by the molecule of an incident radiation leading to an excited state with subsequent deactivation reactions; or (2) electron or energy transfer through an intermediate called a photo-sensitizer. In some cases, photochemical reactions are followed by secondary dark (thermal) reactions. Photochemical absorption can occur only when the electronic changes of the molecule correspond to the wavelength of the incident radiation. Absorption of light energy in terms of photons results in the excitation of an electron from a lower to a higher orbital. The possible transitions of excited electrons from lower to higher orbitals are discussed in literature (ref. 47).

Absorption of light

Absorption of light by a chemical is a prerequisite for any photochemical reaction to take place. A comparison of the spectrum of solar radiation with the characteristic light absorption spectra of organic chemicals will provide a preliminary indication of the available light energy. The spectral distribution of solar energy incident on earth is presented in Fig. 5.13. Integration of the area under the curves would reveal that about 10% of the incident light energy is in the ultraviolet (UV) region and 45% each in the visible and infrared regions (ref. 48). Shorter wavelengths are effectively filtered out by ozone layer.

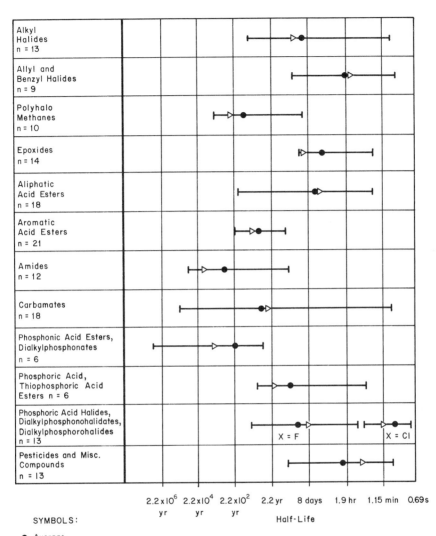

SYMBOLS:

● Average
▷ Median
n No. of Compounds Represented

Fig. 5.12. Hydrolytic half-life ranges for some typical organic compounds at 25°C and pH = 7.
(Source: Reprinted with permission from ref. 14).

TABLE 5.9 Hydrolytic half-lives of a variety of organic compounds in water at pH = 7 and 25°C.

COMPOUND	HALF-LIFE ($t_{1/2}$)
Organohalides	
CH_3F	30 y
CH_3Cl	0.9 y
CH_3Br	20 d
CH_3I	110 d
$CH_3-CH_2-CH_2Br$	26 d
$(CH_3)_2 - CHCl$	38 d
$(CH_3)_3CF$	50 d
$(CH_3)_3CCl$	23 s
$CH_2 = CH\ CH_2\ I$	2 d
$CHCl_3$	3,500 y
$CHBr_3$	686 y
CCl_4	7,000 y (1 ppm); 7 y (1000 ppm)
Epoxides	
CH_2-CH_2 ⟍O⟍	12 d
⬡⊳O	6 m
Esters	
$HCOOCH_3$	2 d
$CH_3COOCH_2CH_3$	2 y
$CH_3COOCH_2C_6H_5$	1.1 y
$CH_3COOC_6H_5$	38 d
$C_6H_5COOCH_3$	118 y
$(O,\ CH_3COO-C_6H_5COOCH_3)$	3.2 y
Amides	
CH_3CONH_2	3,950 y
$ClCH_2CONH_2$	1.46 y
Cl_3CCONH_2	84 d
$CH_3CONH(CH_3)$	38,000 y
Carbamates	
$CH_3CH_2-O-\overset{\overset{O}{\|\|}}{C}-NHC_6H_5$	6,700 y (estimated)
$CH_3-CH_2-O-\overset{\overset{O}{\|\|}}{C}-N(CH_3)C_6H_5$	44,000 y
$C_6H_5O=\overset{}{C}-NHC_6H_5$	170 d (estimated)
$C_{10}H_9OCNHCH_3,\ (\ -Naphthyl)$	8.5 d
Organophosphorus compounds	
$CH_3\ P(O)(OCH_3)_2$	88 y
$C_6H_5\ P(O)(OCH_2CH_3)_2$	440 y
$(CH_3O)_3PO$	1.2 y
$(C_6H_5O)_3PO$	1.3 y
$(\rho-NO_2C_6H_4O)_3PO$	11 m
$(\rho-NO_2-C_6H_4O)_3PS$	3.3 s (estimated)

Continued . . . .

TABLE 5.9 Concluded.

COMPOUND	HALF-LIFE ($t_{1/2}$)
Miscellaneous	
$(CH_3O)_2SO_2$	1.2 m
$ClCH_2OCH_2Cl$	25 s
C_6H_5COCl	16 s

(Source: Reprinted with permission from ref. 46, Copyright (1978), ACS).

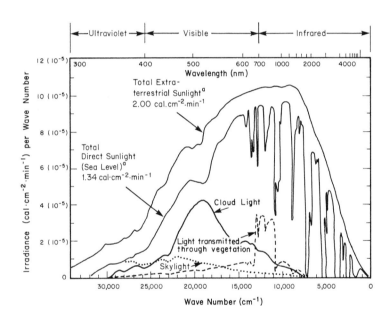

Fig. 5.13. Spectral distribution of extraterrestrial solar energy at sea level on a clear day. (Source: Reprinted with permission from ref. 48, Copyright (1965), Optical Society of America).

At earth's surface, direct photochemical activation using low intensity light <290 nm is improbable. Whereas, UV-visible light >290 nm (frequency $3.45 \times 10^4 cm^{-1}$ or 100 Kcal/Einstein) is available at moderate intensity. For a temperate zone such as in the United States, the mean incident solar energy on horizontal surface ranges from 3000 Kcal/m^2-day in northeast to about 5000 Kcal/m^2-day in southwest.

Fundamental spectral data for organic molecules that undergo such electronic transitions, wavelength of maximum response (λ_{max}), and their molar extinction coefficients (ϵ) (magnitude of the ability to absorb photons) are given in Table 5.10. The higher the value of λ_{max}, the lower is the energy difference in electronic transitions. Thus, the structure of an organic compound will determine whether or not a photochemical reaction takes place in the environment. Ultraviolet absorption is common with many aromatic and unsaturated compounds. Generally, an increase in the number of conjugated double bonds in the molecule will decrease the energy required for an electronic transition.

TABLE 5.10 Spectral data of some chromophores.

Chromophore	Functional group	Electron transition	λ_{max}	ϵ_{max}
$-O-$	CH_3OH	$n \rightarrow \sigma^*$	1830	500
$-S-$	$C_6H_{13}SH$	$n \rightarrow \sigma^*$	2240	126
$-N-$	$(CH_3)_3N$	$n \rightarrow \sigma^*$	2270	900
$-Cl:$	CH_3Cl	$n \rightarrow \sigma^*$	1730	100
$-Br:$	CH_3Br	$n \rightarrow \sigma^*$	2040	200
$-I:$	CH_3I	$n \rightarrow \sigma^*$	2580	378
$-C=C-$	$H_2C=CH_2$	$\pi \rightarrow \pi^*$	1710	15,500
$-C\equiv C-$	$HC\equiv CH$	$\pi \rightarrow \pi^*$	1730	6000
$\diagdown C=O$	$(CH_3)_2CO$	$\pi \rightarrow \pi^*$	1890	900

λ in A° unit, A° = 0.1 nm

$$\epsilon = \frac{O.D.}{c \times d}$$

where O.D. = optical density
c = concentration in moles/L
d = length of optical cell, in mm.

(Source: Reprinted with permission from ref. 47, Copyright (1979), John Wiley & Sons, Inc.).

Thus, the reactions that are normally possible at the far ultraviolet region become feasible at the near ultraviolet-visible range. Fig. 5.14 presents the energies of electromagnetic radiations at different wavelength regions and dissociation energies of some typical diatomic chemical bonds. Comparison of incident radiation energies with bond dissociation energies will provide an estimate of bond cleavage in a given wavelength region.

The excited organic molecule decays rapidly, returning either to the ground state after energy loss through collision and/or secondary radiations and/or chemical changes. The last category includes: (1) ionization of the molecule resulting from ejection of an electron; (2) molecular disproportionation yielding free radicals; (3) molecular isomerization; and (4) dark, thermal reactions involving free radicals and other molecules present in the environment. The rate of loss of a chemical (-dc/dt) by either direct or indirect photochemical reactions may be expressed by simple first-order kinetic expressions.

The solar energy incident on the surface of a natural water body is not uniformly transmitted down as shown in Fig. 5.15. It was noted that the long wavelength absorption was by water and the 400 to 500 nm light, by phytoplankton and organic degradation products in the eutrophic lake (ref. 49). Comparison of the absorption spectra of the organic chemical with the solar spectra profiles in Figs. 5.14 and 5.15 would indicate whether the absorbed light is of any significance.

Rate of disappearance of an organic compound by direct photolysis:

$$-\frac{dc}{dt} = K_p[C] = k_a \phi [C] \qquad (5.43)$$

where k_p = first-order rate constant, ϕ = reaction quantum yield and k_a = rate constant for light absorption by the chemical that depends on the light intensity, chromaticity of light, and extinction coefficient of the chemical.

Rate of disappearance of an organic compound by indirect photolysis:

$$-\frac{dc}{dt} = k_2[C][X] = k'_p[C] \qquad (5.44)$$

where k_2 = second-order constant for the interaction between the chemical and the intermediate, X; for a photosensitized reaction the k_p would be a combined term including the concentration of the excited state species and the quantum yields for the energy transfer to and subsequent reaction of the chemical. In any estimate of k_p or k'_p, values of K_a or $[X]$ should be specific taking into account the variation of the intensity of sunlight with time of the day, season, and latitude.

A simple way of determining the photolytic rate of a chemical is to expose it in aqueous solution or in a thin layer to outdoor sunlight and measure the rate of disappearance. Simultaneously, photolysis of another chemical of known quantum yield (ϕ) with a similar spectral range should be monitored. This method avoids the determination of quantum yield or spectral analysis.

Another method of determining environmental photolysis is to measure ϕ at a single wavelength (λ) in the laboratory. Sunlight intensity (I_λ) data as a function of time of day, season, and latitude are available in the literature. The rate constant in sunlight $k_{p(s)}$ is given by Equation 5.45.

$$k_{p(s)} = \phi \Sigma I_\lambda \varepsilon_\lambda \qquad (5.45)$$

and the half-life in sunlight is given by

$$(t_{1/2})(s) = \frac{\ln 2}{k_{p(s)}} \qquad (5.46)$$

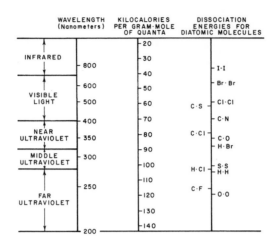

Fig. 5.14. Comparison of chemical bond energies with radiation energy.
(Source: Reprinted with permission from ref. 47, Copyright (1979), John Wiley
& Sons, Inc.).

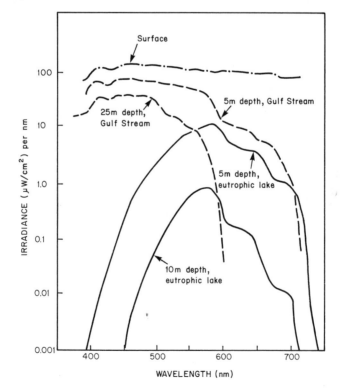

Fig. 5.15. Attenuation of solar energy spectrum in natural waters.
(Source: Reprinted with permission from ref. 49, Copyright (1976), American
Chemical Society).

Both computer and hand methods are available to sum the products of $E_\lambda I_\lambda$ over a wavelength range to plot the photolytic half-life of a chemical in air or water with time and latitude (refs. 50,51). Comparison of the measured and calculated half-lives for direct photolysis in sunlight for eight selected chemicals in water using the above method gave excellent agreement with a factor of two (Fig. 5.16).

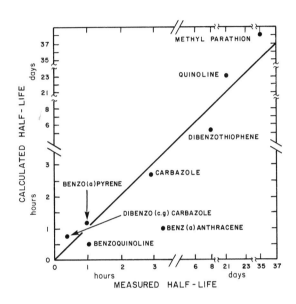

Fig. 5.16. Measured and calculated half-lives for direct photolysis. (Source: Reprinted with permission from ref. 52, Copyright (1980), Butterworths).

Predictive Capability. For screening purposes, Equation (5.45) may be used to calculate the upper limit of k_p by assuming $\phi = 1$. If the calculated rate constant is small relative to other fate processes, no additional photolytic measurements are needed. Prediction of ϕ from structure activity relationship is still empirical. Caution must be used in extrapolating quantum yield from one solvent to the other.

(iv) Halogenation-dehalogenation. Halogenation of organic compounds occurs mostly under synthetic conditions or in drastic environments. Mild chlorination reactions are possible in natural waters in zones of mixing of different effluents or mixing of industrial with municipal effluents containing residual chlorine. Chlorine can be sorbed by algae and released with a time delay, and this could serve as a chlorine reservoir in natural waters.

Dehalogenation reactions occur in the environment and could be due to a combination of reactions such as hydrolysis and disproportionation reactions. The hydrolysis reactions can occur under neutral conditions with water nucleophile attack or under basic conditions, the OH^- ion being the nucleophile. The half-lives of some halogenated compounds at pH 7 and $25^{\circ}C$ are given in Table 5.9. These conditions are relatively closer to the natural aquatic environment. Many halogenated compounds are susceptible to hydrolysis owing to charge separation between halogen atoms and carbon atoms. Chlorinated biphenyls are relatively inert to hydrolysis and consequent breakdown in the environment. Any breakdown of PCBs must be due to processes other than hydrolysis.

Metabolic Transformations

Many microorganisms and biota in general develop resistance to most organic chemicals and transform them to compounds that are not toxic to themselves but may be toxic to the total environment. In general, the following enzyme-catalyzed reactions are possible in the metabolic transformation of organic compounds (Fig. 5.17).

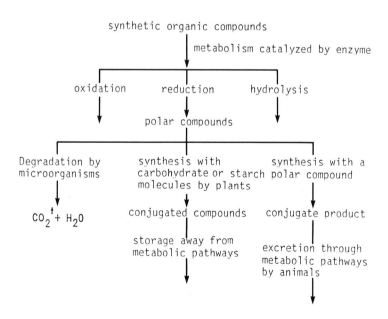

Fig. 5.17. Possible pathways of enzymatic transformations of organic chemicals (Source: Reprinted from ref. 51).

It is essential to determine the kinetics of these transformation reactions as a function of environmental variables to assess the half-life of the chemical under consideration. The rate for the biotransformation will be a function of the biomass and the chemical's concentration under given environmental conditions. When the organic compound is utilized as a carbon source, the growth rate of the organism is dependent upon the concentration of the former.

1. Rate of substrate utilization:

$$-\frac{dc}{dt} = \frac{\mu X}{Y} = \frac{(\mu_m)}{(Y)} \cdot \frac{(CX)}{(K_s + C)} = (k_b) \cdot \frac{(CX)}{(K_s + C)} \tag{5.47}$$

where μ = specific growth rate, X = biomass per unit volume, μ_m = maximum specific growth rate, K_s = concentration of the substrate to support half-maximum specific growth rate (0.5 μ_m), k_b = substrate utilization constant or biodegradation constant, (= μ_m/Y), and Y = biomass produced from a unit amount of substrate consumed. These constants μ_m, K_s, and Y are dependent on the characteristics of the microbes, pH, temperature, and media.

2. Reduced equation for the rate of substrate utilization:
When the substrate concentration $C \gg K_s$, the equation (5.47) reduces to:

$$-\frac{dc}{dt} = k_b X \tag{5.48}$$

This means that the biodegradation rate is first order with respect to all biomass concentration and zero order with respect to chemical concentration.

3. Reduced equation for the rate of substrate utilization:
In actual environmental situations for many pollutants, $C \ll K_s$, hence equation (5.47) becomes:

$$-\frac{dc}{dt} = (k_b) \frac{(CX)}{(K_s)} = k_{b2}[C][X] \tag{5.49}$$

where k_{b2} is a second-order rate constant.

4. Reduced equation for the degradation rate of a chemical:
When the biomass concentration is relatively large compared with the pollutant concentration, the degradation rate is pseudo-first order rate and given by:

$$-\frac{dc}{dt} = k_b' C \tag{5.50}$$

where k_b' is the pseudo-first-order rate constant and dependent on the cell concentration (X_0).

The half-life of the chemical under degradation $(t_{1/2}$ at a given cell concentration) can be calculated. In deriving this equation (5.51) it is assumed that the microbial community has already been acclimated to the chemical and that there is no lag time involved in the production of the necessary level of biodegrading organisms or mutants or the enzyme(s). However, when the chemical is newly introduced to the environment, the overall time required to reduce the chemical to 50% of its initial concentration will be given by:

$$T_{1/2} = t_o + t_{1/2} \tag{5.51}$$

where t_o = acclimation time and $t_{1/2}$ = half-life of transformation of the chemical.

Since the natural environment contains compounds of natural and anthropogenic origin, some biodegradation might require cofactors for microbial metabolism. Hence, cometabolism should be taken into account in the assessment of the environmental fate of a chemical. Half-life gives an estimate of the persistence of the organic compound in the environment (Equation 5.52). If the reactions are different from the first order, appropriate modifications must be made in the equation. Hence, knowledge of kinetics and concentrations of the chemical are essential in the calculation of the half-lives of organic compounds in the environment.

5. Calculation of the half-life of a chemical under degradation

The half-life of the chemical under degradation $(t_{1/2}$ at a given $X_0)$ will be:

$$t_{1/2} = \frac{\ln 2}{k_{b2} X_0} = \frac{0.693}{k_{b2} X_0}$$

where $\tag{5.52}$

$$k_{b2} = \frac{k_b'}{X_0}$$

$(k_b'$ = pseudo-first-order rate constant and X_0 = cell concentration).

5.3 BENCH-MARK CONCEPT

Bench-mark concept involves the selection of one or more chemicals from important classes of toxic chemicals and measurement of their key environmental parameters and physico-chemical properties. This information is then integrated to build an environmental profile (ref. 53) for the particular class of chemical. The new chemical is compared with the corresponding bench mark for structural similarity and by using pattern recognition methods, the behaviour of the new chemical can be predicted (Fig. 5.18).

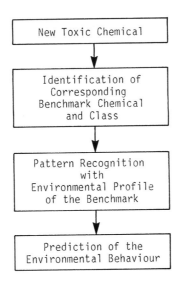

Fig. 5.18. Illustration of the bench-mark concept.
(Source: Reprinted with permission from ref. 52, Copyright (1980), Butterworths).

The environmental parameters and physico-chemical properties included in the bench-mark concept are aqueous solubility, vapour pressure, aqueous hydrolysis, sorption-desorption, biotic and abiotic transformations, and partitioning measured under standard conditions. Chemicals with high log P_{ow} and high environmental persistence value will be flagged for their potential toxicity through bioaccumulation and relatively long periods of exposure to humans and the environment, respectively. Fig. 5.19 shows a hypothetical environmental profile of a chemical that could be used to predict its behaviour with time. Further development is needed for field data, validation, and extension of the concept to effects and toxicity pattern.

Using the information on production volume, use pattern and method of disposal and applying fate processes models, the persistence, distribution among the different environmental media such as air, water, soil and biota can be estimated with a fair degree of accuracy. With the knowledge of the kinetic data on the fate processes such as volatilization, hydrolysis, photolysis, and bioaccumulation the distribution of the chemical and its fate can be predicted

TABLE 5.11 Rules of thumb for biodegradability.

CHEMICAL STRUCTURE	FACTOR(s)
1. Branched structures	Highly-branched compounds are more resistant to biodegradation. 1. Unbranched side chains on phenolic and phenoxy compounds are more easily metabolized than branch alkyl moieties. 2. Branched alkyl benzene sulfonates degrade more slowly than straight chain.
2. Chain length	Short chains are not as quickly degraded as long chains. 1. Rate of oxidation of straight-chain aliphatic hydrocarbons is correlated to length of chain. 2. Soil microbes attack long-chain mononuclear aromatics faster than short-chain. 3. Sulfate-reducing bacteria more rapidly degrade long-length carbon chains than short-length carbon chains. 4. ABS detergents increase in degradability with increase in chain length from C_6 to C_{12} but not $> C_{12}$.
3. Oxidized compounds	Highly oxidized compounds, like halogenated compounds, may resist further oxidation under aerobic conditions but may be more rapidly degraded under anaerobic conditions.
4. Non-ionic compounds	With active halogens present, are likely to be degraded by nucleophilic displacement reactions like hydrolysis.
5. Saturated and unsaturated compounds	Unsaturated aliphatics are more easily degraded than corresponding saturated hydrocarbons.
6. Substituents on simple organic molecules	1. Alcohols, aldehydes, acids, esters, amides and amino acids are more susceptible for biodegradation than the corresponding alkanes, olefins, ketones, dicarboxylic acids, amines and chloroalkanes. 2. Increased substitution, higher chlorine content, more than three cyclic rings hinder or greatly reduce biodegradation. 3. More chlorine on the aromatic ring, the more resistant the compound to biodegradation. 4. Aromatics with substituents are not available for bacterial utilization. Para substituents is more utilized than the meta or ortho substituents. 5. Mono- and dicarboxylic acids, aliphatic alcohols and ABS are decreasingly degraded when H is replaced by CH_3 group. 6. Ether functions are sometimes very resistant to biodegradation.

with time. Bench-mark concept could be a valuable tool in expressing toxicity of a new chemical in relation to an existing chemical and communicating the associated risk to the public.

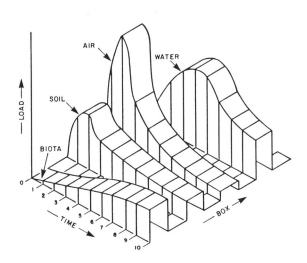

Fig. 5.19. Hypothetic environmental profile of a chemical's distribution in the environment as a function of time.
(Source: Reprinted with permission from ref. 52, Copyright (1980), Butterworths).

5.4 STRUCTURE-ACTIVITY RELATIONSHIPS

During the past two decades, the study of Quantitative Structure-Activity Relationships (QSAR) has been applied in pharmacology and drug design (ref. 53). The last few years have seen a growing interest in the use of QSAR to predict (eco) toxicological properties of organic compounds from their structural and physico-chemical properties (refs. 54-56). The demand is due to ever-increasing number of organic chemicals with the current number around a few hundred thousand chemicals. However, because of the limitations on time, cost and the number of existing testing facilities, only a small number of chemicals can be tested adequately. According to one U.S. EPA's former administrator, "less than 2% of the more than 65,000 chemicals in commerce have been adequately tested for their effects on human health and the environment" (ref. 57). These circumstances have sparked a growing interest in formalized schemes and procedures such as QSAR to flag chemicals that are suspected of potential adverse effects on human health and the environment.

5.4.1 QSAR Studies

QSAR studies attempt to mathematically define the relationship between a specific biological end point induced by a chemical and its physical and/or chemical properties. The requirements are: (1) reliable measurement of a specific biologic effect derived from the dose-response data; and (2) one or more molecular descriptors which quantitatively describe the physical properties and/or chemical structure of the chemical. QSAR studies have used different sets of physico-chemical properties and structural descriptors, and use several statistical computer-based methods in the analysis for QSAR relationships. Several physico-chemical and structural parameters of a wide range of chemicals have been correlated to biological end points such as carcinogenicity, mutagenicity, toxicity, bioconcentration, enzyme activities and others. The accuracy and reliability of measurements, the significance and relevance of the biological end point and the accuracy of descriptor measurement/calculation must be verified before using the QSAR information. Once validated for its quality, QSAR data will be a valuable tool along with the screening methods to identify those chemicals which may pose a significant hazard and require experimental confirmation followed by regulation.

There are three main types of QSAR studies which have been used to obtain structure-activity relationships (SARs). They are: (1) the systematic or intuitive approach; (2) the thermodynamic approach; and (3) the connectivity approach.

1. ### The Systematic/Intuitive Approach

   The systematic approach studies a particular biological response to a homologous series of compounds such as chlorinated dioxins and furans. The difference among the compounds should be systematic so that the change in biological response can be attributed to a particular structural change. The difference include chain length, nature of functional group at a specific position of the molecule or the nature of the functional groups at several selected positions on the molecule. It is difficult to assign biological response if the molecular difference is very complicated. Hence, this approach can cover only small groups of closely-related chemicals. In spite of this limitation, systematic QSAR studies have provided valuable insights into the mechanisms of action and structural features of a few classes of chemicals (refs. 58-60).

2. ### The Extrathermodynamic Approach

   This approach developed by Hansch and Fujita (ref. 61), involves the correlations of physico-chemical properties with biological response.

The parameters which may be used include: (1) hydrophobicity (log K_{ow}); (2) electronic parameters; (3) steric properties (molecular shape, volume, molecular weight, density, topological characteristics); and (4) quantum variables (ref. 62). These descriptors are incorporated into a mathematical relationship which can then be used to predict the biological response of an untested chemical. Since detailed molecular features are not used as descriptors, this approach can be used only with congeneric databases (ref. 62). Many of the physico-chemical properties are inter-related which result in colinearity among variables, leading to statistical bias. This approach may not be suitable for new chemicals due to lack of much of the required information on physico-chemical properties.

3. Connectivity Approach

In this approach, descriptors developed from physical structure or substructure of the chemical is used. Most commonly used descriptors are molecular connectivity indices of the non-hydrogen atoms, the degree of structural branching and the number of valence electrons of each skeletal atom (ref. 63). This method is computer-driven and hence, can handle very large databases. Many studies have been carried out combining the extra thermodynamic and connectivity approaches.

5.4.2 Biological End Points Tested by QSAR

(i) Carcinogenicity. The following three major computer assisted QSAR systems have been used to relate chemical structure and carcinogenicity:

- (a) Enslein Method;
- (b) Automated Data Analysis Using Pattern Recognition Techniques (ADAPT); and
- (c) Computer Automated Structure Evaluation (CASE).

(a) The Enslein Method

A large number of compounds for which the biological response is known are used as the "training set", which the computer program analyzes in order to determine which particular structural and physico-chemical features are related to carcinogenicity. Structural and physico-chemical information describing a chemical of unknown carcinogenic potential may be entered and will be compared with the training set data and a prediction of biological activity will be made. This method has been tested on 343 compounds from the IARC database, 223 of which are known carcinogens and 120 of which are known non-carcinogens (ref. 64). The system correctly classified 87 to 91% of the carcinogens and 78 to 80% of the non-carcinogens. Some compounds were seriously misclassified if they did not possess features present in the training set (ref. 62).

(b) The ADAPT Method

The ADAPT program has been used to analyze several carcinogen databases. Various combinations of descriptors including fragment, substructure, molecular connectivity, environment (based on nearest neighbouring atoms), atomic changes, hydrophobicity and molar refractivity have been employed (ref. 65). The ADAPT program uses pattern recognition techniques to search for a discriminant which separates carcinogens from non-carcinogens. This program correctly separated 90 to 95% of carcinogens from non-carcinogens within a group of 209 chemicals. Using a random set of 30 chemicals, its predictive value was 85.3%, with carcinogens being identified 90% of the time and non-carcinogens being identified 78% of the time (ref. 66).

(c) CASE Method

This uses the concept of structural analogy to identify molecular descriptor structure fragments in the training set of chemicals that are associated with carcinogenic or mutagenic activity (or lack thereof). The method then proceeds to analyze a new molecule for potential activity against a set of descriptors.

The activity of a new compound is predicted based on the probability that fragments overlapping with those in the training set are relevant to activity. A database containing 200 PAHs that was analyzed using ADAPT (ref. 67) was also analyzed using CASE, to compare the two systems (ref. 68). With ADAPT, 95% of 200 PAHs were correctly placed as carcinogens using 28 descriptors, while 89% were correctly placed using CASE. Although, CASE did not predict as well as ADAPT for this database, CASE was more versatile since only structures of the compounds were required. ADAPT requires prior knowledge on the compound from the researchers and is therefore more accurate with well-studied databases. CASE is also less restricted than the Enslein approach since CASE creates its own set of fragments and does not rely on an independent dictionary (ref. 62).

The other biological end points include mutagenicity, toxicity, bioaccumulation, enzyme induction and other biological effects.

Toxicity

QSAR studies have been used with a variety of chemicals in the field of aquatic toxicology. Various structural and physico-chemical parameters have been correlated with toxic effects on several aquatic organisms.

A congeneric series of 28 unsubstituted PAHs were assessed for toxic effects in Daphnia. A negative correlation was found to exist between log LC_{50} and a lower order molecular connectivity index ($r = 0.9972$ to 0.9970) as well as between log LC_{50} and log P ($r = 0.9989$ to 0.9975). These high correlation coefficients are encouraging but they may be somewhat misleading since a small data set was used (ref. 69).

Molecular shape (ring number or chain length) was correlated with toxicity. Log K_{ow} was shown as a poor descriptor of toxicity for a heterogeneous group of chemicals. More molecular structure descriptors are needed to split the chemicals into toxicologically significant functional groups.

Structure toxicity relationships were used to determine whether LC_{50s} could be predicted from LD_{50s} which are better basis for structure-activity relationships (ref. 70). LD_{50s} and LC_{50s} for rainbow trout for 48 organic chemicals were measured to determine whether LC_{50} could be predicted from LD_{50}. A simple linear-regression of log-transformed data provided a good fit ($r = 0.70$) but it accounted for only 50% of the variability in LC_{50s}. Since LC_{50s} are strongly associated with molecular size, factors such as molecular weight and parachor were included in the analysis. It was found that these were not true independent variables and were not used further. Instead, a multiple regression analysis using both LD_{50} and K_{ow} predicted LC_{50} with greater certainty ($r = 0.92$) than did either factor alone (Fig. 5.20). LC_{50s} are used extensively in aquatic hazard assessments.

The relationship between 48-h fish LC_{50} and log K_{ow}, molecular weight, organic and inorganic characteristics and molecular connectivity indices were studied for a heterogeneous set of 123 organic chemicals (ref. 71). Correlation of molecular connectivity indices and log LC_{50} gave a very good fit ($r = 0.829$) and it was further improved by combining molecular connectivity indices with log K_{ow} ($r = 0.876$). This shows that a simple and reliable method to predict the behaviour of a new chemical is to measure its log K_{ow} and derive its molecular connectivity indices.

In another study (ref. 72) on the acute toxicity of p-substituted nitro-benzene derivatives, it was confirmed that the toxicity depended on the differential of the charge built-up on the oxygen atoms (dQOx) of the nitro group. With this single independent variable (computed from ab initio STO-3G molecular orbitals calculations), a highly significant linear correlation, covering over three orders of magnitude of toxicity, was obtained.

For p-substituted aniline compounds, it was shown that the compounds have to be subdivided into groups of electron withdrawing and electron donating substituents. Overall, the results indicated a significant process in the ability to predict the acute toxicity of nitro and amino group containing molecular descriptors.

$$\log \text{ LC50} = -0.1014 - 0.6846 \text{ log KOW} + 0.8315 \text{ log LD50}$$

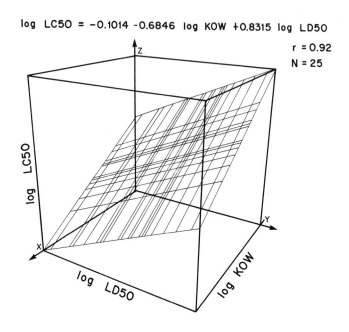

r = 0.92
N = 25

Fig. 5.20. Relationship between LD_{50}, K_{ow}, and LC_{50} for rainbow trout; N = 25, r = 0.92.
(Source: Reprinted with permission from ref. 70).

Structure-activity relationship are being applied to interspecies toxicity extrapolations, in order to gain better understanding of the variability. Analyses are being performed to reveal structural feature characteristics of chemicals that deviate substantially from the interspecies regression (ref. 73).

The main problem with these techniques described here is that predictive values is limited to group of chemicals and their defined boundaries. This requires a prior knowledge about a chemical for comparison with chemicals of its own class which may not be available for a new and untested chemical.

REFERENCES

1   OECD, Existing Chemicals - Systematic Investigation, Organization for Economic Cooperation and Development, Paris, France, 1986, 223 p.
2   R.V. Thoman, Can. J. Fish Aqua. Sci. 38 (1981) 280-296.
3   J.R. Roberts, M.F. Mitchell, M.J. Boddington, and J.M. Ridgeway-Part I: J.R. Roberts, M.T. McGarrity, and W.K. Marshall-Part II, A Screen for Relative Persistence of Lipophilic Organic Chemicals in Aquatic Ecosystems - An Analysis of the Role of a Simple Computer Model in Screening, National Research Council of Canada, NRCC Publication No. 18570, 1981.
4   H. Konemann and R. Visser, Chemosphere 17 (1988) 1905-1919.
5   D. Mackay and S. Paterson, Environ. Sci. Technol. 15 (1981) 1006-1014.
6   M. Timmer, H. Koneman, and R. Visser, Chemosphere 17 (1988) 1921-1934.
7   Ontario Ministry of Environment (OME), Vector Scoring System for the Prioritization of Environmental Contaminants, Final Report-I, OME, Ontario, Canada, 1988, 84 p.
8   Ontario Ministry of the Environment (OME), Scoring System - A Scoring System for Assessing Environmental Contaminants, January 1990.
9   D. Mackay and A.W. Wolkoff, Environ. Sci. Technol. 7 (1973) 611-614.
10 P.S. Liss and P.G. Slater, Nature 247 (1974) 181-184.
11 D. Mackay and P.J. Leinonen, Environ. Sci. Technol. 9 (1975) 1178-1180.
12 C.T. Chiou and V.H. Freed, Chemodynamics Studies on Benchmark Industrial Chemicals, MSF/RA-770286, MTIS PB 274263, 1977.
13 J.H. Smith, D.C. Bamberger, and D.S. Haynes, Environ. Sci. Technol. 14 (1980) 1332-1337.
14 W.J. Lyman, W.T. Reehl, and D.H. Rosenblatt, Handbook of Chemical Property Estimation Methods - Environmental Behaviour of Organic Compounds, McGraw Hill, New York, U.S.A., 1982.
15 Y. Cohen, W. Coccio, and D. Mackay, Environ. Sci. Technol. 12 (1978) 553-558.
16 T.P.H. Gowda and J.D. Lock, J. Environ. Eng., 111 (1985) 755-776.
17 R.E. Rathburn and D.Y. Tai, J. Env. Eng. Div., ASCE 108(EE5) (1982) 973-989.
18a J.H. Smith and D.C. Bomberger, Jr., Chemosphere, 10 (1981) 281-289.
18b J.H. Smith, W.R. Mabey, N. Bohonos, B.R. Holt, S.S. Lee, T.-W. Chou, D.C. Bomberger, and T. Mill, Environmental Pathways of Selected Chemicals in Freshwater Systems, U.S. EPA, Publications Nos. 600/7-77-113 and 600/7-78-074, 1978.
19 A.J. Dobbs, Chemosphere, 13 (1984) 687-692.
20 A.J. Dobbs and M.R. Cull, Environ. Pollut. (Series B) 3 (1982) 289-298.
21 S. Ramamoorthy and B.R. Rust, Environ. Geol., 2 (1978) 165-172.
22 R. Van Blodel and A. Moreale, J. Soil Sci., 28 (1977) 93-102.
23 E.E. Kenaga and C.A.I. Goring, in J.G. Eaton, P.R. Parish, and A.C. Hendricks (Editors), Proceedings of the 3rd Symposium on Aquatic Toxicology, American Society of Testing Materials, Philadelphia, U.S.A., 1980, pp. 78-115.
24 S.W. Karickoff, D.S. Brown, and T.A. Scott, Wat. Res., 13 (1979) 241-248.
25 C.T. Chiou, L.J. Peters, and V.H. Freed, Science, 206 (1979) 831-832.
26 P.S.C. Rao and J.M. Davidson, in M.R. Overcash and J.M. Davidson (Editors), Environmental Impact of Non-point Source Pollution, Ann Arbor Science Publishers, Ann Arbor, Michigan, U.S.A., 1980.
27 G.G. Briggs, in Proc. 7th British Insecticide and Fungicide Conf., The Boots Company Ltd., Nottingham, Great Britain, Vol. I, 1973.
28 T. Mill, in R. Haque (Editor), Dynamics, Exposure and Hazard Assessment of Toxic Chemicals, Ann Arbor Science Publishers, Ann Arbor, Michigan, U.S.A., 1980, pp. 297-322.
29 A.J. Lieb, D.D. Bills, and R.O. Sinnhuber, J. Agri. Food. Chem. 22 (1974) 638-642.
30 R.J. Hall and E. Kolbe, J. Toxic. Environ. Hlth, 6 (1980) 853-860.
31 R.P. Davies and A.J. Dobbs, Water Res. 18 (1985) 1253-1262.
32 P.Y. Lu and R.L. Metcalf, Environ. Hlth. Persp. 10 (1975) 269-284.

33 C.T. Chiou, V.H. Freed, D.W. Schmedding, and R.L. Kohnert, Environ. Sci. Technol. 11 (1977) 475-478.
34 G.D. Veith, K.J. Macek, S.R. Petrocelli, and J. Carroll, in Aquatic Toxicology, ASTM STP 707, 1980, pp. 116-129.
35 R.L. Metcalf, I.P. Kapoor, P.Y. Lu, C.K. Schuth, and P. Sherman. Environ. Hlth. Persp., 1973, pp. 35-44.
36 K. Kobayashi, Proceedings of OECD Workshop on the Control of Existing Chemicals, Unwelltrandesant, Berlin, 1981, pp. 141-163.
37 W.B. Neely, D.R. Branson, and G.E. Blau, Environ. Sci. Technol. 8 (1974) 1113-1115.
38 G.D. Veith, D.L. Defoe, and B.V. Bergstedt, J. Fish. Res. Bd. Can. 36 (1979) 1040-1048.
39 J.C. Skea, H.A. Simonin, H.J. Dean, J.R. Colquhoun, J.J. Spagnoli, G.D. Veith, Bull. Environ. Contam. Toxicol. 22 (1979) 332-336.
40 W.T. Waller and G.T. Lee, Environ. Sci. Technol. 13 (1979) 79-85.
41 Y.A. Greichus, A. Greichus, and R.J. Emerick, Bull. Environ. Contam. Toxicol. 9 (1973) 321-328.
42 J.L. Hamelink, R.C. Waybrant, and P.R. Yant, in R. Suffet (Editor), Fate of Pollutants in the Air and Water Environments, Part 2, John Wiley & Sons, New York, U.S.A., 1977.
43 A. Spacie, J.T. Hamelink, Environ. Sci. Technol. 13 (1979) 817-822.
44 S. Banerjee, S.H. Yalkowsky, and S.C. Valrani, Environ. Sci. Technol., 14 (1980) 1227-1229.
45 G. Kortum, W. Vogel, and K. Andrussow, Dissociation Constants of Organic, Acids in Aqueous Solution, Butterworths, London, U.K., 1961.
46 W. Mabey and T. Mill, J. Phys. Chem. Ref. Data, 7 (1978) 383-415.
47 I.J. Tinsley, Chemical Concepts in Pollutant Behaviour, Wiley, New York, U.S.A., 1979, 265 p.
48 D.M. Gates, H.J. Keegan, J.C. Schleter, and V.R. Weidner, Applied Optics, 4 (1965) 11-20.
49 Tyler, J.E., Transmission of Sunlight in Natural Water Bodies, in Symposium on Abiological Transport and Transformation of Pollutants on Land and Water: Processes and Critical Data Required for Predictive Description, National Bureau of Standards, Gaithersburg, U.S.A., May 11-13, 1976.
50 W.M. Mabey, T. Mill, and D.G. Hendry, Test Protocols in Environmental Processes: Direct Photolysis in Water, U.S. EPA, Publication No. EPA-68-03-2227, 1979.
51 J.W. Moore and S. Ramamoorthy, Organic Chemicals in Natural Waters. Applied Monitoring and Impact Assessment, Springer-Verlag, New York, U.S.A., 1984, 289 p.
52 R. Haque, Dynamics, Exposure and Hazard Assessment of Toxic Chemicals, Ann Arbor Science, Ann Arbor, Michigan, U.S.A., 1980, 496 p.
53 C. Hansh and A. Leo, Substituent Constants for Correlation Analysis in Chemistry and Biology, Wiley, New York, U.S.A., 1979.
54 N.A. Egarova, G.N. Krasovskij, and R. Koch, Chemosphere 11 (1982) 915-919.
55 K.L.E. Kaiser (Editor), QSAR in Environmental Toxicology, D. Reidel Publishing Co., Dordrecht, Holland, 1984, 406 p.
56 K.L.E. Kaiser (Editor), QSAR in Environmental Toxicology, D. Reidel Publishing Co., Dordrecht, Holland, 1987, 465 p.
57 J. Arcos, Environ. Sci. Technol. 8 (1987) 743-745.
58 S. Balaz, E. Sturdik, I. Dibus, L. Stibranyi, and M. Rosenberg, Chem-Biol. Interact. 55 (1985) 93-108.
59 E. Sturdik, M. Rosenberg, L. Stibranyi, S. Balaz, O. Cherno, L. Ebringer, D. Ilavsky, and D. Vegh, Chem-Biol. Interact. 53 (1985) 145-153.
60 W.A. Vance and D.E. Levin, Environ. Mutagen 6 (1984) 797-811
61 C. Hansch and T. Fujita, J. Am. Chem. Soc. 86 (1964) 1615-1626. Cited in ref. 62.
62 M.R. Frierson, G. Klopman, and H.S. Rosenkvanz, Environ. Mutagen. 8 (1986) 283-327.
63 R. Koch, Chemosphere, 9 (1982) 925-931.
64 K. Enslein and P.N. Craig, J. Toxicol. Environ. Health, 10 (1982) 521-530.

65 A.J. Stuper, W.E. Brugger, and P.C. Jurs, in B.R. Kowalski (Editor), Chemometrics: Theory and Application, ACS Symposium Series 52, American Chemical Society, Washington, D.C., 1977, pp. 165-191, cited in ref. 62.
66 P.C. Jurs, J.T. Chou, and M. Yuan, J. Med. Chem., 22 (1979) 476-483.
67 M. Yuan and P.C. Jurs, J. Toxicol. & Appl. Pharmacol., 52 (1980) 294-312.
68 G. Klopman and M.R. Frierson, CASE Analysis of Dipple Database of 200 PAHs, 1986, In preparation, Cited in ref. 62.
69 H. Grovers, C. Ruepert, and H. Aiking, Chemosphere, 13 (1984) 227-236.
70 P.V. Hodson, D.E. Dixon, and K.L.E. Kaiser, Environ. Toxicol. & Chem., 7 (1988) 443-454.
71 Y. Yoshioka, T. Mizuno, Y. Ose, and T. Sato, Chemosphere, 15 (1986) 195-203.
72 K.M. Gough and K.L.E. Kaiser, in J.E. Turnes (Editor) QSAR-88, Proceedings of the 3rd International Workshop on QSAR in Environmental Toxicology, NTIS. Conf. 880520, 1988, pp. 111-121.
73 K.B. Wallace and G.J. Niemi, Environ. Toxicol. Chem. 7 (1988) 201-212.

Chapter 6

HAZARD EVALUATION

Hazard evaluation is strictly a scientific process which estimates the probabilities of hazard using the best available scientific information about the dispersion of a chemical in the environment and the associated effect on the ecosystem and human health. Once the hazards of a chemical and the exposure routes are determined, the prevention and control of the exposure and the adverse effects is a judgemental process involving socio-economic and political considerations. Each society will have a particular legal, economic and administrative framework for making regulatory decisions on the control measures either mandatory or advisory.

6.1 HAZARD IDENTIFICATION

Hazard is defined as a set of circumstances with a potential for causing adverse health effects or harm on humans. In the case of chemicals, adverse health effects (toxicity) can be produced at some dose or under specific exposure conditions. For a chemical to be hazardous, it has to be toxic at the level of environmental concentration and for the duration of the exposure. In brief, the dose makes the chemical a hazard. In contrast, there are chemicals whose exposure at all levels of concentrations will produce a particular type of toxicity called genotoxicity, such as carcinogenicity, teratogenicity, etc. These are also hazards. Hazard identification requires both qualitative and quantitative information on genetic toxicity and non-genetic toxicity of chemicals acting either singly or in groups. This information is derived from chemical, physical, toxicological, clinical, and epidemiological data. Hazard assessment requires the knowledge of exposure concentration of the chemical to correlate against the toxic effects. The adverse effects rate the chemical as intrinsically hazardous but its presence in the environment <u>makes</u> it hazardous. A very toxic chemical with no exposure potential is not hazardous in the environment. Conversely, a chemical with low toxicity but high exposure level with multiple pathways of exposure could be much more hazardous.

In the last decade, attention was focussed on the capability of physico-chemical processes of a chemical in predicting its fate in the environment (refs. 1-4). This is an essential screening part of hazard identification which has been dealt with in detail in the previous chapter.

6.1.1 Different Aspects of the Hazard Identification Process

   (i) Basic Aspects. In the assessment of the hazards of a chemical substance, at least four distinct aspects may be taken into consideration (ref. 5):

   1. Assessment of the intrinsic properties which play a major role in determining the intrinsic hazards of the chemicals; the classification given in the EEC directive 79/831 is based on intrinsic properties.

   2. The evaluation of further data requirement which are necessary for a more complete evaluation of the intrinsic properties.

   3. Risk Assessment which includes the intrinsic danger in the real world context involving factors such as volume, plurality of exposures, environmental dispersion, persistence, bioaccumulation and size of the population at risk.

   4. Priority ranking of chemicals
      Items (1) and (2) will be discussed in this chapter, and items (3) and (4) are discussed elsewhere in this book.

   (ii) Specific Aspects. Among intrinsic properties, flammability or explosivity relate to direct physical danger. Whereas, properties such as water solubility, lipid solubility, boiling point, relative density with respect to water or air, etc. strictly correlate to ecotoxicological effects. Properties such as vapour pressure and lipid solubility influence inhalation and dermal toxicities and dermal absorption, respectively. It logically follows that physico-chemical properties, toxicological and ecotoxicological properties should be taken into account for hazard identification and hazard assessment.

   Some of the early studies reported in literature examined the relationship of physico-chemical properties of pollutants to their environmental behaviour such as persistence, resistance to degradation, and biomagnification in the food chain. Although it could be argued that fate processes are part of the exposure assessment exercise, they still have a well-deserved place in the hazard identification process, because these properties often dictate their presence in the environment and hence their potential hazards.

   Table 6.1 lists the tests that need to be conducted as screening tests in hazard identification for new chemicals under the Toxic Substances Control Act (TSCA) .

TABLE 6.1 Testing protocol for ecological hazard identification of new
chemicals under TSCA.

I. Chemical fate (transport, persistence)
   A. Transport
      1. Adsorption isotherm (soil)
      2. Partition coefficient (water-octanol)
      3. Water solubility
      4. Vapour pressure
   B. Other physicochemical properties
      1. Boiling/melting/sublimation points
      2. Density
      3. Dissociation constant
      4. Flammability/explodability
      5. Particle size
      6. pH
      7. Chemical incompatibility
      8. Vapour-phase UV spectrum for halocarbons
      9. UV and visible absorption spectra in aqueous solution
   C. Persistence
      1. Biodegradation
         a. Shake flask procedure following carbon loss
         b. Respirometric method following oxygen (BOD) and/or carbon dioxide
         c. Activated sludge test (simulation of treatment plant)
         d. Methane and CO_2 productions in anaerobic digestion
      2. Chemical degradation
         a. Oxidation (free-radical)
         b. Hydrolysis (25^oC, pH 5.0 and 9.0)
      3. Photochemical transformation in water

II. Ecological Effects
   A. Microbial effects
      1. Cellulose decomposition
      2. Ammonification of urea
      3. Sulfate reduction
   B. Plant effects
      1. Algae inhibition (fresh and seawater, growth, nitrogen fixation)
      2. Duck weed inhibition (increase in fronds or dry weight)
      3. Seed germination and early growth
   C. Animal effects testing
      1. Aquatic invertebrates (Daphnia) acute toxicity (first instar)
      2. Fish acute toxicity (96 hr)
      3. Quail dietary LC_{50}
      4. Terrestrial mammal test
      5. Daphnia life cycle test
      6. Mysidopsis bahia life cycle
      7. Fish embryo-juvenile test
      8. Fish bioconcentration test

(Source: Reprinted from ref. 6).

Table 6.2 presents the industry chosen fate processes for evaluation of three existing chemicals.

TABLE 6.2 Fate processes chosen to evaluate some selected chemicals.

TEST TYPE	NTA[a]	TYPE A ZEOLITE[b]	LAS[c]
Screening Tests			
CO_2 evolution	95% (TCO_2)	N.A. (inorganic)	>95% (TCO_2)
Octanol-water partition coefficient	N.A.[d] (ionic salt)	N.A. (insoluble in octanol)	125
Microbial inhibition	N.A. (CO_2 evolution tests demonstrate no inhibition)	N.A. (insoluble, unreactive)	N.A. (CO_2 evolution test demonstrate no inhibition)
Semicontinuous activated sludge	92% removal efficiency	80-90% removal	>91% removal efficiency
Settling test	N.A. (water soluble)	40-60% removal	N.A. (water soluble)
Confirmatory Tests			
Adsorption isotherms	<30% on organic and inorganic solids	N.A.	Some affinity for organics and inorganics; effective in removal from water
Hydrolysis rate	N.A. (stable in acids and bases)	Half-life approx. 55 days	N.A. ($TCO_2 \sim$90%)
Metal complexation	Readily complexes metals	Readily complexes metals	N.A.
Ozonation	N.A. ($TCO_2 \sim$90%)	N.A.	N.A. ($TCO_2 \sim$90%)
Chlorination	N.A. ($TCO_2 \sim$90%)	N.A.	N.A. ($TCO_2 \sim$90%)
Photolysis	N.A. ($TCO_2 \sim$90%)	N.A.	N.A. ($TCO_2 \sim$90%)
Biodegradation rates	N.A. ($TCO_2 \sim$90%)	N.A. (inorganic)	N.A. ($TCO_2 \sim$90%)
Continuous activated sludge	>90% removal efficiency	>90% removal efficiency	>90% removal efficiency
Biological inhibition of wastewater treatment process	N.A. (CO_2 tests demonstrate no inhibition)	N.A.	N.A. (CO_2 tests demonstrate no inhibition)
Sludge properties	N.A. (water soluble)	No effects on settleability	N.A. (water soluble)

[a] NTA = Sodium salt of nitrilotriacetic acid
[b] Type A Zeolite = Sodium alumino silicate
[c] LAS = Linear alkyl benzene sulphonate
[d] Guidelines indicate test is not needed or applicable
(Source: Reprinted with permission from ref. 7, Copyright (1981), Academic Press).

A brief discussion of some of the physico-chemical properties and their usefulness in hazard identification is provided below:

Water Solubility

The extent of water solubility of a chemical determines its residence time in water which in turn allows the chemical for long-range transport, as well as undergo biotic and abiotic fate processes related to the aquatic environment. Chemicals with low aqueous solubility will undergo rapid sorption to suspended solids, sediment/soil, or bioaccumulate in aquatic organisms. Hence, a knowledge of the chemical's water solubility along with its volatilization rate from the water column (Henry's law constant) will help to formulate appropriate experimental designs to test its ecotoxicity. In many cases, inaccurate values of water solubility for a chemical has led to false-positive toxicity information. Table 6.3 presents the volatilization rate and the half-life for volatilizational loss for lindane from water along with the calculated value of H, Henry's constant (ref. 8). The partitioning of lindane in an aquatic system and the various fate processes operating in that system are given in Fig. 6.1. A mass balance showed < 1% of the total added lindane was in the water column. The fate processes and their role in the residual aquatic concentration of the chemical have to be assessed in interpreting dose-response relationship for a given chemical. Many other fate processes such as hydrolysis, redox reactions, biodegradation, and photodegradation are interdependent on each other and, to a greater extent, influenced by the aqueous solubility of the chemical (Fig. 6.2). The difficulties in measuring accurately the aqueous solubility of organic chemicals are discussed elsewhere (refs. 12,13).

Hydrolysis and biodegradation are considered to be the most important fate processes for organic chemicals in the aquatic environment and photodegradation is most important in the vapour or gaseous phase (Fig. 6.2). In the soil environment, biodegradation, and to some extent, chemical degradation are considered important in the fate of organic chemicals. Therefore, for chemicals of concern in the aquatic environment or soil, hydrolysis and biodegradation tests should be conducted first. If the chemical is resistant to all degradation processes, including direct photodegradation (where the chemical absorbs light in the ultraviolet region (<300 nm), then the chemical is likely to persist in the environment leading to eventual bioaccumulation.

TABLE 6.3 Henry's law constant, volatilization rate constant (K^v) from water and the half-life ($t_{1/2}$) for volatilizational loss from water for lindane.

PARAMETER	EQUATION USED	CALC. VALUE	LIT. VALUE
H, Henry's law constant	$H = \dfrac{vP(mm\ Hg) \times M.W. \times 16.04^a}{Tk \times S}$ where vP = Vapour pressure MW = Molecular weight Tk = Temperature in 0 Kelvin and S = Solubility in water in ug mL^{-1}	0.202*	
k^v, volatilization rate constant from water	$k^v = \dfrac{1}{d[3.1407 \times 10^{-4}\sqrt{MW} + (2.0413 \times 10^{-4} \times Tk \times Sx\sqrt{MW/vP})]}{}^{a}$ where d = Depth in cm MW = Molecular weight Tk = Temperature in 0 Kelvin S = Aqueous solubility (moles L^{-1}) at T^{0}K vP = Vapour pressure (mm Hg) at T^{0}K	0.365* cm day^{-1}	0.240^b cm day^{-1}
$t_{1/2}$, half-life for volatilization loss from water	$t_{1/2} = \dfrac{0.693 \times d}{k^v}$ where d = Depth in cm k^v = Rate constant for volatilization of lindane from water	1.9 days (for 1 cm depth) 199 days (1 m depth)	2.89 days^c (1 cm depth) 289 days (1 m depth)

a Ref. 9; b Ref. 10; c Ref. 11; * Vapour pressure of 9.4 $\times$ 10^{-6} mm of Hg and aqueous solubility of 7.3 ug mL^{-1} for lindane at 25°C were used.

(Source: Reprinted with permission from ref. 8, Copyright (1985), Springer-Verlag).

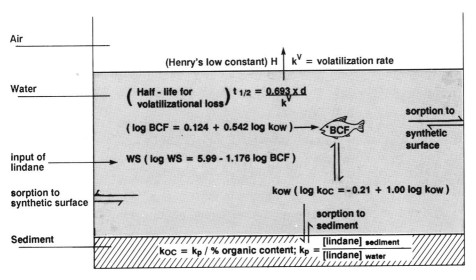

Fig. 6.1. Partitioning of lindane in an aquatic system.
(Source: Reprinted with permission from ref. 8, Copyright (1985), Springer-Verlag).

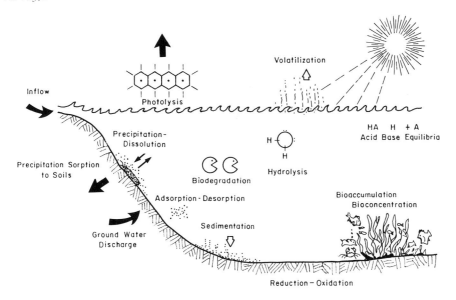

Fig. 6.2. Pathways of degradation and migration of xenobiotics in the environment.
(Source: Reprinted with permission from ref. 14, Copyright (1985), John Wiley & Sons, Inc.).

TABLE 6.4 Terms and definitions commonly used in aquatic toxicology studies.

TERM	DEFINITION
Uptake	Active movement of a chemical into or onto an aquatic organism from surrounding water column.
Depuration	Elimination of a chemical from an organism by several pathways such as excretion, metabolism with subsequent clearance, diffusion, etc. Depuration takes place when the previously exposed organisms are held in water free of any contaminants.
Half-life	Time taken for an organism to eliminate 50% of its total concentration of the chemical when it is held in clean water devoid of exposure.
Steady-state condition	The equilibrium point at which the rates of uptake and clearance of a chemical by an organism are dynamically equal. The concentration of the chemical is essentially constant during a continuous exposure.
Partition coefficient K_{ow}	Ratio of concentrations of a chemical between n-octanol and water. Characteristics of n-octanol closely resemble lipid of aquatic biota such as fish.
Bioavailability	Fraction of the total chemical that is available for uptake by biota from the encompassing environment such as water, sediments, suspended solids.
Bioconcentration	The accumulation of a chemical in a living organism to levels higher than the surrounding aqueous concentration. Bioconcentration factors (concentration in biota/concentration in water) are measured at the steady-state conditions and values could range from $10-10^6$, depending on the lipid solubility of the chemical.
Biomagnification	The process by which a chemical concentrates in an organism in amounts greater than the surrounding ecosystem through food chain and via bioconcentration, e.g., invertebrates bioconcentrate sediment-bound chemicals which are eaten by small fish which, in turn, are consumed by larger fish which are eaten by birds or humans.

(Source: Adapted with permission partially from ref. 15, Copyright (1985), Hemisphere Publishing Corp.).

Fate processes such as direct and indirect photodegradation, bioconcentration, volatilization, redox reactions and metabolic transformations have been discussed in detail in Chapter 5. The predictive capabilities of fate processes for the estimated presence of chemicals in environmental media such as air, water, soil and biota, their residence time in each media have also been discussed in Chapter 5.

The various testing procedures listed in Table 6.1 to determine the persistence of a chemical in the environment will be briefly discussed here.

Biodegradation

Biotic species such as microorganisms and particularly bacteria and fungi, use their metabolic activities to break down complex organic chemical molecules to simple end-products. This process is called biodegradation which can occur in soil, sediment and the water column. Depending upon the structure of the parent chemical and on the type of biodegradation process, the type of end-products could vary. For example, in an aerobic biodegradation (in the presence of oxygen), the end-products are carbon dioxide and water and may also include: (1) the normal metabolic products of aerobic microorganisms; and (2) nitrates and sulphates. In the case of anaerobic biodegradation (where oxygen is absent) the total degradation could yield end-points such as methane, carbon monoxide, and carbon dioxide. End-products might also include some organic compounds that are commonly encountered in the anaerobic microorganisms involved in the normal metabolic process (ref. 16).

Carbon Dioxide Evolution Test Methods

This is a test recommended to evaluate the extent of biodegradation of xenobiotics to carbon dioxide and water in natural systems. The test is applicable to all chemicals irrespective of water solubility or vapour pressure. The measure of biodegradation is given by the ratio of the amount of carbon dioxide produced over a given period over the theoretical amount that could be produced from that chemical. Results are rated positive if the carbon dioxide produced exceeded 50% of the theoretically expected amounts from the test chemical. Positive test results indicate that the test chemical will not persist indefinitely in the soil system, but reliable biodegradation in the environment may not be assumed (ref. 16).

Whereas, the negative results from the test (less than 50% of CO_2 (theoretically) expected from the test chemical) cannot be used to make definitive conclusion on the fate of the xenobiotic in soil. A range of possible scenarios could exist; molecular resistance, resistance because the chemical is sequestered by complexation or sorption, partial breakdown, incomplete breakdown, i.e., breakdown but not all the way to carbon dioxide and water, etc. In short, this test is only a screening test. When screening test is negative, tests should be run to analyze for partial breakdown to end-products other than CO_2 and H_2O, and also degradation should be tested under different operating conditions (refs. 14,16).

Extrapolation of laboratory-generated biodegradation results to the natural environmental conditions is difficult because of the difficulty in simulating the environmental variables such as temperature, pH, oxygen level, viable microorganisms and the type of microbial species (ref. 6). The test concentrations of the chemical in most laboratory studies are much higher than the field conditions, thus making the kinetic data on degradation rates non-extrapolatable to natural environment. Use of a radio labelled test chemical or use of an analytical technique specific for the test chemical, allows the determination of lower test concentration of the chemical. This allows low-level reactions and toxicity to become operable. It also makes the extrapolation of laboratory results to the natural environment to be as close as possible and valid.

A study on the effect of microbial life stages on the fate of methyl mercury under conditions similar to natural water incorporated these requirements. They were: (1) use of radio labelled methylmercuric chloride $(CH_3^{203}HgCl)$; and (2) use of concentration of 100 $\mu g/L$ of mercury concentration in sediments which simulated severe mercury contamination conditions in natural waters (ref. 17). The purpose of the study was to investigate the degradation of methylmercury by living or thermally killed bacteria (Escherichia coli) and pseudomonas fluorescens), or the blue-green algae, Anabaena flos-aquae. In addition, degradation of methylmercury by growing bacteria was also studied (ref. 17).

Living microorganisms had a strong effect on the fate of methylmercuric chloride (MMC). A suspension of Pseudomonas fluorescens sorbed 81.3% of the added MMC in the first 12 h and degraded it to mercuric chloride (MC), about 90% in 72 h. The overlying waterphase contained very small amounts of MMC and MC (Table 6.5). E. coli took up MMC rapidly but degraded it slowly; about 50.6% in 7 d. The rate of degradation increased with the increasing concentration of bacterial cells (Table 6.5).

Anabaena flos-aquae sorbed 81.8% of the added MMC in the first 12 h and degraded 83.4% of MMC to MC in 7 d (Table 6.5). Whereas, sediment sorbed all of MMC in 7 d and degraded 35% of it to MC after 7 d and 55% in 28 d (Fig. 6.3).

TABLE 6.5   Distribution of mercury species in different phases of natural
water systems at 7th day.

PHASES	MC (%)	MMC (%)
Deionized water	12.3	86.0
Deionized water[+]	27.9	71.6
Ottawa River water	11.6	87.2
Ottawa River water[+]	28.1	71.2
Water column overlying sediment	1.2	0.5
Sediment	34.1	62.8
Water column overlying living Pseudomonas fluorescens	4.6	1.5
Living Pseudomonas fluorescens	90.0	3.7
Water column overlying thermally killed Pseudomonas fluorescens[+]	1.7	32.4
Thermally killed Pseudomonas fluorescens[+]	14.5	51.4
Water column overlying living Escherichia coli	2.0	2.0
Living Escherichia coli	50.6	44.5
Water column overlying thermally killed Escherichia coli[+]	1.9	35.2
Thermally killed Escherichia coli[+]	14.2	48.7
Water column overlying living Anabaena flos-aquae	4.8	0.6
Living Anabaena flos-aquae	83.4	8.7

Amount of sediment = 10.0 gm in wet weight
Amount of biota = 0.45 gm in wet weight
Added mercury concentration = 0.10 ppm (μg/mL)
MC = Inorganic mercury
MMC = Methylmercury
[+] = Experiments done 10 months later.
(Source: Reprinted with permission from ref. 17, Copyright (1982), Springer-Verlag).

Results of studies on degradation of MMC and MC to the volatile form of
mercury by growing bacterial cultures are given in Fig. 6.4.

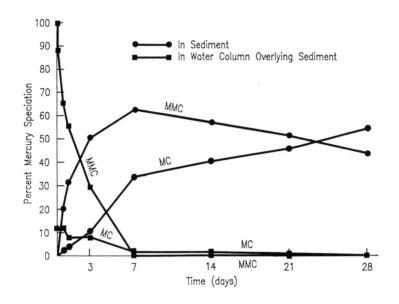

Fig. 6.3. Stability of methylmercury in river water-sediment system.
(Source: Reprinted with permission from ref. 17, Copyright (1982), Springer-
Verlag).

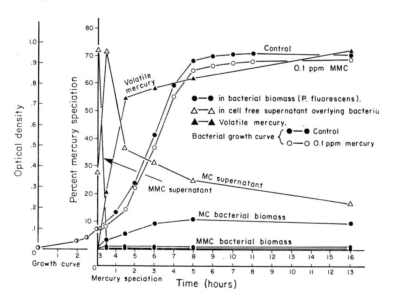

Fig. 6.4. Transformation of methylmercury in cultures of growing bacteria in
Peptone-Yeast Extract Broth medium.
(Source: Reprinted with permission from ref. 17, Copyright (1982), Springer-
Verlag).

The results from this study show that the physiological state of micro-organisms can greatly affect the way in which they deal with contaminants including organic chemicals, their speciation and hence, the amounts of the toxic compounds present.

Abiotic processes such as hydrolysis, photodegradation and oxidation can transform organic chemicals but the accompanied structural changes are only minor alterations. Whereas, biodegradation process using the metabolic processes have the energy and specificity to impact major alterations in the chemical's structure and stability (ref. 6).

Algal Assay

Algae are simple photosynthetic organism found in habitats which receive sufficient sunlight and moisture. They include moist soils and surfaces exposed to air, to freshwater ponds, lakes, reservoirs, stream, estuaries, and oceans (ref. 18). It is probable that a significant portion of the global photosynthesis is carried out by algae and they play a major role among the aquatic components in the fixation of energy from sunlight. The important role played by algae in the ecosystem are outlined below:

1. The oxygen generated in the photosynthetic process is utilized by aquatic organisms and also becomes a part of the global reservoir of atmospheric oxygen.
2. Algae assists in transforming organic wastes to stable effluents (ref. 18).
3. Algae are the foundation of most aquatic food chains and are utilized by many herbivores as a major food source.
4. Algae are very important in the dynamic operation of aquatic ecosystems (ref. 19,20). For example, algal growth rate, diversity, abundance, maximal standing crop and photosynthetic rate have profound effects on aquatic food chains and other pathways of aquatic food web (ref. 14).

The toxicity of heavy metals to freshwater algae is well documented (refs. 21-23) and also laboratory experiments have shown that freshwater algae concentrate heavy metal ions (refs. 24,25). Studies have been reported on the excretion of extra-cellular water-soluble chelators (refs. 26-28). A long-term study was conducted in situ in a low-nutrient status lake to determine: (1) whether there was a correlation between algal biomass and heavy metal-binding in natural lake systems; and (2) which species were actually responsible for the binding (ref. 29). Large polyethylene containers (each 10 m deep and 1 m diameter) were subjected to a variety of treatments and manipulations to relate changes in metal binding to algal community distributions. The results are given in Fig. 6.5 and Tables 6.6 and 6.7.

244

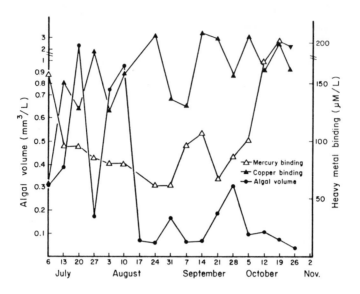

Fig. 6.5. Weekly fluctuations of total algal volume and binding activity of Cu^{2+} and Hg^{2+} in surface samples from an enriched enclosure in contact with sediment.
(Source: Reprinted with permission from ref. 29, Copyright (1978), Can. J. Fish. Aquat. Sci.).

Long-term experiments conducted on a low nutrient status lake in Canada, showed that the binding capacity for the metal ions, Cu^{2+}, Hg^{2+}, Pb^{2+}, and Cd^{2+} to be related to algal species composition rather than to total algal biomass or physico-chemical parameters. Most of the binding could be accounted by certain species of green algae, diatoms, and chrysomonads that usually constituted only a minor fraction of the total algal volume (ref. 29).

Interference with the normal algal production from nutrient enrichment lead to overproduction of algal communities. This may cause taste and odour problems and more seriously, oxygen-depleted situations in surface waters. This condition might be lethal to fish and adversely affect commercial and sport fishing. Some algae under stress release extracellular chemical compounds which could be harmful to aquatic organisms. Hence, it is important to assess the effect of the chemical on this group of organisms, namely, algae eventhough the results may not exactly be extrapolated to natural environment.

TABLE 6.6 Positive correlation coefficients (r ≥ 0.30) between heavy metal binding activity and phytoplankton species volume in 504 samples from enclosures and lake. Statistically significant correlations indicated as follows: *for P<0.05; **for P<0.01; ***P<0.001.

ALGAE	METAL			
	Cu	Hg	Pb	Cd
Greens				
Ankistrodesmus falcatus			0.31	
Coelastrum microporum		0.44*		
Cosmarium impressulum				0.35*
Elakatothrix gelatinosa	0.54	0.51		
Euastrum insulare	0.47*			
Scenedesmus dimorphus			0.32	
S. obliquus		0.31***		
S. quadricauda		0.44**		
Schroederia setigera			0.91***	
Staurastrum paradoxum			0.30	
Tetraedron minimum		0.33		
Blue-greens				
Anabaena spiroides	0.30*	0.52***		
Diatoms				
Stephanodiscus niagarae		0.44		
Cyclotella meneghiniana		0.34		
Cymbella sp.		0.73***		
Melosira granulata			0.32	
Rhizosolenia eriensis			0.30**	
Others				
Cryptomonas ovata		0.64*		
Dinobryon bavaricum	0.60	0.43		
D. divergens	0.53		0.46	0.52

(Source: Reprinted with permission from ref. 29, Copyright (1978), Can. J. Fish. Aquat. Sci.).

TABLE 6.7 Percentage contribution of specific algae to total algal volume in surface samples from an enriched enclosure in contact with sediment. Data correspond to those on which Fig. 6.5 is based.

ALGAE	JULY				AUG.					SEPT.				OCT.			
	6	13	20	27	3	10	17	24	31	7	14	21	28	5	12	19	26
Ankistrodesmus falcatus	2.0	--	0.1	--	--	--	1.3	--	--	--	--	--	--	--	--	--	--
Coelastrum microporum	--	40.8	--	--	--	0.6	--	--	--	--	--	--	--	--	--	0.7	--
Cosmarium impressulum	--	62.7	--	--	37.4	70.4	--	--	--	--	--	--	--	--	--	--	--
Elakatothrix gelatinosa	--	--	--	--	--	--	--	--	--	--	--	--	--	--	--	--	--
Euastrum insulare	--	--	--	--	--	--	--	--	--	--	--	--	--	--	--	--	--
Scenedesmus dimorphus	--	0.2	--	--	--	--	--	--	0.2	--	11.8	--	--	--	--	--	--
S. obliquus	--	--	--	--	--	--	--	--	3.5	9.1	--	2.4	2.6	1.1	0.5	2.3	8.7
S. quadricauda	--	--	--	--	--	--	--	--	11.8	--	--	--	--	--	--	--	--
Schroederia setigera	--	--	--	--	--	0.3	20.0	--	15.6	28.9	27.1	--	--	--	--	--	--
Staurastrum paradoxum	--	--	--	--	--	--	--	--	--	--	27.1	53.2	--	--	--	--	--
Anabaena spiroides	--	--	0.6	--	--	--	--	--	--	--	--	--	--	--	--	--	--
Stephanodiscus niagarae	--	7.2	--	31.2	--	--	--	--	--	--	--	--	--	--	--	--	--
Cyclotella meneghiniana	43.4	2.7	0.4	--	--	--	6.1	--	--	--	--	--	--	--	--	7.2	--
Cymbella sp.	2.0	--	--	--	--	--	--	--	--	--	--	--	--	--	--	--	--
Melosira granulata	--	--	--	--	--	--	--	--	--	--	--	--	--	0.4	--	--	--
Rhizosolenia eriensis	--	--	--	--	--	--	--	--	--	--	--	7.3	--	--	--	--	--
Cryptomonas ovata	--	--	0.5	--	--	--	--	--	--	0.2	--	--	--	--	--	--	--
Dinobryon bavaricum	--	1.2	--	--	--	--	--	--	--	--	--	--	--	--	--	--	--
D. divergens	--	4.1	--	--	--	--	--	--	--	--	--	--	--	--	--	--	--
Total	47.4	56.2	64.3	31.2	37.4	71.3	27.4	--	31.1	38.2	38.9	62.9	2.6	1.5	0.5	10.2	8.7

(Source: Reprinted with permission from ref. 29, Copyright (1988), Can. J. Fish. Aquat. Sci.).

Elements of Hazard Identification

Hazard identification should include a review of available information on the following elements (ref. 30):

1. Physical-chemical properties and routes and patterns of exposure.
2. Structure-activity relationships - correlations that support or argue against the prediction of potential toxic effects.
3. Metabolic and pharmacokinetic properties - Information on the mode of action (direct-acting or the converted form is active), metabolic pathways for such conversions, fate (transport, storage and excretion) and variability of effects among species should be discussed and evaluated. Pharmacokinetics determine the biologically effective dose.
4. Toxicologic Effects - Short- and long-term effects on ecotoxicity and genetic toxicity of the chemical.
5. Epidemiologic Studies - Descriptive epidemiologic studies can be used to form hypotheses and provide supporting data but can hardly be used to make any causal deductions. Whereas, analytical epidemiologic studies of the case-control or cohort variety are useful in evaluating risks to the exposed populations compared to the control groups. The criteria for conducting an adequate epidemiologic study include factors such as (i) proper selection and characterization of exposed and control groups; (ii) adequacy of duration; (iii) proper identification and characterization of confounding factors and bias; (iv) consideration of the latency period; (v) valid confirmation of morbidity and death; and (vi) ability to detect specific effects. The weight of evidence from an epidemiologic study increases greatly with confirmation of the chemical's effect on humans from other studies conducted under different conditions but exposed to the same chemical (ref. 30).

Toxicology Testing

Aquatic Toxicity Tests

Aquatic toxicity tests are designed to assess the toxic effects of chemicals, anthropogenic substances, and xenobiotics on aquatic organisms. Toxic effects may include both acute effects (mortality) and chronic effects such as behavioural changes, physiological changes, biochemical changes and histological changes. Aquatic toxicity tests are carried out to determine the concentration of the chemical and duration of exposure to cause a criterion effect. High concentrations of a chemical can cause acute toxicity in relatively short period of exposure. Whereas, chronic effects develop over a period of exposure at concentrations relatively much lower than the acutely lethal concentration.

Toxicity tests have been performed on a variety of freshwater and saltwater species representing algae, fish and invertebrates. Table 6.8 lists the species commonly used in acute toxicity tests (ref. 31).

TABLE 6.8 Species commonly used in acute toxicity tests.

Freshwater

Vertebrates

Rainbow trout	Channel catfish
Brook trout	Bluegill sunfish
Fathead minnow	

Invertebrates

Daphnids	Crayfish
(Daphnia pulex	Snail
Daphnia magna	Amphiphods
Ceredaphnia sp.)	

Saltwater

Vertebrates

Sheepshead Minnow	Stickleback
Mummichog	Pinfish
Silverside	

Invertebrates

Copepods	Blue Crab
Shrimp	Oysters
Grass Shrimp	Polychaetes

(Source: Reprinted with permission from ref. 31, Copyright (1985), Hemisphere Publications).

Criteria on Toxicity Testing

The criteria used in selecting a test procedure may include some of the following elements:

1. The test should be widely accepted by the scientific community.
2. The test should be able to predict the effects of a wide range of chemicals on different species.
3. The test procedures should be statistically sound and should be repeatable in various laboratories producing similar results.
4. The test should be economical and easy to conduct.
5. The test should be sensitive to detect and measure the effect. The data should be amenable for quantification.

For detailed discussions on various aspects of toxicity test procedures such as design, criteria for the selection of species, influence of external factors on toxicity testing, the readers are referred to the treatise on "Fundamentals of Aquatic Toxicology" by Rand and Petrocelli (ref. 31).

Exposure Systems

The exposure of organisms to chemicals can be conducted by the following four different test systems:

1. Static test. In this test, the organisms are exposed to still but aerated water held in a test chamber containing the chemical at desired exposure concentration. Concentrations are adjusted using dilution water. In this design, water is not changed during the test.

2. Recirculation test. This is similar to static test design (1) except that the test solutions and control water are recirculated through a pump. This is to maintain the water quality but not to change the chemical's concentration. This test design is not commonly used for reasons of set-up and maintenance cost and uncertainty about the chemical's concentration due to possible losses at filter, pump, etc.

3. Renewal test. Again, this test design is similar to (1) and conducted in still but aerated water, but the test solution and control water are replaced periodically (usually 24 h). This is done by either transferring the test species to chamber with freshly prepared test solutions or changing the test solutions in the original chambers.

4. Flow-through test. In this design, the test solutions and control water flow in and out of the holding chambers. Metering pumps or diluters control the flow of dilution water and stock solution of the test chemical so that proper proportions of each will be mixed. The flow can be intermittant or continuous. For further details, readers are referred to ref. 31.

The static and flow-through techniques are the most widely used designs of exposure.

Acute Toxicity Testing: Acute toxicity tests are designed to evaluate the adverse effect of a chemical on aquatic organisms and is expressed as the lethal concentration of the chemical which kills 50% of the exposed population of test organisms in a relatively short period of exposure time (LC_{50} 96 h). The exposure period could vary from 24 h to 14 d (ref. 31). In the early developmental stages of acute toxicity testing, information was expressed as the median tolerance limit (TL_m or TL_{50}) which represented the test chemical's concentration at which 50% of the test species survived the specified exposure time (24 to 96 h). This term TL_m or TL_{50} has been replaced by median lethal concentration LC_{50} and median effective concentration EC_{50}. Common effect criterion for fish is mortality; for invertebrates, immobility and loss of equilibrium; and for algae, growth.

Subchronic Toxicity Testing: Subchronic effects are adverse effects that an aquatic organism develops on a relatively long-term exposure or repeated single exposure over a period of time to a chemical. The exposure period is longer than the exposure period for the acute toxicity testing and often up to 90 d in duration. The exposure concentration of the chemical is kept low (usually 1/10 of acute LC_{50} concentration). Because of the length of the exposure period, studies are also conducted to determine time required for clearance or depuration of the chemical by fish in the absence of exposure (in clean water free from the test chemical). This information is essential in determining the effect level since both uptake and clearance processes will proceed in natural waters where fish could migrate over a distance long enough to meet both exposure and clearance conditions. In this test, the test organism is exposed for only a portion of a life cycle including several sensitive life stages, like reproduction and growth in the first year but do not include exposure to very early juvenile stages.

Chronic Toxicity Testing: Absence of acute adverse effects does not rule out the toxicity of the chemical at all concentrations and exposures. Chronic toxicity testing permit the assessment of the possible adverse effects of the chemical during long-term exposure at sublethal concentration of the chemical. In this test, the test organism is exposed for an entire reproductive cycle to at least five concentrations of the test chemical. The exposure cycle will generally begin with an egg or zygote and continues through development and hatching of the embryo, growth and development of the young organism, reaching of sexual maturity and reproduction to the second generation offspring. Tests may also initiate with the exposed adult and continue through egg, fry, juvenile and adult to egg. With fish, exposure begins with fertilized eggs and criteria for full range of effects include: (1) physiological changes (growth reproduction, development, maturity, spawning success, hatching success, and survival of larvae or fry); (2) behavioural changes (swimming pattern, attraction-avoidance, etc.); and (3) biochemical changes (blood enzyme and ion levels). The duration of chronic toxicity testing is approximately 21 d for the water flea Daphnia magna and can be 275 to 300 d for the fathead minnow, Pimphales promelas. Common test species used in chronic toxicity tests are listed in Table 6.9.

TABLE 6.9 Commonly used test species in chronic toxicity testing.

Fathead minnow	Silverside
Daphnia sp.	Sheepshead minnow
Ceredaphnia sp.	Mysid shrimp

Chronic aquatic toxicity testing is often necessary to evaluate the full range of possible adverse effects on aquatic organisms on repeated long-term exposure of the test chemical. Some effects such as growth may be reversible, diminish or non-detectable with time and some other effects are not detectable at acute exposures. These aspects have been described elsewhere (refs. 31,32).

AVIAN TOXICITY TESTING

The development of hundreds of pesticides in the last four decades has created an urgent need to evaluate their potential adverse effects on wildlife, particularly birds. By 1979, the U.S. EPA, under the Federal Insecticide, Fungicide, and Rodenticide Act (FIFRA) established the guidelines for determining the potential adverse effects on avian species (ref. 14).

Avian Dietary LC_{50}

Toxicity testing of birds is somewhat similar to that of aquatic species. Under FIFRA, toxicity testing is required on two avian species, one species of wild waterfowl (preferably mallard) and one species of upland game bird (preferably Bobwhite, native quail or ring-necked pheasant). Birds used in these tests should be 10 to 17 d old at the beginning of the test period and should be examined every 8-d intervals. Birds are fed treated diet for the first 5 d, followed by clean diets for 3 d with observation. The results are used for setting acceptable application levels and for identifying doses for further testing.

Avian Reproduction

Reproductive toxicity testing is usually carried out on bobwhite and the mallard. Avian reproduction testing is mandatory under FIFRA if any one of the following conditions apply:

1. Pesticide residues resulting from the proposed use are persistent in the environment to the extent that toxic amounts are expected on avian feed.
2. Pesticide residues are stored or accumulated in plant or animal tissues.
3. Pesticide is proposed for use under conditions where birds may be subjected to repeated or continued exposure to the pesticide, especially preceding or during the breeding season.

To meet this last condition, birds are fed treated diets not less than 10 weeks before egg laying and extending throughout the laying season, using at least two treatment level groups. Concentrations for the test chemical should be based on residues expected under the proposed use and a multiple, such as 5. A cost effective multiple-level testing, using at least three exposure levels, to determine effect and no-effect levels, may be useful for new pesticides that show promise on several crops and where avian exposure may vary or where levels of environmental exposure are not established, or both.

Pen Field Studies

Simulated testing and actual field testing for mammals and birds are likely to become routine for those chemicals that have significant toxicity or where there is persistence. The decision to conduct field tests is usually based on consideration of the physico-chemical properties of the pesticide, the proposed use pattern, the likelihood of wildlife exposure to the pesticide under field conditions and at levels expected to be toxic to wildlife, and on review of laboratory data. But, field studies are cumbersome, difficult to analyze, and very expensive (ref. 14).

MAMMALIAN TOXICITY TESTING

Acute Mammalian Toxicity Test

This test is designed to assess the acute toxicological effects on mammals on exposure to high concentrations of the test chemical. In addition, the test will identify the target organ and also set the design dose levels for prolonged exposure studies. A battery of tests under different exposure routes are conducted on chemicals to which humans may be routinely or occasionally exposed. This battery of tests includes primary exposure routes such as oral, dermal, inhalation and also other exposure routes such as acute preneonatal, neonatal and phototoxicity depending on the likely degree of human exposure. An acute oral toxicity testing may require up to 50 animals, whereas fewer animals are used in dermal and inhalation studies. Standard protocols are available with regulatory agencies and should be used if the information is intended to support a regulatory criteria or registration of a chemical for use. The results are expressed as LD_{50} or in a range of LD_1 (lowest reported lethal dose), LD_{10} and LD_{30}.

Subchronic Mammalian Toxicity Test

Subchronic tests are designed to assess adverse effects resulting from repeated exposure to a chemical over a portion of the average life span of an exposed animal. Adequately designed subchronic studies provide useful data on the sublethal effects at relatively low doses (doses lower than the LD_{50} concentration) of the test chemical. Sublethal effects include information on the target organ, physiological effects, cumulative toxicity of the test chemical and metabolism of the chemical. Results from subchronic studies can be used to design dose levels for chronic, reproductive and carcinogenic studies. These data are also valuable in establishing no adverse effect level

(NOEL) which is an important element in risk assessment of a chemical. Chemicals to which chronic low level human exposure is likely, must be assessed for their subchronic effects.

The subchronic toxicity tests for rodents are 30 to 90 d in duration and might vary depending on the biological end point, species chosen for study, and the route of administration. Generally, subchronic studies do not exceed 10% of the animal's life span. Oral and inhalation subchronic testing last for three months in shorter-lived animal (rodents) and one year for longer-lived animals (dogs, monkeys), whereas, dermal studies take one month or less. Wherever feasible, subchronic toxicity tests should expose test animals by routes which are likely to be the same as for humans (oral, dermal, and inhalation)(ref. 33).

Chronic Mammalian Toxicity Testing

This long-term testing is designed to cover greater than 10% of animal's life span and hence, longer than three months of exposure period. This test covers lifetime toxicity studies, multigeneration reproduction studies, and carcinogenicity studies. Chronic testing is designed to identify a myriad of potential toxic effects of a test chemical's structural and functional characteristics. It uses a holistic approach, unlike carcinogenicity testing, to define an etiology of an adverse effect to identify No Observed Effect Level (NOEL) for the test chemical and estimate the safety factor at the ambient exposure level of the chemical (ref. 34). Rodents are used in chronic testing for mammalian toxicity assessment and a typical study will involve three treatment groups and a control group with equal number of animals in each group. The chemical is administered 7 d/wk for at least 2 y. The second non-rodent species to assure safety is usually the purebred beagle. A larger animal might be advantageous for clinical investigation purposes instead of rodents. But caution must be exercised since the larger animal (such as dog) could be a carnivore and often metabolizes chemicals different from rodents (ref. 34)

There are several approaches in the selection of test dose levels. The approach of the National Cancer Institute's Bioassay Program is to conduct a 3-month-range-finding study with enough dose levels to find a level that will suppress the body weight gain by 10%. This dose is called the Maximum Tolerated Dose (MTD) and is chosen as the highest dose. Usually, 1/4 MTD and 1/8 MTD are chosen as the other two test doses (ref. 14).

Mammalian Developmental Toxicity

Once known as teratology tests, these tests are now defined appropriately as developmental toxicity tests (ref. 35). The following terms are used to describe the results of developmental toxicity tests: (1) teratogenic - used for chemicals which produce gross structural abnormalities; (2) embryotoxic - used to identify chemicals, which due to several possible toxic actions destroy the embryo; (3) fetotoxic - less severe effects; toxic or degenerative effect on fetal tissues and organs. Whereas, EPA guidelines on developmental toxicants (ref. 35), have suggested that embryotoxic and fetotoxic terms describe a wide range of adverse effects, and the two terms differentiate the time when the toxicities are apparent.

Mammalian Reproductive Toxicity Testing

These tests assess the chemical's ability to affect adversely the fertility of either parent. The following parameters are used to assess the toxic effects on reproductive function of both sexes.

1. Functional parameters which includes reproductive efficiency, cogenesis, and fertilization;
2. Morphological parameters are gross pathology and histopathology; and
3. Biochemical parameters are molecular aspects such as normal synthesis and metabolism, accessory cell function and hormonal status.

To assess species survival, events and processes such as oogenesis, spermatogenesis, and fertilization are studied and the reproductive process is evaluated (ref. 36). Typically, these reproductive toxicity tests are conducted for three generations of the test species. Depending on the protocol, the parent may undergo continuous exposure throughout the critical periods prior to and after conception. So far, the three-generation protocol has successfully identified reproductive toxicants.

Carcinogenicity Hazard Identification

Guidelines prepared by regulatory agencies, International Agency for Research on Cancer (IARC), and others are available for conducting adequate tests to identify the carcinogenic hazard of a chemical. The guidelines developed by U.S. Environmental Protection Agency are the result of a two-year agency wide effort which included many scientists from the larger scientific community. These guidelines set the principles and procedures in the conduct of risk assessment and to inform the decision makers and the public about the procedures. The case-by-case approach requires expert review of the scientific information on each chemical and uses the most scientifically appropriate interpretation to assess hazard and the eventual risk. Table 6.10 presents the EPA guidelines for carcinogenic risk assessment of which Part B is carcinogenic hazard identification process. Hazard identification is a qualitative risk assessment, dealing with the process of determining whether exposure to a chemical has the potential to increase the incidence of cancer. Both malignant and benign tumours are included in the evaluation of carcinogenic hazard. The hazard identification component qualitatively answers the question of how likely an agent is to be a human carcinogen (ref. 37).

Mutagenicity Hazard Identification

Similar to the guidelines on carcinogenicity hazard assessment, U.S. EPA also developed guidelines for mutagenicity hazard identification (ref. 38):

Qualitative Assessment (Hazard Identification)

The assessment of potential germ-cell mutagenic risk is a multi-step process. The first step analyzes the evidence for a chemical's ability to induce mutagenic events. The second step analyzes its ability to produce these events in a mammalian gonad. All relevant information is then integrated into a weight-of-evidence scheme for the chemical's potential ability to produce mutations in human germ cells.

For hazard identification, it is essential to have the following tests conducted: mouse specific-locus test for point mutations and the heritable translocation or germ-cell cytogenetic tests for chromosomal aberrations. Where data are not available, alternative evaluation is required. When evidence exists that a chemical has both mutagenic activity and ability to attack the mammalian gonads, it is reasonable to deduce that the agent is a potential mutagen.

While mammalian germ-cell assays are presently primarily performed on male animals, a chemical cannot be considered to be a non-mutagen for mammalian germ cells unless it is shown to be negative in both sexes.

Mutagenic Activity

In evaluating chemicals for mutagenic activity, the following factors are to be considered: (1) genetic end points (e.g., gene mutations or chromosomal aberrations) detected by the test systems; (2) sensitivity and predictive value of the test systems for several classes of chemicals; (3) number of test systems used for detecting each genetic end point; (4) consistent results from different test systems and different species; (5) dose-response relationship; and (6) use of recommended test protocols.

TABLE 6.10 EPA Guidelines for carcinogenic risk assessment.

I.   Introduction

II. Hazard Identification

     A. Overview
     B. Elements of Hazard Identification
        1. Physical-Chemical Properties and Routes and Patterns of Exposure
        2. Structure-Activity Relationships
        3. Metabolic and Pharmacokinetic Properties
        4. Toxicologic Effects
        5. Short-Term Tests
        6. Long-Term Animal Studies
        7. Human Studies
     C. Weight of Evidence
     D. Guidance for Dose-Response Assessment
     E. Summary and Conclusions

III. Dose-Response Assessment, Exposure Assessment, and Risk Characterization

     A. Dose-Response Assessment
        1. Selection of Data
        2. Choice of Mathematical Extrapolation Model
        3. Equivalent Exposure Units Among Species
     B. Exposure Assessment
     C. Risk Characterization
        1. Options of Numerical Risk Estimates
        2. Concurrent Exposure
        3. Summary of Risk Characterization

IV. EPA Classification System for Categorizing Weight of Evidence for
     Carcinogenicity from Human and Animal Studies (Adapted from IARC)

     A. Assessment of Weight of Evidence for Carcinogenicity from Studies in
        Humans
     B. Assessment of Weight of Evidence for Carcinogenicity from Studies in
        Experimental Animals
     C. Categorization of Overall Weight of Evidence for Human Carcinogenicity

V.   References

(Source: Reprinted from ref. 37).

Categorization of weight of evidence-classification scheme.

1. Positive data from human mutagenicity studies will constitute the highest level of evidence for the chemical's human mutagenic potential.

2. Valid positive results from studies on heritable mutational events in mammalian germ cells.

3. Valid positive results from mammalian chromosome aberration studies excluding an intergeneration test.

4. Sufficient evidence must be reported from two assay systems, within which one is mammalian (in vitro or in vivo). The positive results may include both tests for the same effect or one of each, gene mutation or chromosome aberration. The criterion is both tests must be on mammalian systems.

5. Results from (4) could present either a strong positive evidence for mutagenicity or less strong evidence for mutagenicity combined with sufficient evidence for a chemical's interaction with mammalian germ cells.

6. Positive mutagenicity test results of weaker strength, combined with suggestive evidence for a chemical's interaction with mammalian germ cells.

7. In the absence of definite proof, a chemical could be classified operationally as a non-mutagen for human germ cells, if it gives valid negative test results for all end points of concern.

8. Evidence lacking for either mutagenicity or chemical interaction with mammalian germ cells.

Note: Categories are in decreasing order of strength of evidence (ref. 38).

Table 6.11 presents another approach for prioritizing the existing chemicals based on European Economic Community Commission directive (EEC 79/83). On the basis of a set of physicochemical, toxicological and ecotoxicological properties, the proposed system developed a scoring system for each property in both the presence and absence of datum (ref. 39).

6.2 DOSE-RESPONSE RELATIONSHIP

(i) <u>Concentration-response relationship</u>. The objective in conducting toxicity tests is to estimate as precisely as possible the chemical concentration that produce an observable and quantifiable response on test organisms under controlled laboratory conditions. The correlation of concentration with the percentage of organisms exhibiting the defined response is commonly known as a concentration-response relationship. This relationship used in aquatic toxicity measurements is analogous to the dose-response

TABLE 6.11 Toxicity scoring profile for available data and unavailable data.

	AVAILABILITY OF DATUM	SCORE	UNAVAILABILITY OF DATUM	SCORE
	TOXICOLOGICAL PROPERTIES			
Acute toxicity (oral LD_{50}, cutaneous LD_{50}, inhalatory LC_{50}	Not harmful	0	On the basis of chemical structure or other acute toxicity data:	
	Harmful	1		
	Toxic	3		
	Very toxic	5	possible to exclude acute harm through the three exposure routes	0
			Acute harm is suspected	1
			Acutely non-lethal effects could be expected	3
			Acutely lethal effects could be expected	5
Skin irritation/ corrosion and/or eye irritation/ corrosion	Negative	0	On the basis of chemical structure:	
	Irritating to skin (score ≥ 2)	1		
	Corrosive to skin within 4 hr	2	Possible to exclude irritant or corrosive potency	0
	Irritating to eyes	2	Faint indications of irritant potency	1
	Corrosive to skin within 3 min.	3	Clear indications of irritant potency	2
			Evidence indications of corrosive potency	3
			Classified as very toxic	3
Sensitization according to the EEC "Guide on classification and labelling"	Negative	0	On the basis of chemical structure:	
	Positive cutaneously	1	Possible to exclude sensitization	0
	Positive by inhalation	2	Information is unavailable	0.5
			Generic indications of sensitization	1
			Specific indications of sensitization	2
			Classified as very toxic	3

Continued . . .

TABLE 6.11 Continued.

	AVAILABILITY OF DATUM	SCORE	UNAVAILABILITY OF DATUM	SCORE

TOXICOLOGICAL PROPERTIES

	AVAILABILITY OF DATUM	SCORE	UNAVAILABILITY OF DATUM	SCORE
Subacute, subchronic, chronic toxicity	No effect level (NEL), orally >1000 mg/kg and/or NEL by inhalation >10 mg/L and/or NEL cutaneously >1000 mg/kg	0	According to the severity of the possible effects, as deducible from the chemical structure	1-5
	NEL orally 100-1000 mg/kg and/or NEL by inhalation 1-10 mg/L and/or NEL cutaneously 200-1000 mg/kg	1		
	NEL orally 10-100 mg/kg and/or NEL by inhalation 0.25-1 mg/L and/or NEL cutaneously 25-200 mg/kg	3		
	NEL orally <10 mg/kg and/or NEL by inhalation <0.25 mg/L and/or NEL cutaneously <25 mg/kg	5		
Mutagenicity, according to the EEC "Guide on classification and labelling"	Proved as not mutagenic agent	0	Data are not significant or are lacking	2
	Classifiable in Cat. 3	2	On the basis of the chemical structure: there are indications for an equivocal mutagenic activity	6
	Classifiable in Cat. 2	6		
	Classifiable in Cat. 1	10	On the basis of chemical structure, there are evident indications for mutagenic activity	10
Carcinogenicity, according to the EEC "Guide on classification and labelling"	Proved as not carcinogenic agent	0	Data are not significant or are lacking	2
	Classifiable in Cat. 3	5	On the basis of the chemical structure: there is general suspicion for carcinogenic activity	5
	Classifiable in Cat. 2	10		
	Classifiable in Cat. 1	15	On the basis of the chemical structure, there are indications for carcinogenic activity	10
			On the basis of chemical structure, there are evident indications for carcinogenic activity	15

Continued . . .

TABLE 6.11 Continued.

	AVAILABILITY OF DATUM	SCORE	UNAVAILABILITY OF DATUM	SCORE

TOXICOLOGICAL PROPERTIES

Effects on reproduction including teratogenicity, according to the EEC "Guide on classification and labelling"	Proved as effect-free	0	Data are not significant or are lacking	2
	Classifiable in Cat. 2	5	On the basis of the chemical structure: there are indications for potential effects	5
	Classifiable in Cat. 1	10	On the basis of chemical structure, there are evident indications for potential effects	10

ECOTOXICOLOGICAL PROPERTIES

Acute toxicity for fish	LC_{50} >1000 ppm	0	Water solubility <0.01 g/L	0
	LC_{50} 100-1000 ppm	1		
	LC_{50} 10-100 ppm	3	Water solubility 0.01-1 g/L but there is rapid degradability	0
	LC_{50} <10 ppm	5	Water solubility 0.01-1 g/L but there is no rapid degradability	1
			Water solubility >1 g/L but there is rapid degradability	3
			Water solubility >1 g/L but there is no rapid degradability	5
Acute toxicity for Daphnia	EC_{50} >1000 ppm	0	Water solubility <0.01 g/L	0
	EC_{50} 100-1000 ppm	1		
	EC_{50} 10-100 ppm	3	Water solubility 0.01-1 g/L but there is rapid degradability	0
	EC_{50} <10 ppm	5	Water solubility 0.01-1 g/L but there is no rapid degradability	1
			Water solubility >1 g/L but there is rapid degradability	3
			Water solubility >1 g/L but there is no rapid degradability	5

Continued . . .

TABLE 6.11 Continued.

AVAILABILITY OF DATUM	SCORE	UNAVAILABILITY OF DATUM	SCORE

ECOTOXICOLOGICAL PROPERTIES

Acute toxicity for birds	Oral LD_{50} >1000 mg/kg	0	There is rapid degradability and the spread is merely localized	0
	Oral LD_{50} 100-1000 mg/kg	1		
	Oral LD_{50} 10-100 mg/kg	3		
	Oral LD_{50} <10 mg/kg	5		
			There is not rapid degradability but the spread is merely localized	1
			There is not rapid degradability and there is wide environmental spread	3
			There is not rapid degradability and there is generalized environmental spread	5
Toxicity for higher plants	Not phytotoxic	0	Gaseous substance and rapidly degradable	0
	Selective phytotoxic	1	Water solubility and/or fat solubility <0.01 g/L	0
	Generally weak phytotoxic	3	Water solubility and/or fat solubility 0.01-1 g/L	1
	Generally phytotoxic	5	Water solubility and/or fat solubility >1 g/L, but there is rapid degradability	3
			Water solubility and/or fat solubility >1 g/L, and there is not rapid degradability	5
Effects on algae	Proved as effect-free	0	Water solubility <0.01 g/L	0
	Weakly altering activity (positive or negative)	3	Water solubility 0.01-1 g/L and rapid degradability	0
	Highly altering activity (positive or negative)	5	Water solubility 0.01-1 g/L and not rapid degradability	1
			Water solubility >1 g/L and rapid degradability	3
			Water solubility >1 g/L and not rapid degradability	5

Continued . . .

TABLE 6.11 Concluded.

	AVAILABILITY OF DATUM	SCORE	UNAVAILABILITY OF DATUM	SCORE

MULTIPLIER PARAMETERS

Environmental spread	Generalized spread, such as: pesticides used in agriculture, fertilizers, industrial emissions, and vehicle emissions	2		
	Extensive spread, such as: environmental residues from medicinal, fodder additives, integrators employed in zootechny, emissions from domestic heating plants, urban waste, emissions from incinerators	1		
	Localized spread	0.5		
	No spread	0		
Persistence	Biotic degradability within 5 days and/or abiotic degradation		On the basis of chemical structure:	
	BOD/ThOD >90% and/or T/2 >1 hr	0.5	Assumed as highly reactive	0.5
	BOD/ThOD 60-90% and/or T/2 1-24 hr	1	Assumed to be easily decomposable	1
	BOD/ThOD 30-60% and/or T/2 24 hr-1 month	1.5	Assumed to be slowly decomposable	1.5
	BOD/ThOD 30% and/or T/2 <1 month	2	Assumed to be stable	2
Bioconcentration	n-Octanol/water partition coefficient		Fat solubility <0.01 g/L	0.5
	Log P <0	0.5	Fat solubility 0.01-1 g/L	1
	Log P 0-3	1		
	Log P >3	1.5	Fat solubility >1 g/L	1.5

MULTIPLIER PARAMETERS

Size of risk population	Whole population	2		
	Partial population sectors	1.5		
	Workers in industry and neighbouring populations or agricultural workers	1		
	Workers only, with exclusion of external contamination (closed cycle)	0.5		
	No risk population	0		

(Source: Reprinted with permission from ref. 5, Copyright (1986), Academic Press).

relationship used in mammalian toxicity testing. In the latter case, the exposure is due to the chemical directly delivered inside the animal by routes
such as oral, dermal, and intrapretonial. The measured amount of chemical
delivered inside the animal is the dose which is a known quantity and can be
correlated to the response.

The concentration of a test chemical in water is usually expressed in parts
per million (mg/L) or as volume percent of an industrial effluent. The
concentration-response relationship is the most fundamental concept in aquatic
toxicology. It extends from acute toxic response to chronic response and
demonstrates that for every chemical there exists a threshold concentration
below which, under defined conditions, no adverse effects is observed. Using
this concept, a concentration-response curve is drawn from which median lethal
concentration or No Observable Effect Levels (NOELs) can be established
(Fig. 6.6).

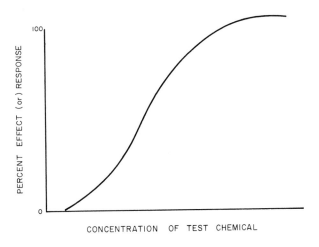

Fig. 6.6. Typical concentration-response curve.

The steeper the slope of the central portion of the curve, the sharper the
threshold of the effect--that is, the more intense the response over a narrow
range of concentration.

Dose-Response Relationship

The terms "effect" and "response" are often considered interchangeable. But in fact, the term "response" refers more specifically to the portion of the exposed population that demonstrates a defined effect. The dose received by the species can either be expressed as the "total dose", integrated overtime or as the "actual dose" that is the amount of the chemical arrived at the target organ at a given point in time. The critical dose and the critical organ are usually the most relevant factors to relate to the magnitude of the observed effect.

The total dose is important in relating to the quantal effect where the dose induces the occurrence of an effect. Quantal effects cannot be graded and can only be expressed as present or absent, or in other words, occurring or non-occurring at the dose level. For these effects, there is no dose-threshold below which the effect will not occur, but the probability of experiencing the effect increases with increasing dose (ref. 39). Hereditary effects and carcinogenicity are considered to be quantal effects.

Observed effects are evidence of adverse biological effects of a chemical as illustrated in Figs. 6.7 and 6.8. These figures illustrate the relationship between the integrated dose of lead in blood (given as concentration) and the observed range of health effects in children and adults.

A dose-response relationship in the case of carcinogenic assessment, defines the correlation between the dose of a chemical and the probability of induction of a carcinogenic effect in the animal species exposed. The primary objective in a dose-response relationship for carcinogens is the need to estimate human risk at low doses. Typically, the only data available are the experimental results of animal studies at high doses, perhaps supplemented by scanty epidemiological information along with the results from a battery of short-term results. The exercise in analyzing these data is aimed in demonstrating conclusively the existence or non-existence of dose-response related aspects of the effect. This identification would make further processes such as regulatory control and communication of such control simpler and credible (refs. 40, 41). When a threshold dose level, below which there is no response, exists, the regulatory options are straightforward. But there are compounds or chemicals for which there is no threshold dose level, which will lead to judgemental process involving socio-economic and societal elements to decide on an acceptable level of exposure.

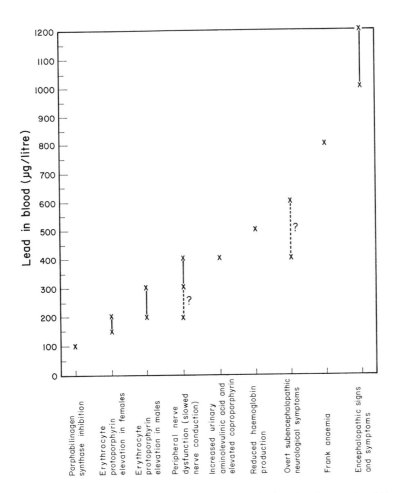

Fig. 6.7. Lowest observed levels for lead-induced adverse health effects in adults.
(Source: Reprinted with permission from ref. 41, Copyright (1987), World Health Organization).

There are other areas of importance in the dose-response relationship such as low doses that give experimentally measurable responses, non-linear response, etc.

6.3 THRESHOLD LEVEL AND SAFETY FACTORS

In the last four decades, the safety factor approach has been used successfully to identify the dose at the No Observable Adverse Effect Level (NOAEL) derived from animal experimental toxicity studies (refs. 42-45). This approach is much less complicated than the mathematical models developed later for carcinogens, developmental toxins and other genotoxicants. However,

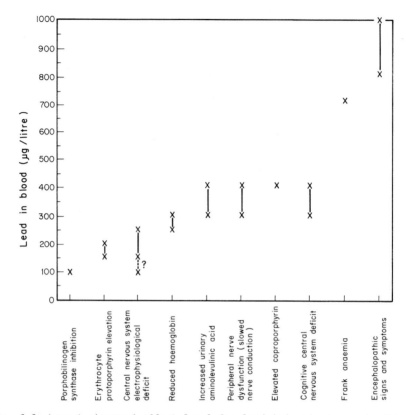

Fig. 6.8. Lowest observed effect level for lead-induced adverse health effects in children.
(Source: Reprinted with permission from ref. 41, Copyright (1987), World Health Organization).

exposure limits based on NOAEL have shown to be generally effective in protecting human health among exposed workers (refs. 44, 46-48).

6.3.1 Threshold Effect Level

Threshold effect is represented by a dose level below which the exposure to a chemical does not cause any adverse effect in biological species including humans. This dose level is known as NOAEL. Different types of dose-response curves are presented in Fig. 6.9. Curve 1 represents the NOAEL situation, where there is no adverse effect until a certain level of chemical exposure is reached at which point, the curve takes off from absessa.

Curve 2 represents a more prevalent and yet complex dose-response situation. Low doses for this curve exhibit some adverse effects which increase minimally with increase in dose up to a point.

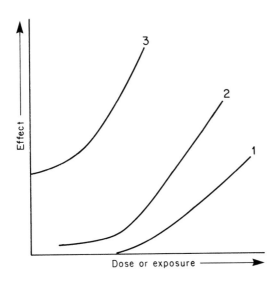

Fig. 6.9. Different types of dose-response curves exhibiting a threshold level. (Source: Reprinted with permission from ref. 41, Copyright (1987), World Health Organization).

After that point, the response increases relatively sharply with increase in concentration. This situation is typical of difference in response to a chemical's exposure between a sensitive subpopulation and the general population which remains unaffected until a certain level of exposure above NOAEL is reached.

The regulatory options will be linked to the differences between curves 1 and 2. In the case of curve 1 scenario, it would be appropriate to keep exposure levels below the threshold level. Whereas, for curve 2, it may not be practical to keep the exposure level to zero in order to protect the relatively small portion of susceptible population affected at low doses. The cost-effective and health-protective approach will be to set standards at or somewhat lower than the inflexion point (marked X), with additional steps to safeguard or reduce the exposure to susceptible subpopulation. An example is the case of methylmercury levels in fish; there are two possible scenarios for higher exposure level to subpopulation: (1) high fish consumption than the rest of the population; and (2) normal consumption but higher levels of methylmercury residue in fish.

The regulatory approach for health protection of this subpopulation would be to recommend/impose fish consumption guidelines for this subpopulation so as to keep the weekly/daily exposure below the threshold limit.

Curve 3 illustrates a more complicated situation where effects due to exposure of the chemical are inseparable from similar effects arising from background exposure.

A number of factors interfere in specifying accurately the threshold level dose. They include the variation in sensitivity among individuals, physiological diversity in human populations, measuring techniques and their limitations, and difficulty in detecting the effect at very low exposure levels. Fig. 6.10 presents a generalized exposure-response curve and shows the various extrapolation estimates from middle range (dose-response) observations.

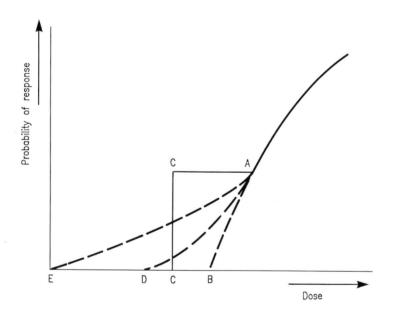

Fig. 6.10. Generalized exposure-response relationships.

The solid line A is the dose-response curve obtained from multiple dose-response animal studies. Point A is the NOAEL in mg or μg/kg.bw/day for the most sensitive biological adverse effect, as determined from a chronic animal study. Curves AB, AD, and AE are the possible dose-response curves at lower dose range with points B, D, and E being the respective threshold points for the adverse effect in human population. For setting an acceptable daily intake (ADI) concentration or acceptable exposure concentration in aquatic environment, represented by point C on the dose scale, a safety factor is applied to the dose at point A. If the extrapolated curve AB is the true dose-response curve, then the safety factor has an adequate margin of safety and so is ADI. However, if AD or AE is the true dose-response curve, then the safety margin is small and the calculated ADI is too high. This might put some individuals in the population at some level of risk in terms of adverse effects. The magnitude of the gap between points C and B correlates to the cost and technology involved in control methods to bring the exposure from B to C.

6.3.2 Safety Factors

Although results of animal studies can predict with reasonable degree of certainty the effects on human populations, the extrapolation suffers from a number of factors including variability in species, design of the study and the type of extrapolation method used. The two major problems or uncertainties associated with extrapolation of animal data to human populations are:

1. Uncertainties in response sensitivities between test animals and humans; and

2. Uncertainties in extrapolation from high dose-response data to low dose range encountered in ambient environment.

Hence, the safety (uncertainty) factor should reflect these problems which must be taken into account to minimize the errors in extrapolations. When the quality and quantity of dose-response data are high, the safety factor is low; when the data are inadequate or equivocal, higher safety factors must be used. The safety factors are not applicable to non-threshold effects such as carcinogenicity. It is replaced by "acceptable risk". The following general guidelines (Table 6.12) have been accepted by the U.S. National Academy of Sciences-Safe Drinking Water Committee and the U.S. Environmental Protection Agency in the development of drinking water standards (ref. 49). This system is also used by several other regulatory agencies around the world. These guidelines are not meant to be rigid and scientific judgement should be exercised depending on each particular case in using the specific numbers for the safety factor. For example, the term "reserved coefficient" is used in USSR which can be viewed as safety factor incorporated in each standard between the threshold level and the maximum permissible concentration (MPC). According to Izmerov (ref. 50), every MPC should have a built-in safety factor of 30% lower than the threshold level. This means that in case of a threshold effect, the next level tested will be 30% lower. If no adverse effect is found, no further testing is required, and this level becomes the MPC. This may seem very small compared to factors used by other international agencies, but it must be noted that USSR uses this method to protect the most sensitive indicator of exposure and not necessarily the pathological response. A standard that protects the high risk section of the population will also protect the rest of the population (ref. 42).

The safety factor methodology has been criticized on the grounds that the NOAEL will depend on the sample size, different response rates affecting the toxicological and statistical inferences (refs. 51,52). Also, there is a chance of not observing the effect (even as high as 1% of the population) in animal studies because a limited number of animals are exposed (ref. 53). Considering all the above points, it has been suggested

TABLE 6.12 Recommended safety factors and rationale.

10 factor	Applied to data from valid experimental studies on prolonged human intake, with no indication of carcinogenicity. This 10-fold factor protects the sensitive members of the population.
100 factor	Applied when experimental results from studies of human intake are not available, or are scanty; valid results of long-term intake studies on one or more species of experimental animals; no indication of carcinogenicity.
1000 factor	Applied when there are no long-term or acute human data; scanty results on experimental animals; no indication of carcinogenicity.

that Probit model plus a safety factor must be used (ref. 54). This approach may be applicable to carcinogens which act through a non-genotoxic mechanism such as promoters and cytotoxicants (ref. 55). Another shortcoming of the safety factor methodology is that it does not account for the variance in the slope of the dose-response curve. In other words, it might be adequate if the dose-response curve has a steep slope but may be insufficient in case where the slope is relatively shallow and covers a range of dose levels for very small incremental change in response.

6.4   NON-THRESHOLD HAZARDS

The existence of a threshold for carcinogenicity is a contentious issue among risk assessors. Biological argument against a threshold level for carcinogenesis is based on the assumption that a single-point mutation in a single-somatic cell can lead to irreversible and uncontrolled growth that eventually becomes cancer. Arguments against this position are based on the existence of metabolic detoxification, DNA repair mechanisms, immunological defences and other related mechanisms which may neutralize the effects at low doses. Another argument based on probability is that while an individual may have a threshold, different individuals may have different thresholds, or may have no threshold at all. Thus, the determination of a population threshold is a difficult statistical exercise (refs. 51,56).

Dose-response relationship and the curves generated will show the existence of a non-threshold adverse effect of a chemical (Fig. 6.11). All the curves shown in Fig. 6.11 represent possible non-threshold response. Curve 1 is the classical (or ideal) linear dose-response relationship where a non-threshold adverse effect is clearly shown. Existence of an effect or response exists at all levels of exposure beginning with zero exposure.

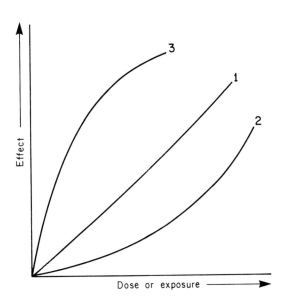

Fig. 6.11. Illustration of non-threshold dose level.

Curves 2 and 3 are sublinear and supra-linear responses to a similar dose exposure. Curve 2 shows small incremental response to increase in dose at low dose levels. In other words, there is a reduced sensitivity of the species to the exposure at lower doses. Whereas, curve 3 shows sharp increase in response to small variation in dose at lower dose levels. This curve represents a group of species that are hyper sensitive to exposure at lower dose levels. But all the curves show an existence of a non-threshold effect.

The U.S. National Academy of Sciences (NAS)-Drinking Water Committee has outlined the following four principles in the identification of non-threshold hazards involving chronic irreversible toxicity or effects of a long-term exposure (ref. 49). These are intended primarily to cancer hazards from pollutants that cause somatic mutation. These principles, may also apply in the identification of mutagenic and teratogenic effects.

(i) <u>Properly qualified effects in animals are applicable to human</u>. Virtually, every form of human cancer has an experimental counterpart in animals and every form of multicellular organism is susceptible to cancer. There are differences in sensitivities or susceptibilities among animal species and humans, different strains of the same species and different individuals of the same strain. However, extensive data generated in the past few decades indicate that substances that are carcinogenic to animals are likely to be carcinogenic to humans and vice versa.

(ii) <u>Adequate methods are not available at present to establish a threshold dose level for the chronic toxicity of chemicals</u>. It is not possible to develop a threshold level that will protect the entire population from carcinogenic hazard. Even studies using large number of animals are likely to detect only powerful carcinogens. Also, there is variation in individual threshold levels among the population.

(iii) <u>High dose exposure to animals is a necessary and valid method of assessing the carcinogenic potential of a chemical</u>. The use of high dose exposure of chemical has two distinct advantages: (1) it positively identifies the target organ susceptible to carcinogenesis; and (2) reduces the number of animals that have to be used in the exposure study. An incidence as low as 0.01% would represent a risk to 20,000 people in a population of 200 million; whereas, the lower limit of reproducibility in common animal studies would be an incidence at 10%. Therefore, the best solution is to assume a direct proportionality between dose and tumorogenesis with no threshold present.

(iv) <u>Chemicals should be assessed for human health risk rather than safe or unsafe</u>. Risk acceptance and risk management is a judgemental process evaluating risk vs benefits of a chemical in the environment. Considering the long latency period for carcinogenesis to fully develop and the irreversibility of the process, it would be improper to expose the entire population to an increased cancer risk when benefits are either small or questionable or limited to particular segments of the population. These considerations require hard scientific evidence but also must be ethical and use as broad a population base as possible in the decision-making process (ref. 42).

Guidelines are also available for the hazard assessment of carcinogenicity, mutagenicity, and developmental toxicity from the United States Environmental Protection Agency Publications (refs. 35,37,38), International Agency for Research on Cancer (IARC - ref. 57) and other agencies.

In addition, short-term tests must be conducted as part of the initial screening for chemical carcinogens. Short-term tests for point mutations, numerical and structural chromosome aberrations, DNA damage and repair, and in vitro transformation provide supportive evidence of carcinogenicity and may also provide an understanding of the carcinogenic mechanism. For example, if a chemical is tested to be non-mutagenic but involved in carcinogenesis, then the chemical must be a cancer promoter and not a cancer inducer. All carcinogenic inducers are mutagenic and hence, act directly on the genetic molecule. Whereas, a non-mutagen promotes cancer in a non-direct mechanism. 2,3,7,8-TCDD is such an example.

Short-term in vivo and in vitro tests that can give indication of initiation and promotion activity, may also provide supportive evidence for carcinogenicity (ref. 37). Table 6.13 presents the representative short-term tests for genotoxicity (ref. 58).

It is clear from this chapter that hazard evaluation requires detailed testing for exposure and toxicity information on the chemicals. If needed, this information can be scored to arrive at a prioritized list of compounds, which can be assessed further for more detailed information. The threshold-type hazards for which no observed effect level can be established have to be separated from non-threshold hazards such as carcinogenicity for which only an acceptable level of exposure can be developed.

TABLE 6.13 Representative short-term tests for genotoxicity.

TYPE OF TEST	SPECIFIC TEST	ORGANISMS USED
DNA Damage in Microbes	Pol A test rec test Mitotic recombination, mitotic crossing over, or mitotic gene conversion in yeast (D3, D4, D5, or D7 Assays)	Escherichia coli Bacillus subtilis Saccharomyces cerevisiae or Schizosaccharomyces pombe
DNA Damage in Mammalian Cells	Unscheduled DNA Synthesis (UDS)	WI-38 strain human cells or various rodent cells Various cell lines or animal sources

Continued . . . .

TABLE 6.13 Concluded.

Gene Mutation in Bacteria and Fungi	Ames test WP2 Assay Yeast "forward" and "reverse" assays Miscellaneous	Salmonella typhimurium Escherichia coli Saccharomyces cerevisiae; Schizosaccharomyces pombe Aspergillus nidulans Neurospora crassa
Gene Mutation in Higher Systems	HGPRT, TK, and Na/K-ATPase Assays Sex-linked recessive lethal assay Plant tests	L5178Y mouse lymphoma cells; Chinese hamster ovary cells (CHO) Chinese hamster lung cells (V-79) Drosophila melanogaster Tradescantia; maize waxy locus
Chromosomal Effects in Isolated Cell Systems	In vitro cytogenetics assays	Wl-38 strain human cells; Chinese hamster ovary cells (CHO)
Chromosomal Effects in Whole Organisms	In vivo cytogenetics Micronucleus test Nondisjunction assay Heritable translocation assay	Various rodent species Various rodent species Drosophila melanogaster Drosophila melanogaster
Oncogenic Transformation	Transformation assays (clonal or focus)	Syrian hamster embryo cells (SHE); BALB/c3T3 mouse cell line; C3H10T1/2 mouse cell ine
Tumor Formation	Mouse skin tumori-genesis Mouse pulmonary adenoma Rat tracheal transplant	Sencar mice Strain A mice Various rat strains

(Source: Reprinted with permission from ref. 58, Copyright (1979), U.S. EPA).

REFERENCES

1 J. Cairns, Jr., K.L. Dickson, and A.W. Maki, Estimating the Hazards of Chemical Substances to Aquatic Life, STP 657, American Society for Testing and Materials, Philadelphia, PA, U.S.A., 1978.
2 R.A. Kimerle, in R. Haque (Editor), Dynamics, Exposure and Hazard Assessment of Toxic Chemicals, Ann Arbor Science Publishers, Ann Arbor, Michigan, U.S.A., 1980, pp. 451-457.
3 A.W. Maki, K.L. Dickson, and J. Cairns, Jr. (Editors), Biotransformation and Fate of Chemicals in the Aquatic Environment, American Society of Microbiology, Washington, D.C., U.S.A., 1980.
4 G.C. Veith, K.J. Macek, S.R. Petrocelli, and J. Carrole, in J.G. Eaton, P.R. Parrish, and A.C. Hendricks (Editors), Aquatic Toxicology, ASTM, Philadelphia, PA, 1980, pp. 111-129.
5 A. Sampaolo and R. Binetti, Reg. Toxicol. & Pharmacol., 6 (1986) 129-154.
6 U.S. Environmental Protection Agency (USEPA), Toxic Substances Control Act-Premanufacture Testing of New Chemical Substances, Fed. Regist. 44 (1979) 16240-16292.
7 L.W. Beck, A.W. Maki, N.R. Artman, and E.R. Wilson, Regul. Toxicol. and Pharmacol., 1 (1981) 19-58.
8 S. Ramamoorthy, Bull. Environ. Contam. Toxicol., 34 (1985) 349-358.
9 J.R. Roberts, J.F. Mitchell, M.J. Boddington, and J.M. Ridgeway - Part I; J.R. Roberts, J.T. McGarrity, and W.K. Marshall - Part II, A Screen for the Relative Persistence of Lipophilic Organic Chemicals in Aquatic Ecosystems - An Analysis of the Role of a Simple Computer Model in Screening, National Research Council of Canada, Ottawa, Canada, NRCC No. 18570, 1981, p. 302.
10 National Research Council of Canada Associate Committee on Scientific Criteria for Environmental Quality, Polychlorinated Dibenzo-p-dioxins; Criteria for Their Effects on Man and His Environment, NRCC Publication No. 18574, 1981, p. 57.
11 D. Mackay and A.W. Wolkoff, Environ. Sci. Technol., 7 (1973) 611-614.
12 D.E. Orr, G. Ozburn, and J. Todd, Can. Tech. Rep. Fish. Aquat. Sci., 975 (1980) 215-219.
13 A. Bharath, C. Mallard, D. Orr, G. Ozburn, and A. Smith, Bull. Environ. Contam. Toxicol., 33 (1984) 133-137.
14 D.J. Postenbach (Editor), The Risk Assessment of Environmental and Human Health Hazards: A Textbook of Case Studies, John Wiley & Sons, New York, U.S.A., 1988.
15 A. Spacie and J.L. Hamelink, in G. Rand and S. Petrocelli (Editors), Fundamentals of Aquatic Toxicology, Hemisphere Publishing Corporation, New York, U.S.A., 17 (1985) pp. 495-525.
16 U.S. Food and Drug Administration (USFDA), Environmental Assessment Technical Handbook, Center for Food Safety and Applied Nutrition and the Center for Veterinary Medicine, U.S. FDA, Washington, D.C., U.S.A., 1984.
17 S. Ramamoorthy, T.C. Cheng, and D.J. Kushner, Bull. Environ. Contam. Toxicol., 29 (1982) 167-173.
18 C.M. Palmer, Algae and Water Pollution - The Identification, Significance, and Control of Algae in Water Supplies and in Polluted Water, Castle House Publications Ltd., England, 1980.
19 G.C. Miller and R.G. Zepp, Environ. Sci. Technol., 13 (1979) 860-863.
20 E.D. LeCren and R.H. Lowe-McConnell (Editors), The Functioning of Freshwater Ecosystems, Cambridge University Press, Cambridge, 1980, 588 p.
21 P.T.S. Wong, Y.K. Chau, and P.L. Luxon, J. Fish. Res. Board Can., 35 (1978) 479-481.
22 C.F. Sigman, H.J. Kania, and R.J. Reyers, J. Fish. Res. Board Can., 34 (1977) 493-500.
23 B.A. Whitton and P.J. Say, in B.A. Whitton (Editor), River Ecology, Blackwell Scientific Publications, London, 1975, pp. 286-311.
24 D.R. Trollope and B. Evans, Environ. Pollut., 11 (1976) 109-116.
25 M. Fujita and K. Hashizume, Water Res., 9 (1975) 889-894.

26 W. Lang, Can. J. Microbiol., 20 (1973) 1311-1321.
27 G.E. Fogg, in R.A. Lewin (Editor), Physiology and Biochemistry of Algae, Academic Press, Inc., New York, U.S.A., 1963, pp. 475-489.
28 T. Murphy, D.R.S. Lean, and C. Nalewajko, Science, 192 (1976) 900-902.
29 F. Briand, R. Trucco, and S. Ramamoorthy, J. Fish. Res. Board Can., 35 (1978) 1482-1485.
30 U.S. Environmental Protection Agency (USEPA), Guidelines for Carcinogen Risk Assessment, Fed. Registr., 51, No. 185 (September 1986), pp. 33991-34003.
31 G.M. Rand and S.R. Petrocelli, Fundamentals of Aquatic Toxicology, Hemisphere Publications Co., Washington, D.C., U.S.A., 1985, 666 p.
32 F.L. Mayer and J.L. Hamelink, Aquatic Toxicology and Hazard Evaluation, American Society of Testing and Materials, Philadelphia, PA, U.S.A., 1977.
33 A.W. Hayes, Principles and Methods of Toxicology, Raven Press, New York, U.S.A., 1982.
34 K.R. Stevens and M.A. Gallo, in A.W. Hayes (Editor), Principles and Methods of Toxicology, Raven Press, New York, U.S.A., 1982.
35 U.S. Environmental Protection Agency (USEPA), Guidelines for Health Assessment of Suspect Developmental Toxicants, Fed. Regist., 51 CFR 2984, No. 185 (1986) 34028-34041.
36 R.L. Dixon and J.L. Hall, in A.W. Hayes (Editor), Principles and Methods of Toxicology, Raven Press, New York, U.S.A., Chapter 4, 1982.
37 Federal Register, Guidelines for Carcinogen Risk Assessment, U.S. Environmental Protection Agency, Fed. Registr., 51, No. 185 (Sept. 24, 1986), p. 33993.
38 U.S. Environmental Protection Agency (USEPA), Guidelines for Mutagenicity Risk Assessment, Office of Health and Environmental Assessment, Washington, D.C., U.S.A., EPA/600/8-87/045, 1987, pp. 2-1 to 2-9.
39 World Health Organization (WHO), Principles and Methods for Evaluating the Toxicity of Chemicals - Part I, Geneva, WHO, Environmental Health Criteria No. 6, 1978.
40 U.S. Congress, Office of Technology Assessment, Identifying and Regulating Carcinogens, OTA-BP-H-42, U.S. Gov't. Printing Office, Washington, D.C., U.S.A. 1987.
41 World Health Organization (WHO), in H.W. de Koning (Editor), Setting Environmental Standards - Guidelines for Decision-Making, WHO, MacMillan, England, Chapter 3, ISBN 92-4-154214-4, 1987.
42 L. Zeise, R. Wilson and E.A.C. Crouch, Environ. Health Persp., 73 (1987) 259-308.
43 J.M. Barnes and F.A. Denz, Pharmacol. Rev., 8 (1954) 191-242.
44 M.L. Dourson and J.F. Stara, Reg. Toxicol. Pharmacol., 3 (1983) 224-228.
45 D.J. Paustenbach and R. Lagner, Amer. Ind. Hyg. Assn. J., 47 (1986) 809-818.
46 W.G. Flamm and J.S. Winbush, Fundam. Appl. Toxicol., 4 (1984) S395-S401.
47 S. Friess, in Pharmacokinetics in Risk Assessment: Drinking Water and Health, National Academy of Sciences, Washington, D.C., U.S.A., Vol. 8, 1987.
48 H.E. Stokinger, in Permissible Levels of Toxic Substances in the Working Environment, International Labour Office, World Health Organization, Geneva, Switzerland, 1970.
49 U.S. National Academy of Sciences (NAS), Drinking Water and Health, NAS Washington, D.C., U.S.A., Vol. 1, 1977.
50 N.F. Izmerov, Control of Air Pollution in the U.S.S.R, Geneva, World Health Organization, Public Health Paper No. 54, 1973.
51 I.C. Munro and D.R. Krewski, Food Cosmet. Toxicol., 19 (1981) 549-560.
52 K.S. Crump, Fundam. Appl. Toxicol., 4 (1984) 854-877.
53 J. Cornfield, F.W. Carlborg, and J. Van Ryzin, in G.L. Plaa, and N.A.M. Duncan (Editors), Proceedings of the First International Congress on Toxicology, Academic Press, New York, U.S.A., 1978, pp. 143-164.
54 D.W. Gaylor and R.L. Kodell, J. Environ. Pathol. Toxicol., 4 (1980) 305-311.
55 M.E. Andersen, Amer. Ind. Hyg. Assn. J., In Press, Quantitative Risk Assessment and Industrial Hygiene, 1988.

56 C. Brown, Oncology, 33 (1976) 62-65.
57 International Agency for Research on Cancer (IARC), IARC Monographs on the Evaluation of Carcinogenic Risk to Humans, Supplement 4, Lyon, France, 1982.
58 U.S. Environmental Protection Agency (USEPA), Environmental Assessment, Short-Term Tests for Carcinogens, Mutagens, and Other Genotoxic Agents, Health Effects Research Laboratory, Research Triangle Park, North Carolina, U.S.A., EPA-625/9-79/003, 1979.

Chapter 7

EVALUATION OF DATABASES FOR IMPACT ASSESSMENT

7.1 CHEMICAL IMPACT

7.1.1 Regulatory Needs

Regulatory agencies around the world face an enormous challenge in the environmental management of chemicals. This is due to the vast array of chemicals which require evaluation of their potential environmental behaviour, fate processes, and their adverse effects. The regulatory framework is continuing to evolve with the increase in our knowledge about the environmental effects of chemicals. Environmental science must continue in its search for the most appropriate assessment tools. The aim should be to distinguish between present means of meeting legislated regulatory objectives and the scientific knowledge to achieve the ultimate goals set forth in the legislation. Thus, scientific data and understanding of the chemicals and their effects are needed not only to support the existing regulations but, more importantly, also to guide the continuous process of developing better regulations and guidelines.

Specific data requirement varies with the type of chemical, applicable regulation, and the component of the environment to be protected. Regulations dealing with biocide chemicals differ significantly from all other toxic-related legislations (e.g., FIFRA, U.S. Federal Insecticide, Fungicide, and Rodenticide Act). The differences are: (1) FIFRA regulates chemicals that are designed and known to be toxic and are deliberately placed in the environment; and (2) the ecosystem type (forest, surface waters, and agricultural environment) and the biocide's mode, rate and timing of entry into that environment are known and can be regulated. Requirements for environmental testing under FIFRA, therefore, have been less controversial than other legislations (ref. 1).

Registration of chemicals under FIFRA requires sufficient information so that U.S. EPA can determine that neither the product its uses, or by-products, will cause an unreasonably adverse effect on the environment. Considerable emphasis is placed on the environmental chemistry data on fate processes of the biocide. Also required are the laboratory information on degradation, metabolism and mobility, field dissipation studies conducted under actual conditions of use (ref. 2). Three major sets of data required under this Act pertain to ecological effects: hazard to wildlife and aquatic organisms, non-target plants and non-target insects. Each dataset includes short-term acute toxicity, subacute toxicity, reproduction, simulated field and full-field studies. The tests are hierarchically organized with the evaluation of results of each tier together with environmental fate data, to determine whether additional testing is needed (ref. 1). Special testings under this Act could include long-term field monitoring studies, studies on endangered species, and effects on microbial functions related to soil fertility.

Regulations on toxic substances control and environmental protection deal with an array of chemicals that may or may not prove to be toxic, may have levels at which they do not cause adverse effects, and may or may not enter ecological systems. Manufacturers are required to report information on chemical identity, intended use(s), total amount to be manufactured or processed, by-products, use pattern, and modes of disposal. The USEPA has identified different types of data to be developed by manufacturers before the actual production of the chemical. This "recommended base set", given in Table 7.1, is similar to the "Minimum Pre-Market Data" recommended by the Organization of Economic Cooperation and Development (OECD). It basically contains three types of data required in assessing environmental effects of the chemical: (1) physical/chemical data; (2) ecotoxicity data; and (3) degradation/accumulation data.

TABLE 7.1 Data requirements for the premanufacture testing of new chemicals.

---

1. Physical/chemical data

Melting point/melting range
Boiling point/boiling range
Density of liquids and solids
Vapor pressure
Water solubility
Partition coefficient, n-octanol-water
Hydrolysis (as a function of pH)
Spectra (ultraviolet and visible)
Soil adsorption/desorption
Dissociation constant
Particle size distribution

2. Acute toxicity data

Acute oral toxicity
Acute dermal toxicity
Acute inhalation toxicity
Skin irritation
Eye irritation (for chemicals showing no skin irritation)

3. Repeated dose toxicity data

14-28 days, repeated dose test(s) using probable route(s) of human exposure

---

Continued . . . .

TABLE 7.1 Concluded.

---

4. Mutagenicity data (screening tests)

    Gene (point) mutation
    Chromosome aberrations

5. Ecotoxicity data

    Acute toxicity, LC_{50} study, fish (96 hour)
    Daphnia reproduction study (3 broods)
    Growth inhibition study, unicellular alga (4 days)

6. Degradation/accumulation data

    Ready degradability
    Bioaccumulation (uptake from medium)

(Source: ref. 3).

Mandatory testing, even the minimum type proposed by the OECD, has not been accepted by many regulatory agencies including the USEPA (ref. 1). Risk assessments of most new chemicals are carried out in USEPA using: (1) the minimum required data provided by the premanufacturing notification; and (2) structure-activity relationships for environmental behaviour and toxicity.

Regulations for protecting the water quality require development of criteria or guidelines which accurately reflect the latest scientific knowledge (refs. 4,5). In addition to discussions on known adverse effects, the protection of raw water for specified uses such as: (1) raw water for drinking water supply; (2) recreational water quality and aesthetics; (3) freshwater aquatic life; (4) agricultural uses ((a) irrigational and (b) livestock watering); (5) industrial water supplies, have been assessed in order to develop numerical concentration limits or narrative statements. The U.S. national water quality criteria were criticized for three main reasons: (1) inadequate database on aquatic toxicity for using either single-species laboratory bioassays or using limited number of laboratory-reared species or for using sensitive species. Lack of tests on multiple species or community, not accounting for physico-chemical characteristics of the water column, not factoring sediments into the experiments, not giving attention to long-term effects and effects of reproduction and behaviour; (2) chemical impacts on the ecosystems and the role of ecosystems on the fate and transport of pollutants, sediment-water interactions, physico-chemical speciation altering the effects of the chemical were not accounted for in the water quality numerical or narrative criteria; and (3) these deficiencies were passed onto the state levels since the national criteria were used as the basis for the state standards. In other words, over protection and under protection of particular systems were the end results.

However, the USEPA revised its policy in 1980 and adopted methods to include large number of species (at least eight) from various trophic levels, different physico-chemical characteristics of the water, chronic effects, effects on reproduction and sensitive lifestages (ref. 1). However, the guidelines "have been developed on the assumption that the results of laboratory tests are generally useful for predicting what will happen in field situations." They also suggest that "field studies are more useful in reviewing criteria than in deriving criteria" (ref. 5). The U.S EPA and Environment Canada encourage states or provinces to identify specific waterbodies where toxic pollutants may be affecting a designated or specific use and then develop criteria or guidelines for those chemicals in those region-specific waterbodies. The questions of extrapolating from the laboratory data to natural waterbodies would be the responsibility of the state or provincial governments to derive guidelines and translating them to regulatory or management strategies.

The scientific information has to meet two entirely different regulatory needs. One is short-term regulatory objectives in terms of issuing permits and licences for industries to operate. The other function of the scientific information is to provide the scientific understanding required to fulfill the ultimate goal of the environmental acts and regulations. This is similar to the toxicity testing on a chemical for its acute effects and chronic effects or in other words, the short- and long-term effects of a chemical. Bearing in mind, the enormous amount of testing to be done on thousands of chemicals, the hundreds of rivers to be monitored and numerous enforcement actions demanding attention in terms of time and resources, if ultimate goals are to be realized, what will be needed is the "intellectual efficiency and generality of results" that is derived from understanding fundamental principles that determine the ways the ecosystems respond to chemical stress (ref. 1). A framework using the results from the current testing protocols should develop appropriate and viable approaches to environmental assessment. One aspect of that is the development of information base on how the ecosystem modifies the fate and dispersion of chemicals among the various media of the environment.

Most of the laws of U.S. EPA require protection of human health and environment. It is likely that the laws are stated differently. The office of Pesticides and Toxic Substances is concerned about potential impacts of pesticides and toxic chemicals on organisms including aquatic and terrestrial communities. Its legal mandate originates from the Federal Insecticide, Fungicide and Rodenticide Act (FIFRA) and the Toxic Substances Control Act

(TSCA). FIFRA assessments are usually data-rich, whereas TSCA assessements tend to be data-poor with only limited ecological effects data provided by the companies. The reason for the difference is FIFRA is a registration law that gives EPA legal authority to demand up-front testing of chemicals. TSCA is only a "review and approval law" and a case must be made before any substantial testing for adverse effects can be demanded (ref. 6).

Because of the large numbers of industrial chemicals to be tested, the Office of Toxic Substances (OTS) has developed a method for identifying chemicals for testing for ecological hazards. Assessment factors are used in conjunction with the hazard assessment to calculate a concentration level which is actually a concern level. When these values are equaled or exceeded, further testing is clearly required. Assessment factors are not the same as safety factors. Four assessment factors are used: 1, 10, 100, and 1000 and they are used solely to review premanufacture notifications to identify those chemicals which require full ecological assessment (ref. 7).

The Office of Pesticide Programs (OPP) uses a four-step preliminary assessment of ecological risk: (1) review and evaluate hazard data; (2) identify and evaluate the observed quantitative relationship between dose and response; (3) identify conditions of exposure; and (4) combine the dose-response information with that of exposure for evaluating the adverse effects on the non-target populations. The exposure data are normally derived from model-estimated environmental concentrations (EEC). If the ratio of EEC/LC_{50} equals or exceeds certain fixed criteria, actual or simulated field testing is required. Currently this framework is not used because of its inability to estimate the level of uncertainty. The framework is intended to provide a safety factor which would allow for the differential variability among fish and wildlife (ref. 8). Since 1985, OPP has developed the weight-of- evidence approach for determining unreasonable ecological risk. This includes consideration of quality and adequacy of the data, as well as the magnitude of the estimated or observed effect (ref. 6).

The Water Quality Act of 1987 (P.L. 100-4) amended the previous Clean Water Act (CWA) and changed its focus from end-of-pipe standards to full scale ambient water quality approach. The new Act requires detailed assessments of: (1) tropic status and trends in lakes; (2) additional non-point source control to reach the set water quality standards and waters not meeting standards due to priority toxic pollutants. Control actions and management plans are being updated (refs. 9,10). State water quality standards in U.S.A. form the backbone of water-quality based approach with biological end-points as the basis. The end-points that are commonly used in risk assessments are chemical-specific risk criteria and whole-effluent toxicity criteria (refs. 11-13).

Tier toxicity testing approach is used for hazard assessment in assessing the quality of the effluent. Estimated effect threshold levels are compared with EEC using the quotient method to flag an unacceptable effluent discharge and trigger either higher tier testing or implementing controls. Thus ecological risk assessment is increasingly becoming an integral part of most of the regulations and also at EPA.

7.1.2 Environmental Databases

The public demand for quantitative data on the state of the environment is relatively recent. Consequently, these data are not well developed, in contrast to the years of data gathering in fields such as health and economy. The feedback between the user community and the data managers not only improves the specification of the required data, but also the techniques and the methods of data collection. In the environmental field, the linkage between the analyst and data producer is still in the developmental stage. Hence, the specifications of data collection are still driven by operational and administrative needs (ref. 14). In natural resource areas such as forest inventories, mineral and hydrocarbon exploration, hydrological surveys for water utilization, the databases, although fairly complete, are often site-specific and user-oriented in terms of economic viability and resource management. They are often inadequate for a comprehensive environmental assessment and ecological sustainability and integrity. However, a potential exists to develop a more integrated natural resource database for assessing the state of the environment.

Environmental complexity and scientific uncertainty about the choice of parameters in monitoring have contributed to the datagap between what is required and what actually exists. Some salient points on this topic are: (1) environmental variability; (2) non-convergence; (3) space and time correlations; (4) cause and effect relations; and (5) biased perspectives (ref. 15).

Organization of data in environmental and natural resource area have been developing over the years based on their nature and use pattern. The following are the major frameworks: (i) stock-flow systems; (ii) mapping and spatial integration; (iii) monitoring system; and (iv) stress-response environmental statistical system (ref. 1).

(i) <u>Stock-flow systems</u>. Stock-flow systems are complex data compilations based on the "rules" that link stock characteristics with flow parameters. This structure is useful for environmental/economic interaction analysis.

(ii) <u>Mapping and spatial integration systems</u>. These systems are databases generally described by geographical coordinates or grid matrices. The Canadian Land Use Monitoring System (CLUMP) and Canada Forestry Inventory are examples of the coordinate and grid systems, respectively. Ecosystem mapping, forest inventories and land use patterns are particularly well suited for this kind of data assembly.

(iii) <u>Monitoring systems</u>. They are important in analyzing environmental conditions and trends. These are characterized by time series (trend analysis) and spatial sampling (distribution analysis). Health statistics databases are examples of this type of data organization.

(iv) <u>Stress-responses environmental statistical systems</u>. These systems integrate data on human and natural activities with data on environmental change.

The following is a list of Canadian federal government databases relevant in assessing the state of the environment and human health. The content and intended uses of these databases are discussed in detail in ref. 1.

LIST OF CANADIAN FEDERAL GOVERNMENT DATABASES

1. Environmental and Natural Resource Statistics
2. National Air Pollution Surveillance (NAPS)
3. National Water Quality Data Base (NAQUADAT)
4. National Hydrometric Data Bank (HYDAT)
5. Canada Land Data System (CLDS)
6. Canada Land Use Monitoring Program (CLUMP)
7. Ecological Regionalization Data Bases
8. Canadian Forest Resource Data System (CFRDS)
9. Canadian Fisheries Statistics Data Base (in preparation)
10. Municipal Waterworks and Waste Water Data (MUNDAT)
11. Industrial Water Use and Municipal Water Use Data Base
12. National Emissions Inventory System (NEIS)
13. National Inventory of Pollution Sources (NIPS)
14. Major Projects Inventory
15. Canadian Network for Sampling Precipitation (CANSAP)
16. Canadian Air and Precipitation Monitoring Network (CAPMoN)(Air)
17. Canadian Air and Precipitation Network (CAPMoN)
18. National Climatological Archives
19. Ice Climatology Data Base
20. Canadian Soil Information System (CANSIS)
21. National Mineral Inventory (NMI)
22. Canada Sport Fishing Data Base (in preparation)
23. Canadian Migratory Birds Population Studies
24. Marine Environmental Data Systems (MEDS)
25. Historical Earthquake File
26. Health Statistics
27. Pesticide Information System

28. National Registry of Toxic Chemical Residues (NRTCR)
29. National Analysis of Trends in Emergencies (NATES)
30. Ocean Dumping Permit Control (ODUMP)
31. Chemicals in Canadian Commerce (CCUBE)
32. Restricted Information System for Chemicals (RISC)

Although epidemiology may be valuable in revealing the health status of the exposed population, it is often of uncertain or limited use due to many uncontrollable factors which could confound conclusions drawn from it (refs. 16-18). Most important factors include sample size, assembling an unexposed control group, memory bias in reporting the essential information on exposure, problems related to length of the latency period and numerous lifestyles such as smoking, eating habits, use of alcohol or drugs, and sex and age differences. In addition, the exposure could be due to mixtures of chemicals at low-level and poorly-defined exposure regimes.

In spite of these difficulties, more encompassing monitoring information is needed through cooperation among agencies, cross-sectoral data gathering, reduction of redundancy, increased comprehensiveness and clearer objectives for the use of the data.

7.1.3 Data Evaluation

(i) OECD framework. Organization for Economic Cooperation and Development has prepared a set of criteria through expert groups for screening chemicals for health and environmental purposes (ref. 19). A number of selection elements were identified including both primary parameters, as well as surrogates which can be used to estimate the former element. Production volume is an example of a surrogate selection element for estimating potential exposure.

Aspects common to both processes (priority-setting for health and environmental purposes) are as follows:

1. Identification of the purpose and scope of the selection exercise which may influence the inclusion or exclusion of chemicals in or from the exercise, the choice of selection elements and other practical considerations. Clarification is essential on the following items, such as time in which results are required, resources available, national priorities, regulatory requirements, policies, effects of interest, targets of interest (consumers, sensitive subpopulation, aquatic organisms, etc.) or broad chemical groups (chemicals in water, chemicals detected in waste disposal site, etc.).

2. The four stages in the priority-setting process, namely, compilation, screening, refinement, and review.

3. Quantity and depth of information required increases from the compilation to the review stage.

4. Output matrix separately sets out priorities by types of toxic responses, target organisms, specific exposure situation, and information needs.

5. The need for expert judgement involving techniques, such as structure-activity relationship and other methods to provide estimates of missing information.

6. Repeating the selection process at regular time intervals to reconsider excluded chemicals based on new information and also to correct for possible errors.

At the screening stage, chemicals are assessed for their potential for environmental exposure and effects. Selection elements for environmental exposure cover three categories of information:

1. Data on the presence of a chemical in the environment (air, water, soil, and biota) -- Selection element - Detection in the environment.

2. Data on the potential release of the chemical into the environment depending upon its use pattern -- Selection elements - production and import volume, environmental release during manufacturing and processing, use patterns, and mode of disposal.

3. Data on the environmental fate of a chemical once it is released into a given media (air or water) of the environment -- Selection elements - environmental distribution, transformation/degradation, bioconcentration, and metabolic products.

Detection in the Environment

Data required for this selection element include:

1. Identity of the chemical detected in environmental samples;

2. Concentration of the chemical;

3. Change in concentration with time;

4. Sampling protocols and analytical methods used (detection limits, statistical data).

Use of data:

Data is critically evaluated to determine the concentration ranges in each medium (air, soil, water, and biota), number of surveys and number of locations involved in the surveys. If monitoring data are available, the trend (concentration increasing or decreasing) is determined, after checking the quality of the monitoring data.

Chemicals found in the environment may not necessarily be the primary chemical but could be products resulted from transformation and/or degradation of the parent compounds. Examples are the products from combustion processes, pulp and paper mill operations or water treatment processes. Microbial interactions could also transform chemicals, like formation of methylmercury (from inorganic mercury) which accumulates in fish.

Chemicals detected in the environment cannot be distinguished for their anthropogenic or man-made origin. Literature data older than 10 y should be carefully assessed with respect to valid/invalid sampling and analytical protocols used. Caution should be exercised in interpreting such data.

Release Potential to the Environment

Data needed for the selection element include:
1. Annual production data;
2. Annual import data;
3. Annual export data;
4. Calculated annual consumption data.

The primary data type required for assessing release potential are sources, quantity and duration of release. In the absence of such information, production volume data, in conjunction with use pattern information, will provide surrogate information.

Environmental Release during Manufacturing and Processing

Data required are information on source emission (rate and duration) into air and water. Also, information is needed on whether the production is continuous or intermittant. Expert judgement is required to estimate fugitive emissions from the plant. If such information is not available for a certain industrial process, plant emission can be estimated based on the knowledge of basic manufacturing process. A methodology has been developed that categorizes emissions, discharges and product contamination for 23 unit processes employed in the production of synthetic organic chemicals (ref. 20).

Data for air emissions and water discharges are available for major air and water pollutants. In some industrial regions, emission registers (environmental emission data) exist, indicating identity and sometimes also quantity of chemicals released to the environment and duration of release.

Use Pattern

Use patterns refer to the qualitative and quantitative description of the variety of uses of a chemical. It provides information on the extent of the chemical release during its use and on the possible location(s) of that release.

Quantitative figures of consumption (tons/year) and percentages in different use categories are available for many metals and some organic chemicals in literature (refs. 21,22).

For environmental purposes, the following five categories of use may be most relevant (ref. 23):

1. Destructive uses (e.g., fuels, fuel additives, chemical intermediates);
2. Contained uses (i.e., no release to the environment), e.g., catalysts used in closed processes, certain photographic chemicals, capacitor fluids;
3. Open, non-dispersive uses (i.e., release to the environment unlikely), e.g., printing inks, finishing chemicals for textiles, dyes, plasticisers, adhesives, paints, varnishes;
4. Dispersive uses (which result in release to the environment), e.g., cutting fluids, fabric softeners, automobile tire rubber; and
5. Highly dispersive uses in the environment (e.g., pesticides, fertilizers, de-icing salts, solvents, detergents).

Chemicals which are used exclusively as intermediates can be classified at a lower level of environmental concern, unless they are frequently detected in the ambient environment.

Mode of Disposal

This selection element evaluates possible losses into the environment after disposal of the chemical. Data on the quantities of the chemical targetted for disposal, method of disposing the chemical (such as neutralization, incineration, landfilling, biological treatment, etc.) and other information on physico-chemical properties which might contribute to release of the chemical following the disposal are required for evaluation of this element.

Uncontrolled releases resulting from incomplete incineration, incomplete breakdown in biological treatment plants, leachates from landfill sites contribute significantly to environmental distribution of chemicals.

Environmental Fate

After release of the chemical into the environment, its distribution is governed by a number of physical, chemical, and biological processes which are known as environmental fate processes. Transport of the chemical and its subsequent partitioning between different media, such as air, water, soil/ sediment, and biota distribute the chemical widely in the environment. Equilibrium partitioning of many organic chemicals can be estimated by using their physico-chemical properties, such as vapour pressure, water solubility, n-octanol/water partition coefficient, Henry's law constant, and soil sorption coefficient. For ionizable compounds, their dissociation constants should be considered. Some of the physical properties are inter-related to a certain extent and can therefore be estimated from each other. The stability of a chemical determines the extent of its distribution in the environment either locally or globally. Only chemicals of reasonable stability will have the time required to reach equilibrium partitioning among the various environmental media.

Transport Processes

Data on transport processes of chemicals are available to the extent indicated below:

1. Vapour pressure: Generally available from handbooks and compendiums (ref. 24).
2. Water solubility: Qualitative information generally available but quantitative and reliable data are less readily available (ref. 24,25).
3. n-octanol/water partition coefficient: Data on some several hundreds of chemicals are listed in literature (refs. 24-26).
4. Henry's law constant: Limited data are available (refs. 24,27,28).
5. Soil sorption coefficients: Limited data are available (refs. 24,29).
6. Dissociation constant: Quantitative data available for several hundreds of compounds (ref. 30).

In the absence of experimental values, reliable estimates for several chemicals can be obtained by using appropriate estimation methods listed in literature (refs. 28,31).

Transformation Processes

The residence time of a chemical in its original form determines its level of persistence in the environment. Biotic and abiotic processes can cause the chemical to transform (minor or major alteration of the original chemical form) and even undergo degradation to its fundamental building units of water, carbon dioxide, ammonia, etc. The greater the resistance of a chemical to the transformation and/or degradation processes, the longer is the persistence of the chemical in its parent form in the environment.

The accumulation of a chemical in the environment will be decided by the ease with which the chemical can be transformed or degraded by biotic and abiotic processes. Most of the transformation data available in the literature have been generated at laboratory conditions, simulating field conditions using microcosm study approaches. However, differences will surface since field conditions are more complex, thus making extrapolations less accurate. In addition, kinetic data on transformation processes relevant to natural conditions are not readily available.

Bioaccumulation/Bioconcentration

Bioaccumulation is a selective process by which a chemical is concentrated in an organism in quantities greater than the surrounding medium. Bioconcentration results when the uptake rate far exceeds the clearance rate by an organism. Biomagnification is a descriptor of a process by which the chemical increases its concentration between steps in the food ladder in the environment.

The bioconcentration factor (BCF) is the ratio of the concentration of a chemical in the whole organism to the concentration in the test medium which surrounds the organism at steady-state conditions. Hence, BCF is an indicator of the ability of a given chemical to accumulate in the lipid compartment of an organism. N-octanol is very close to the properties of the lipid compartment of many biota (about 7% fat). Hence, BCF of a chemical can be predicted with reasonable accuracy from its partitioning coefficient between n-octanol and water mixture (K_{ow}). It should be pointed out here that speciation of the chemical might change between water and n-octanol, thus invalidating the use of K_{ow} values in further calculation.

The net concentration (exposure concentration) of a chemical in the environment is given by the equation (5.1):

$$\frac{dc}{dt} = \frac{k_i C}{1+k_s} \tag{7.1}$$

where C = original concentration of the chemical, k = partition coefficient between two phases, k_i = rate constant for various fate processes, and s = mass of the sorbent in a particular compartment or media. Neely et al. (ref. 32) first reported a semi-empirical relationship between log K_{ow} (logarithm of the octanol-water partition coefficient) and the bioconcentration factor (BCF) for many organic chemicals.

$$\log (BCF) = 0.542 \log [K_{ow}] + 0.124 \tag{7.2}$$

Laboratory studies have shown a similar relationship for ecological magnification (EM) (ref. 33) which is as follows:

$$\log [EM] = 0.7825 + 0.6335 \log K_{ow} \tag{7.3}$$

It should be noted that these are semi-quantitative correlations only and may fail for low K_{ow} value or for chemicals whose speciation is not the same in both water and n-octanol phases.

The transport and transformation processes provide valuable information on the distribution and persistence of chemicals in the environment. Figure 7.1 illustrates the role of various transport processes in concentrating the chemical in one medium and the role of transformation processes in distributing the chemical into other media, such as biota and air or totally degrade the chemical.

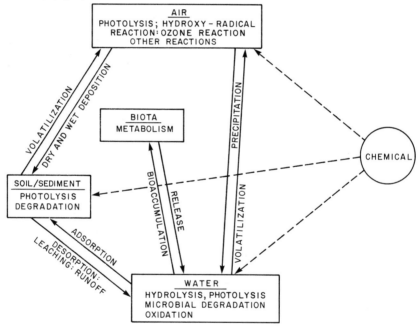

Fig. 7.1. Schematic illustration of transport and transformation processes of a chemical in the environment.
(Source: Reprinted with permission from ref. 34, Copyright (1980), Butterworths).

Data sources listed in the OECD document (ref. 19) include 230 handbooks and tables, 401 monographs, reports and other printed documents, 58 computerized databases, totalling to 689 data sources in the form of a microfiche. However, care must be exercised in using these sources because the quality of the data varies among the documents.

Handbooks and Tables

- transcription errors are common since these are usually copied from other sources.
- do not claim to have "most recent data" since such set of data are generated frequently and published in journals and periodicals.
- usually include data which were not critically assessed in the inclusion process.

Monographs, Reports, and Other Printed Documents

- usually present original data from primary publications or research studies.
- often provide comparative tables of data.

Computerized Databases

- include primary, secondary, or tertiary data whose quality might vary depending upon the protocols under which they were collected. The primary data usually should have been critically reviewed for use for a specific purpose.

Since infinite amount of resources will be needed to assess all use patterns for all chemicals, it is imperative to set a limit which is credible for scientific purposes. Although some 55,000 chemicals are on the list, an analysis of the U.S. inventory shows that only 1,000 chemicals account for about 99.5% of the total volume and 5,000 chemicals make up 99.9% of the total volume. Hence, from public health protection point of view, the initial stages of screening should address the major uses of these high volume chemicals. On the other hand, information on the vast majority of small-volume chemicals is much more hard to obtain. For low-volume chemicals which are assessed as priority chemicals, information on possible end uses from the manufacturer can be identified through either Buyers' Guides or chemical directories. Large computerized databases often include Chemical Abstracts Service (CAS) numbers which can be used in cross-referencing with U.S. TSCA and E.E.C. inventories. Several international systems currently in use for prioritization of chemicals have been reviewed in the OECD document (ref. 19).

(ii) U.S. EPA has been developing the environmental fate exposure data base (EFEDB) since 1979, recognizing the difficulty in obtaining information on identifying environmental release, fate and exposure (ref. 35).

The components BIOLOG and BIODEG contain microbial toxicity and degradation information, whereas the FATE/EXPOS file contains information on fate processes and exposure pathways. EFEDB has greatly expanded since inception.

The EFEDB system consists of three files: (1) DATALOG - a data index file containing chemical identification information with an indication of data type and abbreviated reference; (2) XREF - a full reference file with authors, data, article title, and citation; (3) CHEMFATE - an experimental data file on rates, concentrations, and experimental conditions on various types of environmental fate processes. Table 7.2 lists the type and number of records available as of 1985 in DATALOG and CHEMFATE. At that time, there were more than 63,000 records covering 5,455 chemicals in DATALOG which represented a tripling of records and doubling of the number of chemicals since 1982. As of 1989, these numbers were 180,000 (records) and 12,000 (chemicals) in DATALOG and CHEMFATE contained 24,000 records for 900 chemicals (personal communication, ref. 36). Table 7.2 also gives a breakdown of records by data type. It has to be noted that the number of chemicals considered and the data types vary for the two files in Table 7.2. The FATE/EXPOS file contains information on production and use, fate and monitoring of chemicals in ambient environment (Table 7.3).

TABLE 7.2 Summary of records in CHEMFATE and DATALOG (1985).

DATALOG			CHEMFATE		
Data type	Total records	Average no. of records per chemical	Data type	Total records	Average no. of records[a,b] per chemical
			Identity	650[a]	
Water solubility	5,783	1.07	Octanol/water partition		
Octanol/water partition coefficient	3,727	0.69	coefficient	415	0.83
Vapour pressure	6,532	1.21	Dissociation constant	155	0.31
UV spectra	722	0.13	Soil adsorption	533	1.06
Dissociation constant	804	0.15	UV spectra	254	0.51
Adsorption	3,265	0.60	Vapour pressure	295	0.59
Bioconcentration	1,847	1.45	Water solubility	515	1.03
Evaporation	843	0.16	Bioconcentration	344	0.69
Henry's Law constant	1,297	0.24	Evaporation	189	0.38
			Henry's Law constant	138	0.28

Continued . . . .

TABLE 7.2 Concluded.

	DATALOG			CHEMFATE	
Data type	Total records	Average no. of records per chemical	Data type	Total records	Average no. of records[a,b] per chemical
Biodegradation	13,588	2.51	Soil column	65	0.13
Hydrolysis	1,100	0.02	Soil thin-layer		
Photooxidation	7,032	1.30	chromatography	62	0.12
Monitoring	13,584	2.51	Ecosystem	47	0.09
Ecosystems	259	0.05	Hydrolysis	147	0.29
Field studies	716	0.13	Microbial		
Food monitoring	744	0.14	degradation	1,028	2.06
Occupation			Natural systems		
monitoring	339	0.06	degradation	2,537	5.07
Effluent			Oxidation	651	1.30
monitoring	1,409	0.26	Photolysis	223	0.45
TOTAL	63,591	12.68	Air monitoring	794	1.59
			Biomonitoring	260	0.52
			Field studies	157	0.31
			Soil monitoring	69	0.14
			Water monitoring	947	1.89
			TOTAL	10,475	19.64

[a] Comprehensive literature searches for data in all fields have been performed for only 464 chemicals.

[b] There is more than one record for a parameter type for some chemicals. Total number of chemicals considered: about 5,400 (DATALOG); 500 (CHEMFATE).

(Source: Reprinted with permission from ref. 35, Copyright (1986), Pergamon Press Plc.).

TABLE 7.3 FATE/EXPOS file format.

CAS registry no.: Chemical name
Product volume (millions of lbs.):
Number of producers (TSCA 1977):
Number of producers (DCP):
Workers exposed (NOHS):
Workers exposed (NOES):
Commercial uses:
Use/source: (Pesticide, drug, priority pollutant, natural product, combustion product, commercial product)

Physical-chemical properties:
    Octanol/water partition coefficient (log) =
    Water solubility (ppm) =
    Vapour pressure (kPa) =
    Dissociation constant (pK_a) =

Continued . . . .

TABLE 7.3 Concluded.

Chemical fate data
    Adsorption   (   )
    Bioconcentration   (   )
    Evaporation   (   )
    Henry's Law constant   (   )
    Biodegradation   (   )
    Hydrolysis   (   )
    Photooxidation   (   )

Monitoring data
    Occupational   (   )
    Food   (   )
    Effluent   (   )
    Effluent   (   )
    Air   (   )
    Surface water   (   )
    Ground water   (   )
    Drinking water   (   )
    Soil   (   )
    Human   (   )
    Aquatic organisms   (   )
    Terrestrial organisms (   )

CAS, Chemical Abstracts Service; TSCA, Toxic Substances Control Act Inventory; DCP, Directory of Chemical Producers; NOHS, National Occupational Hazard Survey; NOES, National Occupational Exposure Survey.
(Source: Reprinted with permission from ref. 35, Copyright (1986), Pergamon Press Plc.).

(iii) <u>Decision tree</u>. Neely (ref. 37), in 1979, developed a decision tree (Fig. 7.2) based on a chemical's distribution profile that is an extension of several previous studies on compartmental analysis. The profile gives the estimated distribution of the chemical in air, water, biota, and soil. Decisions on environmental exposure can be made by comparing this profile with the existing or intended use pattern. The "YES" output from boxes K, L, and M suggests the need for further information on biotic and abiotic fate processes.

A. Use Pattern

Information on the different uses of the chemical, medium of entry (air, water, soil, etc.), and the estimated rate of discharge into the environment are required.

B. Confined Use

If the chemical is used in a closed mode with no possible entry into the environment, no further testing is required.

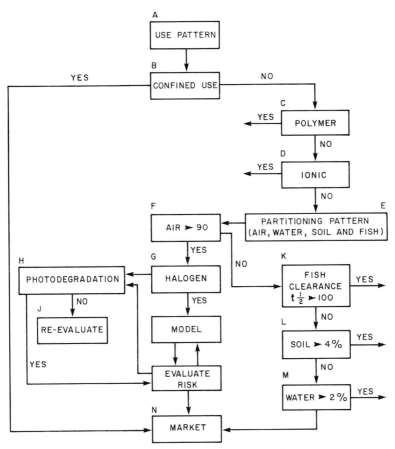

Fig. 7.2. Decision tree to assess environmental distribution.
(Source: Reprinted with permission from ref. 37, Copyright (1979), Amer. Fish.
Soc.).

C. Polymer

If the chemical is an insoluble polymer, then further testing is required
for interactions associated with its disposal process.

D. Ionic Material

Ionic interaction, such as sorption to sediments and suspended solids and
possible transformation to other species, should be investigated.

E. Partitioning Pattern

Migration of the chemical into media other than its medium of origin and
its distribution profile in air, water, biota, and sediment is to be
calculated from values of solubilities, vapour pressures, and half-life for
clearance $(t_{1/2})$ from fish. Using known values of solubilities and vapour

pressures for a wide range of organic chemicals from toluene to DDT, Neely (ref. 38) developed four regression equations to calculate the percent distribution of a chemical which was statistically significant.

$$\text{Percent of chemical in air} = -0.247(1/H) + 7.9 \log S + 100.6 \tag{7.4}$$

$$\text{Percent of chemical in water} = 0.054 (1/H) + 1.32 \tag{7.5}$$

$$\text{Percent of chemical in sediment/soil} = 0.194 (1/H) - 7.65 \log S - 1.93 \tag{7.6}$$

$$\text{and } \log t_{1/2} \text{ (hours)} = 0.0027(1/H) - 0.282 \log S + 1.08 \tag{7.7}$$

where,

$$H(\text{mm Hg } m^3 \text{ mole}^{-1}) = \frac{\text{Vapour pressure x molecular weight}}{\text{solubility (mg } L^{-1})} \tag{7.8}$$

$$S (\text{mm } L^{-1}) = \frac{\text{Solubility mg } L^{-1}}{\text{molecular weight}} \tag{7.9}$$

$t_{1/2}(h)$ = half-life for clearance from fish in this ecosystem.

Table 7.4 presents the chemicals tested and their relevant physico-chemical properties, and Table 7.5 lists the actual and percent distributions predicted from the above regression equations. The agreement seems to be good.

F. Air

Depending upon the results from E, either go to G (air > 90%) or proceed to K for other interactions.

TABLE 7.4 Chemicals tested for the predictability of the regression equations and their properties.

Chemical	Molecular Weight	Vapour Pressure (mm Hg)	Water Solubility (mg L^{-1})
Toluene	92	30	470
p-Dichlorobenzene	147	1	79
Trichlorobenzene	180	0.5	30
Hexachlorobenzene	285	10^{-5}	0.035
Diphenyl	154	9.7×10^{-3}	7.5
Trichlorobiphenyl	256	1.5×10^{-3}	0.05
Tetrachlorobiphenyl	291	4.9×10^{-4}	0.05
Pentachlorobiphenyl	325	7.7×10^{-5}	0.01
DDT	350	10^{-7}	1.2×10^{-3}
Perchloroethylene	166	14	150

(Source: Reprinted with permission from ref. 37, Copyright (1979), Amer. Fish. Soc.).

G. Halogen

If the chemical is a halogenated compound, any suitable model (refs. 39,40) should be used to estimate the mass transfer of chlorine from the troposphere

TABLE 7.5 Actual and predicted distribution of chemicals tested.

Chemical	Water, %	Soil, %	Air, %	$t_{1/2}$ from fish (hours)
Toluene	0.9 (1.33)	0.4 (0)	98.6(100)	10(7.6)
p-Dichlorobenzene	1.24 (1.31)	1.28(0.24)	97.5(98)	15(14)
Trichlorobenzene	1.33 (1.34)	2.06(4.09)	96 (94)	17(20)
Hexachlorobenzene	3.57 (1.98)	39.4 (31)	56 (68)	162(164)
Diphenyl	2.27 (1.59)	5.4 (9)	92.2(89)	27(29)
Trichlorobiphenyl	1.38 (1.33)	15.2 (26)	83 (71)	96(134)
Tetrachlorobiphenyl	1.5 (1.34)	17 (27)	81 (71)	104(139)
Pentachlorobiphenyl	1.5 (1.34)	21 (33)	77 (65)	229(226)
DDT	1.26 (3.17)	67.5 (46.5)	28 (49)	915(517)
Perchloroethylene	1 (1.32)	1 (0)	98 (100)	14(12)

(Source: Reprinted with permission from ref. 37, Copyright (1979), Amer. Fish. Soc.).

to the stratosphere. This step will evaluate the relative risk that halogen atoms will cause by damaging the ozone layer. If the volatile chemical does not contain halogen in its structure, proceed to Box H.

H. Photodegradation

In this step, the potential for the photolytic breakdown of the chemical in the troposphere by hydroxy radicals will be estimated. Such breakdown will eliminate the tropospheric buildup of the parent chemical. If there is no concern, proceed to Box N.

J. Re-evaluation

Once a chemical reaches this box, a continuous re-evaluation examining other possible fate processes must be undertaken.

K. Fish Clearance

Values of $t_{1/2}$ more than 100 hours indicate a potential for bioconcentration of the chemical in water. This decision is arbitrary and based on benchmark concept of comparing with chemicals having $t_{1/2}$ values more than 100 hours and are known to bioconcentrate in fish. As a result, additional tests on the metabolism, type and toxicity of the metabolic products should be undertaken. If $t_{1/2}$ is less than 100 hours, proceed to Box L.

L. Soil/Sediment

If the amount of the chemical in soil/sediment is $\geq 4\%$, then degradation products should be evaluated using the bench-mark concept and comparing to structurally and functionally related compounds.

M. Water

If water holds >2% of the chemical, then aquatic fate processes of the chemical, such as hydrolysis, microbial degradation, sorption to suspended solids should be investigated.

If no long-term environmental impact based on the chemical's use pattern is predicted from this decision tree approach, then the production and use of this chemical should be either continued or permitted if it is a new chemical. It should be noted that this model is developed to assess environmental as opposed to human health hazard.

(iv) Applied examples of decision tree approach. After an accidental discharge of Kepone (a pesticide) into the James River, Virginia (U.S.A.), a decision tree analysis was performed (ref. 37), and Box E was identified as the critical compartment. The internal profile predicted that bioconcentration ($t_{1/2}$ >100 hours)(Table 7.6) and sorption-desorption processes will determine the distribution and persistence of Kepone in the environment. The analysis only used the physico-chemical properties and not the data on degradative processes since they were not available. Further tests on degradation of Kepone confirmed the importance of bioconcentration and supported the preliminary analysis. In this case, the decision tree analysis focussed quickly on the critical compartments of the environment for further monitoring.

TABLE 7.6 The distribution profile of chemicals predicted from Box E of the decision tree analysis.

Chemical	% of Chemical in			$t_{1/2}$ for clearance from fish (hours)
	Soil	Air	Water	
Kepone	62	23	14	231
Mirex	37	60	1.4	320
Chlorpyrifos	74	8.5	18	335
Monochlorobenzene	0	100	1.34	8

(Source: Reprinted with permission from ref. 37, Copyright (1979), Amer. Fish. Soc.).

Mirex, a chlorinated hydrocarbon (dodecachloropentacyclodecane) was used as a flame-retardant in many polymer preparations and also as an insecticide to control fire ants in Southern United States. Mirex behaved similarly to Kepone in the decision-tree analysis except for one important property. Mirex has a relatively high volatility rate and hence, distributed widely through the atmosphere. Thus for Mirex, air compartment and atmospheric fate processes were critical in determining its environmental distribution. The third chemical tested was an insecticide called chlorpyrifos (O-O-diethyl 3,5,6-trichlor-2 pyridyl phosphorothioate). The initial $t_{1/2}$ value of 335 hours was shown to be incorrect by analysis including all relevant fate process data. The corrected value of $t_{1/2}$ <100 hours, showed that chlorpyrifos was not persistent in aquatic environment. The last chemical tested was mono-chlorobenzene (MCB) whose resident phase is air, with a very high fish clearance rate of 8 hours. (Table 7.6). Data showed that MCB degraded rapidly (>99%) in the lower troposphere (ref. 41) with very little MCB entering the stratosphere to damage the ozone layer. In summary, using the decision-tree analysis, it is possible to predict with reasonable accuracy the resident phase of the chemical. However, the user of this model should be aware of the fact that the applicability of the end-results from this decision-tree model will depend upon the data available for the various boxes.

7.1.4 Environmental influence on the fate and transport of chemicals

Evaluation of the natural rates of transport of elements in the environment is necessary in the determination of fate and transport of chemicals discharged into the ecosystems. Sources such as geothermal volcanic activity, forest fires, etc. can cause local effects on the environment in addition to contributing to global inputs. Removal mechanisms such as flocculation, volatilization, hydrolysis, and complexation with dissolved organic matter of natural origin may determine the residence time of a chemical within an environmental compartment.

Residence times of chemicals are usually longer in soils than in water or air due to the virtual unstirred conditions of the soil environment. However, leaching into groundwater or surface waterbody or microbial breakdown could lead to reduced residence time of chemicals in soils. The important factors that affect the retention and solubility of chemicals in soil include the soil temperature, pH, redox (particularly waterlogging and reducing conditions), organic matter content, cation exchange capacity (CEC) and calcium carbonate levels. Acid input into soil will likely lead to enhanced leaching of divalent cations such as lead, zinc, manganese, etc. and trivalent cations such as aluminum and iron.

Residence times can be used to compare the fate and distribution of chemicals in the ecosystems. Although the values of residence time are usually imprecise, an order of magnitude variance is still useful for comparison purposes. Residence times vary as a function of both the chemical and the component of the environment. In general, residence times follow the order: atmosphere (1 day to several years) < soils and sediments (100 to 1000 years) < oceans (10^5 years). Residence times in biota are not well understood and require further precise data gathering. With longer residence times, chemicals have the potential for bioaccumulation.

Residence time in the atmosphere depends upon: (1) the nature of the chemical (particle size, physical state, etc.); (2) regional environmental conditions; and (3) the altitude of entry into the atmosphere. For example, residence times for aerosols at ground levels are about 5 days, whereas aerosols discharged at high altitudes, may have residence times of 100 days (ref. 42) (Table 7.7).

TABLE 7.7 Residence times of pollutants in the atmosphere.

Particulate metals	Residence times (days)		Other Substances	Residence Times
	La Jolla	Ensenada		
Pb	7	8	O_3	0.4-90 days
Cd	0.7	0.5	NO	4-5 days
Ag	0.2	0.1	NO_2	2-8 days
Zn	0.4	0.3	NO_3	4-20 days
Cu	0.5	1	NH_4	7-19 days
Ni	3	0.8	H_2S	0.08-2 days
Co	1.2	0.2	SO_2	0.01-7 days
Fe	1.0	0.4	SO_4	3-5 days
Mn	0.8	0.2	CH_3I	1 day
Cr	0.8	0.4	CO	0.9-2.7 years
V	-	0.6	CCl_4	1 year
Al	1.0	0.2	CH_4	1.5-2 years
Pb210	5	-	Freon	16 years
Pb239+240	1	-	CO_2	2-10 years

(Source: Data on metals reproduced with permission from ref. 43a and data for other substances are from ref. 43b where cross-references are cited in).

Residence times can vary among ecosystems. For example, the half-life for litter decomposition in tropical rain forests is 0.12 y and increases with latitude. The $t_{1/2}$ for litter decomposition in boreal conifer forest is 7.0 y (ref. 44). Litter decomposition half-life values are critical in evaluating the rate of release of organically-bound elements into bioavailable forms.

Table 7.8 indicates the residence times for metals in agricultural soils compared to water column.

TABLE 7.8 Comparison of residence times of metals in agricultural soils* and in water column.**

Metals	Residence Time	
	Soil (y)	Water (d)
As	2000	415
Cd	280	-
Cr	6300	-
Cu	860	560
Fe	-	12
Hg	920 (volatilizes)	340
Ni	2300	-
Pb	400-3000	25
Se	2500	-
Zn	2100	550

* British soils
** Water column-Lake Washington.
(Source: Reprinted with permission from ref. 42, Copyright (1979), Academic Press).

Chemicals which have a relatively short residence time in water column are sequestered in the aquatic sediments resulting in fairly longer residence times. The top 4 cm of the bottom sediment are the chemically and biologically active sediment-water interface providing a habitat for bottom-living organisms, microbial activity rooting area for macrophytes as well as a site for fish reproduction.

Residence time in biota or biological half-times for chemicals are important in assessing the potential metabolic alterations and consequent human health hazard or lack of it. Hence, it is critical to gather more data in this area of the chemical's fate.

Several factors can modify the toxicity of the chemical such as speciation, complexation, etc. and the process appears to be complex to be incorporated in the regulatory assessment process. In reality, not all abiotic factors significantly influence the chemical's nature. The identification of the dominant abiotic factors that are likely to alter the chemical's toxic effects could benefit the regulatory decision-making process. Redox reactions, photochemical transformations, complexation and speciation are the likely abiotic factors which could modify the toxicity and environmental behaviour of most chemicals. Abiotic and biotic transformations have been dealt in detail in earlier chapters.

7.1.5 Models, their predictions and comparison with field data

Integrative fate and transport models may be useful surrogates to the regulatory process in estimating the chemical fate in the environment. A major effort is needed to evaluate the models currently in use, with focus on their predictive value and their sensitivity to parametric change. A fixed system of models is needed ranging from generic ones to specific ones which would be the factor to local environmental parameter variances.

Aquatic fate models are formulated to predict the residual concentration, critical transformation pathways, distribution among components, and specific time scales of xenobiotic chemicals. Most models are constructed as systems of differential equations organized on mass balances. Their primary function is to simplify complex abiotic and biotic transformation data into useful and interpretable forms. The models combine chemical partitioning and kinetic data to yield a set of differential equations which can be analyzed to predict the environmental behaviour of a chemical as a function of time, space and intrinsic chemical loadings.

The input data can be classified as chemical, environmental and loading data sets. The chemical data can be obtained from laboratory studies on chemical reactivity and speciation. The environmental data can be obtained from site-specific limnological field studies or summarized from literature. Chemical loadings can be obtained from worst-case estimates from terrestrial models or from direct field measurements. Utilizing these inputs, aquatic fate models can construct individual output for exposure, fate and persistence of the chemical.

When a synthetic chemical is discharged into an aquatic system, transport, fate, and transformation processes start to play their role. Transport from the point of discharge into the bulk of the waterbody requires advection and dispersion. Simultaneously, transformation processes, most of them irreversible, take place. Finally, the chemical gets distributed with time throughout the environmental system, with concentration gradients arising from dilution, speciation, and transformation. The available aquatic fate models include EXAMS 1/EXAMS 2 (The Exposure Analysis Modelling Systems), HSPF (Hydrological Simulation Program (FORTRAN)), PEST (Rensselaer Polytechnic Institute's Ecosystem Analyzer Model), WASP (Water Quality Analysis Simulation Program), TOXIWASP, WASTOX, etc. and the data needs and applicability has been discussed in detail in ref. 45.

Environmental fate models require information on the distribution of chemicals over time and space. Sources can be described based on their dimensionality and releases and in terms of their temporal distribution. The following Fig. 7.3 illustrates the dimensionality of sources in air pollution. Point sources such as smokestacks, discharge chemicals at (almost) a single point in space described by its geographic coordinates and height above the sea level or surface. Line sources are unidimensional and in aggregate, can be described as a nearly uniform line source (Fig. 7.3). Area source, a group of residences burning wood for heat energy, can better be described as two-dimensional area source; distribution of gas stations in an urban area probably fits under this category of source. Photochemical smog produced over a volume of air could be called a volume source, although one might argue that it could be part of a fate model.

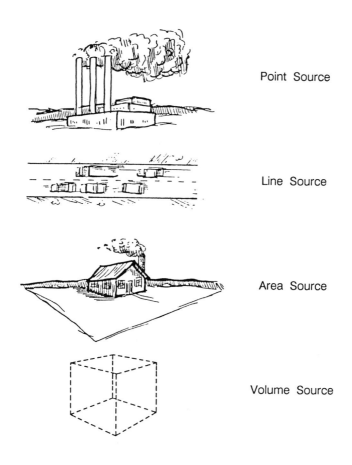

Point Source

Line Source

Area Source

Volume Source

Fig. 7.3. Dimensions of different sources.
(Source: Reprinted with permission from ref. 45, Copyright (1983), ACS).

306

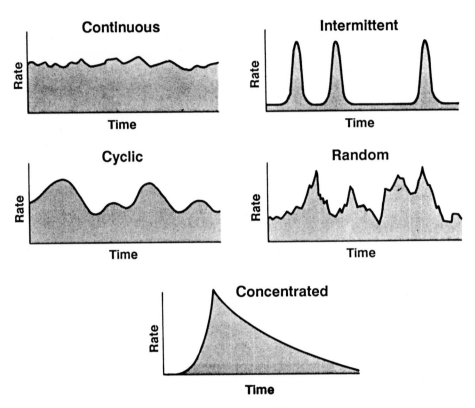

Fig. 7.4. Different patterns of chemical or effluent release.
(Source: Reprinted with permission from ref. 45, Copyright (1983), ACS).

For surface waters, an industrial outfall is a point source, runoff to a river is a line source and atmospheric deposition is an area source (ref. 46).

Fig. 7.4 illustrates the several patterns of release of chemicals over time. Accidental releases are best described as instantaneous release of the total amount (kg per event) whereas most releases are described as rates; kg/sec (point source); kg/sec-m (line source); kg/sec-m^2 (area source). A dimensional analysis will often indicate whether a factor or constant is missing in a fate model. Many releases are more or less continuous and "uniform" such as stack emissions from a power plant. Others are intermittant but fairly regular and predictable as when a coke oven is opened or a chemical vat purged. Some releases are cyclic, although continuous, such as automobile emissions in a day and some are random (continuous or intermittant) like the overflow from a wastewater pond after a rainfall.

It is not always easy to estimate the above release quantities from readily available database. Major types of estimating techniques are direct measurement, material balance, use of mathematical models, and ad-hoc estimating techniques (ref. 46). The following broad topical areas could be improved in order to obtain reliable estimates of release.

1. Measurement. Increase in number of samples and variety of measurements will help to reduce the uncertainty in release rates. Release rate data measuring use are especially needed.

2. Statistics. Actual-on-plant emission and effluent rates, although could be sensitive data, but better summarization of distributions of such releases could be made available for scientific use. Surveys of degrees of use to combine with measured releases will also be valuable.

3. Materials balance. Better characterization of all pathways and chemical steps with accurate flow measurements through these pathways will help to greatly reduce the uncertainties in the data used.

4. Models. Several model-measurement comparisons can be used to calibrate source term assumptions as well as model parameters.

The fugacity concept has been employed in compartmental modelling of chemicals discharged into the environment (refs. 47,48). Fugacity, a thermodynamic property of a chemical, can be conceived as an escaping tendency or pressure with units of pressure, Pa. The key decision in environmental modelling is to first identify the required or acceptable level of model complexity. Then the problem is conceptualized and next the dominant processes are included in the model followed by others in decreasing order of importance. The acceptability of the model is demonstrated by applying the evaluative model successfully to microcosms, to well controlled field environments such as small ponds, rivers, and lakes. Evaluative models are particularly successful for assessment of new chemicals for comparing chemicals and for obtaining the general chemical behaviour profiles. Real models are best suited to contamination situations and assess remedial actions. The following determinants of complexity will help to choose the appropriate level of a model subject to the availability of data:

1. Number of compartments considered;

2. If phase equilibrium is assumed to operate;

3. If degradation reactions are considered;

4. If advection processes are included; and

5. If a steady-state is assumed or time dependence of concentration and emissions is included (ref. 48).

A fugacity level I calculation is an equilibrium, steady-state approach; a level II may be equilibrium, with reaction and advection-steady-state;

308

level III may be non-equilibrium, with reaction and advection-steady-state; and level IV and EXAMS are non-equilibrium, with reaction and advection-non steady-state. Diverse processes such as volatilization, sediment deposition, fish uptake and stream flow can be converted into identical units and their relative importance can be established directly and easily.

The evaluative fugacity models and their various levels are illustrated in Fig. 7.5.

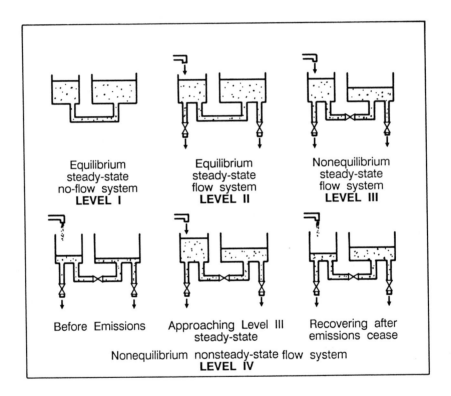

Fig. 7.5. Tank analogy of levels I-IV fugacity calculation conditions.
(Source: Reprinted with permission from ref. 47, Copyright (1982), ACS).

Model Level	Output
I	Distribution of chemical at equilibrium at constant amount of chemical.
II	Equilibrium distribution of a steady emission balanced by an equal reaction rate and the average residence time or persistence.
III	Non-equilibrium steady-state distribution in which emissions are into specified compartments with possible restriction of transfer rates between compartments.
IV	Same as III except that emissions vary with time and a set of simultaneous differential equations to be solved numerically (not algebraically).

The fugacity models were applied to evaluate a hypothetical lake environment, consisting of a 1 km square area with an atmosphere 6000 m high, a water column of 80 m deep containing suspended solids (5 ppm by volume) and biota (fish) of 1 ppm by volume and a bottom sediment layer 3 cm deep with a 4% organic carbon. This was similar to the "unit world" described in ref. 12. Chemicals entered by two routes: (1) by emissions of 0.001 mol/h directly to the water column; and (2) by advection into air with a net inflow of 0.0003 mol/h. Thus, the total emissions added up to 0.0013 mol/h. The advection rate corresponded to an air residence time (volume/flow rate) of 100 h. Reaction rate constants for various processes were taken from the literature.

Level I fugacity model calculation identified the sediment compartment with 57% of the chemical as the dominant compartment. This was followed by air (25%), water (10%), and suspended solids (7%). Although the fish concentration was 30,000 times that of water, absolute concentrations were treated as non-significant since they involved assumed amounts and volumes. Level I calculated equilibrium distribution with no reaction of 1 mol of trichlorobiphenyl.

The fate and distribution of trichlorobiphenyl calculated by fugacity level II was similar to that of level I. Atmospheric distribution of PCBs was identified as the likely important process. The residence time of 400 h was largely controlled by air advection. Level II calculated equilibrium distribution accounting for reactions and advection.

Level III calculation showed that air-water volatilization rate constraint reduced air advective loss and other reaction processes gained predominance (Fig. 7.6). The residence time was calculated by level III model to be 2.2 y which was in fair agreement with observations (ref. 48). Also, the calculated concentrations of tricholorobiphenyl in air, water, sediment, and fish were within an order of magnitude observed in contaminated lakes such as Lake Michigan (Fig. 7.6).

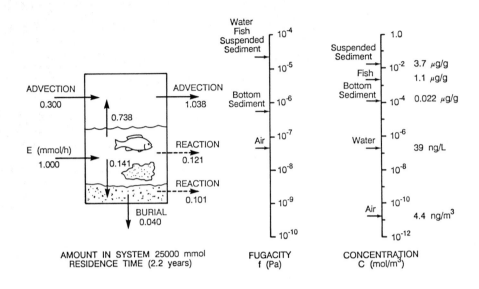

Fig. 7.6. Distribution of trichlorobiphenyl calculated by level III fugacity model.
(Source: Reprinted with permission from ref. 48, Copyright (1983), ACS).

Level IV model was similar to level III calculations up to the build-up in concentrations and fugacity up to the steady-state followed by decay. Compared to water, suspended solids, and bottom sediment were slow to respond to build-up and decay of the chemical. A ten-fold drop in sediment concentration of trichlorobiphenyl would require 15 y. Thus, fugacity models are capable of identifying persistent chemicals and the associated environmental medium prior to their discharge into the environment.

Application of fugacity model level III to the fate of PCB congeners in an ecosystem

Level III model was applied to mono, di, tri, and tetrachlorobiphenyls. The effect of increasing chlorine substitution was widely brought out by the model. The lower congeners are fairly short-lived, partition less into sediments and biota and most reaction tends to occur in the water column. With increase in chlorine substitution, the amounts and persistence increase, more chemical partitions into the sediments and biota, while water column degradation becomes less important. Ultimately, sediment burial and advection dominate the chemical's fate. It is clear that congeners will suffer quite different environmental fates and equal emissions of each will result in very different concentrations and thus exposures. These differences should be reflected in changes in congener distribution of commercial PCB mixtures. With higher chlorine content, PCB congeners are very persistent in the environment leading to long-term hazards (Fig. 7.7).

In a recent study (ref. 51), the fates of two chemicals, 2,4-Dichloro phenoxy acetic acid butoxy ethyl ester (2,4-DBEE) and 1,4-Dichlorobenzene (1,4-DCB) were studied in situ microcosms placed in a pond and compared with the fates in the pond itself. Experimental data obtained were compared with predictions made by an aquatic fate and transport model. The model chosen was EPA's EXAMS (Exposure Analysis Modelling System) which has been described extensively in literature (ref. 52). EXAMS uses several internal transformation and transport process models to compute volatilization, ionization, sorption, photolysis, hydrolysis, biolysis, and oxidation. The input data include information on physical, chemical, and biological data from the chosen aquatic system, as well as characteristics on the chemical including available rate-constants. Outputs from EXAMS include the concentration profile of the chemical as a function of time for all environmental compartments, the relative contribution of each fate process to the total environmental dynamics of the chemical and the longevity of the chemical in the environment after loading has discontinued (ref. 51).

Fig. 7.8 shows the measured concentrations of 2,4-DBEE in microcosms and pond (Ln-transformed data) together with the predicted values from EXAMS. The concentrations measured and predicted from EXAMS agree well. Closeness of slopes indicate similar decay rates. Microcosms concentrations were 10 times lower than pond concentrations which could be due to incomplete mixing of pond when microcosms were placed. However, non-significant difference between the slopes (Table 7.9) indicate similar decay rates between the two data sets.

The decay rate of 1,4-DCB in the microcosms was significantly lower than the rate for the pond and lower than the rate predicted by EXAMS (Fig. 7.9).

312

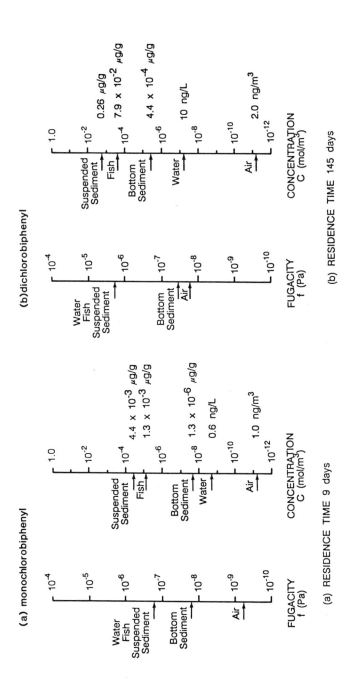

Fig. 7.7. Fugacity level III model calculation of the distribution of PCB congeners. (a) monochlorobiphenyl and (b) dichlorobiphenyl. (Source: Reprinted with permission from ref. 50, Copyright (1983), ACS).

(c)tetrachlorobiphenyl

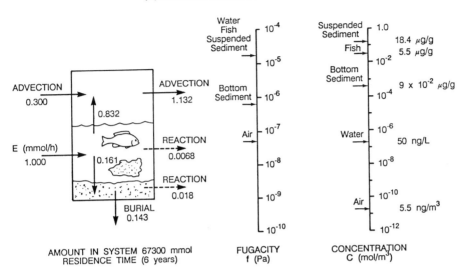

Fig. 7.7. Fugacity level III model calculation of the distribution of PCB congener. (c) tetrachlorobiphenyl.
(Source: Reprinted with permission from ref. 50, Copyright (1983), ACS).

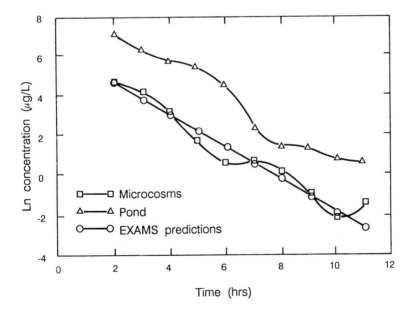

Fig. 7.8. Decay of 2,4-DBEE in microcosms (measured and predicted) and pond.
(Source: Reprinted with permission from ref. 51, Copyright (1983), ACS).

314

TABLE 7.9 Statistical comparisons of slopes of different systems for 2,4-DBEE.

Data	Regression Equation[a]	R^2(%)	Slopes test[b]
Pond	y = 8.86-0.830x	93.7	Do not reject Ho
Microcosms	y = 5.70-0.726x	92.0	
EXAMS	y = 6.37-0.837x	100.0	Do not reject Ho

[a] Least square regression of Ln-transformed data.
[b] Ho: Slopes not significantly different; $p < 0.05$.
(Source: Reprinted from ref. 51 with permission from American Chemical Society).

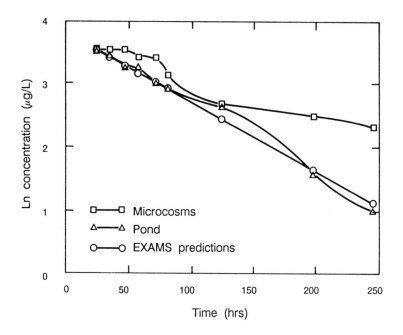

Fig. 7.9. Decay of 1,4-DCB in microcosms (predicted and actual) and pond. (Source: Reprinted with permission from ref. 51, Copyright (1983), ACS).

The difference between the slopes are statistically significant. The low volatility of 1,4-DCB in microcosms was attributed to difficulties in simulating the hydrodynamic aspects of natural water systems. Thus, EXAMS model successfully simulated the decay profile of 2,4-DBEE in both microcosms and pond. But it did not predict accurately the microcosm observations for 1,4-DCB, probably due to the lack of microcosm-specific input parameters, especially hydrodynamic values to the model. The microcosms were not successful in simulating the pond for the volatilization of 1,4-DCB.

Model Testing

The process of field validation and testing of models has been discussed extensively in literature (refs. 53a,b). The model user is often faced with the responsibility to analyze for reasons (errors) for the differences between model prediction and field measurements. This involves assessment of the accuracy and validity of the model input data, parameter values, system representation and output data. Fig. 7.10 schematically illustrates the comparison of sources of errors between the model and the natural system.

Input errors in a model are often significant sources of discrepancies. The natural system receives the "true input" (Fig. 7.10), whereas the model receives the "observed" input as determined by analyses.

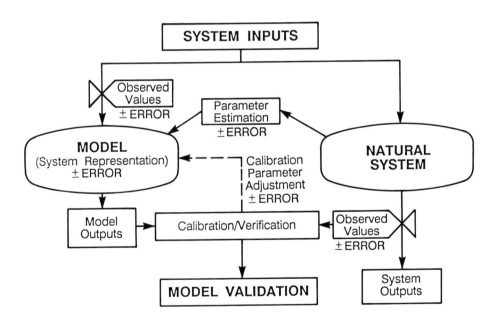

Fig. 7.10. Comparison of inputs, outputs, and errors between the model and the natural system.
(Source: Reprinted with permission from ref. 53a, Copyright (1982), Butterworths).

Analyses are always associated with some degree of error and analytical values are averages of multiple point values. System inputs usually vary continuously both in space and time. A typical example is the error associated with input loading of chemicals. For a watershed modelling exercise, these errors would be associated with chemical input via rainfall or dry deposition. Assumption on chemical application rates, methods, and timing were shown to have a major impact on the loads measured at the watershed outlet. For a detailed discussion on these sources of errors, readers are referred to refs. 53a and 53b. Similar input errors can occur to an aquatic fate and transport model of a chemical in determining the loadings from point and non-point sources.

System Representation Errors

These errors refer to the differences in processes and the time and space scales operated in the model against the determinants of the response in the natural system. The differences between the model output and field data should be analyzed in terms of the limitations of the model algorithm to represent a critical process and that all critical processes are accounted for in the model to some appropriate level of detail (ref. 53b). For example, a lake model that is supposed to simulate dissolved oxygen (DO) levels without accounting for biological components will not be able to predict DO levels close to observed DO levels during algal blooms. Similarly, if sediment-water interface interactions are not included in the aquatic fate model, then the predictions cannot account for the sorption-desorption processes.

Parameter errors which arise from (i) the inability to accurately determine many of the parameters that are characteristic of the natural system; and (ii) the relevant chemical processes under natural conditions. Output errors are similar to input errors. They could result in biased parameter values or misrepresentation of the natural system. The discrepancies between model output and field data should not always be assigned to model errors; measurement errors in the field data gathering can contribute significantly to the discrepancy and must be evaluated. The observed data are measurements at a particular point on a stream, whereas the model simulates an average concentration in an assumed, totally-mixed section of the waterbody. Hence, sampling methods, locations, events like unusual runoff following a heavy rainfall or absence of it in the season and representative sampling have to be considered in calculating the chemical loads. The frequency of sampling will affect the validity of the resulting calculated load. Comparisons between observed data and model predictions must be made on a consistent and a common-denominator basis. Hence, the model user should be aware of the frequency of sampling, statistics applied, and how observed chemical loads are calculated in order to assess the accuracy of the values. The above discussions do not mean all models are accurate or all field data are questionable. In reality, in most cases, field data are our best real indicator of a field system behaviour. Awareness of possible deficiencies of both the model and the observed data can result in a better overall understanding of modelling of natural system.

7.2 BIOLOGICAL IMPACT

Biological impact could occur as a result of natural processes and also due to stress from exposure to chemicals in the environment. The naturally occurring processes include selection, competition, predation, and succession that may vary the size of the population in the absence of any chemical stress.

The ability to translate information obtained from laboratory experiments, using a single species, to field studies of communities and ecosystems decreases greatly because of influences such as population characteristics and biological organization. Each organism with its own population has particular characteristics that have evolved over time. Various mechanisms and processes at the organism level are affected by natural selection which acts towards the improvement of the individual that is part of the population. A major change then occurs between each individual organism and its population because each unit has to compete with others within that population and also with other units from other populations. Characteristics such as age structure, mortality rates, and replacement rates may affect the population; however, the individuals in the population are affected through natural selection and protective genetic mechanisms that they tend to grow fast, as large as possible and produce as many offsprings as their environment would support. This excessive production then becomes a resource for higher trophic levels.

Impacts may also occur at the community or ecosystem level which has additional characteristics (such as diversity, energy transfer, nutrient cycling, etc.) that are not exhibited by populations. Communities with few diversified species in which most have similar life spans usually suffer greater impacts when compared to a more diversified ecosystem with species of both short and long life spans; the latter are more resilient and also show less conspicuous changes.

In order to determine the chemical effects on the biotic system, testing should be carried out at the different biological levels. It is important to determine the effects at the tissue, organ, and cellular level, however, tests are also required at the population and ecosystem levels. Testing should include (i) dose variations (to determine acute and chronic effects), body burden measurements, multi-generation studies, and physiological and neuro-logical effects and (ii) life function processes such as metabolic rates, reproduction, life span, growth, and adaptability.

Field studies allow for the detection of subtle ecological changes, such as the variation of the structure in an ecosystem because of detrimental effects to a specific population. This ultimately affects species at the top of a food chain which are not only aesthetically valuable but they are also indicators of changes to a complex but fragile ecosystem. Natural ecosystems are open and they experience the movement of biota, and chemicals from one to another. Thus, the effects of a chemical on one system could diffuse and affect several neighbouring systems.

7.2.1 Field Monitors

Studies of field monitors are executed on naturally occurring species populations of plants or animals in their own niche. There are basically two types of systems that are used for field studies. They are:
- the use of field enclosures such as temporary greenhouses, limnocorrals, and closed systems; and
- studies carried out in site-specific ecosystems.

Field enclosures are basically confined systems that involve the partitioning of portions of the natural environment. This allows for testing to be carried out in the natural yet controllable environment and eliminates many difficulties that may have been encountered as a result of the influences of natural processes. These systems are ideally used for testing the fate and effects of chemicals under field conditions because they provide the scientist with the convenience of developing control systems within proximity of the test facility. These systems also allow for testing at the ecosystem level of different biological communities, and provide realistic results that may include a wide range of predictive capabilities. These studies have been used successfully for various systems including lakes (refs. 54,55) and forests (ref. 56).

Studies that are carried out in natural ecosystems provide results that require no extrapolation to the field environment. These studies are usually done in areas that are representative of the specific situation, utilizing indigenous species, so that few, if any at all, extrapolations may be required in order to draw some accurate conclusions regarding the effect of particular chemicals or effluents. Also, the mode of entry, insofar as the impact of other contaminants is concerned, will be more realistic if field studies have been conducted to understand the interactions of components within the ecosystem (ref. 57).

Although field tests might produce results that are more realistic, they are not free from limitations. The limitations include: (i) the naturally occurring variables and environmental conditions that are not uniform; (ii) inability to replicate the study because of ever-changing nature of natural environmental conditions and seasonal variation and timing which could have different effects on the test species.

The choice of the right population within any affected site depends to some extent upon several concerns which include the following:

- economic value or social importance of the species within the population (e.g., food source for humans, rare or endangered species, an economical resource, or an amenity);
- sensitivity of the species to the chemical that is being studied (e.g., some species may react more dramatically to a chemical than another species);
- ability of the species to magnify and/or bioconcentrate the chemical (e.g., position of the speices in the food chain, economic value of the species);
- ability of the population to avoid the effects of the chemical under study;
- migrating patterns of the population; and
- the strength or how well established is the population within the study area.

As indicated, there are variables both with the behaviour of the chemical and the species in the population that could affect the results of the assessment of the chemical under study.

Fig. 7.11 illustrates these types of reaction between two substances. Chemical antagonism might occur in which one chemical inactivates the other through a chemical interaction, such as chelation of some metals like calcium which reduces heavy metal's toxicity to aquatic life. On the other hand, synergistic effects may occur between two chemicals or between a chemical and a physical activity creating additional effects to the exposed population, e.g., synergism between chemical and excessively high temperatures.

Table 7.10 lists various criteria that are measured on individuals of the population. These criteria allow an assessment of the population in order to arrive at the best possible estimate of biological response. The use of these criteria enables changes to be monitored at sensitive location like the edges of the range. Sometimes it is difficult to observe changes in the size of a population for species that produce more offspring than are needed to replace adult that might have died from the effect of a hazardous substance. In these cases, the biologist should look at trends that indicate changes in the age structure of the population.

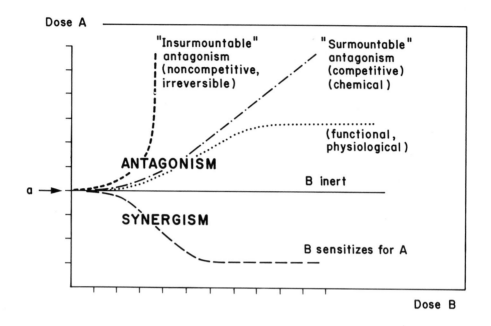

Fig. 7.11. Isoboles (curves of equal biological response) for combinations of a substance A that is active on its own and a substance B that is inactive when given alone, but influences the action of A. Synergism (increased sensitivity for A by the action of B) and antagonism (decreased sensitivity for A by the action of B) are indicated.
(Source: Reprinted with permission from ref. 58, Copyright (1976), Academic Press, Inc.).

Population studies normally are expensive and take a long time to carry out and in many cases, this makes it not possible to design and execute secondary or back-up studies except for microbial and invertebrate populations. Even efficiently designed and well-implemented programs may not reveal all the effects that a chemical may have on a population, especially those that are subtle, unusual, and takes a long time or several generations to show effects.

Lentic Systems

Lentic enclosures are designed for the purpose of evaluating the chronic effects of a chemical to a biological system. It permits an assessment of important ecological interactions that are not possible through single-species

TABLE 7.10 Criteria used for defining biological performance in a population.

MEASUREMENT OF INDIVIDUAL IN A POPULATION	DETERMINATION OF POPULATION RESPONSES
Age Growth Biomass	Age structure Average size of species Health assessment
Numbers Location	Size and distribution of a population Geographical range Migration patterns
Age Fecundity Maturity	Age structure Reproductive success Off-spring size and numbers
Behaviour	Survival patterns Behavioural changes and patterns Changes in courtship and mating rituals Maternal behaviour
Age Mortality Pathology	Life expectancy Factors affecting population Health of population Mortality rates Body burden estimation and population response
Phenology	Seasonal timing of biological phenomenon Movement of population Migration patterns

bioassays or other laboratory-type testing. Field enclosures provide an experimental bridge between laboratory test systems and natural ecosystems because they include a high degree of ecological realism commensurate with control-versus-treatment experimentation and a closely regulated dosing regime (ref. 59). These systems portray naturally occurring processes and the effects on ecological conditions and biotic systems reasonably well; however, factors such as the design criteria and experimental variability could influence the end results.

Design and Operation

Table 7.11 outlines parameters which need to be considered during the design and operation of a lentic enclosure. These include: (1) the enclosure's size and shape; (2) movement within the system; (3) settling; (4) light

322

penetration; (5) nutrient addition; and (6) length of experiment/study. The most important factor regarding a lentic enclosure involves the size of the study area. Enclosure effects are directly related to the degree of scaling down from the natural to the experimental system (ref. 60). Table 7.11 outlines some of the concerns that may arise as a result of scaling down. For example, the exclusion of some predator species may result in the prolifera-

TABLE 7.11 Parameters and concerns in lentic enclosures.

PARAMETERS	EFFECTS/CONCERNS
Enclosure size and shape	- Degree of down scale - Representative producer consumer ratios and nutrient cycling - Adequate size to sustain sampling without disturbance - Capable of accommodating nutrient requirements - Size and number of individual in stock - Consumption-production relationships - Representative surface sediment to water volume ratio - Sidewall sorption and surface area. - Unnecessary build-up of micro-communities - Problems in cleaning
Turbulence/Mixing	- Wind shear - Thermal water movements - Wall movements
Sedimentation/Settling	- Increased water clarity - Decreased primary protection - Altered toxicity depending on chemical
Nutrient Addition	- Planktonic blooms - Reduction in dissolved oxygen concentration - Increased stress levels to test species
Lighting/Shading	- Reduced light intensity in temperate zone - More shading in temperate zone - Reduced light due to limnocorral walls - Reduced primary production - Effect on photosynthesis
Experimental Durations	- Increased/reduced stresses to biota - Seasonal changes/timing - Species choice/adaptation/behaviour - Acclimation period

tion of others. This may be observed in a productive system where the removal of a planktivorous fish may cause increase in bacterial standing stock, phytoplankton volume, and numbers of rotifers and cladocerans (ref. 61). Scaling down and sizing of the lentic enclosure should consider the type of biota that are to be included. For instance, if a fish species is to be chosen, the following criteria should be considered:

- size of the fish at maturity;
- life history cycles and behavioural patterns;
- numbers required for the enclosure (Note overpopulation);
- feeding requirements or prey species and quantity;
- mortality rates;
- adaptability to enclosure environment; and
- persistence, bioaccumualtion and biomagnification of toxicants.

Enclosures should be chosen and designed to accommodate fish growth, and possibly fish production, depending upon the length of the study period.

It is necessary to ensure that there is adequate sediment/water exchange and sidewall surface area to enclosed water volume ratio in lentic enclosures that are similar to the ecosystem that is being simulated. These ratios assist in the maintenance of epilimnetic phytoplankton production, attached growing material and material sorption. Sidewall designs and their influences can be especially important towards pollutant fate and transport (ref. 62). The shape of lentic enclosures are usually rectangular or circular, however, triangular systems have been used. Enclosures with tightly angled or steep corners should be avoided because of poor circulation, difficulties in cleaning and possible collection or irregular build-up of micro-flora and fauna communities.

The horizontal and vertical movements of currents within a lentic enclosure could influence the data during a chemical assessment. Such influences include thermal water movement, windshear, and wall movements. In smaller enclosures, however, the effects of wind shear are limited. Therefore, mixing as a result is reduced, but for larger limnocorrals the use of flotation collars or other types of baffles will effectively reduce these influences.

Turbulence and mixing may also affect phytoplankton populations. For instance, changes in vertical mixing may alter plankton production through increases in photosynthetic activity and efficiency. Waste may become more transparent due to increase settling rates, resulting in changes in primary production.

Settling or sedimentation may substantially affect the concentration of a test chemical and nutrients in a lentic enclosure. For example, inorganic mercury decreases over time in the presence of organic particulates in a marine enclosure (ref. 63). Increases in sedimentation or settling may result in the depletion of nutrients through changes or shift in planktonic species composition. Efficient settling may also affect the production of forage species as a result of less photosynthetic activities.

The addition of artificial nutrient must be carried out with care in order to avoid possible shift of planktonic species composition. Addition of excessive nutrients may result in possible biomass increase which may trigger phytoplankton reproduction. Nutrient addition may also cause reduction in the dissolved oxygen concentration through increases in biochemical oxygen demands. This may exert undue stresses in the test species within the system.

Because of the design of lentic systems shading may occur in certain latitudes which may affect the composition of the biota. This is of particular concern in the northern or southern hemispheres where the sun is not directly over head and as such, one section of the enclosure may receive shaded or diffused light during the entire test. Shading of this nature may reduce primary production and may cause modification to the vertical distribution of biota.

The response of the test species in a limnocorral is dependent upon the time for acclimation to exposure of chemicals. If initial exposures and adaptation periods are too short, species may not have adapted to the new environment and as such their behavioral responses may influence the results obtained. Different species may also require different acclimation time; for instance where fish are the test species, acclimation period is dependent upon the chemical and concentration of test substance, the species of fish, size, life history cycles/processes, metabolic rates and feeding behaviour. It is also important to ensure that seasonal changes and timing are considered during experimental exposures.

Data Assessment

The fate and cycling of toxicants can be monitored in field enclosures with greater precision than in open habitats because of the spatial containment and control of sources, sinks, and processing elements (ref. 59). The quantity of a chemical and its effects on biological and physical processes are also easily monitored. Studies can be carried out in particular areas, such as litoral zones, where sorption may be occurring to sediment or suspended solids using lentic enclosures. However, results obtained for fate and cycling of toxicants from lentic enclosure are usually only an approximation when compared to results from open natural areas. For example, lower cadmium uptake by plankton was indicated as a result of enclosure induced stresses (ref. 64).

There is also the possibility of retention of toxicants to the walls and to attached biota. Sidewalls have accounted for 65 to 79% of mercury loss in marine enclosures (ref. 62) and 40 to 60% loss of radionuclides in fibreglass marine tanks (ref. 65). Settling of particulate together with the sloughing of build-up material on the sidewalls could cause higher rates of sorption and deposition of toxicants in enclosures.

When exposed to a chemical, a synergistic interaction may occur between the toxicants and diseases or parasites in biota that are within lentic enclosures. This is especially observable with species of fish that might have contracted some disease or parasite and these may still be latent at the time of exposure to the toxicant. The additional stress from the chemical may increase the effects. There is also evidence that, depending upon the chemical, a synergistic effect resulting in immunosuppressive action (ref. 66); this type of effect, however, has not been very common.

The investigations of long-term chronic effects of a chemical on fish species have been successfully carried out in lentic enclosures. Apart from general toxicology on specific species, chronic effects have been observed during various life history activities, under the influence of predation and disease stresses; progressive mortality as an indicator of toxicological stress have also been studied on young of the year fish in enclosed systems (ref. 67).

With regards to fish species that are introduced into limnocorrals, only a few can be used successfully because of size limitations and length of life history activities. Lentic enclosures may have positive influences on early life stages resulting in higher survival rates than in a natural environment. Thus, the influences of the test chemical to the early stages of the biota may alter the results significantly with regards to what might have occurred in the field situation.

7.2.2 Terrestrial and Aquatic Plants

Plant communities are stable and are quite resilient to short-term influences. These establishments are relatively slow and their occurrences in various locations are determined by certain environmental parameters such as temperature, sunlight, daylight, etc., the presence or absence of certain pollutants (e.g., high phosphate, nitrates, iron, organic matter, etc.), and soil/sediment composition. The exposure of plant communities to toxic chemicals may result in the following effects: the reduction or elimination of a single or multiple species within the community and the appearance of new and more resilient species to the specific toxicant.

Plants on the whole are more sensitive than other organisms and they receive the effects of the pollutant in exactly the same manner in which it was delivered, so they tend to be more sensitive indicators or early warning systems of the chemical.

(i) Uptake and accumulation. Terrestrial plants may uptake chemical through direct contact of the chemical or through air or water that is transporting the chemical. Absorption may take place through the leaves or from the soil or sediment.

Access of a pollutant through the leaves takes place through the stoma and this pathway is used principally by gases or chemicals in gaseous form (e.g., sulphides, nitrogen oxides, chlorine, fluorine, ammonia, etc.). Other chemicals in dust such as lead or particulate may collect on the leaf surfaces. However, they may only enter the plant in a soluble form.

Some heavy metals such as arsenic may accumulate in plant tissues when high concentrations are available. In some cases, this type of effect may alter the community structure through species elimination, or be hazardous to foraging animal species (ref. 68). Other heavy metals may reach toxic levels in the soil if the acidic levels are sufficiently high. For instance, metals such as zinc, copper, and aluminum become soluble due to acid precipitation and may be available in the soil for uptake.

Some chemicals may produce two entirely different effects depending on plant species. High concentrations of heavy metals and organochlorines have resulted in the reduction of photosynthetic rates (ref. 69). At lower concentrations, however, although inhibition may be observed in one species, others have proliferated through growth stimulation.

Toxicity of aquatic plants are variable because the effects are dependent to a large extent upon the physico-chemical properties of the water column. Variation in accumulation factors for blue-green algae, for instance, have been recorded as high as 1710 for lead accumulation (ref. 70). Studies on Elodea showed that uptake was directly proportional to the time the plant was in the water medium and also the concentration of the chemical in the water. Daily measurement of uptake was found to be related to water concentration and the weight of the plant tissue (ref. 71).

(ii) Toxicological responses. Toxicological effects of a chemical to plant life usually commences by affecting photosynthesis or respiration through possibly an enzymatic reaction. Fluoride may affect various enzyme systems and metabolic processes (ref. 72). Photochemical pollutants oxidize sulphydryl groups which impairs protein synthesis and inhibits carbon dioxide fixation (ref. 68). Sulphur dioxide interferes with the formation and conversion of cysteine and methionine in peptides and proteins (ref. 73). The initial effects of these enzymatic reactions are usually sublethal; they are sometimes followed by terminal effects and finally by interaction with others in the community.

Early response systems in plants have been used as indicators for detecting toxicological responses. Visible foliage damage patterns on sensitive species are noted for the detection of sulphur dioxide. In aquatic algae, exposure to polyaromatic hydrocarbons results in a rapid loss of chlorophyll. These early response systems are dependent upon the dose of the chemical, type of species, stage of growth, age, kind of tissue, and genetic tolerance. Younger plants with softer tissue and newly-developed stoma are usually more susceptible to toxic effects of chemical than older, more mature flora. Plants with blossoms and/or fruits may lose their production if exposure takes place during this stage of their life history.

It is possible that the toxic chemical might eliminate organisms such as pathogens, fungus, or virus and as a result, indirectly affect the floral community by altering the disease interactions (ref. 68). A similar impact could occur if the toxicant affects insects, pests, or parasites from a particular community; the effects may result in various shifts in community size and structure.

Field communities may react in an entirely different manner than that indicated from laboratory toxicological studies because of the influences of environmental variables, interaction by other species, and adaption by the community in question to long-term exposures. Studies on the effects of a pulp mill effluent showed that a prolonged lag in algal growth was required for physiological adaptation before the species started to increase significantly (ref. 74). No loss in the toxicity of the effluent was observed. Initially, the algae only accepted low concentration of the effluent, but after repeated exposure and gradual increases, much higher concentration were tolerated later in the experiment. Both physicochemical factors and physiological adaptation processes of the algal species are likely involved.

(iii) Assessment variables. In order to predict the effect of a chemical on plants or communities of plants, it is important to know the growth and reproductive rates of the species within the community. These are obtained through initial studies and monitoring programs of the plant community before the influence of a chemical. The influence of the community to the toxic chemical must also be known in order to develop early warning systems/species, and signs. This could be obtained through controlled exposures and known doses of the chemical to terrestrial plots and/or lentic enclosures. This information could be useful in order to predict both long-term effects and also effects to similar communities and plant families. Other parameters that have been used to measure the effect of a chemical on a community include:

- community structure/diversity;
- species composition;
- growth and reproductive rates;
- mortality rates;
- physiological state of species;
- genetic variation of the community;
- the presence of other toxicants/chemicals on the site; and
- synergistic and antagonistic effects.

The parameters for studying the effects of a chemical on algal communities include:

- growth rates;
- species composition;
- gamete production;
- cellular division;
- CO_2 fixation;
- protein synthesis; and
- mortality.

7.2.3 Invertebrates

Invertebrates have been consistently used for assessing the effects of chemicals, mainly in the aquatic environment. Some species, however, have been suggested for air quality assessment, but they have not been used on a regular basis for that purpose. In the aquatic environment, the lower animals are common indicator species because they have been found to be more susceptible to the effects of many chemicals than species of fish or other wildlife.

Invertebrates cover a wide range of organisms; for this section, however, the topics will include discussions on: (i) plankton, (ii) microorganisms, and (iii) macroinvertebrates. The information obtained could then be utilized towards the protection of aquatic life and their habitat. These toxicity tests require standardized procedures in order to ensure that the information obtained is reproducible and acceptable for the purpose of comparison and possible standard development.

(i) Toxic response by plankton. Plankton are free swimming or drifting organisms that inhabit both saltwater and freshwater ecosystems. Within the group of planktonic animals, there are meta-, macro-, meso-, micro-, nanno-, and ultra-plankton. These are divided into either phytoplankton or zooplankton species. Phytoplankton are organisms with chlorophyll, mainly from the plant kingdom, while zooplankton are the animal forms. Some assessments of phytoplankton have been covered in the previous section regarding the impacts on plants, therefore more attention will be given to the effects of a chemical or zooplankton.

Zooplankton comprises of detritivores, herbivores, and carnivores, which are common in both fresh and saltwater systems. Many species of zooplankton are commonly used in bioassays because they are key organisms in the ecosystem, and have been found to be more sensitive to chemicals than many of the other species that are higher in the food chain. Some species such as amphipods and copepods are sensitive to a wide variety of chemicals; they are also relatively easy to collect from the field, therefore, are excellent specimens for use in bioassays.

The toxic effect of a chemical may affect both reproduction and fertilization processes in zooplanktonic species. When the early developmental stage of the mussel (Mytilus edulis) was exposed to sevin the results were characterized by reduction in rate of development and unaligned cleavages (ref. 75). Exposure to DDT in Daphnia caused inhibition in reproduction (ref. 76) and exposure to DDE resulted in both reduction in growth rates and egg production in the copepod (Tigriopus sp.) (ref. 77).

The effect of a chemical on zooplankton species may result in structural changes at the community level when processes such as production, predation rates, lifespan and life cycle, and population density and variation, are affected. Chronic doses of a chemical may affect the normal behavioral patterns of prey species making them unable to avoid predatory species. This would occur at the lower levels in the food chain because these species are usually more sensitive to toxic chemicals than others higher on the food chain. Also, direct mortality usually occurs first at the planktonic level and the effects on food production might cause structural changes to the community.

(ii) Toxic responses by microorganisms. Microorganisms are involved in various cycles in the environment. They are capable of rapid growth in favourable conditions. They are also able to degrade and decompose many chemicals through microbial actions; their rate of decomposition, however, is dependent upon the physical and chemical properties of the chemical and also on the various environmental conditions. Some microorganisms are known to show resistance to heavy metals (ref. 78).

Some microorganisms are good indicators of water quality. One strain of luminiscent bacteria is used in a method known as Microtox (described in Chapter 4). It is a bioassay which uses a strain of bacteria, Photobacterium phosphoreum to measure the toxic concentration of a chemical through a decrease in light output (EC_{50}) by the bacteria. When the sensitivity of the bacterial test was compared to the 96-h LC_{50} fish bioassay, the luminescent bacteria test was found to be about six times more sensitive (ref. 79). However, Microtox cannot be used as a stand-alone test because of likely artefacts. It is used in a battery of tests.

"Interaction of hydrophobic aquatic contaminants with dissolved organic substances and particulate matter can result in physical partitioning of the compound from the water column, bringing the susceptible substrate into closer association with those microorganisms capable of degrading the compounds. Such partitioning can also cause a concentration of the contaminant to toxic levels, thereby suppressing or retarding biodegradation or affecting the biological components of the ecosystem. Thus, solubilization or partitioning of pollutants into dissolved phases can stimulate biodegradation, through availability of co-metabolizable substrates or inhibition of normal decomposition activity." (ref. 80).

7.2.4 Fish

(i) Reproduction. Reproduction may be influenced by a toxic chemical through effects of the various reproductive processes; these include: behavioural alterations, egg

production and sperm viability, teratological and embryonic developmental effects, and hatching time. Although the route or mode of action of the chemical may vary, the effects on any reproductive processes ultimately reduce the number of viable offsprings.

The effects of a chemical on reproductive behaviour may include such activities as migration, spawning site preparation, courtship, mating, and parental care and protection. The only aspect of reproductive behaviour that has been extensively studied in relation to toxicity includes avoidance and/or migration (ref. 81). The other processes are quite complex and include numerous variables and strategies that render them extremely difficult to document or monitor.

Copper (ref. 82) and zinc (ref. 83) have been found to reduce egg production in fathead minnows. Also, copper, lead, or zinc have caused histopathological changes in both testes and ovaries and loss of oocytes in the ovaries. Copper was observed to be more toxic towards the animal as a whole, while zinc and lead produced greater effects to the testes.

Certain chemicals affect ontogenic processes at early levels of growth and metamorphosis. The effects may range from minor retardation of growth rates to massive distortions or teratogenic effects early in the embryonic stage. These affected animals usually do not survive to be productive adults. This could cause serious reduction in the distribution and abundance to fish populations.

One of the chronic effects of embryo toxicants is the reduction of the hatching time of developing embryos. This occurs particularly when the concentration of the chemical is lower than amounts required to impair production all together. Some of the known toxicants that reduce hatching time include cadmium, zinc, and polychlorobiphenyls. The lowering of pH has been known to increase the length of the hatching time; this has been noted for rainbow trout and a few other species. Cyanide reacts similarly to pH with regards to hatching time (ref. 84).

(ii) Locomotion. Locomotion is used by fish for the purpose of various behavioural activities. This include maintenance of position in the aquatic medium, avoidance of predators, capturing food and migratory activities. The most used movement of locomotor activity is swimming and this requires several physiological and behavioural processes to coordinate the action properly. The interference of any one of these processes by a toxic chemical will have adverse effects upon swimming which may, in turn, jeopardize the survival of the species.

The monitoring of swimming performance has been suggested as a method for determining sublethal effect of a toxicant. The fish is forced to swim against an applied water current, attempting to maintain a stationary position, and both the critical swimming speed and the maximum sustained speed can be determined. Another method uses the rotation of a water mass to determine the sublethal effect related to swimming by measuring the fish ability to compensate for torque. Sublethal levels 0.06 ppm of zinc in water for 190 d significantly reduced the ability of minnows to compensate for torque (ref. 85).

(iii) Circulation. Chemicals have been known to affect both the heart and the blood. Most pollutants cause bradycardia of the heart (ref. 86) which produces acute internal hypoxia causing the fish to increase ventilation. Only acute exposures of ammonia has been reported to have caused an increase in the rate of the heart (ref. 87), but this occurred under extremely high concentrations.

All substances entering or leaving fish must have had contact with the blood, therefore if these substances were toxic chemicals they might have affected various blood related processes such as gas uptake, osmotic and ionic regulation, hemoglobin synthesis, and hematocrit. Some of the effects of a chemical may be diagnosed through the measurement of hemotological factors. These include: hematocrit, blood cell count, hemoglobin concentration, blood cell differential counts, and serum protein analysis. These are fairly quick screening methods and they provide information that would assist towards an assessment of the condition of the fish.

Many chemicals possess the ability to cause anemia in fish. Some of these include cadmium, lead, mercury, zinc, chloramine, melathion, and pulp mill effluent (ref. 88).

(iv) Osmoregulation. The gills are important sites for osmoregulation processes as well as respiration. They are also constantly exposed to any toxic chemicals in aquatic systems making the gills extremely vulnerable. Various heavy metals have resulted in structural damage to gills causing failure in osmoregulation and disrupting the flow of ion transport across the gill epithelium (ref. 89). Other effects of metals include increases of tissue water, slight increases in sodium and chloride, and inhibition of Na, K-ATPase in the gill epithelia.

It is important to note that handling of fish causes changes in parameters such as sodium chloride levels in blood plasma and osmolality. In some instances, they may take quite some time to return to normal.

(v) <u>Respiration</u>. Ventilation in fish occurs as a result of the expansion and contraction of both the buccal and opercular cavities, which provide a constant flow of water over the gills. The functions of the gills include gas exchange, osmoregula- tion, nitrogenous water excretion, and acid-base balance. The gills, due to their constant movement of large volume of water, are vulnerable to damage by various chemicals.

Acute exposure to some chemicals could result in rapid destruction of the gill lamellae, and death may follow as a probable result of blood hypoxia (ref. 88). However, under lower concentrations (sublethal levels), the fish may cough as a ventilatory response to the toxicant. Increase coughing frequency may occur if the dose of the toxicant is increased. Alterations in cough reflex can be easily monitored using implanted cannulae and pressure transducers and external electrodes for certain chemicals but fish may quickly adjust and the coughing may subside. Thus, the relevance of this sublethal response to population impairment is questionable.

Pathological damage could result from exposure to toxic chemicals and symptoms could include "hyperplasia with lamellar fusion, epithelial hypertrophy, telangiectasia (marked dilation of terminal blood vessels) edema with epithelial separation from basement membranes, general necrosis, and/or epithelial disquamation." (ref. 90).

7.2.5 Wildlife (Mammals and Birds)

There are three principal strategies for assessing the data for xenobiotic effects on wildlife. These are: (1) chemical screening; (2) field ecology; and (3) controlled field studies (ref. 91). Table 7.12 outlines the strengths and weaknesses of these strategies. Results from chemical screening may include "lethality, reproductive impairment, behavioural aberration, alteration in growth and development or changes in physiological indicators (or markers) that may foreshadow effects crucial to reproduction and survival."

The second strategy involves the study of wildlife population that might be affected by the chemical. Details should include population size, distribution, behavioural patterns/changes, absolute and relative abundance, recruitment and mortality rates, interaction with other populations or components of the ecosystem, and indication of body burdens in sampled individuals.

The third strategy "seeks to optimize both control variables and resemblance of test systems to natural environments. It involves the use of field or mesocosms studies. These systems are more complex than standard tests because they may be influenced by various environmental variables that are eliminated from standard testing. Depending upon the system, they may also permit interaction with other component of the ecosystems, allowing more of a natural influence and balance. Mesocosms permit better extrapolation of results to responses of natural systems.

The Office of Pesticides Program (OPP) of the U.S. EPA assesses ecological risk as follows (ref. 92), they:
- review and evaluate hazard data to identify the nature of the hazard
- identify and evaluate the observed dose-response relationship
- identify the conditions of exposure (e.g., intensity, frequency and duration of exposure); and
- combine the information in dose-response effects with that on exposure to estimate the probability that non-target populations will be adversely affected by actual use of a pesticide.

New chemicals are being developed continuously, and on many occasions, the information required to carry out a complete assessment is limited. The U.S. EPA has developed an assessment method to ensure uniformity and consistency in identifying chemicals for testing in order to determine ecological hazards (ref. 92). The agency used assessment factors in conjunction with hazard assessment to determine concentrations of concerns or level of concerns (Table 7.13). "An environnmental concentration of concern is that concentration at which populations of organisms may be adversely affected under simulated or actual conditions of production, use, and disposal." (ref. 92). Variables such as test species, age group susceptibility, acute and chronic exposure, sensitivity and considered in the development of the assessment factor. The assessment factors (Table 7.13) are used to determine concentration that would cause adverse effects, if equalled or exceeded. The four factors that are presently used are 1, 10, 100, and 1000.

The last step compares the toxicological hazard data for test populations or indicator species (LC_{50} or LD_{50}) with exposure data (model-based) that outlines and estimates environmental concentration (EEC) in the media of concern. Table 7.14 illustrates these comparisons in the form of ecotoxicological assessment criteria. If the comparisons equal or exceed the fixed criteria, a risk is inferred and tests are required to confirm the risk (ref. 92). The above framework was developed for the purpose of providing a safety factor that would allow for the differential variability among fish and wildlife species.

TABLE 7.12 Integrated strategies for wildlife toxicology.

TEST SYSTEMS	VOLUME OF DATA PRODUCED PER UNIT COST	REPEATABILITY AND PRECISION OF DATA	CONTROL OF VARIABLES	SENSITIVITY	CONFIDENCE IN APPLICABILITY TO FIELD	SPECIAL CAPABILITIES
Chemical screening	High	High	High	High within confidence of test system	Moderate	Test many chemicals singly and in combination. Utilize many toxic end points (e.g., lethality, reproduction, teratogenicity, growth, behaviour, physiology)
Field ecology	Moderate	Low	None	High for total impact, low for individual variables	High	Evaluate total impact of complex interactions of xenobiotics and other environmental stressors. Determine effects on population distribution and abundance.
Controlled field and mesocosm studies	Moderate	Moderate	Moderate	High	Moderately High	Examine interaction of xenobiotics and other stressors under moderately controlled conditions. Evaluate individual variables. Utilize different end points.

(Source: Reprinted with permission from ref. 91, Copyright (1990), ACS).

TABLE 7.13 Data sources and assessment factors used by OTS[a] to evaluate need
for testing of new chemicals.

DATA SOURCE AVAILABLE	ASSESSMENT FACTOR TO BE APPLIED
Structure-activity derived LC_{50} value	1000
Single LC_{50} value from chemical analog[b]	1000
Single test LC_{50} value for PMN[c]	1000
Two LC_{50} values for same analog (e.g., 1 fish, 1 algal test)	1000
Two LC_{50} values for PMN (e.g., 1 fish test, 1 invertebrate)	1000
Three LC_{50} values for same analog (fish, algae, invertebrate)	100
Five LC_{50} values for same analog (3 invertebrates, 2 fish)	100
Five LC_{50} values for the PMN (e.g., 3 algae, 2 fish)	100
Maximum acceptable toxic concentration for analog	10
Field study	1

a   EPA's Office of Toxic Substances
b   "Analog" is a chemical similar to that proposed for production.
c   "PMN" is the Premanufacture Notification describing the chemical.
(Source: Reprinted with permission from ref. 92, Copyright (1990), ACS).

7.3   ASSESSMENT MODELS

The need to determine the various effects of a chemical in the environment
and human health as a result of their uses and release has been the initiating
factor for various forms of investigations. Acute and chronic effects are
normally carried out in the laboratory, the variables being the concentration
of the chemical and the duration of exposure in the study.

The study of the effects of an existing chemical that has already been
released into the environment requires direct monitoring of the specific
medium of the environment. The knowledge of its chemical and physical
properties will assist in the proper design of the monitoring programs
incorporating the various media that the chemical might potentially impact.

Models are developed based on physical systems with well-defined boundaries
and determinate variables. It requires knowing how the system may respond to
some variables while attempting to predict the responses of others through the
variation of known entities. For example, in air quality models the principle
of mass conservation is considered; while for water modelling, equations of
mass, flow, and volume are important factors. Other information on certain
parameters or the 7Q10 (7-d average over a 10-y period) low flow might be of
importance depending upon the requirements of the model. Therefore, the
ability of the model to predict with some accuracy is dependent upon the
assumptions that have been entered into the model. Fig. 7.12 shows a spectrum
of mathematical models. Environmental-type models appear within the middle
third of the spectrum, in the gray area. It falls between clean mechanistic

TABLE 7.14 Ecotoxicological assessment criteria for pesticides.

PRESUMPTION OF NO HAZARD	PRESUMPTION OF HAZARD THAT MAY BE MITIGATED BY RESTRICTED USE	PRESUMPTION OF UNACCEPTABLE HAZARD

Acute Toxicity

Mammals

EEC[a] $1/5$ LC$_{50}$ mg/kg/day $1/5$ LC$_{50}$	EEC $1/5$ LC$_{50}$ mg/kg/day $1/5$ LC$_{50}$	EEC LC$_{50}$

Birds

EEC $1/5$ LC$_{50}$	$1/5$ LC$_{50}$ EEC LC$_{50}$	EEC LC$_{50}$

Aquatic organisms

EEC $1/10$ LC$_{50}$	$1/10$ LC$_{50}$ EEC $1/2$ LC$_{50}$ EEC $1/10$ LC$_{50}$	EEC $1/2$ LC$_{50}$

Chronic Toxicity

EEC Chronic No effect level	N/A	EEC effect level (including reproduc- tive)

a   Estimated environmental concentration. This is typically calculated using a series of sample nomographs to complex exposure models.
(Source: Reprinted with permission from from ref. 92, Copyright (1990), ACS).

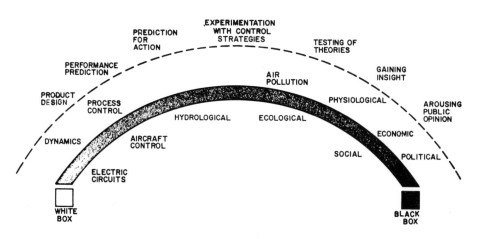

Fig. 7.12. Spectrum of mathematical methods.
(Source: Reprinted with permission from ref. 97).

mechanistic models (electric circuits, dynamics, etc.) and those with totally unknown factors (black box). It is important to recognize, in evaluating and using mathematical models, that each shade of gray in the spectrum carries with it a built-in validity factor. The ultimate use of a model must conform to the expected validity of the model (ref. 93).

The scope of a model is important towards what is expected of it. For example, models are not expected to precisely predict future impacts of a developmental activity; instead they may be capable of assessing various strategies depending upon the different scenarios that were fed into the model.

In other cases, they could be used for the purpose of predicting compliance or non-compliance with a previously established standard or objective. This could be carried out for new or existing developments. In these cases, the models may utilize data submitted by industry together with information of specific variables that may have been obtained from monitoring programs. Details from such a model, if accurately carried out, could result in suggestions or inputs toward equipment design and treatment modification of a system.

Models should be credible and should provide a certain level of confidence; however, this is dependent upon verification, calibration, validation, or post-audit (ref. 94). Fig. 7.13 outlines a process for model testing and validation. The process of validation is composed of a number of steps which results in the model's capability for making predictions that are sufficiently accurate and precise for the intended use (ref. 95).

The initial step is a model construction check, which confirms the correct structure and operation of the model algorithms over the range of conditions and the model parameters expected. Computer runs are also carried out for checking performance over the range of applicability of the model. Calibration involves an adjustment of various model parameters within a certain range until the differences between the model prediction and field data measurements are satisfactory to the application.

Verification indicates how well the model is representing processes in a natural system. It involves checking of computer codes, equations, and programming techniques. This process may also include sensitivity analysis of parameters. Occasionally, previously defined parameters are used to represent a new situation, and the results are then compared to runs using actually recorded field data; this activity has been referred to as model validation or post-audit. It is the ultimate test of the model's predictive capabilities. The degree to which agreement is obtained reflects on both the capabilities of the model and the assumption that were used by the modeller to represent the proposed situation.

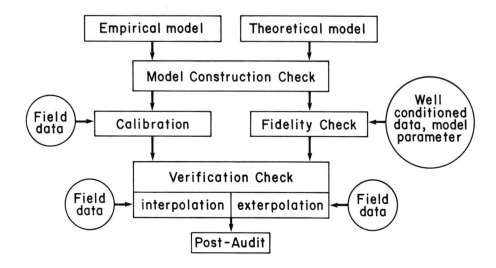

Fig. 7.13. The process of model testing (validation).
(Source: Reprinted with permission from ref. 95, Copyright (1982), Butterworths).

Chemical Releases

Chemical releases into the environment include: natural sources, manufacturing, use patterns, accidents, and disposal methods. Release of the various chemicals occur as a result of the use of the chemical or product containing the chemical. Uses include: industrial, domestic, commercial, agricultural, and transportation. With regards to the application of the chemical, release could occur instantaneously into the environment (e.g., aerosols, pesticide application), or more slowly (e.g., leaky underground storage tank).

7.3.1 Model classification

The U.S. Environmental Protection Agency have categorized air quality models into four generic classes: (1) gaussian; (2) numerical; (3) statistical or empirical; and (4) physical (ref. 96). Other types include Eulerian (diffusion-advection equation), Lagrangian, and Box models.

Gaussian models have been established about 25 y ago (Pasquill-Gifford equations). They can be either short to medium or long-range dispersion models. They assume normal distributions of pollutants along vertical, horizontal, and perpendicular to the direction of the wind. They permit assessments of continuous or instantaneous releases of pollutants with or without a linear rate or decay (ref. 97). These are most widely used for the purpose of estimating impact of pollutants that are non-reactive. In certain cases, Gaussian models have been modified to include special features such as:

- the introduction of different sources such as point sources, line sources, fugitive sources, etc.;
- settling of particles;
- topographical effects;
- alternate wind effects (sea breezes);
- changes in meteorological conditions;
- uptake by vegetation and water;
- reflection of chemical at the ground level; and
- effects of inversions.

Numerical models, on the other hand, are more appropriate for area source urban application for reactive pollutants; they are more complex and require extensive input databases. Because of this, and higher costs, they are not as widely utilized.

Statistical or empirical models are usually used when there is a lack of information and/or understanding of the physical and chemical processes or insufficient database to use one of the previously mentioned models. In some cases, Gaussian assumptions of normal distributions may not be true representatives of a convective boundary layer. Instead, these could be distinct, statistically independent distributions of down- and updraft plumes; in these cases, empirical models might be most applicable.

Physical models are used for fluid modelling such as wind tunnels or for evaluating impact of a single or group of sources in an area limited to only a few kilometres. This type of modelling is quite complex and usually requires technical experts or modellers with extensive experience and knowledge.

Eulerian models are based upon the conservation equation, using a coordinate system fixed in space (ref. 97). These are also known as gradient transport models and they treat turbulence as diffusion term. The use of these models is not as popular as Gaussian type, but they provide extra possibilities such as the variation of wind field with space and diffusion parameters with height. Windfield must be computed or partially observed at the site, and computation are complex and could lead to numerical problems. Also, diffusion parameters are usually not well known (ref. 97). Eulerian models are usually short to medium range, however, long-range versions have been developed for gradient transport modelling.

Certain models have been used for the purpose of assessing strategies for reducing both long-range and long-term pollution. These are called Lagrangian models and they are based on the computation of trajectories between sources and receptors. In certain cases, these models have also been described as statistical models because they use time average rather than meteorological data (ref. 97).

Box models have derived their name from their design. These are built using several adjacent boxes, each yielding average concentrations with time. The concentration of the plume reduces with distance as the plume disperses within the widening box. The trajectory of the pollutant is assumed to be bounded by the sides of the box. In certain cases, these models have been tested and validated by comparison with a wind tunnel model.

Industrial Source Complex Dispersion Model

The Industrial Source Complex (ISC) Dispersion Model (ref. 98) has been designed to consider factors such as fugitive emissions, aerodynamic wake effects, gravitational settling and dry deposition. The model consists of two computer programs that are quite flexible, economical and easy to use. It is also capable of handling complicated source configurations and special atmospheric effects such as site-specific wind profile, vertical potential temperature gradients, stack-tip downwash, building wake effects, etc. The program has been designed to pre-select default values for the above parameters when these options are not specified by the users.

The ISC Model computer programs are suitable for application to pollutant sources in the following types of studies (ref. 98):
  - stack design studies;
  - combustion source permit application;
  - regulatory variance evaluation;
  - monitoring network design;
  - control strategy evaluation for implementation plans;
  - fuel conversion studies;
  - control technology evaluation;
  - new source review;
  - prevention of significant deterioration.

ISC dispersion models have also been found applicable for industrial source complexes, rural or urban areas, flat or rolling terrain, transport distances less than 50 km and one hour to annual averaging times.

The ISC Model applies user-specified locations for point, line, area and volume sources, and user-specified receptor locations or receptor rings. It is a Gaussian Plume Model and may be used to model primary pollutants. Table 7.15 outlines the various equations that are used by the ISC Model. It also has the capability for modelling urban and rural conditions.

The ISC dispersion model can be used to determine both short- and long-term effects. The short-term model (ISCST) is an extended version of the single source model (ref. 104) called CRSTER. ISCST calculates average short-term concentrations from area point, volume, and line sources. The model can incorporate the effects of stack downwash, building downwash, gravitational settling, dry deposition, and urban and rural dispersion. The model uses sequential hourly meteorological data to calculate average concentrations or depositions for time periods of 1, 2, 3, 4, 6, 8, 12, and 24 h. If used with a year of sequential hourly meteorological data, ISCST can also calculate annual concentration or deposition values. Either rectangular or polar receptor grid may be selected.

The ISC Long-term Model (ISCLT) is a sector-averaged model that extends and combines basic features of the Air Quality Display Model, and the Climatological Dispersion Model. It calculates the long-term seasonal and annual pollutant concentration from point area, volume and line sources. Up to 400 receptors may be selected and no sources need be specified by the program. It uses statistical wind speed, and wind direction summaries to calculate seasonal and/or annual ground-level concentration and deposition values.

7.3.2 Acidification simulation model

Regional Acidification Information and Simulation (RAINS) is an International Institute for Applied Systems Analysis (IIASA) integrated model. It was developed by an interdisciplinary research team (ref. 105) as a tool for evaluating control strategies of acidification in Europe. The model has been designed to assess the transboundary aspects of air pollution in Europe and presents a spatial and temporal overview of the problem. The model is currently sulphur-based, however it has been expanded to include nitrogen emissions, transport, depositions, and impacts. RAINS is comprised of seven submodels which are connected as shown in Fig. 7.14. Each submodel is quite simple and deals with pollution generation, atmospheric processes, and environmental impacts.

(i) SO_2-emissions submodel. The RAINS model concentrates on anthropogenic sources because natural origins of SO_2 in Europe are quite insignificant (ref. 106). Sulphur emissions are calculated by mass balance and the emissions from the various sectors together with that from the industrial processes are added to obtain the total emissions from any one country. An option for energy consumption projections for various countries is also included in the model. The main emission producing sectors are refineries, power plants, domestic, industry and transportation; but the fuel utilized by these sectors could include any combination of the following brown coal, hard coal, derived coal, light oil, heavy oil, medium distillate, gas and other fuels (ref. 105).

TABLE 7.15 Equations used in the ISC Model.

EQUATION/PROCEDURES	USE
Steady-state Gaussian plume equation for a continuous source	To calculate ground-level concentrations for stack and volume sources.
Area source equation	Continuous and finite crosswind line source.
Generalized Briggs (refs. 99,100) plume rise equations	To calculate plume rise as a function of downwind distance.
Huber and Snyder (ref. 101) and Huber (ref. 102) procedures	To evaluate the effects of the aero-dynamic wakes and eddies formed by building and other structures on plume dispersion.
Wind-profile exponential law	To adjust the observed mean wind speed from the measurement height to the emission height for the plume rise and concentration calculations.
Single source model (CRSTER) procedures	To account for variation in terrain height over the receptor grid.
Pasquill-Gifford curves (ref. 103)	To calculate lateral and vertical plume spread.

(Source: ref. 98).

Optimization   **Scenario Analysis**

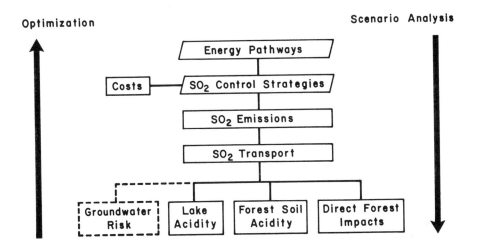

Fig. 7.14. A schematic overview of the RAINS model.
(Source: Reprinted with permission from ref. 112 from Royal Swedish Academy of Sciences).

(ii) Cost analysis submodel. RAINS contains a set procedure to estimate potential reduction in costs for items 2 through 4. "To use the cost submodel of RAINS, one first has to select an existing energy pathway or create a new pathway. Sulphur dioxide emission- control strategies can be specified in three different modes. In the first mode, a user can create a control strategy by applying combinations of three emission-reduction methods: (1) fuel substitution, (2) the use of low sulphur fuels; and (3) the desulphurization. After the user has specified the amounts of energy per sector and fuel to which each of these methods has to be applied, RAINS provides both the related costs and the achieved SO_2 emission reductions. In the second mode, a user specifies amounts of emission reduction per country, and RAINS estimates the optimal abatement costs to achieve these reductions, using its country-specific costs functions. The third mode is used to compute an international cost optimum for reducing deposition to a specific level." (ref. 105).

(iii) Sulphur transport submodel. This submodel for sulphur transport is based on a Lagrangian model of long-range transport of air pollutants and consists of a transfer matrix (ref. 105). It computes the sulphur dioxide concentration in air and the sulphur deposition in each European country. Each country's contribution is then summed to obtain the total sulphur deposition and/or sulphur dioxide concentration. Background contributions are also included.

Uncertainties considered in this submodel include the effects of winds, precipitation, and other meteorological and chemical variables, on both sulphur deposition and air concentrations.

The sulphur transport submodel possesses the capabilities of presenting the total sulphur deposition from previous years. This data could then be compared to various scenarios such as no pollution control, 30% reduction, major sulphur control, and/or deposition limits, to any year in the future. The result could be plotted in the form of deposition maps showing the concentration at various locations throughout the European continent.

Although NO$_x$ transport has complicated atmospheric chemistry, and is more difficult to model, there are long-range transport models with basic chemistry that are showing promising results. IIASA plans to include results of these models in RAINS as transfer matrices with correction factor to account for non-linear chemistry (ref. 105).

(iv) <u>Soil acidification submodel</u>. Acid deposition occurs mainly through air pollution and the affected media are the terrestrial and aquatic environment. Soil varies considerably from area to area with certain types having the ability to buffer acid deposition. In areas where soil do not possess this characteristic, there are major effects to the flora of that particular ecosystem resulting in species alteration, or in extreme cases, forest dieback.

The RAINS soil submodel focusses on a year-to-year development of forest soil acidification in an idealized 50 cm deep soil layer, and the soil acidity is computed by comparing the cumulative acid load to the soil buffering capacity and the yearly rate of acid loading with the buffer rate (ref. 105). If the acid deposition rate is lower than the buffer rate, the model computes and reports a recovery.

(v) <u>Lake acidification submodel</u>. Lake acidification is a major problem in various regions of the European Continent. It is being linked to acidic runoff that is inadequately buffered within the drainage basin of the system. There are also other factors that influence acidification and these include amount of snowmelt, rainfall, runoff pathways, water chemistry and various chemical and physical processes.

RAINS lake acidification submodel attempts to provide a quantitative overview of the key processes which include: (1) the terrestrial catchment segment, which includes snowpack and two soil layers; and (2) precipitation which is routed into quickflow, baseflow, and percolation between soil layers. The same analytical methodology as in the soil submodel is used to calculate the ion concentrations of the internal flows. The leaching of acidity to surface waters is simulated on the basis of simulated concentrations in the soil solution and the discharges from the terrestrial catchment.

The approach for assessing regional lake water impact has two distinct levels. The first is the catchment model which analyzes changes over time in the chemistry of the lake, and the second is a regionalized model which includes characteristics of a large number of lakes within a particular region.

There are four major parameters that determine the dynamics of long-term acidification and recovery: soil thickness, base saturation, silicate buffer rate and forest-filtering factor. The authors of the model caution that the data of the above parameters should be as reliable as possible, and the initialization and parameter estimation should be based on actual field measurements (ref. 105).

(vi) Groundwater acidification submodel. Acid deposition may also lead to the acidification of groundwater as a result of deterioration of the soil's natural buffering capacities. Some of the symptoms include increases in levels of water hardness, aluminum, and sulphate. The groundwater acidification submodel in its initial phase includes a sensitivity mapping system, which produces European maps of aquifer susceptibility to acidification. The sensitivity and risk of groundwater acidification are evaluated by assessing to which extent physical and chemical soil and aquifer properties of a certain region will contribute to the neutralization of acid deposition.

(vii) Forest impact submodel. Forest dieback and degradation have been noted on the European Continent for several years. There are various environmental processes that might have contributed directly towards this depletion and in some areas, in various combinations. Some of these stresses include: soil acidification, damage to foliage as a result of acid deposition, nitrogen overfertilization, climatic alteration, and natural stresses.

In order to assess the forestry impact, three approaches were taken: (1) statistical/empirical models; (2) simulation models of forest environment; and (3) indicator analysis (ref. 105).

The Statistical/Empirical model's principal input is the annual average air concentration of SO_2 (taken from the RAINS transport model), and the output is the accumulated dose of SO_2 to trees which is the simple computation of the product of concentrations and the exposure time. Damage to trees is assumed to occur if the accumulated dose exceeds a threshold level.

The indicator analysis approach uses the sensitivity of forests to specified pollutant impacts based on ecophysiological mechanisms. Some indicators include synergistic impacts of air pollutants with natural stress factors, and the resistance of trees to direct foliage impacts caused by pollutants, either alone or together with natural stress factors. Combined risk of forest diebacks is computed as a function of foliage damage as well as measures of tree resistance to stress (ref. 105).

346

Linkage between Submodels
"The linkages between submodels make the RAINS model more than a loose collection of different models. Since models of one discipline are rarely designed to link with other disciplines, it is critical to give special attention to these linkages." (ref. 105).

Uncertainty Analysis
Sensitivity analyses have been carried out for both the soil acidification and lake acidification submodels. For the soil submodel, it was shown to be particularly sensitive to base saturation, silicate buffer rate, and a filtering factor (allocation of deposition to forested areas). Sensitivity tests indicated the importance of the initial conditions of the soils. The lake acidification submodel was shown to be particularly sensitive to the same parameters as the soil submodel plus an additional soil thickness.

The uncertainty analyses for the remaining submodels are still underway; however, the following conclusions were drawn by Alcamo et al. (ref. 105):

1. In general, it is feasible not only to model the long-range transport of air pollutants but to quantify the uncertainty of model calculations.
2. In many cases, model errors seem to compensate. For example, the uncertainty due to interannual meteorologic variability is ± 32 percent for a single country's contribution to a single receptor location. However, when all countries are included, the typical uncertainty is about ± 13 percent. We may conclude that fairly simple models can therefore produce good results over long time and space scales.
3. To accurately estimate the effect of parameter uncertainty on model output, it is more important to know the range of the parameter uncertainty than the type of their probability distribution. Of these parameter uncertainties, mixing height and wet deposition seem to have the greatest effect on model computations.

7.3.3 Aquatic fate models
Chemicals released in the environment can be traced through extensive monitoring programs of the receiving waters and the various media that might have been exposed to the chemical. In these cases, the effects might be determined after the release of the chemical, resulting in leaving the contamination (if occurred) as is, or developing and executing detailed programs to cleanup and rehabilitate the exposed areas. If, on the other hand, the chemical had not been released, then various studies may be developed to predict impacts and fate of the chemical in the environment. These environmental fate models can be used to assemble chemical and environmental

information into an objective mathematical description of the behaviour of the chemical in aquatic ecosystems (ref. 107). Information from models of this type together with data from actual monitoring studies, toxicological bioassays, fate processes and chemical and physical properties could provide information that would be necessary for a systematic assessment of a chemical.

Assessment models for aquatic fate are designed to predict the geographical distribution or transport within the system, space and time scale, distribution among trophic levels and species, transformation pathways, and residual concentration of the chemical. The model itself is made up of different equations and the principles of mass conservation, including inputs with transport, transfer and reaction components. Relevant chemical processes include direct and indirect photochemical reactions, hydrolysis, biotransformation, ionic speciation, and hydrodynamic transport. The advantages of developing a model, however, is not for the purpose of accurately predicting the future state of the system, instead, the value lies in the very exercise of stating precisely how much is really known about each pathway, and in the possibility of allocating future research efforts in such a way as to contribute most effectively to quantitative knowledge of the overall behaviour of the system (ref. 108).

Transport Processes

Chemicals can be transported regionally or globally. This could represent movement of a few kilometres to many hundreds of kilometres. Regional distribution would include transport mainly by rivers, while surface runoff and groundwater would account for the local movement of chemicals. In many cases, each particular transport mode might be considered as part of an overall (global) movement of a chemical, and movement on different temporal and distance scales may often be considered as being essentially separate. For example, the movement of a chemical in a river system will typically require that exchanges to and from the immediate atmosphere be considered; it is not necessary, however, that global atmosphere movement be considered simultaneously, because a particular river will contribute negligible amount to the atmosphere, and the latter can be considered a fixed large scale reservoir when studying the river (ref. 109).

Transport of chemicals within any aquatic system is dependent upon the behaviour of the particulates and/or suspended solids in the water column. The hydrodynamic behaviour of the system will also determine if the chemical settles onto the sediment and moves laterally with the sediment movement. This strategy in fate modelling is to "piggy-back" the bound or sorbed chemical on a transport model of the sediment phase.

Space and Time Scales

The quantity of a chemical released into the environment is dependent upon the rate and the duration of the release. The toxic impact of the released chemical depends upon the concentration that reaches the target organism. In the case of short-term releases, such as chemical spills or agricultural runoffs, the event is treated as a sudden release of a specific quantity of a chemical into the system, and the time taken for dilution and breakdown can be modelled. In these cases, the fate of the products and the extent of contamination can be predicted through this sudden-release model. A model of this type was developed for predicting concentration-time profiles for chemical spills in a river (ref. 110). It was based on mathematical formulation for transport and volatilization of soluble chemicals and was used to evaluate the consequence of a chloroform spill in the Mississippi River.

When releases are long term, the impact on the environment is a chronic impact and tends to be more significant. Examples include industrial and municipal effluents, natural releases, and dispersed consumer products. In these cases, the model must possess the capability of assessing the effects over a longer period of time. Kinetic steady state models are usually utilized in these cases.

In order to accurately assess the fate of a chemical, the size and number of the segments that might be affected should be considered in the simulation. Segments should accurately depict their respective sizes in order that the mixing assumptions could be assessed. Well-mixed processes are easier to model and also provide more realistic simulations. Some of the segments that can be physically divided include: air-water interface, sediment-water interface, thermocline, benthos, and ichthyofauna.

Regardless of the temporal and spatial horizons involved, mathematical models designed to evaluate the behviour of chemicals must include disruptions of the physical, chemical, and biophysical process governing the transport and fate of chemicals in the aquatic environment (ref. 110). The models must also include the transfer processes such as ionization, volatization, sorption, and bioaccumulation as they relate to the spatial and temporal scales. They may provide simulations that would depict more closely the fate of a chemical in the environment.

Trophic Level and Species Distribution

In order to predict the distribution of a chemical among trophic levels, it is required that the ecosystems be subdivided into different compartments. This does not allow for studying all species in detail; instead it permits subdivision into large heterogeneous compartments and the prediction of responses that might occur to these specific compartments. In many cases, these compartmental subdivisions allow the trained biologist to frequently predict various responses or add detailed information that ultimately help towards understanding the effects of chemicals. For example, if the concentrations of a particular chemical in fish were predicted to be a certain value, then the trained biologist would conclude that this concentration would be higher in larger, older fish. Further conclusion would indicate that yet higher amounts would be recorded for piscivorous species. In a similar manner, resulting body burdens might be predicted through knowledge of food intake and intestinal absorption and retention functions. The rate of biologically mediated transformations remain one of the areas that is yet to be fully understood. Knowledge of the total toxicity of the species of the chemical is required, and not just the amount of the chemical, if ecotoxicity is to be made a subject of prediction and precise analysis (ref. 110).

Dissolved Oxygen Stochastic Model

Dissolved oxygen mathematical models have been used for water quality assessments and management for many years. The model proposed by Streeter and Phelps (ref. 111) who used a series of differential equations of biochemical oxygen demand (BOD) and dissolved oxygen (DO) and applied them one-dimensionally to rivers and estuaries.

The Dissolved Oxygen Stochastic model (DOSTOC) is used to simulate the biochemical oxygen demand and the dissolved oxygen interaction in river systems (ref. 112). The model is steady state and is restricted to one-spaced dimension, the location in a river or stream, or its related travel time. It is a modification of Dewey's stochastic dissolved oxygen model (ref. 113). The model components are summarized as follows:

- BOD and NOD exert an oxygen demand in the water column;
- DO is supplied by reaeration which is related to the dissolved oxygen deficit and river hydraulics;
- DO is supplied by photosynthesis which varies diurnally;
- DO is decreased by respiration;
- BOD is decreased by sedimentation and decay;
- NOD is decreased by decay; and
- DO, BOD, and NOD are increased by non-point sources along the banks of the water course. (BOD = Biochemical Oxygen Demand; NOD = Nutrient Oxygen Demand).

Rate constants as well as photosynthesis, respiration, and non-point source loadings are treated as random variables in DOSTOC. Conditions above any effluents and concentrations of BOD, NOD, and DO of effluents from treatment plants and "pipe" outlets that are entering the system are also random variables. The solutions are stochastic processes representing the levels of BOD, NOD, and DO in the water courses. Known sources of errors due to simplifying assumptions are listed below (ref. 112):

- longitudinal dispersion is neglected;
- uniform velocity assumed for each river reach;
- uniform rate coefficients assumed for each river reach;
- mixing considered to be instantaneous and complete; and
- DO saturation considered to be temperature dependent only.

Parameter Descriptions

The module can be configured for several reaches of any river system. The reaches are defined on the basis of uniform hydraulic characteristics, and recognition that each reach can accommodate only one point source discharge. River width, depth, velocity and flow are all considered in the module.

The flow rate at the head of each river reach must be defined and these should include flow from upstream reaches, point source flows to the reaches, flow from tributary inputs and diffuse source inflows. Point source inflows are defined separately and they include municipal and industrial effluents and tributary stream. Only one point source flow is allowed for each reach in the model.

The BOD, NOD, and DO concentrations must be defined for each point source and non-point source inflow, and river or tributary head water. There is also the option of defining the correlation coefficient between BOD and DO, BOD and NOD, and DO and NOD for all headwaters and point source inflows. If a correlation coefficient is not defined, the model chooses DO, NOD, and BOD values randomly from the distribution defined by the mean and standard deviation. Although DOSTOC was not originally designed for a fast and/or slow BOD decay, these can be easily facilitated using the model "BOD" term to represent fast BOD and the NOD term to represent slow BOD.

Reaeration rates are calculated from hydraulic variables mean depth and mean velocities. Each reach could have a different reaeration rate because hydraulic conditions may vary from reach to reach. In an ice-cover situation, reaeration potential changes due to severe limitations. This is usually represented as a percentage of the open water value; it might be adjusted, however, to improve oxygen calibration.

The photosynthesis component of the module is defined so that photosynthesis varies over the course of the daylight hours. Input includes the maximum photosynthetic rate and the definition of the daylight period. It is assumed that maximum photosynthesis occurs at the middle of the daylight period, and no such activity occurs at night. Both photosynthesis and respiration rates are corrected for temperature and depth.

The DOSTOC model does not explicitly simulate sediment oxygen demand, however, it does account for oxygen consumption via respiration (ref. 119). Oxygen depleted by respiration is defined by a daily average value. Respiration rate is considered constant over the entire 24-h period and is due to aquatic loads, algae, and sediment.

DOSTOC Calibration and Congruence

A sensitivity analysis was carried out using DOSTOC and comparing its results to that of another model, QUAL2E-UNCAS (ref. 114). QUAL2E-UNCAS was used because it has the ability to perform the necessary sensitivity analysis. Before the analysis, it was demonstrated that the two models were capable of producing the same predictions, therefore, ensuring that results of uncertainty analysis with the two models would be compatible.

Input variables and parameters tested for sensitivity include:
- BOD decay rates;
- sediment oxygen demand;
- reaeration rates;
- head water flow rates;
- head water temperature;
- head water DO;
- head water BOD;
- point load flows (tributaries);
- point load DO (tributaries);
- point load fast BOD (industrial effluents); and
- point load slow BOD (industrial effluents and tributaries).

The runs were carried out in winter under ice-covered conditions, when low dissolved oxygen is expected to be most critical. Fig. 7.15 represents the results obtained from running the two models using the same process rates. Their outputs were very similar and could be made to match perfectly. The results clearly indicate that both models faithfully represent the behaviour of the river and neither contained any major coding errors.

Another model calibration of DOSTOC was carried out to demonstrate and compare observed and predicted conditions during winter ice-cover (Fig. 7.16). The observed dissolved oxygen information is expressed as a mean, plus or minus one standard deviation, while the computer simulation is represented by a continuous line. Surface water quality objective of the province of Alberta in Canada (being revised presently) is indicated by the solid line at 5.0 mg/L dissolved oxygen. The oxygen simulation results closely matched and accurately described the observed profiles, indicating good comparison and calibration.

Toxic Organic Fate Model

The toxic organic fate model chosen for discussion is called PEST. It was developed in the early 1980s at the centre for ecological modelling (ref. 115) at Rensselaer Polytechnic Institute in New York, U.S.A. to predict the fate of toxic organic chemicals in natural aquatic environments. It is considered an evaluative model and is used to indicate the importance of various processes under defined environmental conditions and to determine environmental compatibility of particular organic chemicals.

PEST is capable of simulating the time-varying concentration of a toxic organic material in each of as many as 16 carrier compartments: these variables can be parameterized to represent a variety of toxic organic material carrier, (ref. 115) an association typical of aquatic systems (Fig. 7.17).

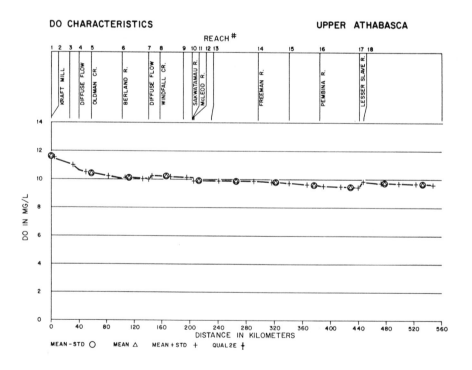

Fig. 7.15. A comparison of QUAL2 and DOSTOC for DO characteristics using the same process rates.

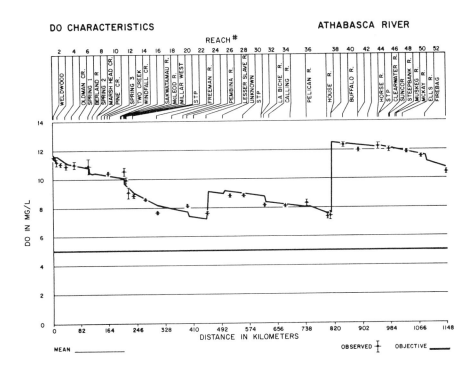

Fig. 7.16. A comparison of observed conditions and predicted DOSTOC simulation for dissolved oxygen.

Broad categories include toxic organics in aquatic plants (phytoplankton and macrophytes); animals (zooplankton, aquatic invertebrates, and fish); dissolved phase, either in the water column or the interstitial water; particulate organic matter, either suspended or bottom sediment; floating organic matter; and clay, either suspended or as bottom sediment.

Output from the model includes (ref. 115):

- the time varying concentration of the toxic material in each carrier (in ppm);
- the percentage distribution of the toxic material among the carriers; and
- the half lives of the toxic material in each carrier.

It is also possible to obtain plots of degradation rates both as they vary through time and also as a function of various environmental factors.

354

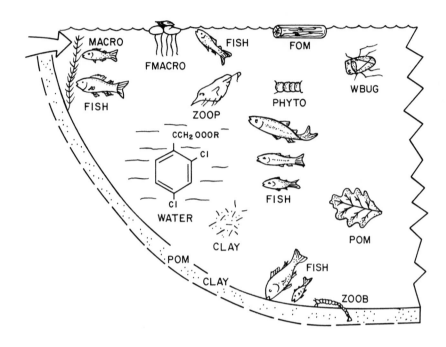

Fig. 7.17. Compartments in the PEST model. FMACRO = floating macrophyte; MACRO = macrophyte; FOM = floating organic matter; POM = particulate organic matter; WBUG = water bug; ZOOB = zoobenthos; ZOOP = zooplankton; PHYTO = phytoplankton.
(Source: Reprinted with permission from ref. 114, U.S. EPA).

Various processes are taken into consideration by the PEST model. These include: hydrolysis, oxidation, photolysis, volatilization, microbial metabolism, gill sorption by aquatic species, consumption, and biotransformation. The model includes highly elaborate algorithms for these various processes. For example, biotransformation is represented via second order equations in bacterial populations density in many other modules. PEST, however, adds to this effect of pH and dissolved oxygen on bacterial activity plus equations for metabolisms in higher organisms.

PEST Verification

Parathion was introduced as a single application of 0.05 ppm to each of two eutrophic fish ponds at Dor, Israel and the experiments were concluded 67 d later (ref. 114). Figs. 7.18, 7.19, and 7.20 represent the predicted and observed concentrations of parathion in the dissolved phase, in zooplankton, and in carp, respectively. The principal source of uncertainty was in the

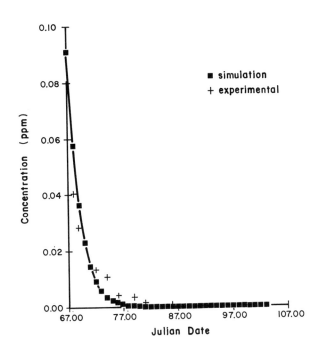

Fig. 7.18. Comparison of predicted and observed concentrations of parathion in dissolved phase in pond.
(Source: Reprinted with permission from ref. 114, U.S. EPA).

diurnal variation of pH, which is important in base-catalyzed hydrolysis of parathion. The authors also found that the mass balance was not being maintained and the toxic organic material was being lost due to a programming error (ref. 114). Uncertainties could have also occurred in the process parameters such as biotransformation, uptake by organisms, photolysis, etc. These reflect a more conservative estimate leading to the simulation of worse case scenarios.

The simulation in Fig. 7.18 was the closest reflection of the experimental data, while that of Figs. 7.19 and 7.20 did not appropriately produce result that were within reason to those of the experimental results. It is also possible that the data might not have been sufficient for validation of the model.

356

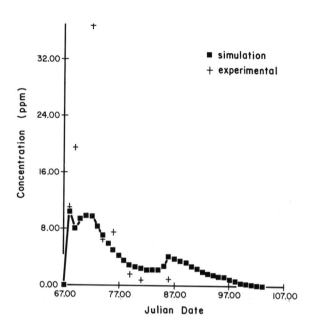

Fig. 7.19. Comparison of predicted and observed concentrations of parathion in zooplankton in pond.
(Source: Reprinted with permission from ref. 114, U.S. EPA).

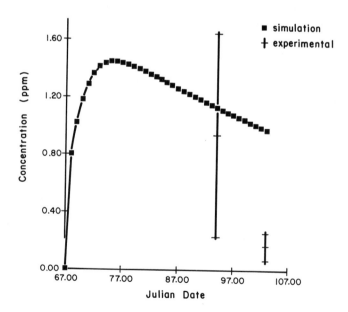

Fig. 7.20. Comparison of predicted and observed concentrations of parathion in carp in pond.
(Source: Reprinted with permission from ref. 114, U.S. EPA).

7.3.4 Accuracy and uncertainty

Mathematical models have been proven to be extremely useful as descriptive and predictive tools providing that "the heart of the model," the mathematical equations are accurate enough to produce results well within required confidence levels. This confidence can be obtained only if the data from the various processes are accurate and sufficient to represent the model application.

Dispersion models usually attempt to estimate the concentration of a chemical at a particular site through the information obtained about various processes and data from monitored parameters. The model is then initialized by the input of information about known events, such as wind speed, emission characteristics, mixed layer height, etc. There are also the inclusion of unmeasured and unknown variations of a specific event such as turbulent velocity, and unresolved details of a atmosphere. These unknowns will result in variations even with the most perfect model. This type of uncertainty may alone be responsible for a typical range of variation in concentration of as much as 50 percent (refs. 115,116).

The prediction of the behavioural aspects of an ecosystem over a long period requires ecosystem modelling. These, in general, have not been concerned with the problem of prediction. Instead, they have been assessed at providing a theoretical framework to aid in understanding the explanation and to provide a system of guidelines for experimentation by identifying key components, processes, and potential effects (ref. 117). These models have not been known for their predictive capabilities because many of their critical processes are not quantifiable and also due to their extreme sensitivity to small changes in the various processes.

The modelling of the behaviour of organic chemicals in aquatic ecosystems is one that requires special consideration. The model should address the fate of breakdown products together with chemical, biological, and physical aspects of a potentially persistent chemical. In many cases, it is not recognized that volatilization is a function of both vapour pressure and solubility and, as such it may be incorrectly modelled. In some cases, the rate of photolysis is influenced by light as well as dissolved organic materials which may also have a catalytic effect.

The occurrence of the chemical in a particular part of the ecosystem may also affect the accuracy of the model. For instance, micro layers of extremely concentrated material might occur at different areas of the water column (e.g., at the surface or just above the sediment layer. In many cases, these may only be a few microns thick, yet they may possess the majority of the compound in the aquatic medium.

It is most important that an appropriate model should be selected for a given situation. Therefore, modelling objectives should be clear and concise and should reflect the requirements of the respective agency. The objectives should be properly defined in order to ensure that the chosen model is capable of producing the required results.

REFERENCES

1 S.A. Levin and K.D. Kimball (Editors), Environ. Management, 8 (1984) 375-442.
2 Fed. Registr. U.S. Environmental Protection Agency, 47, 53912, 24 Nov. 1982.
3 Fed. Registr. U.S. Environmental Protection Agency, New Chemical Substances: Premanufacture Testing Policy, 46 (17) 8986, 26 January 1981.
4 Canadian Council of Resource and Environment Ministers (CCREM), Canadian Water Quality Guidelines, March 1987.
5 Fed. Registr. U.S. Environmental Protection Agency, Water Quality Criteria Documents: Availability, 45 (231), 79318, 28 November 1980.
6 J. Bascietto, D. Hinckley, J. Plafkin, and M. Slimak, Environ. Sci. Technol., 24 (1990) 10-15.
7 U.S. Environmental Protection Agency, Estimating Concern Levels for Concentrations of Chemical Substances in the Environment, Washington, D.C., U.S.A., 1984.
8 D.J. Urban and N.J. Cook, Hazard Evaluation Division, Standard Evaluation Procedure, Ecological Risk Assessment, U.S. Environmental Protection Agency, Washington, D.C., U.S.A., EPA-504/9-85-001; NTIS PD 86-247-657.
9 Fed. Regist., 54 (1989) p. 1300.
10 Fed. Regist., 48 (1983) p. 51400.
11 Fed. Regist., 49 (1984) p. 9016.
12 U.S. Environmental Protection Agency, Guidelines for Deriving Numerical Water Quality Criteria for the Protection of Aquatic Organisms and Their Uses, Washington, D.C., U.S.A., NTIS PB 85-227049, 1986.
13 U.S. Environmental Protection Agency, Technical Support Document for Water Quality-Based Toxics Control, Washington, D.C., U.S.A., NTIS PB 86-150067, 1985.
14 A.M. Friend, in D. Fowle, A.P. Grima, and R.E. Munn (Editors), Information Needs for Risk Management, Environmental Monograph No. 8, Institute for Environmental Studies, University of Toronto, Toronto, Canada, ISBN-0-7727-4409-2, 1989, pp. 63-89.
15 R.E. Munn, The Design of Integrated Monitoring Systems to Provide Early Indicators of Environmental/Ecological Changes, Proc. of the 3rd International Symposium on Integrated Global Monitoring of the State of the Biosphere, UNEP, Tashkent, USSR, October 13-19, 1985.
16 L.A. Spielberg, L.F. Smith, and J.A. Victor, in D. Fowle, A.P. Grima, and R.E. Munn (Editors), Information Needs for Risk Management, Environmental Monograph No. 8, Institute for Environmental Studies, University of Toronto, Toronto, Canada, 1988, pp. 91-99.
17 J.W. Frank, B. Gibson, and M. MacPherson, in D. Fowle, A.P. Grima, and R.C. Munn (Editors), Information Needs for Risk Management, Environmental Monograph NO. 8, Institute for Environmental Studies, University of Toronto, Toronto, Canada, 1988, pp. 129-144.
18 D.B. Chambers and L.M. Lowe, in D. Fowle, A.P. Grima, and R.E. Munn (Editors), Information Needs for Risk Management, Environmental Monograph NO. 8, Institute for Environmental Studies, University of Toronto, Toronto, Canada, 1988, pp. 177-192.
19 Organization for Economic Cooperation and Development (OECD), Existing Chemicals; Systematic Investigation, OECD Publications, Paris, France, ISBN 92-64-12869-7, 1986, 225 p.

20 E.C. Herriek, J.A. King, R.P. Oullette, and P.N. Cheremisinoff, Unit Process Guide to Organic Chemical Industries, Ann Arbor Science Publishers, Ann Arbor, Michigan, U.S.A, 1979.

21 United States Minerals Yearbooks, 1911-1979, Bureau of Mines, U.S. Department of the Interior, Washington, D.C., U.S.A.

22 Canadian Minerals Yearbooks, 1920-1979, Publishing Centre, Department of Supply and Services, Ottawa, Ontario, Canada.

23 Adapted from U.S. Environmental Protection Agency, Instructions Manual for the Pre-manufacture Notification of New Chemical Substances, U.S. EPA, Washington, D.C., U.S.A, 1983.

24 P.H. Howard, Handbook of Environmental Fate and Exposure Data for Organic Chemical, Lewis Publishers, Inc., Michigan, U.S.A., 1989.

25 E.E. Kenaga and C.A.I. Goring, in J.G. Eaton, P.R. Parish, and A.C. Hendricks (Editors), Proceedings of the 3rd Symposium on Aquatic Toxicology, American Society of Testing Materials, Philadelphia, U.S.A., 1980, pp. 78-115.

26 A. Leo, C. Hansen, and D. Elkins, Chem. Revs., 71 (1971) 525-???.

27 Ontario Ministry of the Environment (OME), Volatilization Rates for Organic Chemicals of Public Health Concern, OME, Ontario, Canada, ISBN-0-7729-3983-7, 1984, 72 p.

28 W.J. Lyman, W.T. Reehl, and D.H. Rosenblatt, Handbook of Chemical Estimation Methods-Environmental Behaviour of Organic Compounds, McGraw Hill, New York, U.S.A., 1982.

29 S.W. Karickhoff, Chemosphere 10 (1981) 833-846.

30 L.G. Sillen and A.E. Martell, Stability Constants of Metal-ion Complexes, Supplement No. 1 Special Publication No. 25, The Chemical Society, London, U.K., 865 p.

31 W.J. Doucette and A.W. Andren, Chemosphere, 17 (1988) 345-359.

32 W.B. Neely, D.R. Branson, and G.E. Blau, Environ. Sci. Technol. 8 (1974) 1113-1115.

33 P. Lu and R.L. Metcalf, Environ. Hlth. Persp. 10 (1975) 269-284.

34 R. Haque, J. Falco, S. Cohen, and C. Riordan, in R. Haque (Editor), Dynamics, Exposure, and Hazard Assessment of Toxic Chemicals, Ann Arbor Science Publishers, Ann Arbor, Michigan, U.S.A, 1980, pp. 47-67.

35 P.H. Howard, A.E. Huebert, B.C. Mulesky, J.S. Crisman, W. Meyland, E. Crosbie, D.A. Gray, G.W. Sage, K.P. Howaver, and A. LaMaectria, Environ. Toxicol. Chem., 5 (1986) 977-988.

36 P.H. Howard, personal communication, 1989.

37 W.B. Neely, in K.L. Dickson, A.W. Maki, and J. Cairns, Jr. (Editors), Analyzing the Hazard Evaluation Process, Proceedings of a Workshop, Waterville Valley, New Hampshire, American Fisheries Society, Washington, D.C., U.S.A., 1979, pp. 74-82.

38 W.B. Neely, in R. Haque (Editor), Dynamics, Exposure, and Hazard Assessment of Toxic Chemicals, Ann Arbor Science Publishers, Ann Arbor, Michigan, U.S.A., 1980, pp. 287-296.

39 P.J. Crutzen, I.A.S. Isaken, and J.R. McAfee, J. Geophys. Res. 83 (1978) 345-363.

40 National Academy of Sciences, Halocarbons: Effects on Stratospheric Ozone, Washington, D.C., U.S.A., 1976, 352 p.

41 W.L. Dilling, C.J. Bredeweg, and N.B. Tefertiller, Environ. Sci. and Technol., 10 (1976) 351-356.

42 A.J.M. Bowen, Environmental Chemistry of the Elements, Academic Press, New York, U.S.A., 1979, 333 p.

43a V.F. Hodge, S.R. Johnson, and E.D. Goldberg, Geochem. J., 12 (1978) 7-20.

43b National Academy of Sciences, Atmosphere-Biosphere Interactions: Toward a Better Understanding of the Ecological Consequences of Fossil Fuel Combustion, National Academy Press, 1981, 263 p.

44 E.P. Odum, Fundamentals of Ecology, W.B. Saunders, Philadelphia, 1971, 574 p.

45 L.A. Burns, in R.L. Swann and A. Eschenroeder (Editors), Fate of Chemicals in the Environment, ACS Symposium Series #225, American Chemical Society, Washington, D.C., U.S.A., 1983, pp. 25-40.

46 S.L. Brown and D.C. Bomberger, in R.L. Swann and A. Eschenroeder (Editors), Fate of Chemicals in the Environment, ACS Symposium Series #225, American Chemical Society, Washington, D.C., U.S.A., 1983, pp. 2-21.

47 D. Mackay and S. Paterson, Environ. Sci. Technol., 16 (1982) 654A-660A.

48 D. Mackay, S. Peterson, and M. Joy, in R.L. Swann and E. Eschenroeder (Editors), Fate of Chemicals in the Environment, ACS Symposium Series #225, American Chemical Society, Washington, D.C., U.S.A., 1983, pp. 175-195.

49 D. Mackay and S. Paterson, Environ. Sci. Technol., 15 (1981) 1006-1014.

50 R.L. Swann and A. Eschenroeder (Editors), Fate of Chemicals in the Environment, ACS Symposium Series #225, American Chemical Society, Washington, D.C., U.S.A., 1983, 320 p.

51 C.S. Staley and M.J. Case, Environ. Monitor. Assmnt., 8 (1987) 103-112.

52 L.A. Burns, D.M. Cline, and R.R. Lassiter, Exposure Analysis Modelling System (EXAMS), User Manual and System Documentation, U.S. EPA, Athens, Georgia, 1982.

53a A.S. Donigan, Jr., in K.L. Dickson, A.W. Maki, and J. Cairns, Jr., (Editors), Modelling the Fate of Chemicals in the Aquatic Environment, Ann Arbor Science Publishers, Ann Arbor, Michigan, U.S.A. 1982, pp. 303-323.

53b A.S. Donigan, Jr., in R.L. Swann and E. Eschenroeder (Editors), Fate of Chemicals in the Environment, ACS Symposium Series #225, American Chemical Society, Washington, D.C., U.S.A., 1983, pp. 151-171.

54 W.A. Swenson, J.H. McCormick, T.D. Simonson, K.M. Jensen, and J.G. Eaton, Archives Env. Contam. Toxicol., 18 (1989) 167-174.

55 C.R. Goldman, Limnol. Oceanog., 7 (1962) 99-101.

56 H.T. Odurn and C.F. Jordan, in H.T. Odurn (Editor), A Tropical Rainforest Division of Technical Information, U.S. Atomic Commission, Washington, D.C., U.S.A., 1970, pp. 165-190.

57 J. Cairns, Jr. and K.L. Dickson, J. Test. Evaluation, 6 (1978) 81-91.

58 E.J. Ariens, A.M. Simonis, and J. Offermeir, Introduction to General Toxicology, Academic Press, New York, U.S.A., 1976, 252 p.

59 F.S. Sanders, Environmental Monitoring and Assessment, 5 (1985) 55-99.

60 J.H. Steele, Phil. Trans. Royal Soc. London B. 286 (1979) 583-595.

61 W.C. Kerfoot and W.R. DeMott, in W.C. Kerfoot (Editor), Evolution and Ecology of Zooplankton Communities, Spec. Symp. No. 3, Amer. Soc. of Limnol. and Oceanog., Univ. Press of New England, Hanover, New Hampshire, 1980, pp. 725-741.

62 J.M. Davies and J.C. Gamble, Phil. Trans. Royal Soc. London B. 286 (1979) 523-544.

63 G.D. Grice, M.R. Reeve, P. Koeller, and D.W. Menzel, The Use of Large Volume, Transparent Enclosure Sea-Surface Water Column in the Study of Stress on Plankton Ecosystem, Helgolander Wiss. Meeresunters, 30 (1977) 118-133.

64 K. Krenling, J. Piuze, K. Von Brockel, and C.S. Wong, Mar. Biol., (48) 1978) 1-10.

65 M. Amburer, D.M. Adler, and P.H. Santschi, in G.D. Grice and M.R. Reeve (Editors), Marine Mesocosms, Springer-Verlag, New York, U.S.A., 1982, pp. 81-95.

66 R. Lloyd, Toxicity Testing with Aquatic Organisms: A Framework for Hazard Assessment and Pollution Control, Rapp. P.-v., Reun. Cons. Int. Explor. Mer., 1979, pp. 339-341.

67 J.W.M. Rudd, M.A. Turner, B.E. Townsend, A. Swick, A. Furutani, Can. J. Fish. Aquat. Sci., 37 (1980) 848-857.

68 M. Treshow, in G.C. Butler (Editor), Principles of Ecotoxicology, Scientific Committee on Problems of the Environment (SCOPE), John Wiley & Sons, New York, U.S.A., 1978, pp. 223-237.
69 N.S. Fisher and C.F. Wurster, Environ. Pollut., 5 (1973) 205-212.
70 D.W. Lorch, M. Melkonian, A. Weber, and M. Wettern, Accumulations of Lead by Blue-green Algae, Proc. Intern. Symp. Sandefjord, Norway, 1976.
71 D.C. Mortimer and A. Kudo, J. Environ. Qual., 4 (1975) 491-495.
72 D.C. McCune and L.H. Weinstein, Environ. Pollut., 1 (1971) 169-174.
73 J.B. Mudd and T.T. Kozlowski (Editors), Responses of Plants to Air Pollutants, Academic Press, New York, U.S.A., 1975, 383 p.
74 J.G. Stockner and A.C. Costella, J. Fish. Res. Board Canada, 33 (1976) 2758-2765.
75 D.A. Armstrong and R.E. Millemann, Marine Biol.(Berl.), 28 (1974) 11-15.
76 A.W. Maki and H.E. Johnson, Bull. Environ. Contam. Toxicol., 13 (1975) 412-416.
77 R.D. Burnett, DDT in Marine Phytoplankton and Crustacea, Diss. Abstr. Int. B. Sci. Eng., 34 (1973) p. 533.
78 P.L. Seyfried, in J.G. Eaton, P.R. Parrish, and A.C. Hendricks (Editors), Aquatic Toxicology, ASTM STP 707, Amer. Soc. for Testing and Materials, 1980, pp. 224-232.
79 A.A. Bulich, in L.L. Marking and R.A. Kimerle (Editors), Aquatic Toxicology, ASTM STP 667, Amer. Soc. of Testing and Materials, 1979, pp. 98-106.
80 R.R. Colwell, in G.C. Butler (Editor), Principles of Ecotoxicology, Scientific Committee on Problems of the Environment (SCOPE), John Wiley and Sons, New York, U.S.A., 1978, pp. 275-294.
81 R.L. Saunders and J.B. Sprague, Water Res., 1 (1967) 419-432.
82 D.I. Mount, Water Res., 2 (1968) 215 p.
83 W.A. Brungs, Trans. Am. Fish. Soc., 98 (1969) 272-279.
84 G. Leduc, J. Fish. Res. Bd. Can., 35 (1978) 166-174.
85 B.E. Bengtsson, Bull. Environ. Contam. Toxicol., 12 (1974) 654-658.
86 P. Sawyer, Ventilatory, Cardiac, and Metabolic Responses of Rainbow Trout and Brown Bullhead Catfish to Waterborne Cyanide, M.Sc. Thesis, Virginia, U.S.A., Polytechnic Institute and State University, Blacksburg, 1986.
87 G. Smart, J. Fish. Biol., 12 (1978) 93-104.
88 A.G. Heath, Water Pollution and Fish Physiology, CRC Press Inc., Boca Raton, Florida, U.S.A., 245 p.
89 S.D. Lewis and W.M. Lewis, Trans. Am. Fish. Soc., 100 (1971) 639-643.
90 T.R. Myers and J.D. Hendricks, in G.M. Rand and S.R. Petrocelli (Editors), Fundamentals of Aquatic Toxicology, Methods and Applications, Hemisphere Publishing Corp., Washington, D.C., U.S.A., 1985, pp. 283-331.
91 D.J. Hoffman, B.A. Rattner, and R.J. Hall, Environ. Sci. and Technol., 24 (1990) 276-283.
92 J. Bascietto, D. Hinckley, J. Plafkin, and M. Slimak, Environ. Sci. Technol., 24 (1990) 10-15.
93 W.J. Karplus, Perspective in Computing, 3 (1983) 4-13.
94 J. McLeod, Computer Modelling and Simulation: Principles of Good Practice, Simulation Series Vol. 1, No. 2, Society of Computer Simulation, La Jolla, California, U.S.A., 1982.
95 A.S. Donigian, L.M. Games, S. Hern, R.R. Laniter, and Y. Matsuoka, in K.L. Dickson, A.W. Maki, and J. Cairns, Jr. (Editors), Modelling the Fate of Chemicals in the Aquatic Environment, Ann Arbor Science Publishers, Ann Arbor, MI, U.S.A., 1982, pp. 387-396.
96 US EPA, Guidelines on Air Quality Models (Revised), United States Environmental Protection Agency, Office of Air and Radiation, Research Triangle Park, North Caroline, U.S.A., 1984, 14 chapters.
97 M. de Broissia, Selected Mathematical Models in Environmental Impact Assessment in Canada, Canadian Environment Assessment Research Council, Minister of Supply and Services, Canada, ISBN 0-662-14782-0, 1986, 34 p.

362

98 J.R. Bowers, J.R. Bjorklund, and C.S. Cheney, Industrial Source Complex (ISC) Dispersion Model User's Guide, Vols. 1 and 2 Office of Air Quality Planning and Standards, U.S. Environmental Protection Agency, Research Triangle Park, North Carolina, U.S.A., 1979.

99 G.A. Briggs, Some Recent Analyses of Plume Rise Observation, in Proceedings of the Second International Clean Air Congress, Academic Press, New York, U.S.A., 1971.

100 G.A. Briggs, Plume Rise Predictions, in Lectures in Air Pollution and Environmental Impact Analysis, American Meteorological Society, Boston, Massachusetts, U.S.A., 1975.

101 A.H. Huber and W.H. Snyder, Building Wake Effects on Short Stack Effluents, Preprint Volume for the Third Symposium on Atmospheric Diffusion and Air Quality, American Meteorological Society, Boston, Massachusetts, U.S.A., 1976.

102 A.H. Huber, Incorporating Building/Terrain Wake Effects on Stack Effluents, Preprint Volume for the Joint Conference on Application of Air Pollution Meteorology, American Meteorological Society, Boston, Massachusetts, U.S.A., 1977.

103 D.B. Turner, Workbook on Atmospheric Dispersion Estimates, U.S. Department of Health, Education, and Welfare, National Air Pollution Control Administration, Cincinnati, Ohio, U.S.A., Publication No. 99-AP-26, 1970.

104 U.S. EPA, User's Manual for Single Source (CRSTER) Model, EPA Report No. EPA-450/2-77-013, U.S. Environmental Protection Agency, Research Triangle Park, North Carolina, U.S.A., 1977.

105 J. Alcamo, M. Amann, J.P. Hetterlingh, M. Holmberg, L. Hordijk, J. Kumari, L. Kauppi, P. Kauppi, G. Kornai, and A. Makela, Ambio, 16 (1987) 232-245.

106 A. Semb, Atmos. Environ., 12 (1978) 455-460.

107 L.A. Burns and G.L. Baughman, in G.M. Rand and S.R. Petrocelli (Editors), Fundamentals of Aquatic Toxicology, Methods and Applications, Hemisphere Publishing Corporation, New York, U.S.A., 1985, pp. 558-584.

108 D.R. Miller, G. Butler, and L. Braurall, J. Environ. Management, 4 (1976) 383-401.

109 B. Bolin, in B.H. Svensson and R. Soderlund (Editors), Nitrogen, Phosphorus, and Sulphur-Global Cycles, SCOPE Report 7, Ecol. Bull. (Stockholm), 22 (1976) 17-22.

110 R. Truhaut, Ecotoxicology - A New Branch of Toxicology, in Ecological Toxicology Research: Proceeding of the NATO Science Committee Conference on Ecotoxicology, Quebec, Canada, Plenum Press, New York, 1974.

111 H.W. Streeter and E.B. Phelps, A Study on the Pollution and Natural Purification of the Ohio River, U.S. Public Health Service, Public Health Bull. No. 146, Washington, D.C., U.S.A., 1975.

112 R.J. Dewey, J. Env. Eng., 110 (1984) 412-429.

113 HydroQual Consultants Inc. and Gore and Storrie Ltd., Stochastic River Water Quality Model, Produced for Alberta Environment, Alberta, Canada, 1989, pp. 1-40.

114 R.A. Park, C.I. Connolly, J.R. Albanese, L.S. Clesceri, G.W. Heitzman, H.H. Herbrandson, B.H. Indyke, J.R. Lobe, S. Ross, D.D. Sharma, W.W. Shuster, Modelling the Fate of Toxic Organic Materials in Aquatic Environments, EPA-600/3-82-028, U.S. Environmental Protection Agency, Environmental Research Laboratory, Athens, Georgia, U.S.A, 1982, 163 p.

115 S.R. Hanna, Natural Variability of Observed Hourly SO_2 and CO Concentrations in St. Louis, Atmospheric Environment, 16 (1982) 1435-1440.

116 S.A. Levin and K.D. Kimball (Editors), Environmental Management, 8 (1984) 375-442.

117 M. Posch, L. Kauppi, and J. Kamari, Sensitivity Analysis of a Regional Scale Soil Acidification Model, IIASA, Working Paper W.P.-85-45, Laxemburg, Austria, 1985.

Chapter 8

RISK ASSESSMENT

INTRODUCTION

Risk is defined as the expected frequency of undesirable effects resulting from exposure to chemicals. Risk may be expressed in absolute terms as risk due to exposure to a specific chemical; in relative terms comparing the risk of the exposed population to the unexposed (ref. 1). Risk levels associated with certain common place activities, natural occurrences, voluntary activities, consumption of natural products have been compiled (refs. 2-4). Risk assessment is the process of assigning magnitudes and probabilities to the adverse effects resulting from human activities or natural catastrophes. Risk assessment was originally developed as a part of the actuarial techniques of the insurance industry to estimate probabilities of events that result in claims. Then it was extended to engineering sector to estimate the probabilities of catastrophic failures of engineered systems such as aircraft and nuclear power plants. More recently, risk assessment has been integrated to health industry to estimate probabilities of diseases among the population exposed to a range of toxic chemicals and combinations such as cigarette smoke, dietary patterns, and industrial emissions. Environmental risk assessment deals with hazards arising from pollution of air, water, and soil. The ecological risk assessment, on the other hand, deals specifically with adverse effects on the ecosystem which includes plants and animals and ecosystem properties. Human health risk assessment evaluates the adverse effects on humans resulting from exposure to a chemical and predicts the expected frequency of the effect over a life-time exposure period.

The approach used before risk assessment was hazard assessment. This approach which was in use from late 1970s to middle 1980s calculated a margin of safety by comparing the toxicological end point of interest (usually an estimate of safe concentration) to an estimated exposure concentration. An expert judgement is made on the adequacy of the margin of safety based on the amount of quality toxicological data. Toxicological and exposure data are collected in tiers, thus allowing decisions to be made with minimum data, provided the margin of safety was large enough (about 1000 times), whereas smaller margin is applied with larger databases of good quality. The margin of safety or uncertainty factors applied to safety decisions are basically meant to take into account the variability in specific responses, life stages, short- and long-term biological effects and test methods.

The risk assessment relies on the use of formal techniques such as mathematical or statistical models that define the magnitude of uncertainty in the effect and exposure estimates. The definitions for explicit and uniform use in risk assessment are given in Table 8.1.

TABLE 8.1 Definitions and components of risk assessment.

1. Hazard identification:	The determination of the existence of causal link or the lack of it to particular health effects.
2. Dose-response relationship:	The determination of a relationship between the magnitude of exposure and the probability of occurrence of adverse health effects
3. Exposure assessment:	The determination of the degree of human exposure before and after the introduction of regulatory controls.
4. Risk characterization:	The description of the nature and often the magnitude of risk to human health with associated level of uncertainty.

(Source: ref. 5).

Hazard functions provide a way of expressing individual risks over the exposure period. However, risk assessors in the chronic human health and safety area are often concerned with quantifying the risks to populations rather than to individuals because of the nature of available data. Both epidemiological and laboratory animal studies collect data from samples drawn from large populations and hence only population averages or statistics can be estimated from the above studies. The importance of these two data as key contributors to statistical risk assessment is supported by a recent publication from the U.S. Department of Health and Human Services (ref. 6) (Table 8.2).

Quantifying risk to sensitive/susceptible subpopulations (such as hypersensitive individuals, pregnant women, infants and children, older age groups, etc.) and combining these risks with estimated risks for the larger population to arrive at a number for the total population risk is a key challenge for risk assessors.

TABLE 8.2 Information required in human health risk assessment.

I.   Hazard identification
     A. Human data
        - Monitoring and surveillance (including vital statistics)
        - Epidemiologic studies
        - Clinical studies
     B. Animal data
     C. In vitro tests
     D. Molecular structure-activity relation
II. Hazard characterization
     A. Human studies
        - Epidemiologic studies
        - Clinical studies
     B. Animal studies
        - Minimal effects determination
        - Dose-response modelling
        - Special issues, including interspecies conversion and high- to
          low-dose extrapolation
     C. Phamacokinetic studies (including physiologic rationale)
III. Exposure characterization
     A. Demographic information
     B. Ecologic analyses
     C. Monitoring and surveillance systems
        - Animal
        - Human
     D. Biologic monitoring of high-risk individuals
     E. Transport modelling (mathematical)
     F. Integrated exposure assessments
        - Over time
        - Over hazard (synergy)
IV. Risk determination
     A. Mathematical
        - Unit and population risk estimates
        - Threshold determination (e.g., safety factor approach, NOEL[a])
        - Statistical characterization of uncertainty
     B. Formal decision analysis
     C. Inter-risk comparisons
     D. Qualitative - panel reviews
     E. Qualitative - informal scientific advice
     F. Risk - benefit analysis

---

a   NOEL = No-Observed-Effect Level
(Source: Reprinted with permission from ref. 6).

8.1   ANIMAL STUDIES AND DOSE-RESPONSE

The first step in the risk assessment of carcinogens and non-carcinogens alike, is the hazard identification. This involves the determination of whether the chemical is or is not causally linked to particular health effects. Four general types of information are needed to identify a hazard which include animal bioassay data, epidemiologic data, data on in vitro effects and comparisons of molecular structure and biological activities. Some of the aspects have been discussed in detail in earlier chapters. Much of the required information on the toxicity of chemicals is obtained from studies on animals.

All substances can cause some adverse effects to living organisms under some conditions of exposure. Determination of toxic properties of a chemical is usually carried out in laboratory studies involving animals. Toxic effects are generally classified as acute or chronic (short- or long-term effects and exposure). Acute effects are those resulting from a single exposure of relatively high concentration of a chemical. The effects set in rapidly and could be mild to severe. Chronic effects are those adverse effects which develop over a long period of exposure. Chronic exposure could be intermittant exposures of continuous low-dose exposure of the chemical. Chronic effects include behavioural effects, physiological and biochemical effects including carcinogenicity.

The purpose of animal toxicity studies is to identify the nature of the adverse effect of a chemical and the dose that causes that effect.

Acute Toxicity Studies

Acute toxicity testing is conducted to determine the degree of toxicity of a chemical as related to its exposure dose, to establish its toxic potential with respect to other chemicals. The acute toxicity is expressed as LD_{50} which means the lethal dose of a chemical that is required to kill 50% of the exposed animal population.

Chemicals with lower LD_{50} values are more acutely toxic than those with higher values. Table 8.3 presents a group of well known chemicals and their LD_{50} values to illustrate the above point.

TABLE 8.3 Range of LD_{50} values for some common chemicals.

CHEMICAL	ANIMAL	ROUTE	LD_{50} (mg/kg)
Sucrose (table sugar)	Rat	Oral	29,700
Ethyl alcohol	Rat	Oral	14,000
Sodium chloride (common salt)	Rat	Oral	3,000
Vitamin A	Rat	Oral	2,000
Vanillin	Rat	Oral	1,580
Aspirin	Rat	Oral	1,000
Chloroform	Rat	Oral	800
Phenobarbital, sodium salt	Rat	Oral	162
Copper sulfate	Rat	Oral	300
DDT	Rat	Oral	113
Caffeine	Rat	Oral	192
Sodium nitrite	Rat	Oral	85

Continued . . .

TABLE 8.3 Concluded.

Nicotine	Rat	Oral	53
Aflatoxin B$_1$	Rat	Oral	7
Sodium cyanide	Rat	Oral	6.4
Strychnine	Rat	Oral	2.5
TCDD (dioxin)	Mouse	Oral	0.11

[a] Selected from NIOSH Registry of Toxic Effects of Chemical Substances, 1979. Results reported elsewhere may differ.
[b] Compounds are listed in order of increasing toxicity, i.e., sucrose is the least, and TCDD the most toxic.
(Source: Reprinted with permission from ref. 7, Copyright (1983), Academic Press).

It is evident from the reported LD_{50} values that there is several fold variation in the susceptibility of different species to the same chemical. Not all species exposed to the same dose of a chemical will respond in the same way. Table 8.4 lists the marked difference in the acute toxicity of 2,3,7,8-Tetrachlorodibenzo-p-dioxin (TCDD). There is also a large difference in the whole body clearance half-life of TCDD. Humans are reported to be less sensitive than laboratory animals to the toxic effects of TCDD (ref. 8).

TABLE 8.4 Oral LD_{50} values and $t_{1/2}$ values for whole-body clearance of TCDD in different animal species.

SPECIES	LD_{50} μg/kg	$t_{1/2}$ (half-life) days
Guinea pig	1	30-94
Rat	22-45	31
Monkey	70	455
Rabbit	155	-
Mouse	144	15
Dog	300	-
Hamster	5000	15

(Source: Reprinted with permission from ref. 9, Copyright (1989), John Wiley & Sons, Inc.).

Acute toxicity results of a chemical are useful in understanding and treating systemic manifestations of toxicity in humans which may arise from abnormal or accidental exposure to high concentrations or ingestion of large doses of a chemical.

Subchronic toxicity studies are conducted to identify adverse effects of repeated exposure or continuously for several weeks which is a more common form of human exposure than acute (single) exposure. Such studies provide detailed information on toxic effects, target organs and reversibility of effects. Since several exposure dose levels are used and corresponding effects are observed, the results are used to develop a dose-effect relationship and to determine the "no-observed-adverse-effect-level (NOAEL)". Chronic toxicity studies are conducted to determine the adverse effects in animals which occur only after a prolonged and repeated exposure close to their full life times. Chronic exposure studies can identify adverse effects which become evident only after long latent period. The effects include behavioural changes, physiological and biochemical changes including progressive and irreversible effects such as cancer. Information from chronic exposure studies is particularly valuable in assessing the health risk of a population exposed to long time low-level exposure to a chemical. The major reasons for conducting toxicity studies are summarized below (ref. 8):

1. To identify target organs or systems of the body that are susceptible to injury by a chemical;
2. To identify specific disorders or diseases that a chemical may produce on long-term exposure such as cancer, birth defects, neurological or behavioural disorders.
3. To identify specific biological mechanisms that are involved in the onset of adverse effects detected;
4. To determine the dose, and routes of exposure that give rise to specific effect or disease.

The laboratory test procedures to achieve many of the above goals are available for many years and additional tests continue to be developed. However, all methods are scrutinized for evaluation and refinement. Several protocols and guidelines are available in the literature for conducting non-carcinogenic toxicity tests, in vivo and in vitro short-term tests for genotoxicity and long-term animal studies for carcinogenicity (refs. 10-14).

Evidence from Short-term Tests

Long-term rodent studies are expensive ($1 to 2 million) and time consuming (3 to 4 years), hence, there is growing interest in using short-term tests to predict the results of long-term bioassays. A battery of short-term tests could cost around $10,000 and they are used as screening tests for genotoxic effects of chemicals.

Tests for genetic alterations:

Genetic changes in somatic cells are believed to be closely linked to one or more stages of carcinogenesis and in vitro tests have been developed to detect those changes. Results from bacterial assays for mutation were shown to correlate with carcinogenicity. Many short-term tests (about 100) are available and they involve many organisms ranging from prokaryotes to human cells and can be performed under a variety of conditions ranging from using isolated DNA to cells in vitro and in vivo. These tests can be grouped into three major categories based upon their biological end point (ref. 15):

1. Tests for DNA damage including adduct formation, strand breakage, prophage formation, and DNA repair.

2. Tests for mutagenicity which includes forward and reverse mutation as shown by alterations of DNA, gene products or cellular behaviour, and

3. Tests for chromosomal effects which includes aneuploidy, structural aberrations, micronuclei and sister chromatid exchange.

The use of these tests has increased because of the accumulating evidence that supports the somatic mutation theory of carcinogenesis (refs. 16,17). Another supporting evidence came from reports that many rodent carcinogens are genotoxic in in vitro short-term toxicity tests (ref. 18). As a result of these reported concordances and because of the ever-increasing need to screen chemicals for their carcinogenicity, many countries developed regulatory guidelines requiring submission of short-term tests (STT) data for the registration of new chemicals (ref. 19). A literature-derived study conducted by the Gene-Tox program of the U.S. EPA revealed the two major impediments in the ability of the STT to predict rodent carcinogenicity. For most STTs, there is a dearth of results for documented non-carcinogens and too few chemicals had been tested in multiple STTs to permit any valid comparisons. A recent study (ref. 20) examined the results of four commonly used in vitro STTs in predicting rodent carcinogenicity for 73 chemicals which were recently tested in two-year rodent carcinogenicity bioassay studies by the U.S. National Cancer Institute (U.S. NCI) and U.S. National Toxicology Program. The four STTs chosen were: (1) Ames Salmonella/microsome (SAL) mutagenesis assay; (2) the assays for chromosome aberrations (ABS); (3) sister chromatid exchange (SCE) induction in Chinese hamster ovary cells; and (4) the mouse lymphoma L5178Y (MOLY) cell mutagenesis assay.

It was concluded from the above study that for a set of 73 chemicals evaluated by NCI and NTP, the battery of four STTs was not significantly more predictive than SAL test alone. When all four STTs were positive, the rodent test was positive 82% of the time. However, the predictivity of SAL test is 83% and the concordance of SAL test alone is 62% (Table 8.5), and for all four STTs is essentially the same, i.e., 55 to 66% depending upon the decision rule made (ref. 20). Thus, for the 73 chemicals tested, the predictivity and concordance of the battery of four STTs is similar to that of SAL test alone. In other words, within the limits of the study, there was no evidence of complementarity among the four assays, and no battery of tests constructed from these assays improved substantially the overall performance of the Salmonella assay (ref. 20).

TABLE 8.5 Summary of results of genetic toxicity STTs and rodent tests (positives, negatives, and total tested).

TEST	SAL		ABS		SCE		MOLY	
Carcinogenicity[a]	+[b]	_[b]	+	-	+	-	+	-
+	20	24	24	20	32	12	31	13
-	4	25	9	20	16	13	16	13
Positive predictivity(%)[c]	83		73		67		66	
Negative predictivity(%)[d]	51		50		52		50	
Concordance(%)[e]	62		60		62		60	

[a] Carcinogenicity of chemicals tested in rodents (+ carcinogenic; not carcinogenic)
[b] Results from STTs (e.g., 20 carcinogens tested positive and 24 not positive)
[c] Percentage of STT positives that are carcinogens
[d] Percentage of STT negatives that are not carcinogens
[e] Percentage of qualitative agreements between STTs and rodent carcinogenicity test results
(Source: Reprinted with permission from ref. 20, Copyright (1987), AAAS).

The SAL test does have advantages over the other three STTs in terms of technical ease of performing the assay, wide availability, a sizeable literature and low cost. Although SAL assay is generally regarded as a good screening assay for predicting carcinogenicity in rodents, this test is known not to detect all carcinogens (ref. 20). In the current study, it missed over half of the carcinogenic chemicals (24 of 44 tested). The question then is whether any other in vitro test is capable of detecting SAL-negative carcinogens without concurrent false-positive results (i.e., detecting non-carcinogens as carcinogens). When the results of three STTs (excluding SAL) are analyzed for qualitative correlation with SAL data (Tables 8.6 and 8.7), rodent carcinogenicity shows no association with the results of MOLY, ABS, or SCE.

Combining ABS data with that of SAL, identifies an additional eight carcinogens correctly identified but an additional six non-carcinogens are incorrectly identified as carcinogens. The overall concordance is barely changed. Table 8.7 shows that data from three STTs do confirm positive SAL

TABLE 8.6 Analysis for association of rodent carcinogenicity with data from three sites for 49 chemicals that are SAL negative.

CARCINOGENICITY	ABS		SCE		MOLY	
	+	-	+	-	+	-
+	8	16	15	9	12	12
-	6	19	12	13	12	13

TABLE 8.7 Analysis for association of rodent carcinogenicity with data from three STTs for 24 SAL-positive chemicals.

CARCINOGENICITY	ABS		SCE		MOLY	
	+	-	+	-	+	-
+	16	4	17	3	19	1
-	3	1	4	0	4	0

(Source: Reprinted with permission from ref. 20, Copyright (1987), AAAS).

results effectively: ABS (79%), SCE (88%); and MOLY (96%). When stratified by the SAL outcome, there is no statistically significant association between the results of ABS, SCE and MOLY tests with rodent carcinogenicity. This feature is termed as conditional independence ($P = 0.75$, 0.42 and 0.98 for ABS, SCE and MOLY, respectively, ref. 20).

When SAL test is excluded from the battery of four tests and separate comparisons are made for SAL positive and SAL negative chemicals, Cochrane-Armitage linear trend test analysis shows no significant association between the number of STT positives and rodent carcinogenicity (Table 8.8).

It can be summarized that within the limits of this study, none of the other three in vitro STTs studied is a satisfactory complement to SAL in predicting rodent carcinogenicity. Estimates of correlations between findings in such tests and results of rodent carcinogenicity bioassays depends on the chemical tested, test type, and laboratory. At present, the overall performance of STTs as validated by the proportion of correct results for chemicals classified by rodent carcinogenic bioassay is in the range of 50 to 70% (ref. 15).

Some representative STTs currently in use for genotoxicity are: (1) DNA damage in microbes; (2) DNA damage in mammalian cells; (3) gene mutation in bacteria and fungi; (4) gene mutation in higher system; (5) chromosomal effects in isolated cell systems; (6) chromosomal effects in whole organisms;

372

(7) oncogenic transformation; and (8) tumor formation. The specific tests and organisms used are outlined in Table 6.13 (Chapter 6).

TABLE 8.8 Evaluation of performance of three STTs (excluding SAL) in predictivity of carcinogenicity.

Proportion of STTs positive	Chemicals positive in SAL [proportion of carcinogens (%)]		Chemicals negative in SAL [proportion of carcinogens (%)]	
3/3	14/17	(82)	5/9	(56)
2/3	5/6	(83)	7/14	(50)
1/3	--		6/10	(60)
0/3	1/1	(100)	6/16	(38)
Total	20/24	(83)	24/49	(49)
Cochran-Armitage linear trend test	P > 0.50		P > 0.20	

(Source: Reprinted with permission from ref. 21, Copyright (1988), AAAS).

Chronic experiments are conducted in rodents, and positive results are used to predict the chemicals that may pose a cancer risk to humans. If the carcinogenic response in two closely related species such as mouse and rat does not agree, then extrapolation from rodents to humans is not strong. Conversely, if there is a good agreement between rodent species, then confidence in extrapolation is strengthened. Comparison of carcinogenic response in rats and mice for 392 chemicals by chemical class were analyzed (ref. 22) and data are presented in Table 8.9.

Results of chlorinated compounds were markedly different from other classes of chemicals. For chlorinated compounds, the predictive value of positivity in rats for positivity in mice is 100% (18/18), compared to only 49% (18/37) from mice to rats. When chlorinated compounds were excluded from the dataset, the predictive value of positivity from mice to rats is as accurate as that from rats to mice (75%) (Table 8.9).

Predictivity of carcinogenicity was also evaluated on the basis of mutagenicity of the chemical using Salmonella tests for 294 chemicals from compilations in the carcinogenic potency database (ref. 22). Table 8.9 shows a greater proportion of mutagens are carcinogenic than non-mutagens (72% vs 51%, chi-square P < 0.0001). Also, a large proportion of carcinogens is not mutagenic (79/178, 44%). Prediction from mouse to rat is significantly more accurate for mutagens (64/80, 80%) than non-mutagens (34/63, 54%, chi-square P = 0.001). However, prediction from rat to mouse is not significant (chi-square P = 0.248).

TABLE 8.9 Comparison of carcinogenic response in rats and mice, by chemical class.[a]

CHEMICAL CLASS[b](n)	R+M+ (a)	R+M- (b)	R-M+ (c)	R-M- (d)	PROPORTION OF R+ THAT ARE ALSO M+ [a/(a+b)]	PROPORTION OF M+ THAT ARE ALSO R+ [a/(a+c)]
All chemicals (392)	130	40	56	166	76%	70%
Aromatic amines (65)	30	5	14	16	86%	68%
Halogenated compounds						
Chlorinated compounds[c] (50)	18	0	19	13	100%	49%
Other halogenated compounds (23)	13	1	1	8	93%	93%
Miscellaneous aromatics and aliphatics (47)	11	9	4	23	55%	73%
Miscellaneous carbamates and ureas (37)	5	7	2	23	42%	71%
Miscellaneous heterocycles (36)	12	2	3	19	86%	80%
Nitro aromatics and heterocycles (34)	15	2	9	8	88%	63%
Miscellaneous esters and epoxides (31)	6	2	3	20	75%	67%
Azo compounds (18)	5	5	0	8	50%	100%
Inorganic substances (17)	2	1	0	14	67%	100%
Miscellaneous nitrogen compounds, hydrazines, etc. (17)	7	5	1	4	58%	88%
Mixtures or unidentified structures (10)	0	0	0	10		
Nitroso compounds (7)	6	1	0	0	86%	100%
Salmonella results						
Mutagens (138)	64	19	16	39	77%	80%
Non-mutagens (156)	34	16	29	77	68%	54%

a Among the 392 chemicals tested in both rats (R) and mice (M), 177 were reported only by NCI/NTP, 150 were reported only in the literature, and 65 were reported by both sources.

b Chemical classes are ordered by the total number of chemicals in the class. Each chemical is reported in only one class.

c Compounds composed solely of chlorine, carbon, hydrogen, and optionally, oxygen.

(Source: Reprinted with permission from ref. 22, Copyright (1989), U.S. DHHS).

In view of the vast number of chemicals either already tested positive by STTs or chemicals awaiting screening, it is essential STTs are continuously evaluated and validated for their predictivity of carcinogenicity. This will include continued improvement in the testing procedure, expanding the chemical classes that respond to these tests, use of the larger data base to validate the concordance of the test results with rodent bioassays and possibly extending to human samples to couple with epidemiologic surveys.

Long-term Animal Bioassays for Carcinogenicity

The general approaches and guidelines for conducting chronic toxicity test in animals are well established (refs. 10,12,13,23). However, one of the controversial issues centres around the use of the maximum tolerated dose (MTD) which is defined as the maximum dose that an animal species can tolerate for major part of its lifespan without suffering any acute effects or any impairment of growth. Since there is a long latency period for cancer to develop, it is widely accepted that animal studies should be designed so that species could survive and also maintain good health for the normal duration of their lifetime.

The main reason offered in using the MTD is that it overcomes the "statistical insensitivity" of the small scale experimental studies. For practical reasons, laboratory studies are carried out with relatively small group of animals; in a typical experiment 50 or 60 animals of each species and sex will be used for each dose level tested including the control group. After the completion of the study, the incidence of cancer as a function of dose (including control animal data) is tabulated. Then, the data are analyzed statistically for random errors (random variations in tumor incidence) and for correlation to the chemical dose. In the absence of any control positives, i.e., control animals not exposed to the chemical developing tumor, the lowest detectable cancer incidence in studies of the size mentioned above will be 7 to 10%, which is statistically significant. If control animals develop tumor (as they frequently do), the lowest detectable cancer incidence is even higher. A 10% cancer incidence is very high and yet laboratory studies cannot detect incidence lower than 10%.

Scientists who favour the use of MTD argue that the use of high dose exposure compensate for the weak detection power of the experimental design by positively identifying the critical organ of attack and the dose at which the toxic actions manifest in the animal. More importantly, high doses reduce the number of animals that have to be used in chronic bioassays. The concerns against the use of MTD in chronic bioassay are as follows (ref. 9):

1. The underlying biological mechanism for carcinogenesis may change with changes in dose levels;

2. Current methods of estimating a MTD value for a chronic bioassay does not consider the different mechanisms in the derived MTD; and

3. The biological mechanisms may differ significantly between the exposure at MTD and at actual human exposures.

Greater attention should be paid to the underlying mechanisms for carcinogenesis and their relation to dose. Also, a range of doses should be included in the bioassay design to detect any suppression of detoxification mechanisms at MTD exposure which otherwise would operate at normal doses. Attempts are underway to incorporate biological factors in the design of chronic bioassays.

The recommended design of a cancer bioassay of a chemical (refs. 10,13, 14,24):

- Two species of test animals (usually rats and mice in both sexes) tested at two or preferably three dose regimens; a high dose level (close to MTD) and a lower dose level (usually 1/2 of the MTD) as determined from a 90-d subchronic study;

- Dosing and observation covering substantial portion of the animal's natural lifespan (usually 104 weeks for rodents);

- At least 50 animals in each test group;

- Adequate concurrently run controls;

- Detailed pathologic examination of tissues; and

- Appropriate statistical evaluation of results (dose-response relationships, etc.) (refs. 13,23).

Evidence that can assist in a conclusion of carcinogenicity from animal studies includes the following observations:

- Statistically significant increases in malignant tumors compared to the controls at one or more of the dose levels tested;

- A statistically-significant dose-related increase in malignant tumors from analysis of data on the appearance of tumors and corresponding time of detection;

- An increase in the occurrence of rare malignant tumors which have low or zero incidence rate among historical controls; and/or

- Early onset of cancer in exposed animal species.

False-negatives (identifying a carcinogen as a non-carcinogen) and false-positive (identifying a non-carcinogen as carcinogen) may result from chronic carcinogenicity bioassay. Pathologic examination of many tissues, if followed by simple statistical significance testing might lead to increased "false-positive" identification. Data on the time of onset of tumors and individual animal survival can sometimes assist to reduce the number of false-positives and false-negatives (ref. 23).

The term "carcinogenesis" is commonly applied to include carcinomas (malignant tumors of epithelial cells), sarcomas (malignant tumors of connective tissues and lymphomas) and leukemias (cancers of lymphatic and blood systems). It has been shown that agents that cause one of these types of tumors or benign tumors often have the potential to induce other malignant tumors. Hence, the term "carcinogen" is used for chemicals that cause pathologically related combinations of benign and malignant tumors.

Dose-Response Relationship

Identification of a chemical's potential to cause adverse effects or harm is a first step in risk assessment. This step establishes the fact that the chemical has the intrinsic property to cause harm to human health. Risk is defined as the probability of the specified harm developing as a result of exposure to a chemical. Hence, it is important to estimate the magnitude of risk at specified doses of exposures.

For non-carcinogens, toxic effects are incorporated in the dose-response relationship with established threshold levels. These are levels below which a toxicological response is not observed. This level is often identified as "No Observable Effect Level (NOAEL)". At this level, the organism has the reserve capacity to withstand damage.

The quantitative relationship between the amount of exposure to a chemical and the extent of toxic injury produced is called the dose-response relationship. This fundamental principle in toxicology predicts that no injury will take place if the exposure dose is lower than the "threshold dose value". Such "threshold" values can be demonstrated for acute effects of a chemical. For long-term effects such as cancer, existence of threshold level is controversial for direct genetic carcinogens. For cancer promoters, which are non-genetic carcinogens, such as 2,3,7,8-TCDD, existence of a threshold dose has been recognized by scientists as well as several regulatory agencies (refs. 25,26). Nevertheless, the dose-response relationship may yield very useful information about the potency of a carcinogen or the mechanism by which cancer develops.

The different types of dose-response curves are shown in Fig. 8.1. Curve 2 represents a more common situation where there are some effects observable within a subpopulation where a few members show some effects at low-dose exposure but the rest of the entire population remains unaffected until the take-off is reached. Curve 1 represents a situation where there is no risk

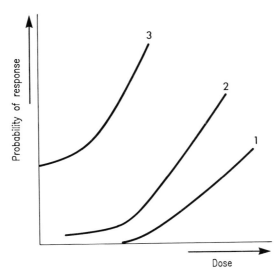

Fig. 8.1. Dose-response curves showing the existence of a threshold dose or NOAEL.
(Source: ref. 27).

until a certain level of exposure is reached when Curve 1 leaves the abscissa. The presence of effects due to background exposure is shown by Curve 3.

Limitations to the use of NOAEL are as follows:

1. With a small number of animals, only relatively strong effects can be identified as statistically significant.

2. Toxicologists may not be able to detect certain biological changes which may nevertheless be present.

3. The threshold dose varies among species. For genetically homogeneous (inbred) group of experimental animals that are studied under well-controlled environmental conditions, the variability in threshold dose may be relatively small.

4. For human populations, which are genetically diverse and for whom the exposure vary greatly in types and quantity of exposures (such as dietary habits, lifestyle habits, occupational environment, state of health), the variability in response to a chemical is likely to be greater than controlled experimental animal population.

Acceptable Daily Intake (ADIs)

The system of ADIs recognizes the uncertainties in NOAEL itself and are accommodated by the application of conservative safety factor to the experimental NOAEL to establish an ADI. When several NOAELs are available from several studies, an additional degree of caution is enforced by selecting the lowest available NOAEL as the basis for establishing an ADI.

While a safety factor of 100 is often used, factors ranging from 10 to 2000 have been used depending upon the nature of toxicity. Larger factors are used to compensate for slight deficiencies in data such as small number of animals tested. On the other hand, available human data may warrant the use of smaller safety factor since human data obviate the need for interspecies extrapolation. Biochemical data relating to absorption, distribution and excretion of the chemical and its biotransformation (detoxification and deactivation) in several species of animals and in humans are valuable in determining the magnitude of the safety factor. Various aspects of safety factors and bases for altering the size of the factor are discussed in WHO documents (refs. 27, 28).

The term Acceptable Daily Intake (ADI) was coined by the Joint FAO/WHO Expert Committee on Food Additives in 1961 (ref. 29). It was subsequently adopted by the Joint FAO/WHO Meeting of the Experts on Pesticide Residues (ref. 30). The ADI is now widely recognized and is used in the environmental field. The ADI is defined as the daily intake of a chemical which during an entire lifetime appears to be without appreciable risk on the basis of all the known facts at that time. It is expressed in milligrams of the chemical per kilogram of body weight (mg/kg.bw). The cautious statements including "appears to be" and "on the basis of all known facts at that time" allow the revision of ADI when new information on the toxicology of a chemical becomes available (ref. 31).

The ADIs have been an integral part in the formulation of national regulation of contaminants and additives in food items in several countries. Furthermore, the ADI serves as a yardstick to check the acceptability of the proposed uses. The ADI is compared with the "potential" daily intake of the proposed use, which is the sum of amounts of the additive in each food calculated on the basis of an average per capita food consumption and the permitted use levels in the food items. If the potential daily intake exceeds the ADI, the use levels may be reduced or some of the uses may not be permitted. A similar procedure is followed for accepting maximum level of pesticide residues in food. The ADI is expressed as:

$$ADI = \frac{NOAEL}{SF} \tag{8.1}$$

where ADI   = Acceptable Daily Intake, mg/kg.bw;

NOAEL = Lowest No-Observable-Adverse Effect Level, mg/kg.bw/day; and

SF   = Safety Factor (>1) for extrapolating animal toxicity results to humans (unitless).

Unfortunately, chronic toxicity data are unavailable for most chemicals because of the time and resources involved in such tests. In contrast, LD_{50}, median lethal dose to a sample population of laboratory animals are easier to obtain and more readily available. It has been recently proposed (ref. 32) to use LD_{50} data to derive provisional ADIs by multiplying oral LD_{50} values (mg/kg.bw) by a factor in the range of 5×10^{-6} to 1×10^{-5} day^{-1}. It was emphasized that this approach was not meant to replace chronic toxicity testing, and it does not identify what non-carcinogenic effects are prevented. It is only a fast-track evaluation of ADIs which could be used to develop management strategies for health risk exposures to contaminated soil, waters, crops, or other material at a particular site (ref. 32). To test this approach, the calculated lower-bound ADI (LB-ADI) were compared with ADIs derived from water-quality criteria set by USEPA for 26 organic compounds (Table 8.10). The last column in Table 8.10 is the ratio of LB-ADI/water quality-derived ADI and only 4/26 ratios were greater than 1 with the largest value being 8.5. When a conversion factor of 5×10^{-6}/day was used, the largest ratio was only 4/26 which shows a good agreement between the two ADIs.

Nature of Toxic Responses

Toxic responses can be of several types (ref. 9):

1. The severity of the injury increases with increase in dose.
2. Severity may not increase with increase in dose, but injury may emerge at an earlier time.
3. Increasing dose increases the probability that adverse effects will develop in an exposed population.
4. With the increase in exposure level, both the incidence and the severity of the injury will increase. The increase in severity is due to increased damage at higher doses while the individual sensitivity variations will increase the incidence of effects.
5. Toxic responses also vary in their reversibility; in some cases, the effects will vanish on cessation of exposure and in other cases, some exposures will result in permanent injury. An example of the latter case is a severe birth defect resulting from a chemical which inflicted an irreversible damage to the fetus at a critical stage of its development.
6. Types of effects that are not clearly a health concern, such as temporary increase in red blood cell count with no other adverse effect. Assessment of such effect is one of the critical issues in chemical risk assessment.

TABLE 8.10 Comparison of calculated lower-bound ADIs and ADIs derived from water-quality criteria of U.S. EPA.

CASID[a]	SUBSTANCE	ORAL LD$_{50}$ (RAT)[b] (mg kg^{-1})	LB-ADI[c] (mg kg^{-1}day^{-1})	DERIVED ADI (mg kg^{-1}day^{-1})	SOURCE[d]	RATIO LB-ADI/DERIVED ADI
107-02-8	Acrolein	46	4.6 x 10^{-4}	0.0155	WQC	0.03
79-06-1	Acrylamide	170	1.7 x 10^{-3}	0.0002	SOC	8.5
108-60-1	Bis(2-chloroisopropyl)ether	240	2.4 x 10^{-3}	0.001	WQC	2.4
1563-66-2	Carbofuran	5.3	5.3 x 10^{-5}	0.005	SOC	0.01
510-15-6	Chlorobenzene	2,910	2.0 x 10^{-2}	0.125	SOC	0.2
87-74-2	Dibutyl phthlate	12,000	1.2 x 10^{-1}	1.25	WQC	0.1
95-50-1	o-Dichlorobenzene	500	5.0 x 10^{-3}	0.089	SOC	0.06
94-75-7	2,4-Dichlorophenoxyacetic acid	370	3.7 x 10^{-3}	0.01	SOC	0.4
117-81-7	Di-2-ethylhexyl phthalate	30,700	3.1 x 10^{-1}	0.612	WQC	0.5
84-66-2	Diethyl phthalate	9,000	9.0 x 10^{-2}	12.5	WQC	0.007
131-11-3	Dimethyl phthalate	6,900	6.9 x 10^{-2}	10	WQC	0.007
534-52-1	4,6-Dinitro-o-cresol	10	1.0 x 10^{-4}	0.00039	WQC	0.2
51-28-5	2,4-Dinitrophenol	35	3.5 x 10^{-4}	0.002	WQC	0.2
115-29-7	Endosulfan	18	1.8 x 10^{-4}	0.004	WQC	0.04
100-41-4	Ethylbenzene	3,500	3.5 x 10^{-2}	0.097	SOC	0.4
206-44-0	Fluoranthene	2,000	2.0 x 10^{-2}	0.0054	WQC	3.7
78-59-1	Isophorone	2,330	2.3 x 10^{-2}	0.15	WQC	0.2
72-43-5	Methoxychlor	5,000	5.0 x 10^{-2}	0.05	SOC	1
608-93-5	Pentachlorobenzene	1,080	1.1 x 10^{-2}	0.016	WQC	0.7
87-86-5	Pentachlorophenol	50	5.0 x 10^{-4}	0.03	SOC	0.02
100-42-5	Styrene	5,000	5.0 x 10^{-2}	0.2	SOC	0.2
95-94-3	1,2,4,5-Tetrachlorobenzene	1,500	1.5 x 10^{-2}	0.0052	WQC	2.9
108-88-3	Toluene	5,000	5.0 x 10^{-2}	0.29	SOC	0.2
71-56-6	1,1,1-Trichloroethane	10,300	1.0 x 10^{-1}	0.54	WQC	0.2
93-72-1	2,4,5-TP(Silvex)	650	6.5 x 10^{-3}	0.0075	SOC	0.9
1330-20-1	Xylene	5,000	5.0 x 10^{-2}	0.063	SOC	0.8

[a]Chemical abstracts identification number; [b]The LD$_{50}$ values are from the RTECS (ref. 33); [c]Lower-bound ADIs are calculated as the product of the oral LD$_{50}$ (mg kg^{-1}) and 1 x 10^{-5} day^{-1}; [d]WQC, ADI derived from water-quality criteria developed by the U.S. EPA (ref. 34); SOC, ADI derived from concentration limits proposed by the U.S. EPA (ref. 35) for synthetic organic compounds.
(Source: Reprinted with permission from ref. 32, Copyright (1984), Academic Press).

Chemicals with Non-threshold Effects

Chemicals which directly cause genotoxic effects such as carcinogenesis belong to this class of chemicals. Theoretically, since a single molecule of a chemical can induce a cancer, there would be no threshold dose for carcinogens. In other words, there is risk of carcinogenesis at any given exposure to a proven carcinogen.

This view, however, is not universally accepted because of the existence of many intervening mechanisms which can prevent the initiation and progression of carcinogenesis. These include detoxification and clearance of the toxic chemical, DNA repair, immunological surveillance and the presence of "protective agents" such as antioxidants (ref. 31). Although these mechanisms would increase the minimal amount of a direct, genotoxic carcinogen to initiate cancer, experiments have failed to demonstrate the existence of a threshold level for cancer initiating chemicals (e.g., the largest experiment conducted was over 24,000 mice on 2-acetylaminofluorene (refs. 36,37)). Hence, in the absence of any reliable procedure to determine a threshold for a direct-acting carcinogen, estimation of the level of risk is considered to be more appropriate.

A number of models have been developed for this purpose. In general, they extrapolate from the observed dose-response relationship to the Virtual Safe Dose (VSD). The extrapolation is based on certain assumptions about the mathematical nature of the dose-response relationship near zero dose. There is no biological method for measuring the possible effect that might theoretically exist at low level of exposure. There is no biological method for predicting or extrapolating the potential effect to the dosage several orders of magnitude lower than the levels tested in the laboratory. The virtual safety level, introduced first by Mantel and Bryan (ref. 38) is defined as a probability of carcinogenicity of less than 10^{-8} at a statistical assurance level of 99%. The U.S. Food and Drug Administration, however, realized that doses associated with such a low-risk level were too small to be detectable and enforceable in most actual situations, and thus adopted a risk level of 10^{-6} (ref. 39). The dose associated with an additional cancer in a million (10^{-6}) is known as VSD.

Non-genotoxic Carcinogens and Promoters

There are numerous examples of substances that increase the incidence of tumors in animals under certain conditions, but they almost certainly are not genotoxic. The promoter does not involve an attack on the genome (genetic material) by the promoter mechanism. Examples include hormones (e.g., estrogen), tumor promoters (e.g., phorbol esters), dioxins and solid-state carcinogens (e.g., implanted metal or plastic foils).

These promoter chemicals most probably act through broad physiological processes that are likely to be arrested by the body's inherent defence mechanisms. These defences are overcome only when some minimum dose is reached. Hence, it is highly likely that thresholds exist for non-genotoxic carcinogens. A safety factor could be applied to the NOAEL for the cancer promoter chemicals to arrive at an ADI. In fact, this approach is commonly used outside the United States for a number of chemicals including nitrilotri-acetic acid (NTA), pesticide permathrin, 2,3,7,8-tetrachlorodibenzo-p-dioxin (2,3,7,8-TCDD).

8.2   UNCERTAINTIES IN EXTRAPOLATION TO LOW LEVELS

In carcinogenic risk assessment, the dose-response assessment determines the dose associated with the acceptable levels of cancer risk in humans based on the data on high dose-cancer incidence in animal studies. This exercise involves the interspecies extrapolation of high-dose incidence to low-dose incidence and by the conversion of dose estimates in animals to equivalent or equipotent estimates of doses in humans (ref. 40). This conversion is defined as dose scaling. Whereas, the estimation of low-dose incidence on the basis of high-dose response data for the same species is known as dose-range extrapola-tion. Various mathematical models are used in these calculations. Dose scaling may refer to animal to animal as well as animal to human. Scaling factor is further defined as any characteristic of a test species or in vitro system that is used as a common denominator for dose scaling. The Life Sciences Research Office (LSRO) of the Federation of American Societies for Experi-mental Biology (FASEB) has recently conducted a symposium under contract with the Center for Food Safety and Applied Nutrition (CFSAN) of the U.S. Food and Drug Administration (FDA) on the issues and current applications of inter-species extrapolation of carcinogenic potency. The topics for review and discussion were: (1) strengths and weaknesses of current interspecies extra-polation methods using metabolic and pharmacokinetic data, identity of data for these methods, bases for choice of extrapolation method and selection of data base, validity and uniformity of interspecies extrapolation from target organ data and strength of the supporting data. The symposium papers were published in "Environmental Health Perspectives, Vol. 77, April 1988".

Numerous investigators, publications and conferences have explored the mathematical-statistical models from which dose-range extrapolations of carcinogenic risk are derived. Little has been published on the subject of dose-scaling including comprehensive reviews on the principles, applications and limitations of dose-scaling method. The symposium focussed on several aspects of dose scaling between test species and humans. They include differentiation of dose-range extrapolation and dose scaling; common methods of scaling based on body mass, surface area, etc.; biological bases of current methods and strengths and weaknesses of current scaling procedures.

In addition, the following concerns were raised which were related to the above topics:

1. Does the choice of biological end point (acute toxicity vs. carcinogenicity) affect the scaling process?;

2. What kind of problems may arise if a common mechanism for carcinogenicity is not operating among species?;

3. Does a difference in slope function of the dose-response curves necessarily imply differing mechanisms of carcinogenesis, that render scaling invalid?;

4. Should dose scaling be based on administered dose or critical tissue concentration?; and

5. Are the statistical methods currently used in extrapolation between species adequate and properly applied?

Experiences with scaling between species show that there is no consistently reliable relationship between species, different chemicals, different routes of administration. In other words, there is no reliable and consistent scaling factor. In addition to body mass and surface area, time has also been identified as a significant variable in deriving scaling factor. The lifespan of a human is approximately 35 times that of a mouse; and one human may represent between 160 to 3000 mice in terms of the number of cells susceptible to carcinogens (ref. 41). Thus, the lifetime chance of a single cell being hit by a carcinogen is estimated to be approximately 100,000 times as great for a human as for a mouse. These assumptions point to a significant variation in sensitivity as a function of body size (number of cells) and longevity.

Another factor that contributes to the present uncertainty of scaling carcinogenic potency results from animals to humans is the duration of the laboratory studies on animals and the latency of tumors as a function of dose. A 1000-fold increase in dose produced 90% decrease in latency (ref. 40). This questions the scaling based on lifespan. The change in absolute dose must be impacting differently among species for the onset of tumors and on the latency period.

Another complicating factor is the differential responses to total dose versus dose rate. Lung cancer were analyzed for 60-y old smokers of two groups; first group smoked for 20 y at the rate of 30 cigarettes/day from age 20 to 40; and the second group for 40 y at the rate of 15 cigarettes/day from age 20 to 60. The longer exposure to a comparable total dose was associated with a 10-fold higher rate than the shorter, more intense exposure (ref. 42).

Species respond differently to the same chemical. For example, pure trichloroethylene (TCE) is only marginally mutagenic or non-mutagenic and its metabolites bind to DNA only at insignificant levels. Mice developed hepatocellular carcinomas at 1000 mg TCE/kg/day by gavage (ref. 43), whereas two strains of rat did not develop hepatocarcinogenicity at this dose. Both species metabolized TCE to trichloroacetic acid (TCA). In rats the metabolism reaches saturation at 500 mg/kg of TCE, whereas, the limit in mice exceeds 2000 mg/kg of TCE. This leads to higher level of TCA 91000 mg/kg in mice blood, seven times higher than in rats. TCA above 50 mg/kg in blood produces peroxisomal proliferation, but only mice developed this effect because of metabolic differences. All these observations and some in vitro results, suggest that TCE is a non-genetic carcinogen and human metabolic data on TCE suggest that humans may not be susceptible to TCE carcinogenicity. This suggests the presence of a threshold dose for carcinogenicity even in susceptible species (ref. 40).

The understanding of the multistage carcinogenic process and isolating critical elements of the process for definitive study will offer solution to the problems in scaling. It might even advance the scaling to arrive at equipotent exposures between test animal species and humans.

The factors that may enhance varied human susceptibility to toxic chemicals including the fact that humans are a highly outbred species that follow a broad variety of diet patterns and divergent lifestyles are discussed by Calabrese in a recent article (ref. 44). The limitation in interspecies extrapolation arises when responses of humans to carcinogens and non-carcinogenic toxicants are currently predicted from highly inbred rodent strains raised on standardized diet regimes and environmental living conditions. Human heterogeneity for a broad range of biochemical characteristics (e.g., arylhydrocarbon hydroxylase activity, epoxide hydrase activity, β-glucuronidase activity, DNA-adduct formation, etc.) was examined with reference to selected animal models (ref. 44). Commonly used mice and rats are estimated to have about 60,000 to 15,000 fold greater β-glucuronidase activity in the proximal small intestine than humans (Table 8.11). This suggests greater enterohepatic circulation of carcinogens conjugated with glucuronic acid and excreted via the bile. It seems rabbit and guinea pig may be closer to humans in terms of certain biochemical characteristics.

TABLE 8.11 Estimated β-Glucuronidase Activity in human and selected animal species small intestine.

SPECIES	ESTIMATED β-GLUCURONIDASE ACTIVITY[*]	
	Proximal Small Intestine	Distal Small Intestine
Human	0.02	0.9
Rabbit	2.4	45.4
Guinea Pig	2.7	139.0
Rat	304.0	1341.0
Mouse	1200.0	5015.0

[*]Activity = $n$moles substrate degraded/h/g.
(Source: Reprinted with permission from ref. 45, Copyright (1974), Academic Press).

It is evident that species differ in their susceptibility to chemical exposures and such interspecies differences provide important pointers to the underlying mechanisms by which chemicals exert their toxic effects. These differences must be well studied in mechanistic terms before truly valid and scientifically credible extrapolations of animal studies to human populations are possible. Identification of the actual mechanisms involved in the chemically induced toxicity should eventually lead to risk assessment models that more adequately reflect the uniqueness of different species-chemical combinations.

Regulatory decisions on carcinogens or potential carcinogens require information on the magnitude of risk at ambient level exposure. Unfortunately reliable quantitative information about risk to humans can come only from epidemiological studies. For carcinogenic hazards and, in general, for most putative hazards, epidemiological information is not available at present and unlikely in the foreseeable future. Therefore, all the information that are available for a given chemical are data from in vitro studies of mutagenicity and data from chronic exposure studies using animals.

Animal experiments are usually conducted at higher exposure levels than those normally encountered in the ambient environment by humans. The quantitative evaluation of the potential risks at the ambient exposure level is carried out by extrapolation of dose-response data from high exposure levels to levels relevant to human exposure. Another step is the interspecies extrapolation of animal data to human population (discussed earlier in this chapter). Both extrapolations suffer from large uncertainties (refs. 46-48).

Several mathematical models have been developed for the low-dose extrapolation, which are quantitatively similar to one another in the experimental dose-response range, yet they may yield substantially different estimates of risks at lower dose ranges where responses are not observable. Estimates of low-dose responses which differ by three to four orders of magnitude are not uncommon (ref. 15). Even among different strains of the same species, dose-response relationships can vary markedly (ref. 49). The inability to assess with certainty, the potential risk at low exposure levels continues to present serious problems in regulatory use of the data. As an example, the National Academy of Sciences (ref. 50), in its report on saccharin, estimated the expected number of additional cancers in the U.S. due to exposure to 120 mg saccharin/day to range from 0.22 to 1,144,000 over a period of 70 y of exposure. This estimated risk span a range of eight orders of magnitude and serve hardly as a guide to regulatory decision-making level (refs. 51,52). Current knowledge does not yet allow the selection of one particular model and animal bioassay data are not sufficient enough to discriminate among the competing models (ref. 15).

Another major source of uncertainty in low-dose extrapolation is the process by which the background is incorporated in the dose-response model of a chemical. The proposed two methods for incorporation are: (1) assuming spontaneous cancer process (background process is independent of process of exposure to suspect chemical); and (2) assuming that the two processes are identical. These two methods yield identical dose-response curves in the measurable range but yield different estimates on extrapolation.

Other sources of uncertainty in low-dose extrapolation include the possible existence of thresholds, mechanism of carcinogenic action and determination of effective critical organ dose at the site of action compared to the adminis- tered dose. Other uncertainties include differing routes of exposure between tested animals and humans and differing susceptibility to the chemical. Experimental animals are genetically homogeneous and share nearly identical environmental conditions. But they are not identical, qualitatively and quantitatively, in their carcinogenic response, as well as in the target organ site of their carcinogenic response. Whereas, humans are genetically outbred species living under widely diverse environmental regimes and exposed to a large variety of carcinogenic and non-carcinogenic modifying factors which may alter the effect of the chemical.

Another limitation in low-dose extrapolation is the dose regime. Experimental animals are exposed to near-constant level of the chemical's concentration for most of their lifetime exposure, whereas human exposure patterns vary considerably during their life time. This might have a significant difference on the mechanism of carcinogenesis, including remedial actions between animal species and humans.

Work is progressing in many laboratories to incorporate pharmacokinetic data, the time between exposure and tumor development, differences between administered doses and the critical organ doses and duration of exposure and competing concurrent risks. Results should clearly state the goodness of the fit and the experimental data, assumptions incorporated in the model accompanied by any uncertainties, most probable estimate and the confidence limits.

8.3 ESTIMATION OF TOTAL ENVIRONMENTAL EXPOSURE

Exposure has been defined as the contact between a chemical or a physical agent and humans (ref. 53). Exposure assessment is the central element in quantitative risk assessment of chemicals and exposure values are used in making regulatory decisions. Essential toxicity data (such as critical organ of attack and the critical concentration of the chemical in that organ related to the onset of an adverse effect) are derived from laboratory animal studies conducted at specific dose levels for specific endpoints.

The exposure assessment provides the human exposure levels for the calculation of risk associated with that level of chemical exposure. Toxicity is defined as an intrinsic property of a chemical and exposure level to humans is an extrinsic property. Toxicity values are rather universal in nature and changes only when new toxicity information becomes available. Whereas, exposure scenarios are very much region-specific and regulatory options and decisions are based on exposure reduction and control. Various approaches are used for exposure control from banning the chemical to provide absolute safety from the chemical exposure, to setting standards for occupational exposure environments or environmental media for ambient exposure, to choosing remedial actions and training and labelling to control exposure during use. Exposure assessment is thus required in risk predictions and to predict effects of the prospective control options (ref. 54).

U.S. EPA has published the general guideline document for carrying out exposure assessments (Table 8.12).

The primary point in the design of an exposure assessment programme is defining the purpose, scope, depth, and approach, elements in any planning exercise. By explicitly addressing these questions in the planning stage, the assessor will be in a better position to consolidate his approach and control the outcome of the assessment. This step will save resources by eliminating unnecessary and unproductive work (ref. 55). This also identifies the boundaries of the exposure assessment process.

TABLE 8.12 General outline for exposure assessments.

---

1. Executive Summary
2. Introduction
   - Purpose
   - Scope
3. General Estimation on Chemicals
   a. Identity
       - Name, synonyms, formula and structure
       - Chemical Abstract Service (CAS) number
       - Grade, contaminants present and additives
       - Other descriptive or identifying characteristics
   b. Chemical and Physical Properties:
4. Sources
   - Production and distribution
   - Uses
   - Disposal patterns
   - Potential environmental releases
5. Environmental Pathways and Fate Processes
   - Transport and transformation
   - Identification of major pathways of exposure
   - Predicted distribution in environment
6. Measured or Estimated Concentration
7. Exposed Populations
   a. Human population
       - size, characteristics, habits and location
   b. Non-human population
       - size, characteristics, location and habits
8. Integrated Exposure Analysis
   - Identification of exposed population and pathways of exposure
   - Human dosimetry and biological measurements
   - Development of exposure scenarios and profiles
   - Evaluation of uncertainty
9. References

(Source: Adapted from ref. 53).

Purpose

There are three possible purposes for conducting an exposure assessment (EA):

1. Most EA are done as part of risk assessment to provide the exposure levels for individuals or populations to estimate the risk. This requires a quantitative or semi-quantitative level of information.

2. Some EAs are used as risk reduction evaluation tools. They can become powerful tools in predicting consequences of a variety of regulatory optional actions. This type of EA requires a different approach from (1) in terms of understanding the causes of exposure in addition to collecting monitoring information.

3. The third purpose of EA is to answer the question of whether there is a significant exposure as a prerequisite for testing of a chemical based on substantial exposure.

In summary, the assessor will be able to clearly define the purpose of the assessment knowing the end use of the information base.

Scope

Scoping questions determine the general outline of the exposure assessment and also plays a critical part in deciding resource expenditure since clear scoping avoids unnecessary expenditure. The questions are of the nature "What should be included or excluded from the assessment?" and should be addressed collectively since the concerns are interrelated.

Examples are:

1. Humans vs non-humans

   Should both be included in the assessment or one only?

2. Individuals vs subpopulations vs general populations

3. Geographic boundaries

   Examples are series of sites, regions, or national when assessing "all plants that make chemical x".

4. Route of exposure

   The route of exposure is the means by which the chemical enters the organisms. For humans, the normal routes are ingestion (via food, drinking water), inhalation and dermal absorption. Other possible route is direct contact with blood during an injury or medical treatment, etc. Assessment may be limited to one or more of the above routes of entry.

5. Media

   The exposure of chemicals can be limited to one medium or could be from multi-media which include air, water, food, soil, etc. A chemical due to its physical and chemical properties might migrate from one medium into other media. The properties such as volatility, lipid solubility, and water solubility are the principal properties that decide the multimedia, potential of a chemical.

6. Exposure settings

   The total exposure can be broken down to several individual settings such as ambient environment. Waste disposal sites, drinking water, occupational environment, consumer products, food categories, accidental spills, etc. The boundaries for each setting can be defined, which in turn, can set the structure and limit for data collection in exposure assessment.

7. Depth of detail

   This is also another critical component in planning exposure assessment. Since exposure assessment is used in decision-making, the level of

390

accuracy and detail has to commensurate with the importance of the
decision being made. Since most exposure assessments are used in risk
assessment, one has to bear in mind that "the risk assessment will be no
more accurate than the least accurate of the two components, exposure
and hazard. It may be wasteful of resources to plan an exhaustive
exposure assessment that is orders-of-magnitude more accurate than the
toxicological data with which it will be combined" (ref. 55). If
exposure assessment will be used to evaluate control options, then more
detailed exposure assessment may be necessary. Increasingly, more
attention is devoted to multi-media exposure assessments with detailed
assessment on one media and less detailed estimate on other media to
arrive at total exposure scenario.

General Information
    A summary description of the chemical and its physico-chemical properties
should be provided, with particular attention to properties which would
dictate its environmental behaviour.

Sources
    The suspected or known points of entry of a chemical into the environment
should be described with details on known rates of entry. The details should
include the list of possible sources, production volume, use patterns and
quantities, destruction/disposal and environmental release and potential for
release of the chemical. The summary of environmental releases should detail
the quantities released into various environmental media, transport and
distribution among media, contaminants in products and contribution from
natural sources. Extremely detailed exposure estimates would help to
characterize each emission source in terms of location, amount of the chemical
released as a function of time to each environmental medium, physico-chemical
characteristics of the chemical released. The uncertainties associated with
the emission estimates should also be provided.

Fate Processes and Environmental Pathways
    This section should describe how the chemical reaches from the source to
the receptor species. The chemical, when released to a environmental medium
such as air or water may undergo one or more fate processes such as physical
transformation (volatilization, sorption/desorption, etc.). It may also
undergo chemical transformation such as hydrolysis, photolysis,
oxidation/reduction, etc., may undergo biotransformation such as
methylation/demethylation, biodegradation, etc., or may bioaccumulate in

biota. Environmental behaviour of a chemical should be assessed before exposures are evaluated. The following factors should be addressed for evaluation of fate processes:

1. The predominant fate process in each environmental medium that determines the residence time of this chemical in that medium.
2. Concentration changes in each medium with time which will determine the critical medium of exposure.
3. The multi-media distribution potential of the chemical, reaction involved in the intermedia transfer and the kinetics associated with such transfer.
4. Are the breakdown products more biologically harmful than the parent chemical? What are the fate processes of the breakdown products?

Based on the above information, environmental media containing the chemical can be identified and also the chemical's movement from the medium of original release to its subsequent fate and "resting" media can be followed. Pathways that result in major concentration of the chemical and high potential for human or environmental contact are the principal environmental exposure pathways.

Models can be used to predict distributions of chemicals in different environmental media and its time dependence in specific reaches such as river basins, streams, etc. Whenever possible, predictions should be validated by available measurements.

Measured or Estimated Concentrations

Measurements are a direct database for exposure analysis and used to estimate releases and ambient concentrations. These data should be evaluated for accuracy, precision and representativeness. In the absence of actual environmental measurements, concentrations in the ambient environment can be estimated either by fate models or by analogy with existing and well-characterized chemicals (bench-mark concept).

Reliable monitoring data can be used to calibrate or extrapolate models to calculate environmental distributions. Concentration estimates should be compared with monitoring data whenever possible. However, it must be remembered that monitoring data, without pathway and fate analysis of the chemical, is not comparable to the modelling results. For example, measured atmospheric concentrations usually represent short-term levels. Whereas, models may forecast annual averages at different locations. Fate analysis information is needed to supplement monitoring data in the following situations.

1. When monitoring data is limited in scope, particularly for organic chemicals;

2. When monitoring data does not relate the source releases with ambient environmental concentrations; or

3. When measured concentrations in the ambient environment cannot be traced to individual sources.

Environmental concentrations should be estimated for all environmental media that might significantly contribute to exposure. If sample size or quality of data are acceptable, then exposure assessment based on actual measurements have precedence over estimates based on models (ref. 53).

The environmental concentration estimates should be presented in a format consistent with available dose-response data and reflect the purpose and depth of the assessment. An estimate of annual average concentration may be adequate for general assessment. Whereas, more detailed assessments may require an estimate of temporal geographic distribution of concentrations of the chemical. When considering regulatory options, prediction of future concentration trends based on current releases will be useful. Determination of background levels will be particularly important when dose-response relation shows a threshold or distinctly non-linear dose-response. Uncertainties associated with the estimates should be evaluated.

Exposed Populations

Populations selected for study could be defined at the outset of the assessment or else selected later on the basis of sources and fate processes studies. Populations at high exposure and subpopulations of high sensitivity such as pregnant women, infants, chronically ill, can be identified and may be studied separately. Census and survey data are often used to identify and describe the population exposed to a chemical. The exposed population may be described on the basis of geographical area, age, sex, and health status.

Although the exposed population is usually described in general terms more specific analysis based on the following is possible:

1. Exposed population size and characteristics (i.e., trends, sex/age distribution);

2. Location of the exposed population;

3. Exposed population life style (e.g., transportation habits, eating and recreational habits, workplace environment, consumer products used, etc.).

Integrated Exposure Analysis

In this section, estimates of environmental concentrations are combined with data on exposed populations to produce exposure profiles and pathway analyses. The calculation of exposure involves two major aspects: (1) identification of the exposed population and environmental objects for which exposure has to be calculated. The degree of detail depends on the concentration gradient over geographic area; and (2) identification of exposure pathways that involves descriptive identification of routes by which chemicals travel from the source to the target population. It also entails quantitative estimates of amounts of exposure through different pathways so that they can be prioritized in terms of their relative importance to human health.

Chemical exposure can arise from several sources and reach humans through several routes. For each exposure route, exposure to population may be calculated by summing up contributions from all sources pertaining to that route. When more than one route of exposure is involved, exposures are kept separate for the following reasons:

1. Relative amounts of a chemical absorbed is route dependent;
2. Target organs and toxicities may differ among exposure routes;
3. Keeping route estimates separate will help formulation and evaluation of control options.

The two basic approaches used in measuring exposure are passive dosimetry and biological monitoring. Passive dosimetry is the measurement of the amount of chemical available for absorption through lung or skin. Dosimetry has been used for several years by industrial hygienists in measuring dermal and inhalation exposures. Dermal exposure measurement involves the attachment of adsorbent pads on the subject's body. At the end of the exposure periods, pads are removed and analyzed for chemical residues (ref. 56). Other techniques include the use of disposable coveralls, washings from hand cleaning which are analyzed for the chemical's residue levels. Fluorescent-dye tracer addition to pesticide formulas, followed by video-imaging analysis is also used. Dermal exposures are calculated from the monitored data with an assumption that the concentration of the chemical found on pads represents the surface concentrations of corresponding parts of the body which are added up.

Inhalation exposures are determined using respiratory or miniature personal air sampling pumps and trapping materials such as charcoal, polyurethane foam or Tenax-GC resins (ref. 57). Inhalation exposures are calculated by: (1) analyzing the chemical residues on the respiratory pads; or (2) analyzing the trapping material and using an estimated breathing rate. The conversion of the external dose into an internal biologically available dose takes into account the properties of the chemical, presence of any solvent(s), any abrasions present on the skin and the extent of skin absorption which varies widely for different regions of the body.

Biological monitoring determines the exposure by direct measurement of body fluids (typically blood or urine) for the chemical in question. Pharmacokinetics is applied to calculate the target organ concentration from the fluid concentration of the chemical. Table 8.13 summarizes the advantages and disadvantages of the above two methods.

TABLE 8.13 Comparison of two exposure assessment methodologies.

METHODOLOGY	STRENGTHS	WEAKNESSES
Passive Dosimetry	1. Exposure routes well defined	1. Must have absorption efficiency data for interpretation
	2. Amenable to inter-studies comparison	2. Must extrapolate to whole body surface to determine total dermal exposure
	3. May provide early warning before actual absorption occurs.	
Biological Monitoring	1. Direct evidence of exposure	1. Must have a knowledge of pharmacokinetics
	2. Absorption data not required for interpretation	2. Exposure routes not known

(Source: Reprinted with permission from ref. 58, Copyright (1986), Elsevier Publishers, BV).

Results of exposure assessments should be presented in a format consistent with dose-response data for use in risk assessment. They could be expressed as annual average exposures, exposures in excess of a given threshold value, etc.

Exposure Setting and Profiles

Total exposure can be classified into specific exposure or "scenarios" as given in Table 8.14.

For each exposure setting, the categories of information essential in quantifying exposure are sources, exposure pathways, measurements, and population characteristics. Usually analysis of one exposure setting will suffice for some assessments, but more scenarios are usually required for more extensive and comprehensive assessment. Integrated exposure assessment involves the summation of independent exposures from different settings. Thus

TABLE 8.14 Information needs for various exposure settings.

EXPOSURE SETTING (SCENARIO)	SOURCE/RELEASE PATTERNS	FATE PROCESSES	POPULATION EXPOSED	MEASUREMENT DATA
Occupational	Site/plant locations; in-plant/on-site materials balance	Physical and chemical properties and multimedia transfer models	Workers, families, populations around sites/plants; age and sex	In-plant/on-site releases and levels around plants; body burden monitoring
Consumer (direct use or inadvertent exposure)	Concentration in product, consumption rates and use patterns	Physical and chemical properties, release rates, intermedia transfer potential	Numbers of users of consumer products; age and sex	Levels in products, releases
Transportation Storage/Spills	Patterns of distribution and transportation; spill frequency	Physical and chemical properties, environmental fate models	Types of storage, transportation and cleanup workers; general population in area	Releases, ambient levels following spills
Disposal (including incineration, landfill, etc.)	Efficiency of method; materials balance for disposal method; releases to environment	Effect of treatment/ disposal method; environmental fate of releases	Workers at site; general population around sites; age, sex	Releases from various points in treatment/ disposal methods; ambient levels
Drinking Water	Groundwater, surface water; distribution system	Aquatic fate; chemical effects of treatment process leachates, stream pipes	Location and size of general population; age and sex	Levels in drinking water, groundwater, surface water, and at treatment plants

Continued . . . . .

TABLE 8.14 Concluded.

| Ambient | Site/plant locations and production volumes; materials balance, emissions factors, or source monitoring; releases to environment; air/water/soil | Environmental fate models | Characteristics of general population; non-human populations | Ambient air, soil, and water; body burden monitoring |

(Source: ref. 53).

integration of scenarios or integrated exposure assessments will often provide exposure profiles, since individual settings usually relate exposure to subpopulation.

An integrated assessment should state the size of the exposed population, the characteristics of the population, exposure pathways, duration, frequency, intensity of exposure and the source of the chemical. Exposures should be related to the source, since it is finally sources that are regulated. The assessor should also evaluate the associated level of uncertainty by analyzing the uncertainties in every step of the whole exposure assessment process.

8.4   METHODOLOGIES IN RISK ASSESSMENT

Risk assessment is a scientific process which identifies and evaluates the hazards of a chemical to the environment and human health. The assessment process determines the likelihood of human exposure to a chemical and characterizes the nature of the adverse effects. Risk assessment, as described in the earlier chapters, can be divided into four major steps: (i) hazard identification; (ii) dose-response evaluation; (iii) exposure assessment; and (iv) risk characterization.

(i) Hazard identification. Hazard is defined as a set of circumstances with a potential for causing adverse health effects or harm on humans. In the case of chemicals, adverse health effects (toxicity) can be produced at some dose or under specific exposure conditions. For a chemical to be hazardous, it has to be toxic at the level of environmental concentration and for the duration of the exposure. In brief, the dose makes the chemical a hazard. In contrast, there are chemicals whose exposure at all levels of concentrations will produce a particular type of toxicity called genotoxicity. Hazard identification requires both qualitative and quantitative information on genetic toxicity and non-genetic toxicity of chemicals acting either singly or in groups. Hazard assessment requires the knowledge of exposure concentration of the chemical to correlate against the toxic effects. The adverse effects alone do not rate the chemical as hazardous but its presence in the environment makes it hazardous. A very toxic chemical with no exposure potential is not hazardous in the environment. Conversely, a chemical with low toxicity but high exposure level with multiple pathways of exposure could be much more hazardous.

(ii) Dose-response evaluation. This is the process which describes the relation between the dose of a chemical and the incidence of an adverse effect in exposed populations. The evaluation takes into account factors such as intensity and duration of exposure, age, sex, and other modifying factors. The dose-response curve obtained at the observable range (high dose) is

extrapolated to low doses. Extrapolation also involves interspecies
extrapolation of data, i.e., from animals to humans and one laboratory animal
species to wildlife species. These limitations should be described in any
dose-response assessment, including a numerical statement on uncertainty
rather than qualitative description.

(iii) Exposure assessment. This process is used to measure or estimate the
intensity, frequency, and duration of animal or human exposure to a chemical
present in the ambient environment. In the case of new chemicals, estimates
are obtained using bench-mark concept and relevant fate processes models.
Exposure assessment should also identify the possible routes of exposure,
size, nature and classes of exposed populations, and the uncertainties
associated with the estimates. Since sources are identified in the process,
the assessment should also include control options and available technologies
for controlling and reducing the exposure to a chemical.

(iv) Risk characterization. This process estimates the incidence of an
adverse health effect under different exposure settings for humans and
animals. This is arrived at by linking exposure and dose-response assessments
(ref. 59). The relation between the four steps of the risk assessment process
outlined above is given in Fig. 8.2.

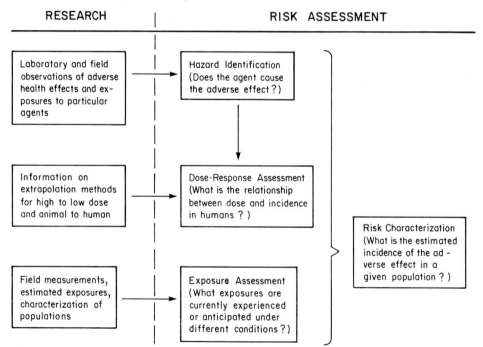

Fig. 8.2. Elements of the risk assessment process.
(Source: Reprinted with permission from ref. 5, Copyright (1983), NAS).

The first step in risk assessment, for carcinogens and non-carcinogens alike, is the gathering of toxicity information on the chemical. This includes basic knowledge on the properties of the chemical and its effects on various biological systems. This information could come from a variety of sources but much of it is derived from animal experiments. Figure. 8.3 illustrates the various data that are required in the risk assessment process.

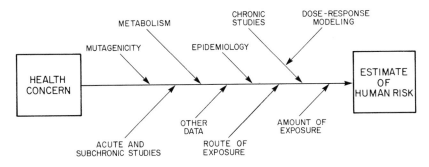

Fig. 8.3. Required data input in the risk assessment process. Some of the factors may not be considered when human risk is estimated (Source: ref. 60).

Non-carcinogenic Chemicals - Safety Factors and Thresholds

It is widely accepted that for the most toxic agents, that do not produce carcinogenic effects, there is a dose below which no toxic response will occur. This dose level is called the "threshold dose". If this dose could be identified with great certainty, establishment of No-Observed-Effect-Level (NOEL) is straightforward and simple. But several factors complicate the determination of NOEL. With a small group of animals studied, only relatively strong effects can be positively identified that are statistically significant. Subtle effects and/or certain biological changes may go undetected in toxicological assessment. Another factor to consider is the variability of threshold levels among individuals in human population. Human populations are also exposed to variety of other environmental chemicals which may modify the risk of the chemical in question.

The ADI is arrived by incorporating a safety factor to the NOEL value to account for the uncertainties associated in arriving at the NOEL value. While a factor of 100 is commonly used, the WHO Expert Committees have used figures ranging from 10 to 2000. The magnitude of the safety factor is decided by the nature of toxicity, slight deficiencies in toxicity results (smaller number of animals tested); available human data and pharmacokinetic information on the fate of the chemical. Aspects of the safety factor have been discussed in Chapter 6. The approach in establishing ADIs has been successfully used for several decades around the world.

Carcinogenic Risk Assessment

Until recently the safety factor approach has been used for carcinogens, developmental toxicants, and all systemic toxicants. Limits based on safety factors have been generally effective in preventing disease among exposed persons (refs. 61,62). This approach is much less complex than the mathematical models developed specifically for estimating the cancer risk of the exposed population. The threshold concept may not be universally applicable to all carcinogens and even if they exist, thresholds are likely to vary among the individuals in the exposed population. In the absence of a reliable procedure to determine a threshold for a carcinogen for the entire population, estimating the levels of risk has been considered to be more appropriate (ref. 31). The safety factor has also been criticized on the basis that the observed no-effect level will depend very much on the sample size. Also, it is possible to record no effects even though the chemical may affect an appreciable portion of exposed population. Importantly, safety factor approach accords little recognition to the shape of the dose-response curve, with steep and shallow slopes being treated almost the same (ref. 63).

Mathematical Models

The direct determination of risk estimates at low levels of exposure would require the use of prohibitively large numbers of animals. Hence, mathematical models are used to overcome this experimental problem. The purpose of the mathematical model is to estimate a virtual safe dose (VSD) or recently termed parameter "a risk-specific dose" (RSD). This involves the development of suitable dose-response data and extrapolation from the observed range to the expected responses at doses encountered at actual exposure situation; this is usually well outside the observed dose-response range and about 3 to 4 orders of magnitude lower than the lowest observed effect level. Statistical models are based on the assumption that each individual in the population has a specific tolerance level to a chemical under testing and this level is presumed to vary in the exposed population. This translates to lack of population threshold level and hence the minimum tolerable level is allowed to be zero. The specification of a functional form of distribution of tolerances determines the shapes of the dose-response relationship curve and thus characterizes a particular statistical model (ref. 58). Figure 8.4 shows the experimental region and the low-dose region of the dose-response curve and the VSD corresponding to some suitably low acceptable level of risk.

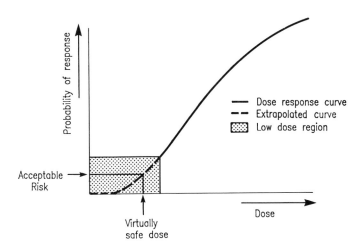

Fig. 8.4. Acceptable risk and virtually safe dose.
(Source: Reprinted from ref. 63).

The shape of the dose-response curve in the low dose area can affect the VSD
value significantly (Fig. 8.5).

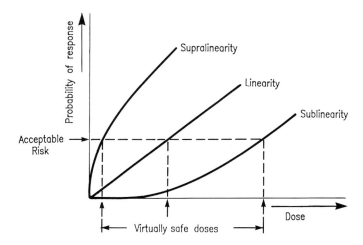

Fig. 8.5. Dose-response curves and VSD.
(Source: Reprinted with permission from ref. 51, Copyright (1981), Pergamon
Press Plc.).

The mathematical models in use today vary in their degree of biological sophistication (ref. 51,63).

The quantitative assessment of the risks arising from exposure to humans to specified doses of chemical carcinogens is performed by estimating the form of dose-response relationship in that specific dose regime. While epidemiological studies of human populations can provide direct evidence of adverse effects on human health, such studies are subject to a wide range of uncertainty. The uncertainty includes variable exposure levels within the population, confounding risk factors, variable tolerance levels of the individuals in the population due to outbred nature of the human population. In addition, the epidemiology analyses the causality after the fact and thus is not consistent with a preventative regulatory philosophy. These problems are overcome by using animal models for humans. The experimental data are fitted to one or more mathematical models of dose-response relationships, which estimate the cancer risk at doses encountered in the ambient medium.

A number of carcinogenic dose-response models have been proposed and their relative merits have been extensively debated (refs. 23,63). The basic assumptions in these models are: that the organism has a number of "critical targets"; that the organism responds biologically if these targets are attacked; and the probability of a hit is proportional to the dose of the chemical carcinogen. Since it is possible to fit any theoretical model to a given dataset, the selection of a model is judgemental in nature.

Description of Models

1. Mantel-Bryan Method (Log-Probit Model)

The Mantel-Bryan extrapolation model was proposed (ref. 38) to estimate the lower confidence limit for VSD for a carcinogen. The term VSD was defined as a probability of carcinogenicity of less than 10^{-8} at a statistical assurance level of 99%. The currently-used risk level is between 10^{-6} to 10^{-8} increase in lifetime risk. The dose-response function in this model is the cumulative distribution that assumes a probit (log-normal) distribution of tolerances in the exposed population. In other words, the sensitivities of individuals of the population follow a normal distribution as a function of logarithm of the dose. This assumption is applicable to acute toxicology, but questionable when applied to carcinogenesis.

This procedure determines the highest dose that is not associated with a response and calculates the maximum risk at this dose at 99% confidence level. The log-probit assumes a unit slope and extrapolates to determine VSDs corresponding to 10^{-6}, 10^{-7}, and 10^{-8} risk levels. This procedure has been modified to account for background incidence assuming independent mode of action. The important features of Mantel-Bryan procedure are that carcinogens may pose some risk at any level of exposure and use of upper confidence limits. The deficiencies of the procedure are that: (1) it does not fit experimental data well; and (2) the slope is not in unity at low-dose range.

2. One-hit Model

This model is based on the concept that cancer is initiated with a single hit on the critical target of the cell. This model was developed initially for radiation-related carcinogenesis. The probability of cancer developing in human is assumed to be proportional to the total lifetime dose of radiation received. The weakness of this method is its assumption of linearity of dose-response in the observed range and resulting very low estimates of VSDs for a given risk level.

3. Multi-stage Model

Multi-stage models are based on the premise that several distinct and heritable sequential changes (stages) are necessary to transform a normal cell to a malignant cell and that one such transformed single cell can lead to human cancer. Mathematically, the incidence of cancer is related to both dose and time. The response is a polynomial function of dose with a number of exponential terms, and the multi-stage model can fit a wide range of experimental data. The model developed by Crump (ref. 64,65) is used by U.S. EPA in their risk assessment of carcinogens. The criticism against multi-stage model is the arbitrary assumption of several stages in the model.

4. Gamma Multi-hit Model

The following assumptions led to the development of this model: (1) a critical site in an organism is destroyed when "hit" by a number (k) of particles; (2) destruction of critical sites will lead to cancer induction in an organism; and (3) the probability of hit is proportional to dose. This model can also fit a wide variety of datasets, but the model can generate a spurious background cancer incidence rate which could discount a possibly significant tumor incidence at low doses. The model has no biological basis if k is not an integer or becomes extremely large. When k is less than 1, the model can yield unrealistically low estimates of VSD due to the slopes becoming very steep at low doses.

5. Time-to-Tumor Models

These models attempt to describe the relationship between dose and the time required for a response to occur. Several models have been proposed (ref. 23). The severe limitation of time-to-tumour models is the inability to determine the actual responses in an experiment. In most cases, internal tumours are usually detected only at necropsy without knowing when exactly the tumours set in. In addition, these models require exact information on the cause of death, whether it was due to tumour or other causes. Pathologists are reluctant to draw such distinctions.

6. Physiologically-based Pharmacokinetic (PBPK) Model

Physiologically-based pharmacokinetic (PBPK) models developed recently (ref. 66) are used to reduce uncertainties commonly associated with extrapolation models such as interspecies extrapolation, across routes administration and low-dose extrapolation to human exposure conditions. These models use actual physiological parameters that describe the metabolic process and quantitatively relate to exposure concentration of a chemical to its effective dose at target tissue(s). When organ dose is known, the mathematical model can calculate the equivalent exposure needed for humans to manifest the same toxic effect as seen in experimental animals. Such estimates of effects can take into account genetic differences, disease processes, development and maturation and variety of other physiological, biochemical and metabolic factors common to humans, and avoid the use of arbitrary judgements. The ability of PBPK models to extrapolate between species significantly improves the ability of risk assessment process to estimate human cancer risks from animal cancer bioassays.

Munro and Krewski have summarized the biological components of some extra-polation models (ref. 51). They also noted that the dose-response curves for the logit, Weibull and multi-hit models can approach zero at a faster rate than linear or supralinear rate, although the biological plausibility of this behaviour seems questionable. The multi-stage model, however, does provide for data that are linear at low doses and exhibit upward curvature at higher doses unlike the one-hit model (ref. 51). Despite their biological rationale, these stochastic models must also be considered somewhat arbitrary until the mechanisms of carcinogenesis are more fully understood. This and other characteristics of multi-stage model (ref. 65) are the reasons for this model being most widely used by U.S. regulatory agencies since 1977.

Figure 8.6 illustrates the determination of VSD in the presence of sponta-neous risk from the background levels. The background may be independent of the induced responses or synergistic in nature but the supporting biological explanation or experimental evidence is not very clear at this time. The added

risk over background at low-dose levels may be estimated by fitting a particular dose-response model to experimental results and extrapolating to the
low-dose region of interest.

Linear response at low doses seem to be acceptable to many toxicologists
based on evidences from some direct acting carcinogens and spontaneous lesions
occurring from background dose. For others showing sublinearity or even
threshold effects, linear extrapolation could provide an upper limit on the
actual risk in the low-dose exposure region. The proposed procedures are
illustrated in Fig. 8.7.

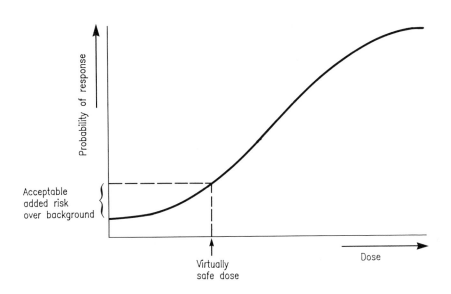

Fig. 8.6. Determination of VSD in the presence of background.
(Source: Reprinted with permission from ref. 51, Copyright (1981), Pergamon
Press Plc.).

The first of the four approaches is by Van Ryzin (ref. 67) which involves
fitting a suitable model to the experimental data and then extrapolating
linearly from some point close to the lower end of the dose-response curve in
the observable range. A second approach is to extrapolate linearly from the
lowest dose for which the observed response exceeded that of the control
group. The third procedure is to smooth out any inversions in the observed
dose-response curve using isotonic regression, and then extrapolate linearly
from the lowest dose at which the adjusted response is above the control
level. The fourth method is the application of 5000-fold safety factor to the

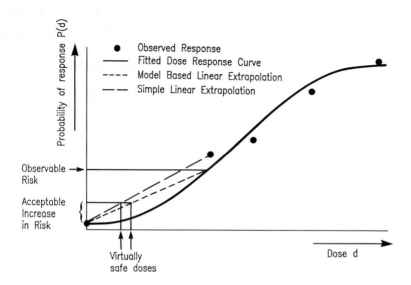

Fig. 8.7. Proposed methods of linear extrapolation of data.
(Source: Reprinted from ref. 63).

lowest dose at which the response is significantly (P <0.05 in Fisher's exact test) above that in the control group (ref. 63). For further discussion of the procedures, the readers are referred to the publication by Krewski, et al. (ref. 63).

Many compounds require metabolic activation before becoming reactive (Fig. 8.8).

Pharmacokinetic models for metabolic activation have been developed to take into account the possible pathways of elimination or activation into a reactive metabolite. The effects of non-linear kinetics in the simple linear extrapolation procedure have been discussed elsewhere (ref. 63).

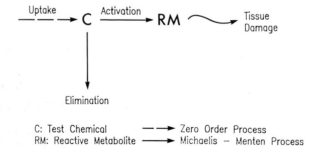

Fig. 8.8. Simplified pharmacokinetic model for metabolic activation.
(Source: Reprinted from ref. 63).

Krewski et al. concluded (ref. 63) that the use of both linear extrapolation and safety factors represent possible approaches to establishing safe levels of exposure with the most suitable of these two methods depending on the biological acceptability of the linear no-threshold hypothesis. When low dose linearity is in doubt, linear extrapolation can be highly conservative, while the safety factor approach may be preferable in this case, the selection of the actual magnitude of the safety factor remains largely a judgemental issue. Although a 5000-fold safety factor may work well in some cases, the performance of this procedure will depend strongly on what the threshold dose actually is.

Shortcomings of Low-dose Extrapolation Models

Although several models are available, all are subject to some criticism. Empirically several different models can be fitted to most datasets and studies using vast number of animals are unlikely to decide between models for their applicability. The multi-stage model is flexible to fit a wide range of empirical data and has a reasonable biological basis. However, its usefulness may not be optimal in all situations.

Based on the scientific uncertainty regarding the different approaches to risk assessment, the following guidelines can be drawn:

- "Threshold" concept should not be applied to carcinogenesis unless dose-response data are available that are not consistent with a non-threshold model;

- The effect of a carcinogen can be assumed to be additive to the background incidence of cancer. The exceptions are when the carcinogen under evaluation acts by a mechanism different to the one for the background incidence or it acts synergistically with other carcinogens in the environment.

- The current knowledge on the carcinogenic mechanisms do not provide clear guidance as to the choice of the model to be chosen. The low-dose linearity for direct carcinogens seems to be more generally accepted.

Fitting Models to Data

Comparisons have been made for the one hit, Weibull, gamma multi-hit and multi-stage models by applying them to tumour incidence data on nine carcinogenic compounds (ref. 68). or to hypothetical data sets. The conclusions drawn were: (1) most models fit most of the data at high experimental dose almost equally well; (2) an impractically large volume of data would be required to conclude which model provides the best fit at low doses; and (3) at low risk levels, 10^{-6}-10^{-8}, the VSDs follow the order one hit > multi-stage > Weibull = multi-hit > Mantel-Bryan (log-probit) (ref. 68). Thus for the same low-dose level, one-hit model yields the highest estimates of risk while the Mantel-Bryan model gives the lowest estimate of risk.

1. The data from the "mega mouse study" conducted with 2-acetylamino-fluorene were used to compare the VSD estimates for risk at 10^{-5} or lower by five different models (Fig. 8.9).

   The corresponding estimates (of the VSD at risks of 10^{-5} or lower) range over several orders of magnitude. The large dataset had little effect on the relative difference between the VSDs estimated by multi-stage and log probit models, normally reported by few datasets.

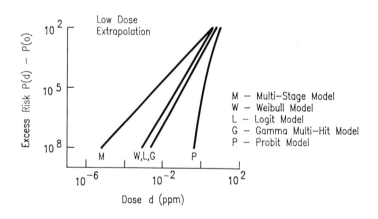

Fig. 8.9. Dose (ppm) VSD estimates by different methods. (Source: Reprinted from ref. 63).

2. Similar substantial differences among six mathematical extrapolation models were observed in the estimates of added risk over the background at low-dose levels for NTA (nitrilotriacetic acid), Saccharin, 2-AAF (2-acetyl amino fluorene) and Aflatoxin (ref. 68). The dose-response curves for saccharin and NTA are very steep, while that of 2-AAF is more or less linear throughout the entire dose range and that of aflatoxin is neither steep nor shallow. The results clearly showed a substantial difference between the methods used. Linear extrapolation was the most conservative in all cases, followed by multi-stage and Weibull models.

Logit and multi-hit models were, although in agreement, less conservative than the Weibull model. The least conservative estimates were from
the probit model.

3. When the five simplistic models, probit, multi-hit, logit, Weibull and
   multi-stage models were applied to data from an inhalation study on
   formaldehyde, the models fitted well at higher experimental doses
   (Fig. 8.10). But at lower dose region, the predictions were dissimilar
   (Table 8.15).

Extrapolation is routinely performed by regulatory agencies although it is
subjected to criticisms, partly due to our lack of knowledge on the mechanisms
of cancer induction. However, in the absence of good human data (almost always
lacking), some reliance on rodent carcinogenicity testing is unavoidable.

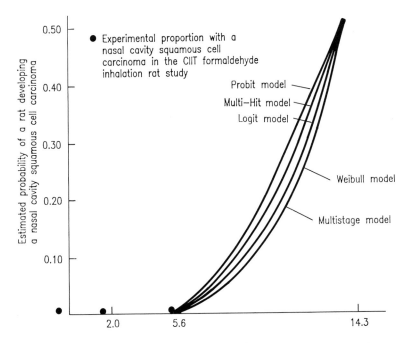

Fig. 8.10. Fitting of mathematical model to inhalation data on formaldehyde at
high experimental doses.
*Multi-stage model is frequently used by U.S. EPA and OSHA (U.S.
Occupational Safety & Health Agency).
(Source: Reprinted with permission from ref. 69, Copyright (1987), ACS).

In spite of deficiencies, the mathematical models hold promise of providing a more orderly and systematic methodology to determine tolerance than using the safety factor approach for carcinogens. Further research in biological and biochemical properties and pharmacokinetics of chemicals in a biological system may assist in developing more realistic and reliable models for extrapolation. Likewise, improved epidemiological procedures could serve as

TABLE 8.15 Dissimilar prediction of risks by models at low doses of formaldehyde.

Dose (ppm)	Ratio =	Risk estimated using fitted multi-stage model / Risk estimated using fitted probit model
5.6		1.0
5.0		1.3
4.0		3.0
3.0		13.3
2.0		260.0
1.0		300,000.0
0.5		1,600,000,000.0

(Source: Reprinted with permission from ref. 69, Copyright (1987), ACS).

important tools in the identification and quantification of human risk. The guidelines intended to select the model closest to the type of data available are listed in literature (ref. 23).

The key aspects of risk assessment are illustrated in the form of a "decision tree" framework as shown in Fig. 8.11. The decision tree approach may not be exactly applicable for some of the toxic end points such as genotoxicity. However, it is a useful concept for making some of the decisions required in risk assessment (ref. 60).

8.5 COMPARATIVE RISK ASSESSMENT

Comparisons of risk provide a perspective about the relative magnitude of the risk. Table 8.16 lists the variety of risks calculated and associated estimate of uncertainty.

The carcinogenic potency of various chlorinated hydrocarbons can be presented in a comparative risk frame. For example, chloroform, which is produced by the interaction of residual chlorine with organic mattter, is shown to produce cancer in animals 20 times as readily as does trichloro-

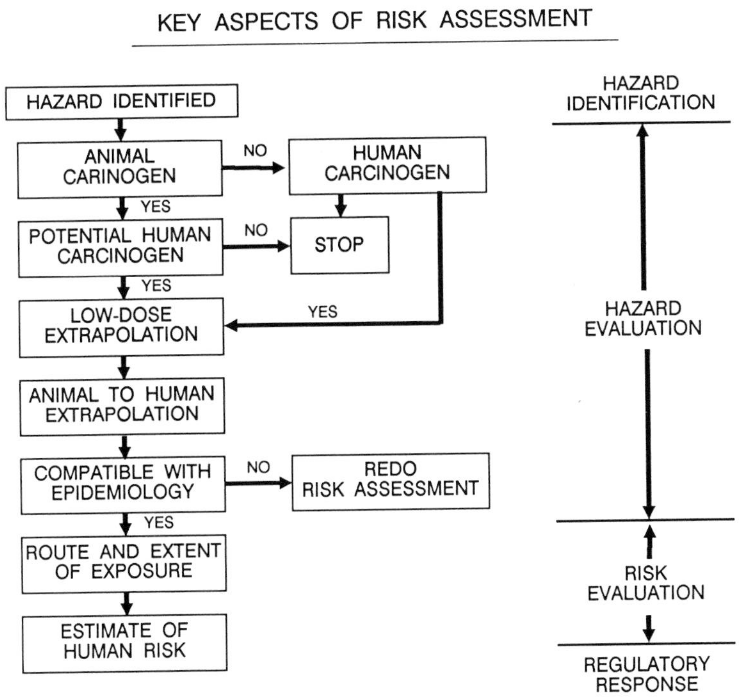

KEY ASPECTS OF RISK ASSESSMENT

Fig. 8.11. Key aspects and major decision points of risk assessment and their relation to risk assessment and management process.
(Source: Reprinted with permission from ref. 60, Copyright (1983).

ethylene (TCE). TCE is an industrial solvent, occasionally detected in well waters due to accidental contamination. Neither of the two chlorinated hydrocarbons is known to cause cancer in humans, however, on a comparative scale, chloroform has 20 times higher carcinogenic risk than TCE.

Comparison of exposures is another way of illustrating the relative risks associated with a single carcinogenic agent. Table 8.17 lists the sources of radiation and associated dose levels and population risks on a yearly basis. The estimate of lethal cancers on a linear hypothesis assumes approximately 8000 mrems per cancer (at low doses) with an uncertainty of 30% or more (ref. 70).

TABLE 8.16 Comparable risks for some categories of activities.

ACTIVITY	MEAN ANNUAL RISK	UNCERTAINTY
Motor vehicle accident (total)	2.4×10^{-4}	10%
Motor vehicle accident (pedestrian only)	4.2×10^{-5}	10%
Home accidents	1.1×10^{-4}	5%
Electrocution	5.3×10^{-6}	5%
Air pollution, eastern United States	2×10^{-4}	Factor of 20 downward only
Cigarette smoking, one pack per day	3.6×10^{-3}	Factor of 3
Sea-level background radiation (except radon)	2×10^{-5}	Factor of 3
All cancers	2.8×10^{-3}	10%
Four tablespoons peanut butter per day	8×10^{-6}	Factor of 3
Drinking water with EPA limit of chloroform	6×10^{-7}	Factor of 10
Drinking water with EPA limit of trichloroethylene	2×10^{-9}	Factor of 10
Alcohol light drinker	2×10^{-5}	Factor of 10
Police killed in line of duty (total)	2.2×10^{-4}	20%
Police killed in line of duty (by felons)	1.3×10^{-4}	10%
Frequent flying professor	5×10^{-5}	50%
Mountaineering (mountaineers)	6×10^{-4}	50%

(Source: Reprinted from ref. 73).

TABLE 8.17 Comparison of common radiation risk levels.

ACTIVITY	DOSE (mrem/year)	CANCERS IF ALL U.S. POPULATION EXPOSED (ASSUMING LINEARITY)
Medical x-rays	40	1,100
Radon gas (1.5 pCi/L, equivalent dose)*	500	13,500
Potassium in own body	30	1,000
Cosmic radiation at sea level	40	1,100
Cosmic radiation at Denver	65	1,800
Dose to average resident near Chernobyl first year	5,000	Not relevant
One transcontinental round trip by air	5	135
Average within 20 miles of nuclear plant	0.02	1

* The radon exposure is to the lungs and cannot be directly compared to whole body external exposure. The comparison here is on the basis of the same magnitude of risk. The uncertainty of the radon is at least a factor of 3.

Ames, McGaw, and Gold (ref. 71) compared the possible hazards from both natural and synthetic carcinogens based on their amounts to which humans might be chronically exposed. This calculation is intended to establish a scale of possible hazards in order to provide a guide to priority setting based on their comparative risk levels.

The measure of potency that was used in this comparison was TD_{50} (daily dose rate in mg/kg.bw) to half the percentage of tumour-free animals by the end of standard lifetime. The lower the TD_{50} value, the more potent is the carcinogen. Human exposure (daily lifetime dose in mg/kg.bw) is expressed as a percentage of the rodent TD_{50} dose for each carcinogen. This ratio is called the percentage HERP (human exposure/rodent potency dose). Since rodent data are all calculated on the basis of lifetime exposure at the indicated daily dose rate, the human exposure data are similarly expressed as lifetime daily dose rates even though human exposure is less likely to be on a daily basis for a lifetime exposure. The authors caution against using the HERP index as a direct estimate of human hazard and list the reasons for it (ref. 71).

The table of HERP value (Table 8.18) can be used to compare carcinogenic hazards within categories and synthetic chemicals against natural carcinogens.

TABLE 8.18 Ranking of possible carcinogenic hazards of natural and synthetic products and human activities.

POSSIBLE HAZARD HERP(%)[a]	DAILY HUMAN EXPOSURE[b]	CARCINOGEN DOSE PER 70-kg PERSON	POTENCY OF CARCINOGEN TD_{50}(mg/kg)	
			RATS	MICE
Environmental Pollution				
0.001[*]	Tap water, 1 L	Chloroform, 83 μg (U.S. average)	(119)	90
0.004[*]	Well water, 1 L contaminated (worst well in Silicon Valley)	Trichloroethylene 2800 μg	(-)	941
0.0004[*]	Well water, 1 L contaminated , Woburn	Trichloroethylene, 267 μg	(-)	941
0.0002[*]		Chloroform, 12 μg	(119)	90
0.0003[*]		Tetrachloroethylene,	101	(126)
0.008[*]	Swimming pool, 1 h (14 h/d)	Chloroform, 250 μg	(119)	90
0.6	Conventional home air	Formaldehyde, 598 μg	1.5	(44)
0.004		Benzene, 155 μg	(157)	53
2.1	Mobile home air (14 h/d)	Formaldehyde, 2.2 mg	1.5	(44)

Continued . . . .

TABLE 8.18 Continued.

POSSIBLE HAZARD HERP(%)[a]	DAILY HUMAN EXPOSURE[b]	CARCINOGEN DOSE PER 70-kg PERSON	POTENCY OF CARCINOGEN TD_{50}(mg/kg) RATS	MICE
		Pesticide and Other Residues		
0.0002*	PCBs:daily dietary intake	PCBs, 0.2 μg (U.S. average)	1.7	(9.6)
0.0003*	DDE/DDT:daily dietary	DDE, 2.2 μg (U.S. average)	(-)	13
0.0004	EDB:daily dietary intake (from grains and grain products)	Ethylene dibromide: 0.42 μg (U.S. average)	1.5	(5.1)
		Natural Pesticides and Dietary Toxins		
0.003	Bacon, cooked (100 g)	Dimethylnitrosamine, 0.3 μg	(0.2)	0.2
0.006		Diethylnitrosamine, 0.1 μg	0.02	(+)
0.003	Sake (250 mL)	Urethane, 43 μg	(41)	22
0.03	Comfrey herb tea, 1 cup	Symphytine, 38 μg (750 g of pyrolizidine alkaloids)	1.9	(?)
0.03	Peanut butter (32 g; one sandwich)	Aflatoxin, 64 ng (U.S. average, 2 ppb)	0.003	(+)
0.06	Dried squid, broiled in gas oven (54 g)	Dimethylnitrosamine, 7.9 μg	(0.2)	0.2)
0.07	Brown mustard (5 g)	Allyl isothiocyanate, 4.6 mg	96	(-)
0.1	Basil (1 g of dried leaf)	Estragole, 3.8 mg	(?)	52
0.1	Mushroom, one raw (15 g) (Agaricus bisporus)	Mixture of hydrazines, and so forth	(?)	20,300
0.2	Natural root beer (12 oz.)	Safrole, 6.6 mg	(436)	56
0.008	Beer, before 1979 (12 oz.; 354 mL)	Dimethylnitrosamine, 1 μg	(0.2)	0.2
2.8	Beer (12 oz; 354 mL)	Ethyl alcohol, 18 mL	9110	(?)
4.7*	Wine (250 mL)	Ethyl alcohol, 30 mL	9110	(?)
6.2	Comfrey-pepsin tablets (nine daily)	Comfrey root, 2700 mg	626	(?)
1.3	Comfrey-pepsin tablets (nine daily)	Symphytine, 1.8 mg	1.9	(?)
		Food Additives		
0.0002	AF-2:daily dietary intake before banning	AF-2(furylfuramide), 4.8 μg	29	(131)
0.06*	Diet cola (12 oz.:354 mL)	Saccharin, 95 mg	2143	(-)

Continued . . . .

TABLE 8.18 Concluded.

POSSIBLE HAZARD HERP(%)[a]	DAILY HUMAN EXPOSURE[b]	CARCINOGEN DOSE PER 70-kg PERSON	POTENCY OF CARCINOGEN TD_{50}(mg/kg)	
			RATS	MICE

		Drugs		
[0.3]	Phenacetin pill (average dose)	Phenacetin, 300 mg	1246	(2137)
[5.6]	Metronidazole (therapeutic dose)	Metronidazole, 2000 mg	(542)	506
[14]	Isoniazid pill (prophylactic dose)	Isoniazid, 300 mg	(150)	30
26*	Phenobarbital, one sleeping pill	Phenobarbital, 60 mg	(+)	5.5
17*	Clofibrate (average daily dose)	Clofibrate, 200 mg	169	(?)

		Occupational Exposure		
5.8	Formaldehyde:workers' average daily intake	Formaldehyde, 6.1 mg	1.5	(44)
140	EDB:workers' daily intake (high exposure)	Ethylene dibromide, 150 mg	1.5	(5.1)

a   Asterisks indicate HERP from carcinogens thought to be nongenotoxic. The amount of rodent carcinogen indicated under carcinogen dose is divided by 70 kg to give a milligram per kilogram of human exposure, and this human dose is given as the percentage of the TD_{50} dose in the rodent (in milligrams per kilogram) to calculate the human exposure/rodent potency index (HERP);

b   Average or reasonable daily intakes is used to facilitate comparison. In several cases, such as contaminated well water or factory exposure to EDB, this is difficult to determine, and the value for the worst found is given. The calculations assume a daily dose for a lifetime; bracketed HERP value indicates drugs taken for a short period. For inhalation exposures, an inhalation of 9600 L/8 h for the workplace and 10,800 L/14 h for indoor air at home are used;

c   A number in parentheses indicates a TD_{50} value not used in HERP calculation because it is the less sensitive species; (-)=negative in cancer test. (+)= positive for carcinogenicity in test(s) not suitable for calculating a TD_{50};

(?) Is not adequately tested for carcinogenicity. TD_{50} values shown are averages calculated by taking the harmonic mean of the TD_{50}s of the positive tests in that species from the Carcinogenic Potency Database. Results are similar if the lowest TD_{50} value (most potent) is used instead. For each test, the target site with the lowest TD_{50} value has been used. The average TD_{50} has been calculated separately for rats and mice, and the more sensitive species is used for calculating the possible hazard.

(Source: Reprinted with permission from ref. 71, Copyright (1987), AAAS).

416

Ideally, the best standard for comparative hazard evaluation would be a substance for which the true hazard from low-level exposure was known with certainty. The true hazard cannot be determined from estimates based on safety factors or from mathematical model extrapolations. Hence, a composite standard whose hazards are acceptable to the consumers may possibly serve as a reference standard. Chlorinated drinking water has been used as a reference standard to compare with other environmental hazards (ref. 72). The resulting composite of hazards defines a zone of hazard which is conceptually equivalent to the U.S. EPA list of Generally Recognized As Safe (GRAS) food additives (ref. 73). Environmental hazards may be comparatively evaluated relative to GRAS zone of commonly acceptable hazards. This process provides insight into the actual hazard of a chemical (or a substance) and also reveals its hazards relative to other substances.

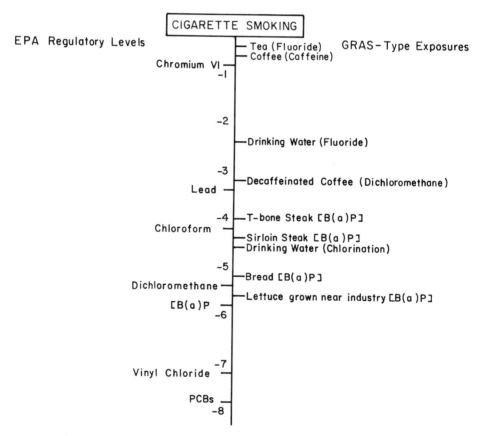

Fig. 8.12. Comparison of hazards relative to cigarette smoking (log scale). Hazards environmental and lifestyle exposures) are normalized to the reference standard of smoking a pack of cigarettes daily.
(Source: Reprinted with permission from ref. 72, Copyright (1990), Academic Press).

Fig. 8.12 shows the GRAS zone of hazards plotted on the right of the log axis and hazards from exposures to the established regulatory levels of drinking water contamination are plotted on the left side of the log axis. It can be seen that the GRAS zone of acceptable hazards are 2 to 6 orders of magnitude below the chosen reference standard, cigarette smoke (a mixture of numerous chemicals reflecting diverse biological mechanisms represents "worst case" complex mixture). However, hazards from vinyl chloride and PCBs are observed to fall 2 to 3 orders of magnitude below the GRAS zone. Whereas, hazards from chromium (VI) is nearly two orders of magnitude above the GRAS zone; roughly equivalent to the hazard from an intake of a litre of coffee or tea per day (Fig. 8.12). From this analysis, one may consider that vinyl chloride and PCBs are over regulated and chromium (VI) may be under regulated relative to other commonly acceptable hazards. Comparative hazards evaluation might improve regulatory consistency.

REFERENCES

1 World Health Organization (WHO), Principles and Methods for Evaluating the Toxicity of Chemicals, Environ. Health Criteria 6, WHO, Geneva, 1978.
2 R. Wilson and E.A.C. Crouch, Science, 236 (1987) 267-270.
3 A.V. White and I. Burton (Editors), Environmental Risk Assessment Scientific Committee on Problems of the Environment (SCOPE) of the International Council of Scientific Unions (ICSU), John Wiley & Sons, New York, 1980, 157 p.
4 B.N. Ames, R. MaGaw, and L.S. Gold, Science, 236 (1987) 271-280.
5 U.S. National Academy of Sciences (NAS), Risk Assessment in the Federal Government: Managing the Process, Committee of the Institutional Means for Risk Assessment of Risks to Public Health, Commission on Life Sciences, Washington, D.C., U.S.A., 1983.
6 U.S. Department of Health and Human Services, Task Force on Health Risk Assessment, Federal Policy and Practice, Auburn House, Dover, MA, U.S.A., 1986.
7 J. Rodricks and M.R. Taylor, Reg. Toxicol. Pharmacol., 3 (1983) 257-307.
8 F.H. Tschirley, Dioxin Sci. Am. 265 (1986) 29-35.
9 Hon-Wing Leung and D.J. Paustenbach, in D.J. Pausenbach (Editor), The Risk Assessment of Environmental and Human Health Hazards: A Textbook of Case Studies, John Wiley and Sons, New York, U.S.A, 1989, pp. 689-710.
10 United States Environmental Protection Agency (U.S. EPA), The Risk Assessment Guidelines of 1986, Office of Health and Environmental Assessment, U.S. EPA, Washington, D.C., U.S.A., EPA/600/8-87/045, 1987.
11 National Research Council (NRC), Risk Assessment in the Federal Government: Managing the Process, National Academy of Sciences Press, Washington, D.C., U.S.A., 1983.
12 Office of Science and Technology Policy (OSTP), Chemical Carcinogens: Review of the Science and Its Associated Principles, Fed. Registr., 50 (1985) 10372-10442.
13 R. Peto, M. Pike, N. Day, R. Gray, P. Lee, S. Parish, J. Peto, S. Richard, and J. Wahrendorf, Guidelines for Simple, Sensitive, Significant Tests for Carcinogenic Effects in Long-term Animal Experiments, in Monographs on the long-term, and short-term screening assays for carcinogens: a critical appraisal. IARC Monographs, Supplement 2, Lyon, France: International Agency for Research Cancer, 1980, pp. 311-426.

418

14 U.S. Environmental Protection Agency (U.S. EPA), Good Laboratory Practices Standards--Toxicology Testing, Federal Register, 48 (1983) 53922.
15 Interdisciplinary Panel on Carcinogenicity, Science, 255 (1984) 682-687.
16 D.S. Strauss, J. Natl. Cancer Inst., 67 (1981) 233-241.
17 B.D. Crawford, in W.G. Flamm and R.J. Lorentzen (Editors), Advances in Modern Environmental Toxicology, Princeton Scientific, Princeton, NJ, U.S.A., 1985, pp. 13-59.
18 B.N. Ames, Science, 204 (1979) 587-593.
19 D.J. Berry and M.H. Litchfield, in J. Ashby et al. (Editors), Evaluation of Short-term Tests for Carcinogens: Report of the International Programme on Chemical Safety's Collaborative Study on in vitro Assays, Vol. 5 of Progress in Mutation Research Sercies, Elsevier, Amsterdam, 1985, pp. 727- 740.
20 R. Tennant, B. Margolin, M. Shelby, E. Zeiger, J.K. Haseman, J. Spalding, W. Caspary, M. Resnick, S. Stasiecoicz, B. Anderson, and R. Minor, Science, 236 (1987) 933-941.
21 J.K. Haseman, B.H. Margolih, M.D. Shelby, E. Zliger, and K.W. Tennant, Science, 241 (1988) 1232-1233.
22 L.S. Gold, L. Bernstein, R. Magaw, and T.H. Slone, Environ. Health Persp., 81 (1989) 211-219.
23 State of California, Health and Welfare Agency, Guidelines for Chemical Carcinogen Risk Assessments and Their Scientific Rationale, Department of Health Services, Berkeley, California, 1985.
24 J.M. Sontag, N.D. Page, U. Saffiotti, Guidelines for Carcinogenic Bioassay in Small Rodents, Bethesda, MD, U.S. National Cancer Institute, 1976.
25 H.P. Stu, D.J. Paustenbach, and F.J. Murray, Reg. Toxicol. & Pharmacol., 7 (1987) 57-88.
26 M. Gough, Risk Analysis, 8 (1988) 337-342.
27 World Health Organization (WHO), Procedures for Investigating International and Unintentional Food Additives, Tech. Report Series No. 348, WHO, Geneva, 1967.
28 World Health Organization (WHO), Risk Assessment (Proceedings of a seminar), Copenhagen, WHO, 1982.
29 World Health Organization (WHO), Evaluation of the Toxicity of a Number of Antimicrobials and Antioxidants, Sixth Report, Tech. Report Series No. 228, WHO, Geneva, 1962.
30 World Health Organization (WHO), Principles Governing Consumer Safety in Relation to Pesticide Residues, Report of a Joint FAO/WHO Meeting on Pesticide Residues, Tech. Report Series No. 240, WHO, Geneva, 1962.
31 Frank C. Lu, Reg. Toxicol. Pharmacol., 3 (1983) 121-132.
32 D.W. Layton, B.J. Mallon, D.H. Rosenblatt, and M.J. Small, Reg. Toxicol. Pharmacol., 7 (1987) 96-112.
33 R.J. Lewis and D.V. Sweet, Registry of Toxic Effects of Chemical Substances: 1983 Supplement to the 1981-1982 Edition, Publication 84-1002, Natl. Inst. of Occup. Safety and Health, Washington, D.C., 1984.
34 U.S. Environmental Protection Agency (U.S. EPA), Water Quality Criteria Documents: Availability, Fed. Regist., 45 (1980) 79313-79341.
35 U.S. Environmental Protection Agency (U.S. EPA), National Primary Drinking Water Regulations: Synthetic Organic Chemicals, Inorganic Chemicals, and Microorganisms, Fed. Regist., 50 (1985) 46936-47008.
36 N.A. Littlefield, J.H. Farmer, C.W. Gaylor, and W.G. Sheldon, J. Environ. Pathol. Toxicol., 3 (1979) 17-34.
37 SOT ED_{01} Task Force, Fundam. Appl. Toxicol., 1 (1981) 26-128.
38 N. Mantel, and W. Bryan, J. Natl. Cancer, Inst., 27 (1961) 455-470.
39 U.S. Federal Register, 42 (Feb. 1977) 10412-10437.
40 W.J. Vosek, Environ. Health Persp., 77 (1988) 49-54.
41 D.P. Rall, Species Differences in Carcinogenesis Testing, in H.H. Hiatt, J.D. Watson, and J.A. Winsten (Editors), Origins of Human Cancer, Book C, Human Risk Assessment, Cold Spring, Harbor Laboratory, NY, U.S.A., 1977, pp. 1383-1390.

42 M.C. Pike, in D.G. Hoel, R.A. Merrill, and F.P. Perera (Editors), in Risk Quantification and Regulatory Policy, Banbury Report No. 19, Cold Spring Harbor Laboratory, Cold Spring Harbor, New York, U.S.A., 1985, pp. 55-64.

43 I.F.H. Purchase, in d.g. Hoel, R.A. Merrill, and F.P. Perera (Editors), Risk Quantification and Regulatory Policy, Banbury Report No. 19, Cold Spring Harbor Laboratory, Cold Spring Harbor, New York, U.S.A., 1985, pp. 175-186.

44 E.J. Calabrese, Environ. Health Persp., 77 (1988) 55-62.

45 B.S. Drasar and M.J. Hill, in Human Intestinal Flora, Academic Press, New York, U.S.A., 1974, pp. 54-71.

46 K.S. Crump, D.G. Hoel, C.H. Langley, and R. Peto, Cancer Research, 36 (1976) 2973-2979.

47 H. Guess, K. Crump, and R. Peto, Cancer Research, 37 (1977) 3475-3483.

48 U.S. Food and Drug Administration and Federation of American Societies for Experimental Biology, Symposium on "Biological Bases for Interspecies Extrapolation of Carcinogenicity Data", in T.A. Hill, R.C. Wands, and R.W. Leukroth, Jr. (Editors), Environ. Health Persp., 77 (1988) 47-105.

49 J.K. Haseman and D.G. Hoel, J. Toxicol. Environ. Health, 5 (1979) 89-101.

50 U.S. National Academy of Sciences (NAS), Committee for a Study on Saccharin and Food Safety Policy - Part I. Saccharin: Technical Assessment of Risks and Benefits, NAS, Washington, D.C., U.S.A., 1978.

51 I.C. Munroe and D.R. Krewski, Fed. Cosmet. Toxicol., 19 (1981) 549-560.

52 E. Somers, Res. Toxicol. Pharmacol., 3 (1983) 75-81.

53 U.S. Environmental Protection Agency, Guidelines for Exposure Assessment, Federal Register, 51, No. 185 (1986) 34042-34054.

54 Fed. Regist., 50 (1985) 10372-10442.

55 M.A. Callahan, G.L. Dixon, S.H. Nacht, D.A. Dixon, and J.J. Doria, "Methods for Assessing Exposure to Chemical Substances", Vol. 1, U.S. EPA Exposure Evaluation Division, Office of Toxic Substances, Washington, D.C., U.S.A., EPA 560/5-85-001, 1985, 106 pp.

56 J.E. Davis, Res. Dev., 75 (1980) 33-50.

57 D.J. Severn, Environ. Sci. Technol., 21 (1987) 1159-1163.

58 J.C. Reinert, et al., Toxicol. Lett., 33 (1986) 183-191.

59 D.J. Paustenbach, in D.J. Paustenbach (Editor), The Risk Assessment of Environmental and Human Health Hazards: A Textbook of Case Studies, John Wiley & Sons, New York, U.S.A., 1989, pp. 27-124.

60 C.N. Park and R.D. Snee, Amer. Stat., 37 (1983) 427-441.

61 W.G. Flamm and J.S. Winbush, Fundam. Appl. Toxicol., 4 (1984) S395-S401.

62 S. Friess, History of Risk Assessment in Pharmacokinetics of Risk Assessment: Drinking Water and Health, Vol. 8, National Academy of Science, Washington, D.C., 1987.

63 D. Krewski, C. Brown, and D. Murdoch, Fundam. Appl. Toxicol., 4 (1984) S383-S394.

64 Food Safety Council, Food Cosmet. Toxicol., 18 (1980) 711-734.

65 K.S. Crump, D.G. Hoel, C. Longley, and R. Peto, Cancer Res., 36 (1976) 2973-2979.

66 D.B. Menzel, Environ. Sci. Technol., 21 (1987) 944-950.

67 J. Van Ryzin, J. Occup. Med., 22 (1980) 321-326.

68 D. Krewski and J. Van Ryzin, in M. Csorgo, D. Dawson, J.M. Rao, and E. Saleh (Editors), Statistics and Related Topics, Elsevier/North Holland Inc., Amsterdam, 1981, pp. 201-231.

69 R.L. Sielken, Jr., Environ. Sci. Technol., 21 (1987) 1033-1039.

70 R. Wilson and E.A.C. Crouch, Science, 236 (1987) 267-270.

71 B.N. Ames, R. MaGaw, and L.S. Gold, Science, 230 (1987) 271-280.

72 B.A. Owens and T.D. Jones, Reg. Toxicol. & Pharmacol., 11 (1990) 132-148.

73 U.S. Fed. Regist., 42 (Mar. 1977) 14640-14659.

Chapter 9

REGULATORY DECISION-MAKING PROCESS

The protection of the environment and human health depend upon pollution control and abatement strategies. General improvements in the environmental quality to date have occurred as a result of adequate control and abatement strategies for hazardous chemicals.

Decision makers ensure environmental protection through the development of various acts and legislations. These are then enforced through federal, provincial, and local regulatory agencies. The developers of legislation and acts must ensure that the information which they use are sufficient to protect human health and the environment; in many cases the data are drawn from standardized procedures which evaluate the effects of chemical on relevant environmental components. This approach also provides comparable, replicable, and reliable data through good laboratory practices which ensures that the information is legally defensible and enforceable.

Risk assessment and risk management are both elements of the decision-making process. The management aspect of risk encompasses various activities that are necessary to reach decisions regarding different levels of the estimated risk. This is followed by the communication of the estimated risk to the affected public, and finally the determination of the risk that is acceptable to the affected community.

9.1 STRENGTH AND BOUNDARY OF INFORMATION

In the past two decades, there has been changes in the attitudes and approaches of scientists, administrators, and the public towards the environmental protection. The publics have been concerned about the quality of the environment as a whole because of the possible risks from the indiscriminate uses of chemicals both industrially and domestically. Thus, the demand from the public has been towards the decision makers to develop adequate and enforceable standards that will protect both the environment and human health from the hazards of these chemicals.

In developing an environmental standard, the decision makers must ensure that the information that was used to make the decisions was scientifically sound and statistically valid, and was at a level of quality that will provide maximum possible protection to the environment and humans. In certain cases where the properties of the chemical might indicate that it is highly persistent, and permeates into more than one environmental compartment, it is possible that multi-tier and multi-media testing might follow in order to determine its critical pathways of exposure and possible health risks.

Variations in mandatory test results for a given chemical for a prescribed test organism are commonly reported in the literature. These tests include both acute and chronic toxicity tests. The former is represented by LC_{50} values and the latter by the onset of chronic or long-term effects.

It is likely that inconsistencies occur because of differences in experimental techniques or possibly due to type, stage, or age of the organisms that was used or using different toxic endpoints for adverse effects.

Data used in decision making are usually obtained through various toxic endpoints such as non-aquatic species testing, aquatic toxicity testing, epidemiological studies and human health considerations from extrapolations of animal studies. With regards to information collected through aquatic toxicity testing: (i) it is desirable that numerous data points are obtained, (ii) data are obtained for several phylogenic levels both from the freshwater and marine environments, and (iii) both chronic and acute toxicity information, should be acquired. The use of multi-tier testing might possibly reduce or eliminate most of the false-positive and false-negative inferences about the effect of the chemical under testing.

Full scale chronic studies should be conducted when the results from the initial acute and subchronic testing are not conclusive. Test procedures should adhere to good laboratory practices and follow the established protocols in order that the test results can be compared to those from other related studies. In certain cases, data might often include embryo-larval or egg-fry exposure studies; these are usually inexpensive and often provide information on the sensitive early-life stages of the test species.

Within the aquatic environment, the movement of toxicants could be variable. Very few will remain in the water column indefinitely. They may accumulate in the biota, dissipate into the atmosphere, bind to the sediment or suspended solids or be degraded. As a result, it is essential to quantify the fate processes that are critical at the sediment-water interface to determine the longevity of the chemical contamination of the aquatic system. The sediment-bound toxicant could be benign in nature until biotic or abiotic processes (such as physical disturbances or leaching due to changes in the chemistry of this water column) change its characteristics.

Physical and chemical properties will influence the fate of the substance and will permit comparison to similar group of substances or family of compounds. Solubility of the chemicals together with its vapour pressure will provide information regarding its residence time in the water column. Octanol/water partition coefficient tends to correlate with the bioavailability of the chemical. For most chemicals with low water solubility and high octanol water partition coefficient, association with suspended solids and bottom sediments are significant removal processes from the bulk water. Other environmental fate processes such as photolysis, oxidation, hydrolysis, and reduction are integral parts of an assessment of the chemical.

For various chemicals, tests might be required using non-aquatic species as test organisms, particularly if carcinogenicity is suspected. These tests are usually quite expensive and are time-consuming. Short-term procedures using a bacterial test (Ames test - Salmonella typhimurium) together with in vitro cytogenetic assay or sister-chromatid exchange test should predict the potential for carcinogenicity. Depending upon the strength of the predictivity of the battery of tests, confirmation might be required using whole rodent species to carry out long-term carcinogenic bioassays.

Based on the use pattern of the chemical, epidemiological data could be valuable in the assessment. However, the critical and difficult to control variables must be taken into consideration in order that valid results are obtained. Epidemiological studies are difficult and expensive to carry out and in many cases, it might not have predictive capability because of after-the-effect analytical approach.

The information from chronic or life-cycle studies should also allow for the protection of both the reproductive processes and offsprings of various living organisms. If there are egg failures or effects on the viability of the sperm, then, possibly the species could be eliminated. Insufficient data could result in the development of protective standards that are not adequate to control physiological stresses to certain species making them less competitive or lethargic, leading to gradual decline of a population. Even the elimination of species that might appear insignificant, such as some small aquatic insect or crustacean could ultimately affect other members of a biological chain because of the dependence of higher members of the food chain upon the lower members as a food source.

9.2 RISK COMMUNICATION

Experts and managers are coming to recognize that the manner in which people perceive a risk determines how they respond to it, which in turn, sets the context for public participation and input into the final decision. It is hard to have proper guidelines when the public ignores serious risks and recoils in terror from less serious ones. The task of risk communication, then, is not just conveying information, although that alone is a challenge, but it is to alert people when they ought to be alerted and reassure them when they ought be reassured (ref. 1). Whatever the job concerns, it is important to clearly outline and explain the environmental risk to the public who are likely to be affected.

Risk statements about chemical that are presented to the public through many media. Some of these media include newspaper, radio, television, mail, meetings, presentations, magazines, pamphlets, films, and audio and video presentations. The two most influential and powerful of all of the mentioned methods of communicating information, however, are the print and television media. Also, the manner in which the information that concerns the public is presented determines the public's reaction. For example, range and accuracy of analytical equipments is breaking new barriers and, as such, ultra-traces of a chemical can be detected in a system. The public does not realize that present-day equipments are capable of measuring background levels that have been present but undetected in the environment for a long time. The public's view of risk is affected by their attitude towards science and technology. A well-informed society might be able to understand the scientific and technical aspects of a particular situation and offer suggestions.

The way in which members of the public perceive risk has been influenced by their intense interest towards good health and longevity. Health has been seen in the United States as being consistently more important politically than any other entity such as clean water, clean air or the preservation of forests or the earth's crust (ref. 2). The Toxic Substances Control Act (TSCA) which was generated to inform the government of the products developed by the chemical industry, was ultimately enacted and shaped as a health-protecting legislation.

The public has been requesting more direct participation in consultative functions of the regulatory process. This indicates that people are more aware of decisions that are being made for them by government, and, in many cases, they prefer to have more input in those decisions. Public awareness about environmental quality has been steadily increasing. As a result, they maintain a reasonable understanding about the various chemicals released into the environment, and the potential impacts associated with these chemicals. In instances, however, where they may not understand the technical information, they are usually provided with some type of monetary support that enables the hiring of independent experts capable of answering and/or explaining in detail, questions and technical details that may enable the public's understanding.

Risk Comparison

Risk comparison has been used to compare the risk of a chemical to that of other substances or possible activities. Because comparisons are perceived to be more intuitively meaningful than absolute probabilities, it is widely believed that it can be used effectively in communicating information about chemical risks and other hazards (ref. 3).

Risk comparison has been used increasingly because it appears to be compatible with intuitive, natural thought processes such as analogies; it avoids difficult and controversial tasks of converting diverse risk into a common unit (e.g., dollars per life lost or per day of pain and suffering); and it avoids direct numerical references to small probabilities, which can be difficult to comprehend and evaluate in the abstract (ref. 4).

Risk comparison has been of interest to government, industry and consultative groups who initially required the use of quantitative information to communicate the possible risks of certain chemicals to the public. The initial methods resulted in lack of understanding of the interpretation by the public who perceived: (i) the regulatory agencies and industry to be uninterested in their concerns, (ii) delays by regulatory bodies to initiate solution towards chemical risks, and (iii) reluctancy to foster participation of the public in activities that might be affecting them.

There are two basic types of risk comparison: comparison of risk of diverse activities and the comparison of risk of similar activities (ref. 3). The comparison of risk of diverse activities involve comparing the risk of a new or existing chemical or activity to that of a diverse set of chemicals and/or activities. An example of this type of risk comparison is when chemicals and their processes are compared to the risks of smoking, driving, flying, dietary habits such as drinking diet soft drinks and eating charcoal boiled steaks (ref. 5a). The second type of risk comparison of similar activities involves comparing the risk of a new or existing chemical or activity to that of a similar set of chemical or activities; for example, the comparison of the risks of consuming natural foods to foods that contain chemical additives and pesticide residues (ref. 6).

Risk comparisons and contrasts are performed sometimes to denote the different manner in which they are treated. An example is the comparison of the carcinogenic effects of aflatoxin B1 and dioxin. "They have similar toxicities and carcinogenic potency (perhaps within a factor of 10, although both measures for both chemicals vary substantially with species tested). The certainty of information for aflatoxin is great. There is less information about carcinogenicity of dioxin. Dioxin may be a promoter and pose a minuscule risk at low doses, whereas aflatoxin is almost certainly an initiator also. Nonetheless, such standards as these appear to be more stronger for dioxin, possibly because dioxin is an artificial chemical and possibly because it was a trace component of a chemical mixture (Agent Orange) that was used in warfare." (ref. 5b).

There are several important limitations of the risk comparison approach. These include: (1) failure to identify and emphasize uncertainties involved in the calculation of comparative risk estimates; (2) failure to consider the broad set of quantitative dimensions that define and measure risk; and (3) failure to consider the broad set of qualitative dimensions that underlie people's concerns about the acceptability of technologies and associated risks (ref. 3). Other limitations include: (1) failing to consider the likelihood for the reduction, redistribution, and/or the mitigation of risk; (2) excluding the costs and benefits of available technological alternatives; and (3) not accounting for the needs and concerns of peoples' education, occupation, employment status, environmental preferences, and other relevant characteristics.

Notwithstanding the limitations outlined above, risk comparisons that are well constructed and well documented can help put risk into perspective and effectively communicate risk information (ref. 7). They can provide a benchmark against which the magnitude of new or unfamiliar risks can be compared, and they also help inform people about the range and magnitude of risks to which they are exposed (ref. 3).

Public Information and Involvement

When dealing with the public, the regulating agency should ensure that communication is a two-way process and that with ethical standards are complied with (ref. 8). The regulatory intention should be clearly outlined and should not be hidden within the message (ref. 9). These activities are not easy to carry out. When an agency's representative is confronted with a difficult or incriminating question from the public, the normal type of reaction is that of defence and the reply is usually camouflaged. Instead, if there is still uncertainty about the risk, it should be expressed indicating that the agency might require more time to assess the data. Although this type of message may not be very positive, it is honest and open and allows for correction or justification at a later date.

The public is made up of a cross-section of people from many different social and educational backgrounds. The message must, therefore, be simple and should be transmitted early in the process, allowing for all segments to understand what is being transmitted before individual becomes disinterested. Details including inferences and valued statements and explanation should be left for the latter part of the process. This style of presentation will satisfy a broad spectrum of the population. The well educated segment which requires more details including technical data and analysis will be able to obtain them later on in the presentation. When simplifying the presentation, special precautions should be taken to ensure that the message is still accurate. This would prevent possible misinterpretations that might occur.

The communication programs should be designed with the receivers in mind. It should be developed to suit the needs of the audience. Most experts who are attempting to design a communication program usually include too much technical details. It should be remembered that the public does not have the desire nor the time to become experts; instead, they require the information and understanding of consequences of risk, the circumstance of its occurrence, the measures to mitigate the risk and the management efforts proposed by the respective regulatory body. Depending on the risk category, the public would want more information about accident or spill management and emergency planning if low-probability high consequence technologies are involved; they would be looking for information on risk distribution and potential health effects for man-made, but routine risk events (such as pollution), and would be concerned about consequences of diffuse risk for future generation such as the greenhouse effects or radioactive waste disposal (ref. 9).

A good communication program should be designed to address different receivers through different transmitters. It should also use different channels of communication with programs designed to suit the type of receivers being addressed. Many regulatory agencies use press releases as a major mode of communication, but there are other ways such as press conferences, public hearings, open letters, and public information brochures. Some of these methods such as press conferences and public hearings receive immediate feedback from the receiver so that the clarifications and recommendations could be addressed on the spot, while other more passive methods such as letters require more time to review and incorporate public's requests and concerns. Although various packages may carry the same message, the method of communication could be different. For instance, manuscripts for scientific columns in newspapers should be more problem-oriented and should often contain various perspectives regarding the analyses of the risk, while a message in the form a of press release would contain more basic facts and some discussion of results.

The message should be well planned and designed in order to include a well tuned balance of facts, inferences, evaluation, and figures. In order to communicate risk effectively, all relevant evidence and factual information should be presented. The procedure and rationale of reaching a conclusion on the basis of the presented evidence is often more important than the inference itself (ref. 10). In many cases, people might disagree with the outlined evidence, however, they could still accept the outcome if the explanations and inferences were reasonable and meet their requirements.

It is important to be honest, open-minded, understanding, and responsive during the message presentation. Honesty may not instantly be rewarded, however, it is a vital condition for the gaining of credibility. Dishonesty on the other hand will, sooner or later, be revealed and will certainly create repercussions and distrust among both transmitters and receivers. In addition to honesty and completeness, information should be responsive to public demands and inquiries. Transmitters expect fast responses and the public likes to be informed immediately after a hazardous event has occurred or after a new study with debatable results has been published (refs. 9,10).

The results of the risk communication processes and activities are difficult to assess and impossible to measure, however, the feeback that is obtained from the receivers usually produce a few indications of the success of the program. At times, it might appear that the receivers may not agree with decisions regarding trade-offs, setting of priorities, or the selection of management options but with a well-planned and well-executed program they may realize that the chosen decisions were agreed upon as a result of open discussions, and well-scrutinized trade-off negotiations.

Possible Guidelines

There are no easy ways that will guarantee successful risk communication. Methods should include, however, a broad concept of risk and continual communication between the transmitters and the receivers. Table 9.1 outlines the seven cardinal rules of risk communication which tend to apply equally well to the public and private sectors. Although many of the rules may seem obvious, they are continually and consistently ignored in practice. The goal of risk communication is to produce an informed public that is involved, interested, reasonable, thoughtful, solution oriented, and collaborative; it should not be to diffuse public concerns or replace action (ref. 11).

9.3 PUBLIC PARTICIPATION IN RISK MANAGEMENT

Risk management issues have become matter of great interest and importance to society as a whole. Industrial accidents such as the Exxon Valdez oil spill, chemical leak in Bhopal, Chernobyl nuclear disaster, and the PCB fire in Quebec affected the public confidence regarding industrial controls and safety in many ways. They have led to the creation of public fear regarding the risk of various industrial and technological developments to both human health and the environment.

TABLE 9.1 Seven cardinal rules of risk communications.

RISK COMMUNICATION	CONSIDERATIONS AND GUIDELINES

RULES

1. Accept and involve the public as a legitimate partner	- Demonstrate respect for public; - Involve the community early before important decisions are made; - Involve stakeholders; - Emphasize sincerity of effort.
2. Plan carefully and evaluate effort	- Begin with clear objectives; - Evaluate risk information; - Know strength and weaknesses; - Classify and segment audience; - Recruit good spokespeople; - Train staff in communication skills; - Pretest effort; - Evaluate efforts and learn from mistakes.
3. Listen to the publics' specific concerns	- Listen carefully and attentively; - Take time to find out what people are thinking; - Use techniques such as interviews, surveys, etc. - Identify with audience; - Recognize peoples' emotions and hidden agendas.
4. Be honest, frank, and open	- State credentials; - If you don't know, say so; - Get back with answers; - Admit mistakes; - Disclose risk information; - Speculate with great caution; - Discuss data uncertainties, strengths and/or weaknesses; - Identify worst-case estimates.
5. Coordinate and collaborate with other credible sources	- Develop good working relationships; - Coordinate with other organizations; - Use credible and authoritative intermediaries; - Use the best qualified authority.
6. Meet the needs of the media	- Be open and accessible to reporters; - Respect deadlines; - Provide risk information tailored to media needs; - Prepare and provide background material; - Establish long-term relationship of trust.

Continued . . . .

430

Table 9.1 Concluded.

RISK COMMUNICATION	CONSIDERATIONS AND GUIDELINES
7. Speak clearly and with comparison	- Use simple non-technical language; - Use vivid, concrete images that communicate on a personal level; - Avoid distant, unfeeling languages about deaths, injuries and illnesses; - Acknowledge and respond to emotions that people express; - Acknowledge and respond to the distinctions that public view as important in evaluating risk; - Use risk comparisons; - Discuss actions that are underway or can be taken; - Tell people what you cannot do; - Promise only what you can do.

(Source: ref. 11).

In the last decade, there has been an increased environmental awareness. Well organized and informed group of environmentalists now represent all sectors and professions of society. These groups have enhanced their capacity to identify, analyze, articulate, and manage their concerns with exceptional effectiveness both at the technical and political levels. Environmental issues, particularly those pertaining to public health and safety are now viewed as important social issues, and the public has taken the step towards action through well organized proactive groups. The results of these activities have led to the development of new or updated legislations and regulatory changes towards environmental management. Both government and industry find themselves having to listen to the public and include the public into their decision-making processes.

Choosing Participants

Participants should include interest groups and individuals who are likely to be affected or influenced by the proposed developmental activity. Limits set on public involvement may be crucial towards the assesssment of risk and the assignment of priorities to this risk; for example, people living near the location of a controversial facility are likely to view risk in a significantly different way from others living farther away, who might be more anxious about abstract environmental concerns that may not be an issue to residents living within proximity of the facility.

The public is also concerned about choosing the most effective method of representation in order to express their views and concerns. Interest groups are, in some cases, disorganized, and the lead role might be taken by an individual who might not be representing the need of the community that is likely to be affected or might be at risk. This can lead to the group ignoring issues that are most relevant to the potentially affected community.

It is essential to include a representative cross-section of the community. This would ensure that vocal special interest individuals or groups do not obsecure the community which would like to express as a whole. The public should be represented in terms of age, sex, education, professional status, income and place and length of residence in the area of concern.

Being present is not representation; it means that at some points the representatives will have to be vocal in a meeting. In such cases, numbers have to be limited, and, it is of prime importance that the chosen speakers deliver messages from the publics' point of view and not their personal views. One way to identify participants for dialogue is to look for community leaders or "influentials". It is essential to include all public or special interest groups as they emerge, since most of those citizens or agencies who desire to be involved seek an organization of like-minded people (ref. 12). However, seeking influentials may fail to deal with those who have not yet emerged as vocal participants but have a stake in the outcome of the involvement process (ref. 13). For this reason, it might be justified to include in the group of representative individuals selected at random from various sectors of the community in question. Furthermore, in order to ensure that all concerns are expressed by the affected community, it is important to request input from the attendees during an allotted period of the meeting or hearing.

Participatory Approaches

There are various approaches available to encourage community participation. Most of these are expensive and they consume a great deal of time and requires a lot of patience and virtue. There is no single mechanism to encourage the public to participate. The methods to be used, however should depict the particular needs of the community. It should encourage information exchange, develop consensus building, and show definite interest in representing the concerns of the public that are actually at risk.

Grima (ref. 14) have identified three main approaches to participation, defined according to the manner in which public should be brought into a process. First, he distinguishes participation through the election or appointment of public representatives to different level of the decision-making appratus (public and private) and to administrative bodies, so they may influence the decision making and management processes. This approach by Grima is similar to the participation that is produced through one of Edmond's (ref. 15) types of actions and decisions. He indicated that the legislation should provide the best institutional form for public participation because it enables the public to participate through its representatives. He noted that in the best of cases, national commissions of enquiry could be set up through parliamentary commissions listening to concerns of representatives from major organizations. This type of participation through public representation on advisory councils and consultative committees readily lends itself to cooptation, to the overrepresentation of experts and accredited organizations, and sometimes to manipulation (ref. 16).

The second type (ref. 14) was noted as being legal actions and requests for judicial review of administrative decisions. This approach to participation is similar to Edmond's action regarding formal quasi-judicial procedures and arbitration in order to provide the most effective arenas for public participation. He further indicated that policy implementation decisions involving primarily technical and economic consideration generally gave rise to questions of justice, fairness, or legitimacy. This types of participation, however, is reactive and defensive, involving a restricted public which must demonstrate its direct interest in the issue (ref. 16).

Finally, Grima (ref. 14) dealt with specific mechanisms of participation in decision making, including public consultation and public hearing. He indicated that these are supported by education and information and tend to constitute direct, non-discriminatory relations with the public, within a process leading to a decision or an action.

Another definition of participation outlines that the affected public should be involved in the process of formulating the specific policies, programs, and projects that affect their lives (ref. 17). Participation in this case is restricted to only the public that are to be directly affected, therefore, it also requires a motive for the purpose of involvement.

Participation can be considered also as an instrument for the resolution of conflict (ref. 18). It consists of the recognition of conflict, common identification of legitimate disagreements and the planning of solutions on a community basis with the involvement of all participants. This is considered as a means of community development involving collectivity before individual interests.

There is no single method or approach towards public involvement that would satisfy all the requirements for information exchange, consensus building, consultation and interest involvement. It would be beneficial to apply various techniques in order to arrive at a workable solution. Some of these include door-to-door campaigning, public meetings, task forces, telecommunications, workshops, hearings, petitions, and dog and pony shows. In all cases, however, techniques should enhance consensus and understanding, encourage dialogue, feedback, display flexibility and ensure honesty.

Generally, public participation should be voluntary, however, the agency should render no condition or attempts to misinform the public. The following principles should be taken into consideration during the design and execution of a public information program (ref. 19):
- the process must be capable of meeting the publics' needs;
- the process has to be open and responsive;
- the risk must be fully defined and explained with directions and honesty;
- all publics should receive equal treatment;
- public should be allowed to choose the methods of communication with regulatory agencies;
- public should be involved early in the process;
- the process should be flexible and should provide for the exchange of information between participants;
- participation should occur in a climate of trust and cooperation;
- participation should be integrated with decision making; and
- public participation process should not only meet the publics' needs but it should also appear to meet publics' needs.

Intervenor Groups

The groups that are referred to as the public are socially diversified and are composed of individuals from various social and economical backgrounds. These people would have different levels of education and political affiliations. The publics that are involved in the decision-making process, today, usually do so through intervenor groups which are composed of representatives who are well informed, more politicized, aware of current events, and forceful regarding opposition or modification to technological development. Also, included under this category are traditional conservationists, various professional societies and the established interest groups of environmentalists.

These groups have developed various techniques to attract the attention of both the public and media. These groups are able to attract the support of prominent intellectuals who devote both time and resources in developing their positions.

In some cases, public interest groups are developed for a particular cause, such as the construction of a highway or a dam and life of these groups are usually short (a few months). Generally, decisions regarding policy and standards-setting usually involve the groups that have been established for a fairly long time such as nationally-and internationally-based environmental groups. The group or individuals that are considred the public, however, are usually specialized in the area of expertise that is required for that specific negotiation. These meetings are usually well organized, but it does not mean that the agreement that is negotiated will be accepted by all publics. It is always very difficult to obtain a decision that will be acceptable to all publics.

Intervenor groups have changed with time. The ones with "radical" attitudes have developed into well-trained and experienced negotiators who are aware of the essentials of the regulatory decision-making and standards-setting processes. They have become effective spokespersons through experience and have learned the need for making realistic compromises in order to achieve their desired goals.

Intervenor groups have not only been able to provide their own expertise, but they have been known to utilize the skills of experts who have been sympathetic to their cause. The presence of competent professionals on both sides have led to rational compromization and solutions acceptable to both parties.

Public participation, like any other program could have additional or unforeseen concerns that were not originally anticipated; misconception and errors in judgement could arise that were not expected and participating groups or publics may require more support or information. It is possible to monitor for these shortcomings through several techniques such as reply letters or cards, surveys, and public meetings.

9.4 CONTROL STRATEGIES AND OPTIONS

The choice of a strategy and/or option regarding the control of a particular chemical depends on both its chemical and physical properties, methods of commercial production, its effects on human health and environment, and its ability to degrade and bioaccumulate. Information gathered from initial assessments of the chemical will assist towards a decision regarding the strategy or option for its production, use, and disposal. The following are possible strategies or options:

- No restrictions regarding production, usage, and disposal;
- Restricted use;
- Treatment and disposal practices; and

- Technological options;
- Ban on production and usage.

Control strategies during the production of a chemical are also good environmental practices, towards safety and environmental housekeeping. It minimizes risk and maximizes protection to both human health and the environment.

9.4.1 No restrictions

Following the assessment and evaluation of a chemical, the decision is made regarding its use and disposal practices. Areas covered include: evaluation of safety, benefits, estimation of exposure levels to target systems, effects on humans and the environment, persistence, accumulative and magnification capabilities, and its social and economic implications. Comparisons are also carried out with chemicals of the same family and those of similar chemical structure. If the chemical is acceptable on the above requirements and appears to be safe for use, it could be released with no restrictions.

Although a chemical might be classified as being safe for use, there is always a possibility that there might have been potential gaps and errors in the initial assessment. When the final stage of production and distribution is reached, there should be reasonable and proper assurance of reliability. If, however, there remains a degree of uncertainty, it is essential that appropriate follow-up programs such as monitoring and further research be maintained in order to detect any adverse effects that might have been unavailable or overlooked during the initial assessment.

9.4.2 Restricted use

Polychlorinated biphenyl (PCB) compounds are non-flammable, thermally stable and, electrically non-conducting oils, and hence have been widely used as heat transfer fluids in electrical transformers. Previous to the revelation of its toxicity and persistence, there has been accidental leakages, deliberate dumping, and careless handling of PCBs. As a result, substantial quantities have entered both the terrestrial and aquatic environment, and on occasions, contamination occurred by atmospheric transport (ref. 20). This substance has been found to be acutely toxic to aquatic life at low parts per billion. It has been shown to be bioaccumulative and persistent resulting in lethal doses to many birds which subsist in aquatic biota. Environmental contamination of PCBs is a non-point source and exemplifies the original lack of thorough investigation and inadequate disposal and treatment options. Presently, however, many countries have severely restricted the use of PCBs.

9.4.3 Risk reduction

Table 9.2 illustrates the general strategies for reducing damage from environmental hazards (ref. 21). These strategies encompass approaches that

TABLE 9.2 Ten general strategies for reducing damage from environmental hazards hazards; each is illustrated by three examples.

---

1. Prevent the creation of the hazard in the first place.
    Examples: prevent production of plutonium, thalidomide, LSD.

2. Reduce the amount of hazard brought into being.
    Examples: reduce speed of vehicles, lead content of paint, mining of asbestos.

3. Prevent relapse of the hazard that already exists.
    Examples: pasteurizing milk, bolting or timbering mine roofs, impounding nuclear wastes.

4. Modify the rate of spatial distribution of release of the hazard from its source.
    Examples: brakes, shutoff valves, reactor control rods.

5. Separate in time or space, the hazard and that which is to be protected.
    Examples: isolation of persons with communicable diseases, walkways over or around hazards, evacuation.

6. Separate the hazard and that which is to be protected by interposition of a material barrier.
    Examples: surgeons' gloves, containment structures, childproof poison-container closures.

7. Modify relevant basic qualities of the hazard.
    Examples: altering pharmacological agents to reduce side effects, using breakaway roadside poles, making crib slat spacings too naroow to strangle a child.

8. Make what is to be protected more resistant to damage from the hazard.
    Examples: immunization, making structures more fire and earthquake resistant, giving salt to workers under thermal stress.

9. Begin to counter the damage already done by the environmental hazard.
    Examples: rescuing the shipwrecked, re-attaching severed limbs, extricating trapped miners.

10. Stabilize, repair, and rehabilitate the object of the damage.
    Examples: post-traumatic cosmetic surgery, physical rehabilitation, rebuilding after fire and earthquakes.

(Source: Reprinted with permission from ref. 21).

are usable for the reduction of damage from any environmental hazards, and they are capable of forming the foundation for the consideration of available options for the reduction of risk.

Other options include mass and energy balance which focusses on residuals, i.e., leftovers from varius consumptive and productive activities, and the process that may be executed to change or adapt these residuals so that they could be used for various situations. These residuals are usually known quantities and their uses avert the development of new and unknown products.

There are difficulties with determining which data set to use in calculating the risk reduction and how to weigh the data set that is used (ref. 22). Studies on the health effects of urea formaldehyde points out such contrarieties. A few controlled group studies revealed no significant increases in the risk towards adverse effects but on the other hand, uncontrolled studies indicated a potential health risk (ref. 23). It would be logical to consider the results of the controlled studies in front of those from the uncontrolled experiments because of possible methodological differences and biases.

9.4.4 Technological options

Other options include: technological developments that could reduce or virtually eliminate discharge of toxic chemicals in effluents from entering into the environment. These options would include the use of various scrubbers and filters, recycling and reusing water, incineration of waste as a method of generation energy, changes in engineering designs and other techniques that could prove beneficial to both industry and the environment.

TABLE 9.3 Treatment technologies for removal of inorganics[*].

CONTAMINANT	TREATMENT METHOD	REMOVAL PERCENTAGE	RELATIVE TREATMENT COSTS[**] CENTS/1000 GALLONS		
			0.3 mgd	1.0 mgd	50 mgd
Arsenic					
As V (Arsenate)	AC/F, pH 6-7	90	175	44	19
	IC/F, pH 6-8	90	175	44	19
	Excess LS	90	305	63	40
	Activated alumina, pH 5-6	95	122	62	51
	IE	90	83	51	42
	RO	90	332	164	129

Continued . . . .

438

TABLE 9.3 Continued.

CONTAMINANT	TREATMENT METHOD	REMOVAL PERCENTAGE	RELATIVE TREATMENT COSTS** CENTS/1000 GALLONS		
			0.3 mgd	1.0 mgd	50 mgd
As III (Arsenite)	Oxidations of As III to As V and use same treatment list for As V				
Asbestos	Conventional Filtration	95	141	54	19
	Direct Filtration	95	113	40	13
	Diatomaceous Earth Filtration	95	143	74	35
Barium	IE	90	80	44	22
	LS, pH 11	95	-	63	41
	RC	95	318	201	121
Cadmium	IE	90	80	44	22
	Excess LS	90	-	59	41
	RO	90	318	201	121
	IC/F, above pH 8	80	142	54	18
Chromium					
Cr III (Trivalent)	IC/F, pH 6-9	90-98	146	55	19
	AC/F, pH 7-9	90-98	146	55	19
	Excess LS	98	-	59	41
	IE	90	51	29	15
	RO	92	318	201	121
Cr VI (Hexavalent)	Ferrous sulphate coagulation/filtration, pH 7-9.5	90	146	55	19
	IE	90	80	52	32
	RO	90	318	201	121
Copper	IE	95	80	44	22
	LS	90	-	59	41
	RO	95	318	201	121
	AC/F	50	140	54	18
Fluoride	Activated alumina, pH 5.5	90	47	27	14
	RO	90	206	121	67
	LS	65	-	59	41

Continued . . . .

TABLE 9.3 Concluded.

CONTAMINANT	TREATMENT METHOD	REMOVAL PERCENTAGE	RELATIVE TREATMENT COSTS** CENTS/1000 GALLONS		
			0.3 mgd	1.0 mgd	50 mgd
Lead	IC/F, pH 6-9	95	175	44	19
	AC/F, pH 6-9	95	175	44	19
	Lime or excess LS	97	298	60	40
	IE	95	92	36	23
	RO	95	332	164	129
	Direct filtration	60	134	33	13
Mercury					
Inorganic	LS, above pH 10.5	90	-	59	41
	Granular activated carbon	95	152	59	21
	RO	85	318	201	121
Organic	Coagulation/filtration with PAC	50-75	219	94	37
	Granular activated carbon	95	152	59	21
Nitrate	IE (anion resin)	90	111	75	48
	RO	90	318	201	121
Nitrite	Breakpoint chlorination	90	5	3	1
	IE (anion resin)	90	117	85	59
	RO	90	318	201	121
Selenium					
Se IV (Tetravalent)	IC/F, pH 5.5-7	80	245	78	22
	Activated alumina	95	78	43	23
	RO	75-99	368	228	134
	LS	50	-	64	41
Se VI (Hexavalent)	Activated alumina	95	391	305	232
	RO	75-99	368	228	134
Silver	Ferric sulphate coagulation/filtration, pH 7-9	80	140	54	18
	AC/F, pH 6-8	80	140	54	18
	Lime of excess LS	85	-	59	41
	RO	90	318	201	121
	Direct filtration	60	90	33	11

*   Data derived from draft "Technology and Cost" documents prepared for EPA by V.J. Ciccone & Associates, Inc.
**   Based on constructing new facilities; costs may be lower if existing facilities may be upgraded or optimized.
AC/F = Alum coagulation/filtration; IC/F = Iron coagulation/filtration; LS = Lime softening; IE = Ion exchange; RO = Reverse osmosis.
(Source: ref. 24).

9.4.4 Ban on production and usage

There is also the option of a total ban on production or usage of certain chemicals. An example is dichlorodiphenyl-trichloroethane (DDT) which is a chlorinated hydrocarbon pesticide that is no longer permitted for general use in several countries. This particular pesticide is very persistent, bioaccumulative and is also biologically magnified.

The extremely heavy use of DDT during World War II resulted in the wide spread contamination at trace quantities throughout the world, and because of its persistence, it could persist for a relatively long period of time. DDT has been linked to the declines in certain species of wildlife, thinning of eggshell, etc.

Environmental Safety Evaluation

The Environmental Safety Program is developed to control the quality of a new product that might be released for commercial use.

Initially, the new chemical receives a feasibility study to determine whether it is marketable, economically feasible, and safe to human health and the environment. The safety programs itself incorporates several phases including full toxicological assessments, physico-chemical property evaluation, marketing and economic analysis in order to justify commercial production. At the end of each phase, a decision regarding its acceptance or rejection is made before proceeding to another.

Many products may fail the initial screening because of either a problem with commercial viability or their environmental acceptability. On the other hand, if the product passes the preliminary screening and a decision is made towards its commercialization, both an initial safety audit and a safety assessment schedule is prepared. Safety assessment schedule would include a comprehensive plan outlining studies on physical, and chemical data, description of use patterns, exposure potential toxicological and environmental details and disposal routes and practices that might be required in order to satisfy a final safety audit. Table 9.4 outlines details of a typical safety evaluation program for a new product. These audits are usually conducted by various regulatory departments that might be responsible for its utility and licensing. Some of these include departments of the environment, health and welfare, occupational health, and possibly agriculture.

This safety evaluation schedule provides a step-by-step outline of the plans involved in the assessment of the new product. Tests are scheduled to determine as early as possible the adverse effects of the chemical. Less expensive acute toxicity testing and short-term carcinogenicity testing are carried out prior to expensive chronic and long-term studies, and the latter

TABLE 9.4 A safety evaluation schedule outlining details that might be required in order to test a chemical that might be commercially produced.

PHASE	STUDIES	TEST DETAILS	DURATION
Initial Screening	Acute toxicity	LC_{50}, LD_{50}	24-96 hours
	Aquatic toxicity	Fish, invertebrates, and algae	24-96 hours
Hazard Detection	Short-term carcinogenicity	Salmonella test, chromosome aberration, gene mutation	2 days to 26 weeks
	Mammalian toxicity	Skin and eye sensitivity oral toxicity	
Evaluation and Decisional Level			
Delineation of Hazard Type	Metabolism	Bacterial test Fish and mammal	4 days
	Chemical analysis	Stability Chelation Analytical	4 to 6 weeks
	Biodegradation	Temperature Pilot field test Soil studies Anaerobic systems	1 to 6 months
	Mammalian toxicity	Inhalation Reprodcution Roden bioassay Teratogenicity	2 days to 2 years
	Carcinogenicity/ mutagenicity	Chromosomal effects Organic transformation Rodent carcinogenisis bioassays	
	Expanded aquatic toxicity	Chronic toxicity Ecosystem simulation	7 days to 24 weeks
Final Validation	Aquatic toxicity	Life cycle Chronic tests Ecosystem simulation	1 week to 26 weeks
	Mammalian toxicity	Rodent bioassay Chromosomal effects Gene mutation	3 days to 2 years
	Carcinogenicity/ mutagenicity	Rodent carunogenesis	3 days to 2 years
	Bioconcentration	Biomagnification Bioaccumulation	
Monitoring Level	Aquatic/Terrestrial Epidemiology Occupational/Safety	1 to 3 years	

are pursued only if the product has a reasonable chance for marketing. The final safety evaluation is done prior to a approval to construct a new plant.

Environmental Auditing

Environmental auditing is a management tool that has been designed to evaluate environmental protection and management systems, compliance with relevant regulations, standards, policies and guidelines and anticipated environmental risk. This activity is a control strategy that permits existing organizations and operations to assess their environmental protection systems, improve their overall performance and efficiency, ensure continual compliance, and mitigate environmental risk. Environmental auditing is not the same as an assessment or monitoring program. It observes and analyses the organizational structures and in-place environmental control systems in order to ensure that correct parameters are being monitored, adequate and up-to-date protective equipment are in place, and operation and maintenance procedures are in order, so that the facility will satisfy specification and compliance set by both regulatory bodies and the company itself.

Environmental auditing, like any other auditing (financial or safety) is an examination of existing management systems and controls. It is a diagnostic tool who permits a check on the systems and controls that affect environmental performances. It should be conducted by personnel who are independent from the activity that is being audited; this allows for credibility and objectivity. It should be remembered that any audit of a particular facility is already part of a broader program that should include performance expectations, compliance requirements, frequency of audits, reporting procedures, action planning and follow-ups.

Auditing programs are comprehensive and usually address several areas in detail. These include: air quality management, water quality management, waste management, contaminants and hazardous materials, emergency response and spills, process units, and human health and public concerns. Some programs, however are quite selective and may only address one or two of the areas listed above.

Some auditing programs are very specific and may choose to include only the regulatory requirements for each area listed above. Others may emphasize management systems and controls that would satisfy certain compliances within a specific regulation.

The techniques that are used during an environmental audit are quite variable. A 1984 survey (ref. 25) revealed that auditors structure their information gathering in a number of ways. For example, they:
- use formal protocols, check lists, and questionnaires;
- watch people as they work;
- conduct interviews with employees and management;
- physically inspect unit and facilities;

- take photographs;
- examine records and files; and in some cases,
- collect and send samples for external analysis.

Environmental auditing standards are few, but many are in the developmental stage by both industrial associations and by individual companies or government departments.

9.5 COST-BENEFIT ANALYSIS

In the assessment of chemicals, the expenditures and the benefits to society must be evaluated in order to determine the amount of testitng that is required for the approval of the particular chemical. Chemicals that are frequently used may require more stringent and elaborate testing. Similarly, substances that society considers to be more valuable or more beneficial will receive more acceptability in spite of their known risk to human health and the environment than chemicals that are considered less useful.

The production as well as the introduction of new chemicals will continue in the years to come. This will result in constant scrutiny by both the regulatory body and society concerning safety, costs and benefits. Society continually expects maximum protection from adverse effects and benefits without substantial risks.

In cost-benefit analysis, the decision is quite simple if the net benefit is greater than the options. If there are several alternatives, then the one depicting the most benefits for the same cost and risk level is likely to be selected. Cost-benefit analysis should take into consideration the hazards to both the environment and human health.

In the evaluation of a program, the conditions for choosing the lesser cost pathway are: (1) the end product must be identical, (2) the risk must be reduced, and (3) the benefits must be the same or greater.

9.5.1 Risk benefit

The use of economics in the assessment of risk is not an easy task. It has always been extremely difficult to place a dollar value on human life, and as such, has been a very controversial topic to discuss or develop some consensus.

There are basically three objectives that are use for the purpose of risk evaluation. These are: (1) utility maximization; (2) risk reduction; and (3) risk rationalization (ref. 26). Utility maximization has been described as trying to gain the highest net value from any risk management situation;

theoretically, the risk level is established so that an increase or decrease in risk would lower the net value of the utility. The second, risk reduction is dependent on utility maximization. Risk reduction simplifies the analysis and avoid the problems associated with the methods used to achieve utility maximization. Finally, risk rationalization is used for the purpose of comparison of natural levels, risk alternatives and unrelated risks; it is used in public debates concerning acceptable levels of risk.

Risk-benefit analysis is an approach that focusses on how the risks of a development is compared to its benefits. The risks are described as the disadvantages, liabilities, or harmful effects that could occur to human and the environment, while the benefits are the advantages that are gained by society as a whole or individually through the use of a chemical during day-to-day activities.

Table 9.5 outlines three major categories for both benefit and risk. Benefits include value to the consumer, conservation of natural resources and energy, employment, regional development and balance in trade. The risk, on the other hand, comprises of adverse effects to human health, environmental damage, and misuse of natural resources.

TABLE 9.5 Categories for benefits and risks.

BENEFITS	RISKS

1. Value to the consumer
   a. Practical utility
   b. Aesthetic value
	1. Adverse effect on health
	   a. Acute health effects
	   b. Chronic health effects

2. Conservation of energy, renewable and non-renewable resources	2. Environmental damage
	   a. Air, water, and soil/sediment contamination
	   b. Wildlife/fisheries effects
	   c. Vegetation effects
	   d. Aesthetic effects
	   e. Property damage

3. Economic
   a. Employment
   b. Urban/regional development
   c. Balance of trade
	3. Misuse of energy sources, renewable and non-renewable resources

(Source: modified from ref. 27).

In many cases, time may affect both the benefit and risk of a chemical. Initially, a product may appear to be much required by society because of both social and economic values. Subsequently, it may be viewed as undesirable, unnecessary, or even a liability to both the economy and society. Scientific discoveries and monitoring programs may also discover that a product which has been extremely beneficial is a contaminant and is creating various effects that are exposing both human health and the environment to substantial risks. Regulatory authorities must then assess the benefits and the risks and finally decide upon the restricted use or the non-use of the substance. In some cases, it has been an extremely difficult task exercising judgement as to whether benefits outweigh the risk because a wrong decision either way might be very costly. Normally, the effects as a result of the abandonment of a product are short-lived because substitutes are usually suggested in the short term, and research are always working towards the production of a new, more effective and safer products for future needs.

Dichlorodiphenyldichloroethane (DDT) is an excellent example of a chemical whose benefits had been assessed as a result of the various risks of the product to both environment and human health. In this case, the risks outweighed the benefits with the result various countries banned the use of this chemical. In some other societies (Far east, Africa), however, benefits in terms of eliminating insect-caused diseases for exceed the risks.

An example of an industry or product whose chemicals have been extensively beneficial to society is that of petroleum. It has actually changed the face of the globe both economically and socially. Although there are various risks (water pollution, global warming, etc.) with which society contends, these risks at the present time are outweighed by the benefits.

Social Benefits

The evaluation of the benefits of a chemical to society is dependent upon whether it is a new or existing product. In the case of a new chemical, the social benefits involve evaluating the gain by society by making the chemical available, while, for an existing chemical, evaluation involves the determination of what society might have to forego if the chemical ceases to exist or was not available.

New products will provide new benefits, and in some cases, create additional risk. The uncertainties regarding expsoure and every possible health risks are largely unknown at the onset. Prior to marketing, however, the new chemical undergoes careful testing programs that would allow an assessment before the product is marketed. Because of the substantial time delays between the benefits and the onset of the risks of carcinogenic chemicals, it is not always possible to ensure the safety of society. In many cases, the benefits and the risk may not be received by the same social segments. For example, risks as a result of occupation will be concentrated on

446

the working sector, while the benefit might be enjoyed by the community as a whole.

Once the community enjoys the benefits and rewards of a newly-developed product, returning to the original state prior to the new product is very difficult. Therefore, it is imperative that the initial assessment of the product must be as thorough and accurate as possible to ensure the protection of human health and the environment.

Criteria for Assessing Benefit

For establishing sanctions against the use of certain chemicals, or for imposing certain restrictions on their use, the following criteria which was established by the National Research Council (ref. 27) should be considered:

1. What needs of society are met by the chemical or the class of chemicals in question? In other words, what specific benefit does the chemical or class of chemicals supply?

   The usefulness of a chemical may range from the merely aesthetic to the highly utilitarian: For example, a chemical may be used to make a fiber which is supplied for practical use. A plastic film used to package a product may have a dual purpose; that is, to make the product more appealing, and to keep it in better condition on the way to market (as in the packaging of lettuce). A polymer used in a paint may supply a more attractive gloss without necessarily providing greater protection. If the threat of toxicity is significant, merely aesthetic values may not be sufficient for retention.

2. If a chemical should be allowed or limited in any significant way, are there adequate alternatives for meeting the need and providing the benefits it would have furnished? Are the alternatives likely to be more or less safe, expensive, or difficult to use, or require significant time spans for adjustment?

3. What is the extent of public use established by the substance or likely to be established, in volume or in dollars?

4. What level of employment is or will be involved in making, distributing, and marketing the substance? Could displaced employees be fairly quickly assimilated through other employment? Does the chemical in question have an impact on employment by creating business in other products by making them more useful or more attractive? Would restrictions on the use of the chemical cause unemployment?

5. If changes or substitutions affect the end-use applications of the substances, how will these alter the cost picture and the utility of the product to the public?

6. How do any manpower or economic dislocations measure up in magnitude against the overall impact on the economy, either locally or on a broader scale?

It is important for the decision makers to provide society with the maximum protection from adverse effects of a product without denial of the benefits. Regulators must ensure that testing processes are adequate to provide protection. Over-testing could create excessive economic strain that could result in lengthy delays in providing a potentially beneficial product.

9.6 DETERMINING ACCEPTABLE RISK

There are no single definition that clearly explains the term "acceptable risk," but legal definitions have emerged as a result of court decisions involving this concept.

The two court cases of consequence are the benzene and the vinyl chloride decisions. In both cases, the term "acceptable risk" was used to denote "safe" by the court's definition, and it meant that the societal criteria of the law have been met and there was no significant risk of harm. Acceptable risk in the court's view involves a judgemental decision based on three factors (ref. 28): (1) the statutory criteria; (2) the scientific data; and (3) the risks that are acceptable to society.

The use of the term "acceptable risk" in direct relationship to the cncept of "safe" indicates that it is used as a generic term of broad legal application. For example:

"Where a statute directs a balancing of risks and benefits or consideration of feasibility as in the toxic substance act, the elements that go into a determination based on consideration of scientific data and the benefits, costs and technological feasibility relevant under the statutory criteria, the "acceptable" level of risk represents the outcome of that balancing determination (ref. 28)".

The legal specifications of the term "acceptable" are basically judgemental and involve a case-by-case approach. There are not simplistic shortcuts but each case requires a full legal and judgement assessment of the relevant factors and implications.

Acceptable Level

Following a recent decision in involving vinyl chloride, the United States, Circuit Court of Appeals for the district of Columbia (ref. 29) proposed that EPA must establish a safe level of emissions that will result in acceptable exposure without regard to cost or technical feasibility. The judge further indicated that the EPA administration could not, under any circumstances, consider cost and technological feasibility at this stage of the analysis. The latter factors had no relevance to the preliminary determination of what is safe. It was suggested that the above interpretation by the court was an indirect level of a de manifestis level (i.e., a ceiling above which events are inherently unsafe and should be regulated without regard for cost) to establish an acceptable risk level (ref. 30).

A review of 132 United States federal regulatory decisions for suspected carcinogens (ref. 31) showed that for small populations every chemical with an individual lifetime cancer risk above about 10^{-3} had been regulated historically, while for large populations the risk level dropped to 10^{-4}. This population-based de manifestis level has been considered an appropriate method for establishing risk level because it represents the level of risk that regulatory agencies have deemed acceptable in the past (ref. 30). It is probably not possible to set regulatory risk levels as previously indicated, however, without some knowledge of past regulatory decisions on analogous risks; abstract debates over acceptability need to be anchored in an analysis of real decisions with real consequences (ref. 32).

Defining acceptable risk and exposure standards is not reducible to a mechnical exercise. It requires scientific knowledge as well as an appreciation of the limits of that knowledge. It requires a good understanding of the context of the risk, and it requires a willingness, by the agencies as well as by the critics, to deal openly with such difficult value-laden issues (ref. 32).

A "relative decision-making" technique has been proposed recently (ref. 33) by comparing hazard estimates of individual substances and complex mixtures to one or more well-established reference compounds in a relative potency framework. This concept is called Rapid Screening of Hazard (RASH) which uses data-intensive, model-sparse approach to improve regulatory consistency through comparative hazard (or risk) evaluation. The process generally uses existing toxicity data without the use of theoretical models and without prior categorization as carcinogen or non-carcinogen. For specific details and rules for matching toxicological endpoints, readers are referred to ref. 34. Fig. 9.1 illustrates the comparison of risk of exposures to hazardous chemicals with the risk from ingestion of chlorinated drinking water. These chemicals are suspected carcinogens analyzed by U.S. EPA's Carcinogen Assessment Group (CAG) and by Owen and Jones (ref. 33). A considerable spread is apparent with values seem to vary almost plus or minus three to four orders of magnitude (Fig. 9.1). Because the relative potency factors reflect a fairly high degree of stability when large data are considered, one tends to infer from this analysis that current methods have unexplained inconsistencies in regulation of a group of carcinogens. Also, there is a wide and variable

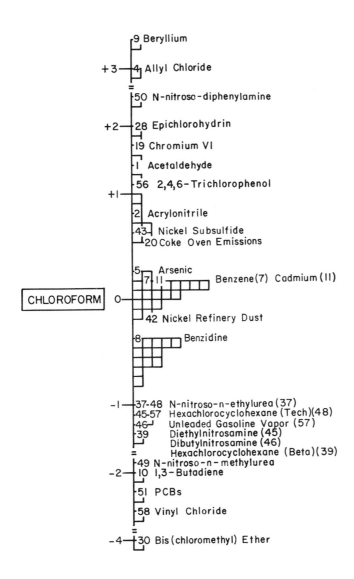

Fig. 9.1. Relation of CAG risk coefficients of suspected human carcinogens to chloroform (log scale). Chemicals in boldface are regulated on epidemiologic evidence. Most fall within an order of magnitude of the degree of control afforded chloroform. The CAG slope estimates for each chemical are converted to permissible oral intake levels of chloroform-equivalent units, and the log variation is plotted here. Numbers refer to the position of the chemical in the CAG table of relative carcinogenic potencies in the acetaldehyde health assessment document.
(CAG = U.S. EPA's Carcinogenic Assessment Group)

range of safety for the analyzed chemicals. The approaches and analysis of RASH-based relative potency approach could offer a different perspective for a consistent level of regulation of hazardous substances. It could also be used as a screening tool to prioritize chemicals and might improve consistency, reduce uncertainties, and bolster public confidence in the regulatory decision-making process.

REFERENCES

1 P.M. Sandman, Explaining Environmental Risk, United States Environmental Protection Agency, Office of Toxic Substances, Washington, D.C., 20460, 1986, 27 p.
2 E.J. Burger, Jr., Risk Analysis, 8 (1980) 309-313.
3 V.T. Covello, Environ. Sci. Technol., 23 (1989) 1441-1449.
4 B. Fischoff, et al., Acceptable Risk, Cambridge University Press, New York, U.S.A., 1981.
5a R. Wilson, Technol. Rev., 81 (1979) 40-46.
5b R. Wilson and E.A.C. Crouch, Science, 236 (1987) 267-270.
6 B.N. Ames, R. Magaw, L.S. Gold, Science, 236 (1987) 271-285.
7 V.T. Covello, P. Sandman, and P. Slovic, Risk Communication, Risk Statistics and Risk Comparisons, Chemical Manufacturers Association, Washington, D.C., 1988.
8 R.L. Keeney and D. Von Winterfeldt, Risk Analysis, 6 (1986) 417-424.
9 O. Renn, Evaluation of Risk Communication: Concepts, Strategies, and Guidelines in Managing Environmental Risks, Proceedings of an APCA International Specialty Conference, Washington, D.C., 1987, pp. 99-117.
10 V.T. Covello, P. Slovic, and D. Von Winterfeldt, Risk Abstracts, 3 (1986) 172-182.
11 V.T. Covello and F.W. Allen, Seven Cardinal Rules of Risk Communication, United States Environmental Protection Agency, Washington, D.C., 1988, pp. 1-4.
12 A.P. Grima, in J.B.R. Whitney and V.W. MacLaren (Editors), Environmental Impact Assessment: The Canadian Experience, Institute of Environmental Studies, University of Toronto, 1985, pp. 33-51.
13 N. Wengert, Nat. Resources J., 1 (1961) 207-233.
14 A.P. Grima, in M. Plewes and J.B.R. Whitney (Editors), The Role of Public Participation in the Environmental Impact Process, Environmental Impact Assessment in Canada, I.E.S., University of Toronto, Toronto, Ontario, EE-5.
15 P. Edmond, Participation and the Environment: A Strategy for Democraticizing Canada's Environmental Protection Laws, Osgood Hall Law Journal, 13 (1975) 783-837.
16 R. Parenteau, Public Participation in Environmental Decision Making, Federal Environmental Assessment Review Office, Ottawa, Canada, 71 p.
17 P. Wilkinson, in D. Wivedi (Editor), The Role of Public in Environmental Decision-Making, Protecting the Environment, Coop. Clark, 1974, pp. 21-250.
18 W.R.D. Sewell and T. O'Riordan, Natural Resources Journal, 16 (1976) 1-22.
19 Alberta Environment, A Proposed Approach to Setting Ambient Objectives in Alberta, Standards Research and Development Branch, Environmental Assessment Division, 1990, 141 p. (Unpublished).
20 S.J. Eisenreich, G.J. Hollod, T.C. Johnson, Accumulation of PCBs in Surficial Lake Superior Sediments: Atmospheric Deposition, Limnological Research Center, University of Minnesota, Minneapolis, MN, 1979.
21 W. Haddon, Publ. Health Reports, 95 (1980) 411-421.
22 G.W. Torrance and A.D. Oxman, in C.D. Fowle, A.O. Grima, and R.E. Munn (Editors), Information Needs for Risk Management, Inst. of Environ. Studies, Univ. of Toronto, Ontario, Canada, Environ. Monog. No. 8, 1980, pp. 39-62.

23 G.R. Normann and M.T. Newhouse, Can. Med. Assoc. J., 134 (1986) 733-741.

24 B.R. Willey, Water/Engineering and Management, 134 (1987) 28-31.

25 J.W. Read, Environmental Auditing in the Canadian Private Sector, Environmental Protection Service, 1984.

26 SCOPE, in A.V. Whyte and I. Burton (Editors), Environmental Risk Prepared by the Scientific Committee on problems of the Environment (SCOPE) of the International Council of Scientific Unions (ICSU) Assessment, John Wiley and Sons, New York, 1980, pp. 67-95.

27 National Research Council, Principles for Evaluating Chemicals in the Environment, requested and funded by United States Environmental Protection Agency, National Academy of Sciences, Washington, D.C., U.S.A., 1975, pp. 33-44.

28 R.C. Barnard, Reg. Toxicol. & Pharmacol., 11 (1990) 201-211.

29 Natural Resources Defense Council Versus U.S. Environmental Protection Agency, 824 F 2d 1146, 1987

30 C.C. Travis and H.A. Hattemer-Frey, Environ. Sci. Technol., 22 (1988) 873-876.

31 C.C. Travis, S.A. Richter, E.A.C. Crouch, R. Wilson, and E.D. Klema, Environ. Sci. Technol., 21 (1987) 415-420.

32 J.P. Dwyer and P.F. Ricci, Coming to Terms with Acceptable Risk, Environ. Sci. Technol., 23 (1989) 145-146.

33 B.A. Owen and T.D. Jones, Reg. Toxicol. & Pharmacol., 11 (1990) 132-148.

34 T.D. Jones, P.J. Walsh, A.P. Watson, B.A. Owen, L.W. Barnthouse, and D.A. Sanders, Risk Anal., 8 (1985) 99-48.

APPENDIX A

GLOSSARY OF TERMS USED

Acceptable Daily Intake (ADI)	The amount of a substance that is considered "safe" for human consumption, on a daily basis, for a lifetime. The value of ADI is decided by a regulatory body, after considering relevant scientific data.
Acclimation:	A physiological adaptation of fish to some selected experimental conditions, including any adverse stimulus.
Acute effect:	A health effect manifested quickly usually of short duration (4 to 7 days).
Acute toxicity:	The harmful effects of a chemical which are demonstrated within a short period (hours to days) of exposure; relevant to lethal effects.
Adsorption:	The concentration of a chemical on the surface of solid particles.
Algicidal:	Elimination of algae through lethal action.
Algistatic:	Control of growth and proliferation of algal cells without killing them.
Amino acids:	Organic compounds that contain acid and amine groups. Amino acids are the building blocks of proteins.
Ampiphilic:	Soluble in both lipid and water.
Antagonism:	An interaction between two chemicals resulting in toxicity less than the expected additive value.
Aromatic:	Compounds that contain one or more benzene rings.
Assimilation:	The transformation of absorbed nutrients into substances which are part of biological cycles.
Atrophy:	To decrease in size or waste away.
Autrotrophic:	The nutrition of those plants that are able to construct organic matter from inorganic.
Benign:	Non-multiplicative, not harmful to the host body.
Bioaccumulation:	Storage of a chemical within an organism at a concentration higher than detected in the environment. This process needs not necessarily harmful.
Bioassay:	This term can be used for toxicity tests with fish, but it is probably reserved for the formalized procedures used in testing the potency of chemicals.

Biochemical Oxygen Demand: (BOD)
A property of water or wastewater, determined by measuring the quantity of oxygen consumed by a sample under controlled conditions ($20^{\circ}C$, neutral pH) for a defined time period. The most commonly used period is 5 days which is sometimes written as BOD_5.

Bioconcentration:
Accumulation of a chemical directly from the water, to a higher concentration in an aquatic organism. The bioconcentration results from simultaneous processes of uptake and depuration.

Bioconcentration Factor: (BCF)
A quotient relating the concentration of a specific chemical in an aquatic organism to the concentration of the chemical in the water surrounding the organism. BCF is usually determined experimentally.

Biodegradable:
Capable of being metabolized by a biologic process or an organism.

Biomass:
The total particulate organic matter present beneath a unit surface area.

Carcinogenic:
Capable of causing cancer in animals and humans.

Chemical Oxygen Demand: (COD)
A concept similar to BOD, except that the measurement of amount of oxygen consumed is based on rapid chemical oxidation of the sample. BOD and COD are generally poorly correlated.

Chlorinated:
Presence of one or more chlorine atoms in a chemical compound.

Chromosome:
One of the group of structures that form in the nucleus of a cell during cell division. Chromosomes, composed of DNA, carry the genetic code for the organism.

Chromosome aberrations: Changes in the number, shape, or structure of chromosomes.

Chronic: Prolonged. Can refer to the effect or the duration of exposure. In mammalian toxicology, usually signifies exposures lasting at least one-tenth of a lifetime. In aquatic toxicology, is simetimes used to mean a full life-cycle test.

Chronic effect: A prolonged health effect that may involve irreversible change or damage.

Criteria (water quality): The relation between the concentration of a pollutant and its measured effect on a target organism.

DO: Dissolved Oxygen. Normally measured in milligrams/litre and widely used as a criterion of receiving water quality.

Dose-response curve: Similar to concentration-response curve except that the dose received inside the animal body is known. Dose is plotted against the response of the test animal.

DNA: A large molecule (Deoxyribonucleic acid) that contains the genetic information responsible for cell growth, function, and reproduction.

EC_{50}: Median effective concentration; the concentration of a chemical which produces some effect in one-half of a test population. The effect could be lethal or non-lethal. Effect and exposure time must be specified.

Ecosystem: An interacting system of all living organisms in a circumscribed region of similar characteristics, and the non-living substrate, nutrients, energy, and other environmental components.

Effluent:

A liquid or gaseous discharge of waste material into the environment.

Enzyme:

A protein that acts as a catalyst to allow a specific chemical reaction to take place in a cell.

Epidemiology:

The science of correlating exposure to a chemical with the appearance of a specific disease or other effect in a human population group.

Eutrophic:

Waters with a good supply of nutrients with a rich organic production.

False-negative:

A test result which indicates that a chemical is harmless when it is actually hazardous.

False-positive:

A test result which indicates that a chemical is hazardous when it is actually harmless.

Fate:

Disposition of a material in various environmental compratments (e.g., soil, sediment, water, air, or biota) as a result of transport, transformation, and degradation.

Gene:

The smallest subunit of a chromosome that contains a genetic message.

Genotoxic:

Able to damage genetic material of a living organism.

Half-life:

The length of time required for the quantity or activity of a chemical to be reduced by one-half to its original concentration or activity.

Hazard assessment:

The evaluation process for determining if a substance is hazardous to humans.

Herbicide:

An agent that kills plant life.

Hormone:	A biochemical secreted by one tissue in the body that exerts an influence on a biochemical function or an organ somewhere else in the body.
In vitro:	Pertains to a procedure that takes place in an artificial medium without the use of live animals.
In vivo:	Pertains to a biological reaction or test which occurs within the body of a life animal.
Insecticide:	An agent that kills insects.
LC_{50}:	Median lethal concentration; the concentration lethal to one half of a test population. Duration of exposure must be specified.
LD_{50}:	Median lethal dose; the dose delivered inside the body which is lethal to one-half of a test population.
LT_{50}:	Medial lethal time; the survival time of one-half of a population in a given concentration of a chemical.
Life-cycle test:	A test in which exposure generally starts with newly-hatched stages and continues at least until they reproduce. Usually, the second generation receives continuing exposure, and is studied for a month.
Malignant:	Refers to the cancerous cells or tumours that may grow, proliferate, and eventually kill the organism.
Mutagenic:	Ability to cause an alteration of the inherited genetic material.
Mutation:	A stable change in the genetic material.
Narcosis:	The state of stupor or unconsciousness produced by a chemical.

NOEL:

No-Observed-Effect-Level. The concentration level below which the chemical does not cause significant adverse effect(s). Identifcal to NOAEL (No-Observed-Adversed-Effect-Level).

Oncogenic:

Able to cause tumours.

Passive dosometry:

The measurement of the amount of chemical available for absorption through the lung or skin.

pH:

The negative logarithm of the hydrogen ion concetration.

Phylogenetic:

Pertaining to organisms related in evolutionary development.

Redox potential:

(oxidation-reduction potential)
The electrical potential of a bright platinum electrode immersed in a solution containing a mixture of the oxidized and reduced states of a substance, compared with a normal hydrogen electrode.

Risk:

Expected frequency of undesirable effects resulting from exposure to a chemical.

Rodenticide:

An agent that kills rodents.

Safety factor:

A numerical value applied to NOEL to arrive at an ADI value. This value compensates for inadequacies in the estimate of NOEL.

Sublethal:

A concentration level that would not cause death. An effect which is not directly lethal.

Synergism:

Attenuation of the effects of one chemical by another one; this explains the increased toxicity of chemical mixture than the calculated individual toxicities.

Telangiectasia: Marked dilation of terminal blood vessels.

Teratogenic: Ability to cause alteration in the developing cells, tissues, or organs at the embryonic stage of development.

Threshold: The point on a dose-response curve above which effects are observed and below which no adverse effects are observable.

Virtually Safe Dose: (VSD)   A long-time daily intake, that is estimated to have very little risk of causing disease or toxic effect. Almost always refers to humans, and usually involves a risk of one in a million.

Xenobiotic: A synthetic chemical or substance found in biological systems but of foreign origin.

Water quality criterion: Commonly refers to the highest concentration of a chemical or a traditional parameter which is not expected to cause an appreciable effect on an aquatic system or its users. The number is derived from available scientific data. There may be several criteria for the same substance, e.g., water for drinking purposes, industrial use, agricultural use, livestock feeding, etc.

Water quality objective: An expression of a desirable goal, and does not have the same force as a standard.

APPENDIX B

I N D E X

A